ISBN 978-1-333-75974-2
PIBN 10104046

FB &c Ltd, Dalton House, 60 Windsor Avenue, London, SW19 2RR.
Company number 08720141. Registered in England and Wales.

For support please visit www.forgottenbooks.com

Systematic Education:

OR

ELEMENTARY INSTRUCTION

IN

THE VARIOUS DEPARTMENTS

OF

LITERATURE AND SCIENCE;

WITH

Practical Rules

FOR STUDYING

EACH BRANCH OF USEFUL KNOWLEDGE.

By the Rev. W. SHEPHERD,
The Rev. J. JOYCE,
And the Rev. LANT CARPENTER, LL.D.

IN TWO VOLUMES.

VOL. I.

London:

PRINTED FOR LONGMAN, HURST, REES, ORME, AND BROWN, PATERNOSTER-ROW.

1815.

J. M'Creery, Printer, Black-Horse-Court,
London.

ADVERTISEMENT.

THE important period of human life, which commences when young persons are freed from the restraint of school discipline, is often ill spent, for want of some useful object of mental pursuit. The living instructor is, perhaps, not at hand to point out a course of study; and many an ingenuous youth falls into the habit of desultory and baneful reading, who, with proper guidance, might have formed a decided taste for the acquisition of wholesome knowledge, in the prosecution of which he might have improved his mind, and have been preserved from frivolity and vice. Influenced by these considerations, the Authors of "Systematic Education" have had it in view to supply those, who are between sixteen and twenty-five years of age, with such guidance. They have endeavoured to offer such elementary instruction as may afford a good preparative for future reading, and to point out the best sources of farther information on the subjects of which they treat. It has been their aim to compress within a narrow compass, a great fund of important knowledge, which could only be obtained by the perusal of a multitude of volumes;

and they flatter themselves that, on some topics, their Elements will supply materials for instruction not unworthy the attention of the Preceptor, who may be engaged in conducting the studies of pupils somewhat advanced in scholastic attainments.

As they have endeavoured to give a correct and familiar introduction to the principal departments of scientific and literary inquiry, they are not without hopes that their work will be found an useful text-book in those schools where instruction comprehends other objects besides the Classics; and that it will be of eminent service to those young persons in the process of whose early education the Classics have been almost the exclusive subject of attention.

This exposition of the work now offered to the public would be abundantly sufficient, if it fell into the hands only of the uninitiated, and of those who are engaged in the business of instructing others. For the former, it is believed, it may be reckoned a safe, if not an ample guide to useful and important knowledge: the latter require no apology, they know the difficulties of compressing into a small compass, a syllabus even, of a great variety of subjects. From both these classes, therefore, the authors of "Systematic Education" expect a candid reception.

To the learned and the critic they have nothing to offer: their aim was to supply a work, which, as far as they know, has hitherto been unattempted, that might assist the unskilful, not only as a guide to what they wished to pursue, but such a one as should afford them a choice of subjects from which they might select subjects adapted to their taste, their acquirements, or their wants; and having made their election, they will find the introductory principles laid down, explained and exemplified, and a course of study pointed out, with references to such elementary works as may be adapted to their wishes, and to the time they have to devote to literature and science. With such views, to have attempted any thing like deep learning, or profound research, would have been out of place. While they have avoided this error, they have kept clear from giving mere abridgments, with which they could have readily filled their volumes at a small expense of time. From works of their own, already before the public, in some shape or other, they have, on some few occasions, freely borrowed, and in a few instances from those of others; but, in every case, it is believed, full and constant references are given, and due acknowledgments are made for the advantages which they have derived, and which they wished their readers to derive from this line of conduct.

Having thus briefly detailed the objects and plan of their Work, they respectfully submit the decision, as to its merits in point of execution, to the candour of an enlightened public.

CONTENTS

OF

VOL. I.

CONTENTS.

DIRECTIONS TO THE BINDER.

OL. I. Plate	MATHEMATICS, .	to face p. 540
II. ——	I. MECHANICS . .	——— 16
——	II. HYDROSTATICS and PNEUMATICS .	——— 44
——	III. OPTICS	——— 74
——	IV. ELECTRICITY and VOLTAISM . . .	——— 104
——	V. ASTRONOMY . .	——— 136
——	VI. CHEMISTRY . . .	——— 174
VII. & VIII.	STRUCTURE and FUNCTIONS OF MAN. .	— 567 & 568

INTRODUCTION.

PRACTICAL ESSAY ON EDUCATION.

IN nothing is man more eminently distinguished from the inferior animals, than in the capacity of increasing in knowledge. The process of instinct is, indeed, rapid, and its results are perfect in their kind; but those results are limited within comparatively narrow boundaries. Though various species of birds construct their nests with exquisite skill, in the manner which is best adapted to their habits, and to the promotion of their security, yet from generation to generation the mode of their construction is exactly the same. The bee is no sooner furnished with wings, than it speeds its flight in quest of its proper food; which it stores up in cells, that, from the commencement of time, have been uniform in size and in figure. Not so with man. The degrees and the species of art and skill exhibited by the human race, are almost infinitely varied; and a long space of time must intervene before any individual can attain to that measure of knowledge which he is capable of acquiring. This apparent disadvantage, however, is amply compensated by the wide range allowed to human intellect; and by the capacity of mental improvement, which is continued almost through the whole of life; and, which, though it may be apparently suspended by the infirmities incident to extreme old age, and by the common doom of mortality, will, as it is hoped, and as we are taught to believe, be continued through the endless ages of eternity. Upon this subject, how beautiful, and at the same time how rational, are the speculations of Addison: "There is not, in my opinion, a more pleasing and triumphant consideration in religion, than this, of the perpetual progress which the soul makes toward the perfection of its nature, without ever arriving at a period in it. To look upon the soul as going on from strength to strength; to consider that she is to shine for ever with new accessions of glory, and brighten to all eternity; that she will be still adding virtue to virtue, and knowledge to knowledge; carries in it something wonderfully agreeable to that ambition which is natural to the mind of man. Nay, it must be a prospect pleasing to God himself, to see his creation for ever beautifying in his eyes, and drawing nearer to Him by greater degrees of resemblance."

It is a striking circumstance, that a being who is born to this high destiny, should, after the period of his birth, continue in a state of helplessness for a longer space of time than any other creature. With relation to man, it may truly, and emphatically be said, that perfection is of tardy growth. The beasts of the field are soon enabled to provide for themselves their proper sustenance and shelter; and when they are arrived at this stage of maturity, they either voluntarily and peaceably quit, or are forcibly driven from, the protection of the authors of their being. The same law holds good with respect to the fowls of the air, and other tribes of inferior beings. But with regard to man, how long does the imbecility of infancy demaud the solicitude of parental care! For how lengthened a season does the ignorance, the inexperience, the levity, and the rashness of youth, occupy the vigilant attention of guardians, instructors, and friends. Even in more advanced life, what lessons remain to be learnt in the severe school of experience, how many errors remain to be corrected by the painful progress of events. Thus feeble in his outset is the Lord of the Creation—thus unpromising is the commencement of a career of improvement which admits of continual advance.

However high and capacious then are the powers which "lie folded up in man," it seems to be the law of nature, or to speak more correctly, it seems to be the will of our all-wise Creator, that those powers must be expanded by degrees, and that their expansion must be effected by the process of education.

In one sense indeed, and that a very important one, the process of Education is perpetually going forward. Man, regarded as a moral agent, and an accountable being, is a compound of habits. According as his habits are good or bad, he is to be esteemed or qualified as virtuous or vicious. Now it is a matter of common observation, that the habits of an individual are generally formed in consequence of the precepts with which he is imbued—and in a much greater degree, in consequence of the examples which are presented for his imitation. Whosoever, therefore, is under the influence either of the conduct, or of the principles of others, (and who is not under such influence?) may be justly said to be so far educated by them to moral good or ill. Much is it to be wished, that those who are interested in the welfare of youth, would attend to this most serious maxim. It would preserve them from many pernicious errors, and would convince them of the folly of entertaining unreasonable and inconsistent expectations. Such is the homage which vice pays to virtue, that many a parent, who is himself by no means scrupulous of violating the rules of morality, is startled at the idea of early profligacy in his offspring. With a view of promoting the mental improvement of his son, he provides for him instructors in various departments of knowledge. He spares no expense to promote his progress in science. He is anxious to receive what he imagines he is entitled to expect as the fruit of his parental attention and care. But he is disappointed. The child of his hopes, instead of a prodigy of learning and of knowledge, is, when far advanced in the season of youth, found to be deplorably ignorant, self-willed, and untractable. He despises the idea of qualifying himself by useful studies, to adorn the station in life which his birth and his fortune entitle him to occupy. He is given up to frivolity, and, having no good qualities, no estimable accomplishments to recommend him to honourable notice, he glories in his vices, and makes a public spectacle of his depravity. Shocked and disgusted, the mortified parent vents his feelings in execrations against the indolence and unfaithfulness of tutors and preceptors, when in reality he himself is alone to blame. His manners may have been comparatively decent, but he has unfortunately disregarded the maxim of the stern satirist,

Maxima debetur puero reverentia.—

—He has thoughtlessly permitted his offspring to witness his irregularities—and by this combination of wickedness and folly, he has at an early age blunted in his child the sense of moral obligation. In the pursuit of what he deemed allowable amusements, he has permitted the heir of his fortune to associate, under little or no restraint, with cunning and profligate domestics, who were ever ready to minister to the vices of their superiors. Thus has he in fact trained him up in low ideas and to mean pursuits, and yet he wonders at his unworthy and unbecoming propensities. But his wonder would cease, could he penetrate the mist which is poured before the mental eye by the power of self-partiality. Then would he be sensible of the capital error into which he has unconsciously fallen; and, however unpleasant the truth might be, he would be convinced, that his ideas on the subject of the training of youth have been incorrect, and inadequate, and that the miserable and disgraceful scenes which he has witnessed with so much pain and concern, are the consequences—the natural and necessary consequences of his son's education having been conducted more in the orgies of his father's dining-room, or in the purlieus of the stable-yard, than in the retirement of the library, or in the apartment of his tutor. In order to form a moral agent to the highest degree of excellence of which he is capable, the most guarded vigilance over the propensities of early youth, is requisite on the part of natural superintendents—and it seems to be the wise ordinance of providence, that the anxiety which parents universally entertain for the welfare of their offspring, is calculated, when properly directed, to become a strong promoter, and a steady safeguard of virtue.

If we may give credence to the records of remote antiquity, the institutions of one ancient nation, in order to obviate the mischiefs produced by the ignorance or the inattention of parents, provided, by compulsory laws, for the public education, according to an established system, of all children born within its precincts; and there have not been wanting philosophers both of ancient and of modern times, who, maintaining the principle, that a state has a paramount interest in the welfare and good conduct of those who are born within its limits, have vindicated and applauded such institutions. Speculations of this description, do not, however, seem to merit any elaborate discussion. It will be superfluous to dwell upon the public education of the Lacedemonians, which, after all, seems to have extended little further than to the provisions of a general military conscription, or to examine the political romance of Xenophon. The dreams of a theorist are of little authority, and the results of the boasted Spartan education, were by no means such as to entitle it to any high commendation. It has been well observed by a judicious author, that, "while the arts of life were improving in all the neighbouring nations, Sparta derived this noble prerogative from her constitution, that she continued the nearest to her pristine barbarity; and in the space of nearly a thousand years (which include the whole period in which letters and the arts were the most cultivated in the rest of Greece) produced no one poet, orator, historian, or artist of any kind. The convulsions of Athens, where life was in some measure enjoyed, and the faculties of body and mind had their proper exercise and gratification, were far preferable to the savage uniformity of Sparta."

A little consideration will convince the man of a thinking mind, that the prescriptions of civil authority universally act as barriers to the improvement of the arts. The language is, "hitherto shalt thou go, but no farther." It is, however, the business of education not to cramp, but to guide the intellect. Its province extends to the inculcating of those fundamental principles upon which the structure of science is to be built: the finishing of the structure ought to be left in a great measure to individual discretion. To the attainment of truth, freedom of inquiry is absolutely essential. A man may as well attempt to penetrate the mazes of an entangled wood in fetters, as to investigate the vast variety of intellectual subjects, with a mind trammelled by the imperative decisions of human institutions. And to the reducing the general mind to this degrading predicament, do the prescriptions of civil authority in matters of literature usually tend. They lead to the fostering of prejudice, and to the perpetuation of error. They necessarily keep a nation stationary in the march of intellect, and repress that expansion of thought which is the parent of excellence. To a certain degree they may be productive of decided and powerful effects; but the uniformity of habit and character, which they are calculated to produce, rather tends to lower man to the level of brutal instinct, than to raise him higher in the scale of the intelligent creation.

On these speculations, however, it is unnecessary to enlarge. We are in this case free from the necessity of wandering through the airy indistinctness of theory. In offering a few hints upon the process of Education, which may be suitable to the condition and circumstances of a Briton, we are happily authorized to assume the position, that the child is left to the disposal of its parent.

Education is, indeed, in the British empire, an object of national concern. Our various universities and public schools, are splendid monuments of the attention paid by our ancestors to the important object of training and enlightening the youthful mind. The provision made for the support of these establishments, especially in England and Ireland, is, generally speaking, munificent. At the same time it is not sufficient to afford a temptation to the indulgence of idleness, by the conversion of responsible offices into sinecures. The dignity hence accruing to their teachers and professors, invests them with high authority, and imparts additional weight to their instructions; while the respect in which they are habitually held by long established prescription, gives a powerful sanction to the system of their discipline. In Scotland the case is somewhat different, but the result is perhaps little less favourable to general improvement. The professors who lecture in the universities of that kingdom, depend for the principal part of their emoluments upon the fees which they receive from pupils, whose attendance upon their instructions is in many instances optional. Their gains being, therefore, in proportion to their reputation, this circumstance is a strong stimulus to exertion, and bids fair to ensure to the superior Scottish seminaries of education, a succession of learned and scientific preceptors. The constitution and utility of the Scottish parish schools, have been ably and feelingly described by that excellent writer and amiable man, the late Dr. Currie; and though the claim of the supporters of Dr. Bell, to denominate his mode of educating the lower orders of the community a "national system," may be disputed, there is every reason to hope that his labours, and those of the indefatigable Lancaster, will, in the lapse of a short time, place the elements of knowledge within the reach of the humblest individual in the British Isles.

Various and extensive, however, as our public establishments for education may be, with the exception of the individuals who dedicate themselves to the ministry in our national churches, and, perhaps, also of those who devote themselves to the study of the law, it may be affirmed of the great mass of our community, that in the momentous article of the education of his offspring, every one is permitted to follow the dictates of his own discretion.

From this circumstance has arisen a question which, though discussed in successive generations from the time of Quintilian, down to the present day, has, by reason of the freedom of our views and of our habits, been no where more frequently and more earnestly argued than in our native country—namely, which is preferable—a public or a private Education. This question certainly involves matter of high importance, and is well deserving of serious consideration.

On entering upon the investigation of this problem, however it may be expedient to remark, that the Roman rhetorician, whose opinions on this subject have been so frequently quoted, does not by any means treat upon it in the abstract. The general scope of his immortal work, is to detail the process by which a Roman youth might attain to excellence in that accomplishment, which in his time, was the means of attaining the highest civic honours, viz. the eloquence of the forum, and of the senate. It would indeed be a species of laborious trifling, to treat this as an abstract inquiry. Its decision in each case must in a great degree depend upon the particular circumstances of the individual interested in that decision. Is it not, for instance, most clearly the height of absurdity to think of committing a youth, feeble in body or in mind, to the discipline of our public schools? The system necessarily adopted in those seminaries does not admit of those relaxations and indulgences, and of that minuteness of attention, which are requisite to mitigate the effects of corporeal or mental infirmity. In so rude a climate, a sickly plant will speedily wither and die. What an affecting picture does the biographer of Cowper delineate, of the subject of his memoir just emerging from an infancy of peculiar delicacy, and sent to encounter, without protection, the contentions and buffetings of a public seminary of education. "The little Cowper was sent to his first school in the year of his mother's death, and how ill suited the scene was to his peculiar character, must be evident to all who have heard him describe his sensations in that season of life, which is often very erroneously extolled as the happiest period of human existence. He has frequently been heard to lament the persecution he sustained in his childish years, from the cruelty of his school-fellows, in the two scenes of his education. His own forcible expression represented him at Westminster as not daring to raise his eye above the shoe-buckle of the elder boys, who were too apt to tyrannize over his gentle spirit. The acuteness of his feelings in his childhood, rendered those important years, (which might have produced, under tender cultivation, a series of lively enjoyments) miserable years of increasing timidity and depression which, in the most cheerful hours of his advanced life, he could hardly describe to an intimate friend, without shuddering at the recollection of his early wretchedness."——

True it is, that at Westminster school, Cowper acquired a considerable store of learning, and imbibed the principles of that just taste, which characterizes all his writings. But at what a price were these accomplishments purchased? What was the effect of the process to which he was there obliged to submit, upon the happiness of his future existence? His health was impaired. His spirits were broken. He withdrew from the active scenes of society into a comparatively useless retirement—and he finally became a prey to that morbid sensibility which, for the long and dreary space of thirteen years, rendered his life a blank in the records of intellectual existence.

They, who are narrowly limited in the means of supporting and establishing their families, must be regarded as hazarding a perilous experiment, when they educate their sons at public schools. There, habits of expense are almost necessarily contracted—habits, which in the heirs to title and wealth, may not be inconsistent or unjustifiable, but which are fatal to the future welfare of those who are less fortunately circumstanced. Here let it be observed, that the moral certainty thus superinduced, of a youth's acquiring views and propensities which will be the sure and copious source of anxiety and distress in coming years, is, in the estimation of discreet judgment, by no means compensated by the prospect with which some parents flatter themselves, that in public seminaries their children may form connexions which will ultimately promote their worldly interests. This principle of action is in itself contemptible. It directly tends to the excitement and the fostering of meanness and hypocrisy—it may produce a parasite and a sycophant, but it will never produce a man of honour and a gentleman—and, notwithstanding some rare exceptions may be quoted to excite the eagerness of the ambitious, the views upon which it is founded will generally end in disappointment and mortification.

Nor is it advisable for those, who, however wealthy they may be, wish to bring up their sons to conduct the details of trade and commerce, to send them to our superior public schools. From the undeviating system of instruction which is there adopted, they will learn perhaps every thing except what will be useful to them in their future destination. Surrounded by companions who are born to what they are led to regard as higher aims and expectations, they will become ashamed of their origin, and discontented with their prospects. Thus will they be induced to rebel against natural authority, and in process of time they will obstinately and wilfully thwart the views, and counteract the wishes of their parents, who, however they may lament the failure of their plans, will have their own folly alone to blame for their unfortunate issue.

Numerous as may be the individuals contained in the classes which are pointed out in the foregoing exceptions, there remains in the ranks of Society an abundant sufficiency of recruits to maintain the numbers of those whose early Education ought, in prudence and discretion, to be conducted at our public schools. The imperious dictate of general opinion has decided, that persons, designed for public life, ought to go through the process of a public Education.

Hence it is expected that the sons of our nobility and of our principal gentry—that they who have a reasonable prospect of obtaining seats in parliament—or of filling the higher, and even the secondary offices of state—that they who are destined to the bar and the church;—and in some cases, to the practice of medicine, should qualify themselves for their respective stations by submitting to the discipline of our public seminaries of Education. And this expectation is far from being supported merely by prejudices of prevailing fashion. It is founded on the nature of things, and the constitution of society, and is therefore reasonable and proper. Generally speaking, it is not indeed absolutely necessary that a particular individual should enter into public life. But if such be his destination or his fortune, it is certainly expedient, and much to be wished, that he should enter upon his station provided with that furniture of mind, and endued with those accomplishments, which will best enable him to discharge its duties with utility to the community at large, and with credit to himself. This happy result may be justly calculated upon, as likely to ensue from the discipline of public Education. In our extensive and well endowed public seminaries, a system of equality prevails among the pupils, which admirably tends to abate the presumption, without controling the spirit of aristocracy, and to enure youth to that patience in suffering, and that manliness of exertion, which are the best preparatives for the scenes of active life. The nature and habits of the society too, which is assembled in these seminaries, produce those easy and unembarrassed manners, which afford an unspeakable advantage in the transaction of business. In the various stages which occur, if the expression may be allowed, in the route of public Education, ingenuous youths proceed by just degrees, and without any violence of transition, to the object of their hopes and wishes. Thus are they enabled without effort, to adapt themselves to their successive circumstances, without being betrayed into improprieties and inconsistencies, which would render them the objects of ridicule and contempt. Novelty of situation will not deprive them of the invaluable faculty of self-command—nor will it on the other hand inspire them with overweening confidence and conceit. And when to these various recommendations, it is added, that the method of instruction practised in our public schools, is skilfully adapted to imbue the youthful mind with the principles of pure taste, and to call into action the innate powers of genius, enough has been said to vindicate their utility and importance to those, who are destined by their birth, or who are devoted by the wishes of their parents, to the duties and engagements of public life.

Some parents, however, influenced perhaps by a mixed feeling of tenderness, and of conscientious regard for the welfare of their offspring, have hesitated to commit them to the discipline of a public school, from an idea that the obligation of attending to numbers of pupils, must necessarily preclude the possibility of the tutors promoting the improvement, and watching over the morals of individuals. Nothing can be more weakly founded than the former of these objections. It is bottomed in absolute ignorance of facts. The vivifying principle of a good mental Education, is steady system, and prompt and vigorous discipline. These are found in perfection in our public schools, and perhaps in them alone. There the ablest teachers have ample scope for their energies, free from the impertinence of interference, or from the benumbing dread of pecuniary loss. There, emulation urges the pupil to labour, and the publicity of honours at once rewards the past, and stimulates to future exertions. In fine, let the appeal be made to facts, and it will be found, that in our public seminaries have been trained the men who have most eminently distinguished themselves by the elegance, the accuracy, and the profundity of their erudition.

As to morals, it must be acknowledged that vice, and even profligacy, are occasionally to be found in our public schools. But, alas! is vice confined to them?—By no means. It is not even excluded from the domestic walls. It is an observation sanctioned by the almost unanimous testimony of those whose opinion is founded upon experience, that the vices of a public school are of a nature to be easily detected, and to be corrected by discipline; while those of private education creep on in concealment, and frequently arrive at a remediless degree of maturity before they are discovered. The remark of the judicious Dr. Barrow on this head is at once striking and just. "The perpetual restraints under which the private pupil lives, and the constant presence of those much older than himself, do not suffer his propensities and passions to appear in their true colours; and consequently their course cannot be sufficiently regulated, nor their excesses restrained. He does not grow open and ingenuous by unreserved communication with his equals; but artful and designing, by watching the sentiments of those more advanced in age; and the self-command which he appears to possess, is often policy, not principle—hypocrisy, not virtue."

Most of the observations which have been applied to the English public schools, are also applicable to the English universities. These are, and necessarily must be, the resort of individuals, whose views are directed to the church or the bar, or of those who claim by their birth, or are likely to attain in consequence of their circumstances, the honours and distinctions of public life. Here the scholar enters upon a wider range of study, and extends his excursions into the field of science. These institutions were indeed first established at a time when learning was the exclusive province of the clergy, and the course of instruction pursued within their precincts was arranged according to this narrow principle. It consisted of the puerile Rhetoric, of the intricate Logic, and of the barbarous jargon dignified by the name of School-divinity, which for several centuries were regarded as comprizing the whole compass of human learning. Hence our universities were formerly rather the parents of pedantry and of unprofitable speculation, than of sound literature and useful science. In consequence of the difficulty of procuring even desirable alterations in established systems, dignified by the veneration bestowed upon antiquity; this continued for too long a season to be matter of merited reproach. The rapid increase, and the general diffusion of knowledge has, however, enforced upon the conductors of those institutions, the necessity of salutary reform. In the course of education, they keep pace with the progress of the times, and it cannot now with justice be said, that the studies pursued in them, are too abstracted, or that they have too little bearing upon the realities of life. The system of our universities may not indeed be perfect: but it is of a high degree of excellence, and is well calculated to strengthen the intellectual powers, and to enable them to act with vigour upon any subject, which, when the student enters at large upon the business of the world, may be practically presented to them.

The tour of Europe was formerly thought absolutely requisite to complete the education of our men of rank, and of the superior order of our gentry. Foreign travel was certainly of great use in rubbing off academical rust, in correcting prejudices, and in enlarging the sphere of mental vision. By comparing the institutions of his own country with those of foreign lands, the observant youth was enabled duly to appreciate the value of the former, and learn in what particulars they were capable of correction and amendment. By making himself acquainted with the characters of the individuals who took an active part in the conduct of politics, and with the circumstances, views, and interests of the continental courts, he qualified himself for the situation of a diplomatic agent, or for the discharge of the arduous duties of the cabinet. The events of the late war have, however, for many years, precluded the young nobility and gentry from availing themselves of this source of improvement. Thus situated, travellers of rank and fashion have directed their excursions to Turkey, Greece, and Egypt. This circumstance has caused those countries to be better known than they formerly were: but it is much to be doubted, whether, by wandering through districts inhabited by hordes of semi-barbarians, and tribes of miserable slaves, our countrymen will be materially improved either in intellect or morals.

The foregoing remarks have, of course, a special reference to the case of individuals, on whom, it is deemed expedient, to bestow a public education. These, however, bear but a small proportion, to the great mass of our community, whose instruction must necessarily be derived from the discipline of private seminaries. Of these seminaries, there are always existing, under various appellations, a countless multitude, the characters of which extend through all the gradations of merit and demerit. This circumstance is, to the serious and considerate parent, a source of great and just anxiety—for what more important topic can occupy the thoughts of a rational being, than the settlement of his offspring in a situation, where the character of his mind, and his moral habits, which must have such a commanding influence over his future destiny, will in all probability be fixed for ever. On the part of parents who are themselves illiterate, and who wish to bestow upon their children those advantages of intellectual culture, the want of which they have themselves had occasion to lament, the utmost care and circumspection are requisite. The province of education opens a wide field for the knavery of quacks and charlatans, who make a practice of plundering the unwary and the ignorant. The wretch, who, by his bold and interested presumption, puts to hazard the health of the body, is a subject of merited detestation and reproach; but he is still more detestable, who tampers with the health of the youthful mind.

Nothing is more lamentable than the irreparable waste of time, and the destruction of intellect, caused by the inattention and mismanagement of unfaithful and incapable teachers. People of this description are justly chargeable with the crime of intellectual murder—a crime which ought to draw down upon its perpetrator the severest punishment. There have not indeed been wanting theorists, who, reflecting upon the mischief occasioned by incompetent pretenders to the art of teaching, have thought it a fit subject for legislative interference and correction. Such interference, however, seems to be incompatible with the genius of our free constitution; and it would be extremely difficult, if not absolutely impossible, to make legislative restrictions, in the matter of education, without opening a wide door for the introduction of oppression and abuse. This being the case, all that can be done, is, to warn parents of their liability to imposition, and of the consequent necessity of caution. If they are not themselves learned, and wish to bestow upon their children a learned education, they will do well to consult some friend who may be qualified to assist and direct them in the choice of a school for the training of their offspring. In the mean time, common sense, and their general knowledge of the affairs of life, should teach them to be suspicious of high professions, and boastful promises—of all short methods for the attainment of knowledge—and of all proposals to conduct the pupil up the hill of science, without subjecting him to the endurance of pain, or to the labour of exertion. These professions are directly incompatible with the laws of providence, to which, the human intellect, invariably, is subject. They are the expedients of adventurers, whose object it is to make a specious shew, and thus to abuse and turn to their profit the credulity of the public.

And here, it may not be inexpedient, briefly to notice, a query which is frequently proposed, and has been variously answered—namely, whether classical literature be a proper object of study for those who are not intended for a learned profession, or for public life—That it would be extremely absurd for an individual of this description, to dedicate so much time to classical literature, as is allotted to that department of knowledge in our public schools, has already been hinted. The writer of this essay well remembers an instance of a youth, who, on being transferred to a mercantile counting-house from the highest form of a public school, which he quitted with a merited reputation for good scholarship, was found to be so ignorant of figures, as not to be able to cast up a bill of parcels. Yet it is by no means advisable for the future representatives, even of the middle classes of society, to forego the study of the classics, during the period of their school-education. It is perfectly practicable to acquire at school a competent, and by competent, is meant, a very considerable degree of classical knowledge, in combination with those studies, which have a more direct bearing upon the affairs of life. The habit of strict and careful analysis, which is formed by the process of judicious instruction in the Greek and Latin languages, is itself a most valuable acquisition, and is an excellent preparative for the exertion of the mental powers, in all other inquiries. The facilities, which a knowledge of these tongues affords, in the acquisition of modern languages, and in comprehending the terms of art and science, is a matter of trite, but at the same time of just remark. In our most favorite and popular English authors, references to classical subjects, and even to classical phraseology, are so frequent, that an acquaintance with this branch of literature is absolutely requisite to a just idea of their meaning, and to a true relish of their spirit. To which may be added, that a correct English style and true delicacy of taste in composition, are hardly ever acquired but by the medium of classical literature. It is presumed then, that it is not an unreasonable opinion, that with regard to the class of the community whose circumstances are now under consideration, a moderate portion of time, dedicated to this object, is well and prudently bestowed.

In the English Universities, and in the University of Dublin, a proficiency in classical literature, and the abstract sciences, constitutes the title to academic honours, and is of course the great object of pursuit. This circumstance naturally takes place, in consequence of the peculiar adaptation of the system of these institutions to the learned professions. But as these professions furnish a comparatively small number of subjects of education, it has from time to time, been proposed, by individuals of no mean acquirements in erudition and science, to provide a course of instruction for gentlemen, who, though they do not aspire after the dignity of a profession, are likely to fill respectable stations in active life. Plans of this nature have uniformly been adopted in the Academies, or, as they are of late denominated, the colleges of the Protestant Dissenters. These plans have usually embraced, besides Classics and Mathematics, which have been rather secondary than primary objects, a course of Logic and Metaphysics—Lectures on Natural and Moral Philosophy, and the Evidences of Christianity—on Civil and Ecclesiastical History; and on the British Constitution.—The utility of such a course of instruction is obvious; and various publications evince, that the lecturers, who have treated on these topics, in the seminaries above alluded to, have executed their tasks with exemplary industry and great ability. It is to be lamented, that the institutions themselves have been invariably short lived. Into the causes of this fact it does not come within the scope of this Essay to inquire. Suffice it therefore to remark, that in addition to the dissenting academies, any one, who wishes his son to have the benefit of instruction, in any of the above-mentioned branches of study, free from the obligation of a minute and laborious attention to classical literature, and from other obligations enforced at our English Universities, may have his wishes amply gratified in the Scotch Universities, and particularly in those of Glasgow and of Edinburgh.

In treating generally on the subject of education, it will be proper to advert to the course of instruction appropriate to the female sex. On this topic, however, brevity will be expedient, as whatever may be the decisions of Essayists, female education will be directed by the arbitrary decree of fashion. It is obvious however to remark, that as modesty and retirement, are the natural characteristics, and constitute the most powerful attractions of the sex, females should seem to be the fittest subjects for private education—and that those parents, whose circumstances will enable them to incur the necessary expense, will do well to have their daughters educated under their own eye. Those alone, who are conscious to themselves, that the manners of their domestic circle, are not the most commendable, or who find it necessary to share with others the expense of the teachers, of what are called accomplishments, are justifiable in sending them from home: and how injudicious are many of the attempts which are made to enforce the acquirement of these accomplishments! The time, which can properly be spared for them is, in the most favourable circumstances, inadequate; but when a young lady, who has neither eye, nor ear, is compelled to drudge at music and drawing, the result of her labours is discomfort to herself, and annoyance to the friends and strangers who are summoned to witness her proficiency; and who, if they possess any relish for the fine arts, are embarrassed between their unwillingness to bestow hypocritical praise, and to utter unwelcome truth. Accomplishments are doubtless a valuable acquirement, and also an acquirement, within the reach of those who are endowed with natural taste, and who have time to bestow upon them. As to those, who are differently circumstanced in the acquisition of facility, in the works appropriated to their sex, in the study of modern languages, of History and Geography, in the perusal of our best English authors, and the formation of a correct style of writing, they will find sufficient employment for the years which are allotted to their school-education.

In former times, it was by no means an uncommon circumstance, for ladies of high rank to receive the benefit of a classical education. Queen Elizabeth's Latin exercise book is still exhibited in the Bodleian library—and the unfortunate Lady Jane Grey is said to have been an accomplished scholar. In our own days too, there have not been wanting parents who have procured for their daughters instruction in the learned languages. This branch of education, however, as applied to females, has been made the subject of much paltry and unmerited ridicule. The capacity of the female sex for the learning of languages, is at least equal to that of the male;

and if classical studies tend to the exercise of the understanding, and to the refinement of taste, why are not these objects as desirable for the one sex as for the other? In point of fact, the course of female education will allow nearly as much time for this pursuit, as is generally dedicated to it by boys, who are intended to enter at an early period into the concerns of active life; and it will be difficult to point out any object upon which that time can be better employed. As to the frivolous objection that classical accomplishments tend to make young ladies conceited, it may be a sufficient answer to observe, that were those accomplishments more commonly diffused among females, they would be proportionably less a subject of pride; and that the emotions of self-conceit are easily repressed by that moral discipline, which, throughout the whole process of education, it is taken for granted, will be strictly enforced. Without this discipline, indeed, every topic of instruction may be perverted into a subject of conceit. With it, no accomplishment will generate those feelings which trench upon the essential virtues of modesty and humility.

But learned females are said not to acquire the good graces of the other sex. It is asserted that they are regarded with a species of dread and jealousy.—If a reputation for literature keeps fools and coxcombs at a distance from a youthful female, is this circumstance a proper subject of lamentation? and is it expedient, for the sake of such characters, to keep down the female mind, in order to reduce it to the ordinary level of intellectual society? In the estimation of reason, a lovely woman cannot be rendered less lovely, by the high cultivation of her talents; and many examples may be quoted to prove, that intellectual attainments are so far from being inconsistent with feminine graces, that they confer upon them additional attractions.

In the mean time, let not domestic accomplishments be despised. On the contrary, let them be cultivated with the most diligent attention. But why should any portion of the field of knowledge be interdicted to any rational creature, who has an opportunity, and who entertains a wish to enter it? and why should females be debarred from a source of elegant amusement, and of useful instruction, peculiarly adapted to their domestic habits? The conduct of learned females is watched, especially by their own sex, with an evil eye. Their foibles are magnified. Their errors are exaggerated, and whatever faults they commit, are laid to the account of literature, with the candour and good sense evinced by the self-complacent ignorant, who, on seeing a man executed for forgery, exclaimed, "such are the consequences of reading and writing!" Many a lady has railed against learned females who, if she had herself received some tincture of learning, would have been enabled to detect the charlatanism of her son's preceptor, who, being himself grossly ignorant, wastes the precious time of his pupil, while he proposes to render him, probably by some short and easy method, a proficient in literature and in science. When we consider what influence the female sex have in directing the early ideas of man, and also upon the habits of his future life, it is surely desirable that they should be endowed with every species of knowledge, conveniently within their reach, which may turn that influence to good.

The preceptors of youth, of either sex, ought, however, to be again and again admonished of the importance of the task which they have undertaken, and also of its difficulty. It is their duty to be patient with the dull, and steady with the froward—to encourage the timid, and repress the insolent—fully to employ the minds of their pupils, without overburdening them—to awaken their fear without exciting their dislike—to communicate the stores of knowledge according to the capacity of the learner, and to enforce obedience by the strictness of discipline. Above all, it is their bounden duty to be ever on the watch, and to check the first beginnings of vice. For valuable as knowledge may be, virtue is infinitely more valuable; and worse than useless are those mental accomplishments, which are accompanied by depravity of heart.

LANGUAGES. Philosophical principles are discovered by

the examination, and by the comparison of a multiplicity of facts. Upon this process is founded the philosophy of grammar, to an acquaintance with which, a knowledge of a variety of languages is absolutely necessary. Hence, the study of languages becomes an object extremely interesting to the man of scientific research, and especially to those who devote themselves to metaphysical inquiries. It is no less so to him, who, declining any recondite examination into the origin of words, and the mechanism of phraseology, is contented with tracing the imagery which, in the literary compositions of different countries, captivates the fancy, and impresses the heart; and thus bounds his views to those investigations, which result in fixing the laws of just taste. The historian, who is not qualified to read the original records of the age and country which are the subjects of his lucubrations, finds himself perplexed at every step. He moves onward through dimness and shade. He is obliged to trust implicitly to guides, who may be, for aught he knows, ignorant or unfaithful. Thus do his difficulties multiply; and he finds himself little qualified to investigate what is embarrassing, and to elucidate what is obscure—and, however penetrating may be his natural sagacity, and however alert may be his vigilance, he is continually liable to fall into the most ridiculous errors.

To say nothing of the peculiar views and circumstances of diplomatists and statesmen, or of those who hold even subordinate situations in our public offices, the occurrences of common life render a familiarity with different languages highly expedient, if not essentially requisite to successful enterprize. Our armies and our fleets have, of late years, carried on their operations in almost every nation of Europe, and in all the quarters of the globe—and it is evident to the perception of common sense, what facilities are afforded to the conduct of those operations, by a knowledge of the vernacular tongue of the country in which they take place. The want of this knowledge was found to be so inconvenient, and in some instances so detrimental, and even fatal in Flanders, at the commencement of the war against the Republic of France, that a vocabulary, containing, in three or four languages, a collection of military terms, and of the forms of speech used in the common intercourse of life, was found to be extremely useful. It is a well known fact, that the first process entered upon by a military cadet in our East Indian possessions, is the learning of the Hindostannee tongue. To all which observations it may be added, that for the management of the extensive concerns of our merchants, manufacturers, and superior tradesmen, it is highly desirable to add to other qualifications that of a good linguist. Hence a few plain and practical remarks upon the study of languages, may in this Essay be esteemed as not altogether useless or uninteresting.

Languages are divided into two classes, the dead and the living—that is to say, those which are no longer used by the general mass of the inhabitants of any country, as the means of oral communication, and the remembrance of which is preserved merely by written documents; such as the Latin, the Greek, the Hebrew, and the Saxon—and those which are still in use in different states as the medium of social intercourse, such as the French, the Italian, the Spanish, and the Portuguese.

With respect to living languages, it is certain, that the most effectual and the most speedy method, whereby a pupil may acquire a facility in them, is to reside for a sufficient time in the countries where they are in vernacular use, and to frequent the company of that class of society where they are spoken in their purity. Much instruction may also be gained by attendance upon theatrical performances, and by listening to legal pleadings in those countries, where the courts of law are open, and advocates are employed to plead. By this means the process of instruction is perpetually going on. Necessity at first compels to exertion; and the pleasures of society give a stimulus to the intellect. The faculty of association puts forth its full influence for the production of the desired effect; and ideas and their corresponding words soon begin to present themselves simultaneously to the mind. Mr. Gibbon describes in the following lively terms, the easy and the rapid manner, in which, during his first residence at Lausanne, he acquired a knowledge of the French tongue: "In the Pays de Vaud, the French language is used with less imperfection than in most of the distant provinces of France: in Pavilliard's family, necessity compelled me to listen and to speak; and if I was at first disheartened by the apparent slowness, in a few months I was astonished by the rapidity of my progress. My pronunciation was formed by the constant repetition of the same sounds; the variety of words and idioms, the rules of grammar, and distinctions of genders, were impressed on my memory: ease and freedom were obtained by practice; correctness and elegance, by labour; and before I was recalled home, French, in which I spontaneously thought, was more familiar than English to my ear, my tongue, and my pen."

It must, however, be observed, as a matter of the highest moment, that unless oral instructions be accompanied and confirmed by grammatical and philological studies, their results will, on quitting the scene of their communication, be lost, with a celerity which is hardly to be conceived. That which is learned merely by rote, soon vanishes from the recollection. It should seem to be the law of Providence, that what is easily attained, makes a slight impression on the tablet of the memory; and that a slight impression is soon erased. No intellectual acquirement is solid and permanent, which is not founded on the knowledge and application of principles.

For those who cannot conveniently fix their residence in the country, the language of which they wish to acquire, the most feasible method of attaining this object, is to procure the assistance of a native of that country in the capacity of tutor. In this case, the choice of the individual is a matter of prime importance. To say nothing of moral character and correctness of manners, it is not every one who is qualified to teach his native tongue. The office of an accomplished preceptor, in any language, requires a rare union of acquirements, it demands an extensive acquaintance with general literature, and a knowledge of the principles of universal grammar and good taste. People, who are not themselves well educated, will experience but little success in educating others. And while our country swarms with foreigners of every description, whose first idea, when they are reduced to difficulties, is to assume the office of teachers, caution on this head is peculiarly necessary. Ignorance and presumption generally go hand in hand; and it is by no means an uncommon incident, that they, who in their native country never rose higher than to the occupation of valets or clerks, profess to imbue their pupils with all the graces and elegancies of its language. It is obvious, that from instructors of this description, little can be learned but vulgarity and barbarism. A faithful and intelligent preceptor, however, may be of the greatest use. He will be enabled to attune the ear of his pupil to a correct pronunciation. He will give him a relish for the best authors of his native country. He will introduce him to a familiar acquaintance, not only with its historians and poets, but also with its more idiomatic, its comic and colloquial writers, whose phraseology will be an excellent guide, and will afford him much facility in speaking their language. At the same time he will instruct him in composition, and qualify him for maintaining an epistolary correspondence in the language which is the object of his study. It is evident that the earlier the period at which a pupil is entrusted to the care of such a tutor as has been described, and the more time he dedicates to his instructions, the more quick and certain will be his progress. To a youth of good parts, daily and domestic intercourse with a preceptor of this description will almost, as far as the acquisition of languages is concerned, supersede the necessity of foreign travel.

The above-mentioned methods are requisite for the acquisitiou of what may be styled a practical use of the living languages. But there is a numerous class of students, who never enter into the concerns of active life—whose views are confined to the closet, and who merely wish to peruse the works of the standard writers of different modern nations, as they read the Latin and Greek classics, without particularly troubling themselves with the study of the colloquial forms of speech. How many scholars are there, for instance, who never held a conversation in Italian, but who experience great pleasure in perusing the poems of Tasso and Ariosto in the original. This degree of acquaintance with modern languages is not a matter of difficult acquirement. A few elementary instructions, from a properly qualified teacher, are required, after which, the student, if he be possessed of tolerable abilities, and of sufficient diligence, and especially if he has previously obtained a grammatical knowledge of the Latin tongue, may, in a great measure, depend upon his own exertions. In this pursuit, however, he must be particularly admonished, above all things, to lay his foundation well—not to be disgusted with the toil of elementary inquiries—to dwell with patient industry upon grammatical inflections—and not to leave any difficulty without due investigation. He must advance into the district of literature, as the skilful and prudent general advances into an enemy's country—with caution and circumspection, being particularly careful to leave no strong place unoccupied in his rear. And during the whole course of his progress he will derive singular advantage from Sir William Jones's method of double translation, that is, from making a version of passages selected from some approved author, of the language which he is studying, into English—and after a proper interval of time, re-translating that version into the original tongue. This process will give him a stock of words, and a facility of expression, and by comparing his second version, with the phraseology of the original author, he will in a manner constitute him his corrector, and thus acquire the aid of a tutor, who will guard him against barbarism, and impart to him a taste for the elegancies of style.

As to the dead languages, the principal of them are the Latin, the Greek, and the Hebrew. These are taught in our

Schools and Universities. The systems of our various public establishments are not exactly alike, but they are all well adapted to the end which they are designed to answer. They are all founded upon patient industry, and accuracy of elementary research, without which, the attainment of any valuable knowledge is utterly impracticable. It does not fall within the province of the present work to enter into any criticism of these systems. Where all are good, it is hardly necessary—it would perhaps be invidious, to inquire which is the best. But for the direction of some masters of private seminaries, and for the guidance of those who may wish to attain to a certain degree of classical knowledge, by dint of their own exertions, it may not be inexpedient to subjoin a method, by which a student may attain to a tolerable acquaintance with the Latin and Greek languages.

Pursuing the common road, he will begin with the Latin tongue. The first requisite will be an acquaintance with the grammar. Latin Grammars are almost innumerable; but Owen's Lilly's Accidence improved, published by Lowndes, London, is particularly adapted to unassisted learners. First, because it exhibits a sufficient variety of forms of the declension of nouns, and is nevertheless concise. Secondly, because the syllables of doubtful pronunciation in the Latin words are carefully accented. Thirdly, because the syntax rules are copious, but clear, and illustrated by a sufficiency of singularly well chosen and classical examples. Of this grammar, the accidence and syntax should be committed to memory.

The examples in the syntax being construed at the end of the book, the student will, by the perusal, acquire a knowledge of a considerable number of words and combinations. When he is thoroughly master of them, therefore, he may proceed to try to construe some easy introductory book. He must henceforth, resolutely forego the help of translations, they are the bane of scholarship. Let him provide himself with Ainsworth's Dictionary, and Valpy's Delectus. This latter most useful book, contains in its first pages a number of easy sentences, through which he will, by the help of his dictionary and grammar, proceed with profit and pleasure. But he must observe, that he ought to keep himself in the constant exercise of analysis, or parsing, *i. e.* declining the nouns and pronouns, forming the verbs which occur, and investigating in the rules of syntax, the reason of the cases, genders, numbers, modes, &c. This will appear at first irksome, but it will soon become easy; and in the formation of verbs, and the declension of nouns, he will find much assistance in Hoole's Terminations.

Those who have not sufficient courage to encounter Valpy's Delectus, will find a succedaneum for resolute study in Bailey's Phædrus, in which the road of the scholar is smoothed by an *ordo,* or an exhibition of the arrangement of the Latin words as they occur in English construction; by an index or dictionary adapted to the author; and by a collection of remarkable phrases. The writer of this article would, however, by no means recommend the use of this, or similar books, as he is persuaded that more real progress in a knowledge of the Latin tongue, will be made by the patient, unassisted investigation of ten lines, than by the perusal of fifty lines thus facilitated by special indexes and ordos.

When he enters on the second part of Valpy's Delectus, which contains more intricate sentences than those which occurred in the former, he will do well to procure Lyne's Latin Primer, where he will find a number of excellent rules for construing Latin. These rules he may apply to Valpy's Delectus, as Valpy's selection of passages is more interesting and classical than Lyne's.

When he feels a consciousness that he has advanced sufficiently into Valpy's Delectus, to have acquired a tolerable facility in investigating sentences, he will be gratified by entering upon the perusal of a classic writer. The general simplicity of the construction of Ovid's periods, is a sufficient ground of recommendation as an introductory author. Let the student then provide himself with the Excerpta ex Ovidii Metamorph.

published by Pote, of Eton. In the notes subjoined to the text, he will find an useful help. It will also be necessary for him to procure Lempriere's Classical Dictionary. This work will throw great light on the mythological and historical allusions which abound in every page of Ovid. Cellarius's maps too will afford him a correct idea of ancient geography.

During the whole of this process, it is absolutely and indispensably requisite that he continue the task of analysis. If he has not the assistance of a master, of course he cannot derive any advantage from the common exercise books. But the method of double translation will be found to preclude the necessity of any help of this kind. By daily translating into English some of the prose sentences in Valpy's Delectus, and on the ensuing day re-translating his version into Latin, he will be able to correct his own exercises, and acquire in time a considerable promptitude in Latin composition.

The prosody contained in Owen's grammar is compendious and satisfactory, but that contained in Valpy's Latin Grammar is still more so. By committing the latter to memory, and applying its rules to Ovid's verses, he will, in process of time, be able to read Latin verse correctly. In order to assist his more early pronunciation, the Gradus ad Parnassum, or Labbe's Catholici Indices Eruditæ Pronunciationis, will be found of signal benefit.

He may now vary his studies by the perusal of Cornelius Nepos. In the notes to the Delphin edition of this author, he will meet with considerable assistance.

When he has read what he esteems a sufficient portion of Cornelius Nepos, he may read a few books of Cæsar's Commentaries. Of this author also, the Delphin edition will be found the most useful.

From Ovid he may advance to Virgil, which author he will do well to read in the school edition of Heyne. The explanatory notes of that indefatigable scholar are, in an eminent degree, clear, useful, and honest—because he turns not from difficulties, "to hold his farthing candle to the sun." He bends the strength of his talents to the faithful elucidation of his author, and thus he is truly an useful editor.

It is to be wished, that Horace had fallen into such industrious hands. In Knox's Horatius Expurgatus, however, the scholar will find a good collection of illustrative notes. The annotations subjoined to Frances's translation also throw much light on various obscure passages in this elegant author. The Variorum edition of Juvenal is an elaborate work, and the annotations throw ample light upon most of his difficulties. The learned veteran, Mr. Owen, in his poetical version of Juvenal, and in his occasional notes, has displayed the various accomplishments of a correct grammarian, and of a scholar of elegant taste. During the perusal of Juvenal, this valuable publication may be consulted with pleasure and profit.

When these works, or considerable portions of them, have been carefully studied, especially if the method of parsing, and double translation recommended above, have been faithfully persevered in, the student

"Nabit sine cortice"

will be qualified to pursue his studies without any further peculiar aid.

In the study of the Greek tongue, the scholar's attention will, of course, be first directed to the grammar. The Eton and Westminster rudiments are the standard Greek grammars of this country. The former, being the more concise of the two, is the more proper to be committed to memory; the latter, exhibiting a much greater variety of the declensions of nouns substantive and adjective, is a very acceptable object of occasional consultation and reference. But it will be by no means necessary for the student to commit to memory the whole of the Eton grammar. He must, however, make himself master of all the paradigms of the declension of nouns, pronouns, and verbs. If he does not accomplish this, he will find himself embarrassed in every subsequent step. It is very desirable also that he should be familiarly acquainted with the rules for the formation of various cases in the fifth declension of simple nouns; and he will derive great advantage from a frequent perusal of the rules for the formation of the tenses of verbs. It may also be useful to him to be informed, that the verbs in μι are more clearly exhibited in the Westminster, than in the Eton grammar.

By statedly writing down the paradigms which he has learnt, he will not only ascertain the correctness of his remembrance, but he will also become familiarly acquainted with the Greek characters.

When he has thoroughly drilled himself in the grammar, he may proceed to the study of Dalzel's Collectanea Græca Minora; a work of modest pretensions, but of transcendent merit, whose author possessed the rarely united accomplishments of profound erudition, and a happy facility and benevolent desire of communicating instruction. Though qualified to expatiate in the widest field of Grecian literature, he condescended to sympathize with the tyro—he felt his difficulties, he perceived the obstructions that stop his progress, and skilfully and satisfactorily removed them. His diligent fidelity, and his careful minuteness of explanation, are beyond all praise. When to all these recommendations is superadded the elegance of his selection from the purest Greek authors, we may congratulate the student on the occurrence of an introductory book of such superior excellence. The index subjoined to this volume supersedes the use of a lexicon.

Whether the tyro wishes to pursue his studies by the perusal of prose or verse, he is happy in the further assistance of Mr. Dalzel. In that gentleman's two volumes, entitled Collectanea Græca Majora, he will find a treasure of explanatory notes, in which the peculiarities of the Greek idiom are accurately developed.

In the use of the prose Collectanea, it will be advisable to adopt the plan suggested by the editor in his preface, viz. to begin with the extracts from the easier authors, such as Xenophon and Ælian, and afterwards to make trial of Herodotus, Polyænus, and Thucydides; and last of all, to peruse the passages selected from the philosophers, orators, and critics.

Till he has formed a tolerably familiar acquaintance with the Greek radicals, he will find Hedericus's Lexicon the best adapted to the exigencies of the general study of Greek authors. In process of time, he will derive more pleasure, as well as profit, from the philosophic arrangement of Scapula.

When he has read the historical extracts from Xenophon, he may, by way of variety, apply himself to the study of the poetic Collectanea. This elaborate work is introduced by extensive extracts from Homer's Odyssey. The diligent perusal of these extracts will, with the assistance of Mr. Dalzel's copious annotations, give him a very competent acquaintance with Homer's style. The constant consultation of the Tabella Dialectorum, in the Eton grammar, will soon familiarize him to the variations from the standard, that is, the Attic dialect, which perpetually occur in the works of the mighty master of epic song.

When he has carefully studied the extracts from the Odyssey, he will be well qualified, and, in all probability, inclined to read the Iliad. The Lexicon of Schrevelius was drawn up with a particular reference to this work: and to the unassisted reader of Homer, this manual will frequently be found of great service. The most convenient edition of the Iliad is Heyne's two vols. 8vo. Many of Clarke's notes are very instructive; but the dangerous allurement of a Latin translation, renders his edition a very ineligible book for a tyro.

During the perusal of the Iliad, however, considerable portions of Dalzel's two volumes of Collectanea Majora should be daily read. These books, the Greek student may be earnestly exhorted

Nocturnâ versare manu, versare diurnâ.

When the first volume has been thoroughly digested, the student will be able with ease and pleasure to read Xenophon's Anabasis. The most useful edition of this interesting work is that printed at Oxford, in 1788, in octavo. In the notes, and especially in the Index Græcitatis, they, who are yet inexpert in the Greek tongue, will find many difficulties elucidated, and many uncommon senses of words and peculiarities of phrase satisfactorily explained.

A very elegant work was printed at Oxford in 1768, entitled Των παλαιων Επιταφιοι, or, Funeral Eulogies upon military men. The index and notes to this work contain a treasure of learning, and the editor has manifested great industry and attention in their composition.

Considerable benefit may also be derived from the notes on a small collection entitled Ποικιλη Ιστορια, published by Pote, of Eton, in 1785. It will, however, be advisable for the scholar to cut out the Latin translation, which in a great measure destroys the utility of this otherwise valuable manual.

During the whole of the course of reading which has been delineated, it is indispensably requisite that the student should daily exercise himself in parsing. Inattention to this exercise will be ruinous in its consequences. The method of double translation recommended in the study of the Latin tongue, may be with advantage practised in the study of Grecian literature. Bos's Ellipsis Græcæ, and Vigerus de Idiotismis, should be always at hand, as they exemplify and interpret a vast variety of instances of difficult phraseology.

It is presumed that this course of introductory study will qualify the scholar to extend, in almost any direction, his researches into Grecian literature.

CHAP I.

ON THE STUDY OF THE BELLES LETTRES.

What is included in the Belles Lettres—Five periods in the progress of knowledge—A fine taste necessary to the accomplished scholar—Utility of the study of the Belles Lettres—The foundation to be laid in Grammar, and the knowledge of the languages—Importance of the Belles Lettres to different characters.

If we examine into the frame of the human mind, we shall perceive that the Supreme Being has not only given us a desire for knowledge, but has also implanted in us a sense of beauty, harmony, and proportion, so that we cannot help receiving a high pleasure from a masterly piece of music, an expressive picture, a sublime poem, and a finished oration, though we are unacquainted with the sources from which the pleasure is derived. But though the liberal and elegant arts afford us an agreeable entertainment, even when we are ignorant of their principles; it is certain that our enjoyment of them will be more just, lively, and delicate, if we have cultivated our taste, and acquired an accurate and enlarged view of the several things which contribute to the excellence of composition. Hence the importance of a general, not to say an extensive and accurate acquaintance with what are denominated the Belles Lettres, which will enable us not only to judge of the works of others, but in a certain degree, to excel in composition ourselves. Every person who has enjoyed a good education, or whose situation in life presupposes the advantages of early and solid instruction, will be expected to speak and to write his own language with fluency, judgment, and taste. To assist the reader in the attainment of this perfection will be the object of the following chapters.

The term Belles Lettres is so vague and indeterminate, that we scarcely meet with two writers who have meant by it the same thing. Some persons have maintained that the true Belles Lettres are Natural Philosophy, Geometry, and other branches of Mathematics: some have included in this department of learning, the polite, or fine arts: and others comprehend under the term, all those useful and instructive branches of learning, which occupy the memory and judgment; such as Geography, Chronology, History, and Heraldry: and some have given it a more confined meaning, including in it, Rhetoric, Criticism, Poetry, and Oratory. We shall follow the latter arrangement in our account of Belles Lettres, without neglecting, in the other parts of the work, those other subjects connected with General Knowledge.

Had we nothing farther to urge in favour of polite learning, than that it furnishes an innocent, easy, and refined amusement, even this would render it worthy of attention. In the present state of our nature, it is a happiness to find recreations which are always within our reach, and which result from the situation of our own minds. The Belles Lettres, in the more extensive use of the term, may be considered in a much superior point of view, than merely as administering a relaxation from severer studies: they deserve to be regarded as matters of no small importance, as having promoted in the highest degree the benefit and glory of individuals and nations. We cannot be insensible, that the periods, and the countries in which the liberal arts have been cherished, and carried to a high degree of perfection, are of all others, the most illustrious and distinguished.

If we look into the history of the world, we shall perceive five periods that have been particularly famous for their progress in knowledge and taste, which are thus enumerated:

I. The *Athenian* period, which began before the battle of Marathon, and continued down to the time of Alexander the Great. This æra produced Herodotus, Thucydides, Xenophon, Sophocles, Euripides, Pericles, Isocrates, Æschines, Demosthenes, Socrates, Plato, Aristotle, Aristophanes, Menander, Phidias, Apelles, and Praxiteles.

II. The second is the *Roman* period, which includes Terence, Lucretius, Cicero, Cæsar, Sallust, Livy, Virgil, Horace, Varro, and Vitruvius. To these have been added, though they are men unquestionably of an inferior reputation, with regard to the purity of their writings, Paterculus, Florus, Lucan, and Juvenal; Seneca, Quintilian, and Pliny.

III. The third is denominated the *Arabian* period, which, though not to be put on a level with the others, is nevertheless too illustrious to be passed over unnoticed. When the Saracens had subdued the countries about them, and had established considerable kingdoms in Asia, Africa, and Spain, like other conquerors, they betook themselves to the arts of peace, and the improvement of the human mind. For this purpose they translated the best Greek Authors into their own language. Though they did not wholly neglect the politer studies, and even excelled in poetry and history, yet they chiefly gave themselves up to the sciences, at once sublime, and of practical utility, viz. Astronomy, Chemistry, and Medicine.

IV. The next is the *Italian*, or *Medicean* period, so called from the great encouragement given to the study, and improvement of the Belles Lettres by the illustrious family of the Medici. This æra took its rise from the revival of learning and taste in Italy, after the capture of Constantinople, and reached down to the close of the 16th century. In this period are included the celebrated names of Petrarch, Boccacio, Ariosto, Tasso, Guicciardini, Machiavel, Davila, Bembo, and Vida; all of whom are illustrious, in some way or other, for their writings; and to these are to be added, as ornaments to the arts, Raphael, Michael Angelo, Corregio, Guido, Titian, and such a constellation of painters and sculptors as the world never produced.

V. The last period is said to have begun about a century and a half ago, and has continued to the present time. This period is, on some accounts, more illustrious than the preceding, and has been especially eminent for the general diffusion of knowledge and elegance, for the simplicity and refinement of the manners of men, and for an extensive improvement in the conveniences and embellishments of life. Without attempting to enumerate all the persons who have adorned these latter times, we may briefly refer to a few of the writers, who by their works have done honour to several countries in modern Europe, particularly to France and England. In the former have flourished a Corneille, a Racine, a Moliere, a Boileau, a Massillon, Flechier, Bossuet, and Fenelon; and in our own country we recognize the names of a Locke, and Newton; a Milton, a Dryden, a Pope, a Tillotson, an Atterbury, Addison, and Swift; a Goldsmith, Johnson, and many others, who deserve to be placed in the same rank, and will receive due honour from posterity.

If it appear strange that the names of Homer and Pindar have been omitted, it should be recollected, that these great poets flourished before the respective æras that we have described. Poetry, and particularly the higher departments of it, arrives sooner at perfection than the other polite arts, or the other branches of general literature.

The cultivation of the Belles Lettres reflects the highest glory on the individuals who have excelled in the study, as well as on nations who have been benefitted by them. The illustrious characters whom we have mentioned, while they have thrown a splendour round the countries and the ages in which they lived, have by their admirable works transmitted their own renown to all succeeding times, and will ever be held in grateful remembrance. Without entering upon the public benefits which flow from the elegant and liberal studies, we may observe, that an extensive acquaintance with, and a just taste for polite literature, will tend to improve the understanding and to refine the affections and manners. It should be remembered, that we must join a just taste to an extensive acquaintance with polite literature, for otherwise our knowledge will not greatly avail us. A load of learning will be of small service, if it be not accompanied with a sound judgment, and a lively feeling with respect to the beauties of composition. There are persons in the world, to whose erudition scarcely any thing is unknown, and yet their real character is well drawn by Mr. Pope, who says

Pains, Reading, Study, are their just pretence;
And all they want, is Spirit, Taste, and Sense!*

But if we apply to the Belles Lettres with a proper degree of discernment, and with hearts disposed to relish the natural and unaffected charms, which are presented to us in the productions of the best ancient and modern writers, we shall find reason gradually improving, and our sentiments of things becoming every day more accurate, enlarged, and liberal. The more we converse with the works which have stood the test of ages, and which are formed upon the principles of Classic purity and elegance, the more will our faculties be strengthened, the greater progress shall we make in good sense, that most valuable acquisition; and the fitter shall we be for acquitting ourselves with credit and dignity, in the common duties of our stations. It is the excellence of polite literature, that the objects, on which it is chiefly engaged, are the usual events and affections of social life, so that we cannot increase our acquaintance with it, without increasing our qualifications for acting with wisdom and prudence in the general intercourse with our fellow creatures.

An extensive acquaintance with, and a just taste for polite literature, will refine the manners, as well as improve the understanding, a circumstance that should recommend it highly to our regard. The Belles Lettres will contribute to mend the heart in a direct way, as the works which are eminent in that branch of knowledge will be found to contain a great number of useful remarks, maxims, and reflections, and as they display a multitude of facts and characters which are calculated to make a deep impression upon the mind, and to inspire it with the true love of virtue and solid glory. But the indirect influence of the liberal sciences is perhaps still more powerful; a steady application to them gradually polishes the human soul, corrects and softens the turbulence of the passions, and introduces a nobleness of thinking, which has a happy effect upon the conduct of life.

Though there is not that strict and close connexion between a taste for natural, and a taste for moral beauty, which some philosophers have imagined, yet they are not entirely without a relationship. The " elegans spectator formarum," with respect to external objects, and the productions of genius, will be better qualified, and disposed to admire the graces of the mind, than others, and even to follow after them, when no extraordinary temptations to the contrary occur in his way. He cannot converse with the sages of antiquity;—the illustrions men of former days, and the works of a fine imagination, without feeling and imbibing in a certain degree, a dignity of sentiment and of action. He will be raised above the inducements of vulgar pleasures, and become a more amiable member of society; accordingly, it may be observed that persons of true taste are seldom deficient in the virtues of politeness and humanity, whatever vices they may possess of any other kind.

Having pointed out the general usefulness of the Belles Lettres, as they are calculated to improve the understanding, and refine the affections and manners, we shall now, in order that we may be the more sensible of their excellence and importance, mention several of the benefits that spring from those branches of polite learning, separately considered, which come under our immediate cognizance.

Although music, painting, and sculpture, do not, in this place, fall within our province, yet we may observe, that if we have an easy opportunity of acquiring a taste for, and proficiency in them, they will contribute to our pleasures, and enlarge our sphere of knowledge, but they may be omitted without any prejudice to our reputation and pretensions as scholars. Nor is it proposed to enumerate all the advantages resulting from the liberal sciences, but to give such a short and comprehensive view of them, as may attract attention, and excite diligence.

It will not be necessary, that every person shall pursue all that is recommended as worthy of attainment, each will select for himself, what he deems most important to his own feelings, or nearest allied to his situation and rank in society. Few, perhaps, of the readers of this Introduction, will think it to their purpose, to pay any attention to the Greek and Latin languages, and still fewer to the Hebrew, yet we shall touch upon the advantages resulting from the study of them all, because to other persons, whose pursuits, taken up, probably, late in life, force an attention to them, it may be important to know, that to be well grounded in these languages, is of the highest moment.

The languages now enumerated, are, to a certain class of persons, justly reckoned the keys of knowledge, and the foundation of good taste, so that without a competent knowledge in them, they will stumble at the threshold, and never make any considerable progress in their pursuits. As few books of importance are written in the Hebrew language, excepting the scriptures of the Old Testament, it is chiefly useful to divines, but with regard to them, an acquaintance with it is absolutely necessary; for it is certainly absurd for persons to take upon themselves the office of explainers of revelation, without being able to have recourse to the tongue in which it was delivered. But the Hebrew language merits attention, as a part of the Belles Lettres, because the Old Testament abounds with the finest strains of poetry and eloquence, the simplicity, grandeur, and beauty of which, cannot be perfectly understood except by those who have an exact and critical knowledge of the original.

As to the Greek, it is useful, not only as it was in this language that the charter of our salvation was delivered, but also with relation to our advancement in polite learning. It was Greece that gave birth to the most eminent poets, orators, historians, and philosophers ; so that to the language of Greece we must apply, if we desire to have a thorough acquaintance with, and a true relish for those natural, unaffected, and sublime beauties of composition, which have been the admiration of all ages. The same may be asserted of the Latin tongue, which likewise presents us with a set of fine writers, the disciples and rivals of Greece, who will be applauded so long as good sense and good taste subsist in the world. But the Latin is also useful, as it is the vehicle of correspondence among men of letters, and a kind of universal language, in which many capital treatises of modern times have been composed, so that unless we are well skilled in it, we can make but an indifferent progress in several important parts of science.

In order to our improvement in polite learning, we must, in the first place, lay a solid foundation in the principles of General Grammar ; we must then enter upon that of Oratory, for the purpose of attaining a clear method in whatever we wish, either by speech or writing to enforce upon others as principles of truth or duty. Our next concern must be to make ourselves acquainted with the rules and art of Rhetoric, contained in works expressly devoted to the purpose. Closely connected with Rhetoric, is the art of Criticism, by which is meant a nice discernment with regard to the beauties and defects of other species of composition besides eloquence. There are several kinds of Criticism, all of which are useful in a certain degree ; even that which relates to the different readings of MSS. and conjectural emendations, is often of great importance to the interests of literature. At the revival of letters in Europe, this art was of the utmost consequence, in order by it to obtain correct editions of the ancient authors, which had been mutilated and injured by the carelessness or ignorance of transcribers. Nor are those persons to be despised, or even lightly esteemed, who continue to labour in the same way, and who endeavour to oblige the world with still more perfect and splendid copies of the noble productions of Antiquity. But a still more interesting part of Criticism, is that which applies itself to the higher excellences of writing, which philosophically displays the sources from which they proceed, and feelingly represent their charms; and which tends both to correct and to refine our taste. We cannot converse too much with those critics who answer to this character, viz. those who are excellent authors, as well as excellent judges. We shall reap substantial benefit from perusing the works of such men as Longinus, Quintilian, Horace, Addison, Hurd, and Lord Kames; to these, and particularly to the latter, we shall in what follows have frequent recourse.

From Criticism, we proceed to one of its prime objects, Poetry, which is well deserving of our attention. Those who are fond of this divine art, generally speak of it with such raptures, as young lovers do of their mistresses. Without, however, losing our reason, or embracing the language of enthusiasm, we may observe, that many solid advantages will result from an acquaintance with the favorites of the Muses. Nothing is better calculated to enliven and strengthen the imagination. Nothing will afford us an equal choice and plenty of words, or give us a superior insight into the variety and force of language. Nothing will furnish us with ampler materials for noble expressions and animated figures. But the higher species will perform much more than all this. The Epic, the Tragic, the Lyric, and the Moral kinds, will inspire us with a number of sublime sentiments and reflections, will instruct us in the movement of the passions, and form us to a striking and pathetic manner of composition. The graces of writing will be acquired from reading the poets, sooner than from any other source, and perhaps, there never was a person wholly unmindful of them, that was a truly elegant author; and it is no mean recommendation of the Poets, that several of them may be ranked among our best prose writers. History, on which we shall soon enlarge, is another very important part of the Belles Lettres, but the benefits derived from the study of it, need not be recounted here, they will be better enumerated hereafter. It may however be observed, that it qualifies us for the right conduct of life, whatever be the station we fill. This, connected with biography, presents to the view a thousand illustrious characters, actions, and events, deserving of our attention. It opens to our mind the great objects of government and morality. It sets before us the discoveries of science, the improvements of art, and the progress of human reason.

Another circumstance well worthy of our attention will be, the obtaining some acquaintance with the sentiments and systems of the ancient philosophers. To this may be added miscellaneous learning, which is almost entirely a modern acquisition. The ancients generally are either poets, or orators, or philosophers, or historians, or critics; but the moderns have produced a multitude of performances which cannot properly be ranked with any of these species, and yet are not to be neglected. Under the denomination of miscellaneous learning, may be ranked the Spectator, the Guardian, Rambler, Adventurer, &c.; fictitious history, productions of wit and humour, together with occasional dissertations and essays.

With regard to the importance of the study of the Belles Lettres, it may be assumed, that it will assist us in attaining a clear, harmonious, and forcible style, which is a matter of great consequence to those who have to convey their ideas to others. Perspicuity is indispensable to the writer or the speaker, and without it, all that a person says or does, in the way of literature, can be of no avail. If we do not express our sentiments in a manner that is easy to be understood, our labour will be lost. Nor is the harmony of language to be considered as a trivial accomplishment. A taste for it is implanted in the human breast, and persons will find themselves pleased and affected by it, though they cannot assign a reason for the influence it has upon them. Besides, the clearness of a discourse will frequently be seen to depend greatly on a just and elegant arrangement of the terms we make use of. As to a forcible style, there can be no doubt about its excellency, since it must be exceedingly important to have our thoughts come with weight upon the minds of our readers or hearers. It may probably be asserted, without fear of contradiction, that none, who were wholly ignorant of polite literature, ever united in their works, a perspicuous, harmonious, and strong manner of expression. They must have been deficient in one or more, or all of these qualities. It is only by conversing with the fine writers of ancient and modern times; it is only by applying to the liberal studies, that we can learn to communicate our sentiments at once with clearness, gracefulness, and strength; and a happy conjunction of clearness, gracefulness, and strength, will add an efficacy to our compositions that cannot be easily described. The ancients were thoroughly sensible of the benefits resulting from the union of the qualities just enumerated, and therefore applied themselves to the acquisition of polite learning with incredible ardour and perseverance. For this purpose they entered into an accurate discussion of the nature and combination of long and short sounds, and the beauty and vigour which a discourse may derive from a judicious management of numerical feet. By these means they brought their eloquence to a surprizing point of perfection, and though it may not be necessary for us to carry the matter so far as they did, yet something of the same care would meet with an ample reward.

With respect to those who would apply themselves to the study of the sacred volume, it may be observed, that a proper knowledge and taste in the Belles Lettres, will enable them to enter with more discernment and spirit into the sense of the Scriptures, in general, and especially into the elegance and force of particular passages. A thorough acquaintance with the sacred records will be of vast importance to those who undertake to explain their meaning, and enforce the doctrines and duties inculcated in them. Nothing, perhaps, will better prepare a person for this acquaintance, than a previous study of the authors who are eminent in the republic of polite learning, hence he will acquire that true genius of criticism, which will enable him to rise above grammatical trifles, and to survey with full scope and energy, the places he has occasion to illustrate; hence he will peruse the writings of the inspired penmen with something of the ardour with which they themselves wrote, which must surely be the most likely way of discovering their design and meaning. Had commentators been usually men of taste, the world would not have been loaded with such a number of tedious and insipid performances. But a competent progress in the liberal studies, will be of signal service in enabling a person to ascertain the beauty and emphasis of many particular passages of Scripture. In this, an accurate knowledge of the Belles Lettres will most eminently display itself. Those who are conversant with the best writers, will frequently, by producing a parallel sentiment or mode of expression, throw extraordinary light and lustre on certain passages in ancient literature. Raphelius, Elmer, Bos, and others, have made excellent use of their learning in this respect. Indeed, it is only the person of taste who is likely to feel strongly, and describe the sublimity, the eloquence, the pathos, and the energy of a thousand places, which are to be met with in the works of antiquity, and especially in the sacred records.

Those who have to plead for, and with their fellow creatures, will find a knowledge of polite literature of great advantage in striking the affections, which is of much cousequence to the writer and orator. Some have held this part of the business as of little moment. If, indeed, men had been framed without passions, we should have had nothing to do but to speak to their reason and understanding; or if the business of the orator were only with the discerning few, who always followed the cool dictates of the rational faculties, it would be quite sufficient to enumerate, as simply and plainly as possible, those facts and arguments by which they ought to be governed. But considering man as he really is, it is of the highest importance to address his feelings as well as his judgment; we should endeavour to touch the strings of his soul, and to awaken his gratitude, his shame, his joy, his fear, and his hopes. This can be effectually done, only by being ourselves under the influence of the principles recommended by the dignity and weight of the subjects that we treat upon, and by the internal strength of the motives with which they are enforced. In the manner of striking the affections, we shall receive much help from a knowledge and taste in the Belles Lettres: we shall learn a more lively and animated strain of composition, and a more suitable and engaging method of appealing to the heart.

History will furnish us with many excellent observations and illustrious facts, which cannot fail, when properly introduced and represented, of making a powerful impression upon those whom we address in our discourses, whether by the press or from the pulpit. The Orators will shew us the way of insinuating ourselves into the good will of those for whom we write, and to whom we speak: they will teach the management of those figures that speak powerfully to the passions. The epic and tragic poets will describe the sublime, the affecting, and tender emotions of the mind, instruct us in the sources of pity and terror, and tell us the language that is fitted to excite them.

Finally; a competent progress in the liberal studies will prevent our compositions, on the one hand, from being careless and incorrect, and on the other from being jejune and spiritless. These are two extremes which ought most studiously to be avoided. If we are remarkably defective in accuracy, though we abound in other excellences, we shall disgust the judicious; but if we are cold and lifeless, we shall be guilty of a more disagreeable fault, and the best method of avoiding both these defects, will be by a diligent application to the Belles Lettres. These will not only teach us to guard against glaring improprieties, but will oblige us likewise to be dissatisfied with a languid correctness. They will instruct us to put our thoughts into their proper place; to introduce them with delicacy and address, and clothe them with decent ornament. In short, the Belles Lettres will give a colouring, a grace, and an energy to our sentiments, which will be highly advantageous to the scholar in every department of literature.

CHAP. II.

OF LANGUAGE.

Definition of language and articulation—Description of the voice, and on what it depends—Of letters, syllables, and words—Rise and origin of language—Names of things, how selected—Interjections—Origin of action—Causes of metaphorical language—Origin of different kinds of writing—Discovery of letters—Account of Cadmus—Methods and materials of writing.

LANGUAGE may be defined to be a set of words that any people have agreed upon, by which to communicate their thoughts to each other. Or, more generally, by language may be understood the expression of our ideas by certain *articulate* sounds, which are used as the signs of those ideas.

Articulation is the form or character which the voice acquires, by means of the mouth, and its several organs and appendages, as the teeth, the tongue, the lips, the larynx, &c. The voice, by articulation, is not made more loud or soft, which are said to be its primary qualities, but it acquires, in addition to these characters, others that may exist with them. The simplest of these new characters, are those acquired through the openings of the mouth, as these openings differ in giving the voice a passage; and from the several configurations of these openings proceed vowels. There are other articulate forms which the mouth makes, not by mere openings, but by different contacts of its several parts, such as it makes by the junction of the lips; of the tongue with the teeth; of the tongue with the palate, and the like. These contacts are preceded, or immediately followed, by some opening of the mouth; and the articulations so produced are denominated consonants.

The voice is produced by the larynx, which is a hollow organ placed between the root of the tongue and the trachea, or wind-pipe, which gives a passage to the air into and out of the lungs in respiration.

The larynx is composed of cartilaginous pieces, moved in various directions by voluntary muscles, on the motion of which, habit and practice confer a vast precision. Thus, voice is to speech, in relation to the muscles of the larynx, what the rude movements of the fingers of the savage, are to the precise and delicate motions of a man employed in the finest mechanical arts. The principle is the same, the results only are different. It is a general law in the organs of voluntary motion, that they acquire perfection by exercise, that they are in short susceptible of education.

Speech, therefore, may be considered as the formation of the voice, produced by means of the organs about the throat, nose, and mouth, into articulated sounds, by which men communicate their thoughts to each other. All animals have a voice, but man alone speaks, in the sense now alluded to.

If a letter be a sound that cannot be resolved into more simple elements, speech is the formation of the voice into the sounds expressed by letters, and the composition of words from these. Letters, as we have seen, are divided into vowels and consonants: the former are produced simply by the voice passing through the mouth, opened to a greater or less degree, without the aid of the tongue. The latter, are sounds pronounced with the vowels, and modifying or limiting them: they have, therefore, either expressed or understood, vowels before or after them. The sound of the vowel in these cases is altered, by the tongue being applied to some part in the cavity of the mouth, striking against the teeth or lips.

The smallest combinations of letters produce a syllable; syllables, properly joined, make a word; words duly combined form a sentence; and from sentences are produced orations, discourses, &c. So that to principles apparently very trivial, as, to about twenty elementary sounds, we owe that variety of articulate words which have been sufficient to explain the sentiments of all the present and past generations of men.

Language may be considered, as signifying the expression of our ideas by articulate sounds, which are used as the signs of those ideas. In a more general sense, the word language is sometimes used to denote the sounds by which animals of all kinds express their particular feelings and impulses, in a manner that is intelligible to their own species. Between, however, the language of man, in a civilized state, and that of other inferior animals, there is but little analogy. Human language is capable of expressing ideas and notions, of which it is probable the brute creation can have no conception. Speech, according to the ancients, is made to indicate what is expedient and what is inexpedient, and in consequence of this, what is just or unjust; and, therefore, it is peculiar to man, who alone possesses a sense of right and wrong, of the expedient and inexpedient.

Few subjects are more difficult than the attempt to account for the rise and origin of language. As there are no facts to lead us to suppose that articulated language is the result of instinct, the inquiry is interesting and important, though embarrassed with much difficulty, how mankind were first induced to fabricate sounds, and employ them for the purpose of communicating their thoughts. Children learn to speak by insensible imitation, and when advanced in life, they learn other languages, than what they hear spoken about them, under proper instructors, or through the medium of books; but the first men had no speakers to imitate, and no formed language to study. By what means then did they learn to speak?—On this question, only two opinions can be formed. Either language must have been originally revealed from heaven, or it is the fruit of human industry. The greater part of Jews and Christians, and some learned and inquiring Pagans, have embraced the former opinion, which seems to be supported by the authority of Moses, who represents the Creator as teaching our first parents the names of animals. The latter opinion is held by Diodorus Siculus, Lucretius, Horace, and many other Greek and Roman writers, who maintain that language was an art invented by man. The first men, they say, lived for some time in woods and caves, uttering only confused and indistinct noises, till associating for mutual assistance, they came by degrees to use articulate sounds, mutually agreed upon for the arbitrary signs or marks of those ideas in the mind of the speaker, which he wanted to communicate to the hearer.

It is certain, that men could not have instituted civil polity, or have carried on by concert any common work, without communicating their designs to each other, and there are four ways by which it has been thought that this could have been done before the invention of speech, viz. (1) By inarticulate cries, expressive of sentiments and passions. (2) Gestures, and the expression of countenance. (3) Imitative sounds, expressive of audible things; and (4) Painting, by which visible objects may be represented. Of these methods of communication, it is plain that only two have any connexion with language, viz. inarticulate cries, and imitative sounds: the latter must probably be abandoned, as having contributed nothing to the *invention* of articulation, though it may have assisted in its progressive advancement. Therefore, inarticulate cries only must be looked to, as having given rise to the formation of language, if it were an art acquired by human ingenuity alone.

Many of our best modern writers, among whom are Warburton, Johnson, Beattie, and Blair, maintain that language was originally revealed from heaven; and they regard the accounts of its human invention as supposititious, depending upon no fixed principle. The opinions of the ancients, as they are called, in their estimation, claim no greater authority than those of other men, because language was formed and brought to a great degree of perfection, long before the æra of any historian that has come down to modern times; of course the antiquity of the Greek and Roman writers, gives them no advantage in this inquiry, over the philosophers of the present or last century.

If, however, the first language were communicated to man by inspiration, it must, it may be imagined, have been perfect, and held in high reverence by those who spoke it; and would, in fact, have become universal, or the language of all mankind. But we know that a vast variety of languages have prevailed in the world, of which some are very imperfect, and others have unquestionably been lost. Now if different languages were originally invented by different nations, this would naturally follow from the mixture of these nations; whereas it should seem, that no motive sufficiently powerful could have been offered, to induce men, possessed of one perfect language of divine original, to forsake it for others of their own invention, that would, in every respect, be inferior to that with which they or their forefathers had been inspired.

In answer to this, it is said, that nothing was given by inspiration, but the faculty of speech and elements of language; and that men have modified it by their natural powers, in the same way as thousands improve what they could not invent. The first language, if given by inspiration, would have been perfect in its principles, but, probably, not copious: it was sufficient that a foundation was laid of such a nature as would support the largest superstructure, which men might ever have occasion to raise upon it, and that they were taught the method of rearing this superstructure by composition and derivation. This theory, while it preserves the language radically the same, admits the introduction of different dialects in different countries over which men spread themselves. Every new region and every new climate suggests different ideas, and creates different wants, which would produce great diversity, even in the first elements of speech, among all savage nations; the words retained of the original language being used in various senses, and pronounced with various accents. When any of these tribes emerged from barbarism, the improvement and copiousness of their language would keep pace with their own progress in knowledge, and the arts of life. Superior refinement may induce imitation, conquest may impose a language, and extension of empires may melt down different nations and different dialects into one mass; but independent tribes, without any other collateral circumstances, naturally give rise to a diversity of languages. The variety of tongues, therefore, the copiousness of some, and the narrowness of others, furnish no solid objection to the divine origin of language; for, whether it was at first revealed from heaven, or, in the course of ages, was invented by men, a multitude of dialects would inevitably arise as soon as the human race was separated into a number of distinct and independent nations.

After all, we pretend not to decide on this controversy, it is sufficient for our purpose to have very briefly stated the arguments on both sides. On either theory, it is admitted that the first rudiments of speech were very contracted, and we may accordingly proceed to inquire in what manner, and by what steps, language advanced to the state in which we now find it. If we suppose a period to exist before any words were invented or known, it is clear that men could have had no other method of communicating their feelings to others, than by cries of passion, accompanied by such motions and gestures as were expressive of emotion. These are the only signs which nature teaches all men, and which, being natural to all, are understood by all. These exclamations, therefore, called, by grammarians, interjections, uttered in a strong and passionate manner, were, undoubtedly, the elements of speech.—*See the following chapters.*

When a more enlarged communication became requisite, and names began to be applied to objects, these names must have been chosen by assimilating, as much as possible, the nature of the object to be named, to the sound which they gave it: thus, to any thing harsh or boisterous, a harsh or boisterous sound would be applied, in the same manner as a painter would represent grass by using a green colour. He could not act otherwise, if he desired to excite in the hearer the idea of that object which he wished to name. To imagine words invented, or names given to things, in a manner purely arbitrary, is to suppose an effect without a cause. There must have been some motive which led to one name rather than another, and no motive would more generally operate upon men, in their first efforts towards language, than a desire to describe, by speech, the objects which they named, in a manner more or less complete, according as it was in the power of the human voice to effect this imitation. In all languages, a multitude of words are evidently constructed on this principle: a certain bird is named a cuckoo, from the sound which it emits; one sort of wind is said to *roar*, another to *whistle*, and we all know what is meant by the terms thus applied; a bullet from a musket is said to make a *whizzing* noise; a serpent is said to *hiss*, a fly to *buzz*; and the falling of a building is said to come with a *crash*: a heavy and violent rain is said to *pour*, and hail to *rattle*. In all these, and a multitude of other cases, the resemblance between the word, and the thing signified, is plainly discernible.

It will be readily admitted, that this principle of a natural relation between words and objects, can only be applied to language in its simple and early state; and though there are remains of it to be traced, it would be vain and hopeless to search for it throughout the whole construction of any modern language. As the number of terms increase among every people, and the vast field of language is filled up, words, by a thousand fanciful and irregular methods of derivation and composition, deviate widely from their primitive roots, and lose all resemblance in sound to the things signified. Such is the existing state of language. Words, as we now use them, may be considered as symbols, not as imitations; as arbitrary, not natural signs of ideas. But there seems to be no doubt, that language, the nearer we can approach to its rise among men, will be found to partake more of a natural expression.

Passionate exclamations, or, as they are denominated, interjections, were the first elements of speech. Men laboured to communicate their feelings to each other, by those expressive cries or gestures which nature taught them. After the names of things began to be introduced, the mode of speaking by natural signs would not be abandoned at once; for language, in its infancy, we can readily imagine, must have been extremely barren, and, for a considerable period, among rude nations, conversation would be carried on by means of few words, intermixed with exclamations and earnest gestures. To this mode of speaking, necessity at first gave rise. But after the necessity had ceased, by language becoming more copious, the ancient mode of speech still subsisted among many nations, and what had arisen from necessity, continued to be used for ornament. In the Greek and Roman languages, a musical and gesticulating pronunciation was retained in a considerable degree: the declamations of their orators, and the pronunciation of their actors upon the stage, approached to the nature of what is denominated *recitative* in music;—was capable of being marked in notes, and supported with instruments. The case was parallel with respect to gestures; for strong tones and animated gestures always go together. The action, both of the orators and players in Greece and Rome, was far more vehement than that to which we are accustomed; and Cicero says, that it was a contest between him and Roscius, whether he could express a sentiment in a greater variety of phrases, or Roscius in a greater variety of intelligent, significant gestures. At length gesture, entirely engrossed the stage; and the favourite entertainment was pantomime, which was carried on by gesticulation only.

The early language of mankind being entirely composed of words descriptive of sensible objects, became, of necessity, extremely metaphorical. To signify any feeling of the mind, they had no particular expression which was appropriated to the purpose, but they were obliged to paint the emotion which they felt, by alluding to sensible objects which had most connexion with it; and which could render it, in some degree, visible to others.

As language became more copious, it gradually lost its figurative style, which was its original characteristic. The vehement manner of speaking by tones and gestures became less universal. Instead of poets, philosophers became the instructors of the world; and, in their reasonings on all subjects, they introduced that plainer and more simple style of composition which is now denominated prose: and, at length, the metaphorical and poetical dress of language was reserved for those occasions only, in which ornament was professedly studied.

Writing is an improvement upon speech, and consequently was subsequent to it in the order of time. Its characters are of two kinds: either signs for things, or signs for words. Thus the pictures, hieroglyphics, and symbols employed by the ancients, were of the former sort; the alphabetical, now employed by Europeans, of the latter.

Pictures were certainly used in the first graphical attempts of mankind, because men are naturally prone to imitation; and, therefore, a rude picture would soon be employed for giving imperfect descriptions of events, and for recording their remembrance of facts, or of a beloved object. Thus, to signify that one man had killed another, they painted the figure of a dead man lying on the ground, and another standing over him with a hostile weapon in his hand. This was the only kind of writing made use of by the Mexicans, when America was first discovered. It was, however, a very imperfect mode of recording facts, since, by pictures, external events could only be delineated.

Hieroglyphical characters may be considered as the second stage in the art of writing. These consist in certain symbols, which are made to represent invisible objects, on account of a resemblance which such symbols are supposed to bear to the objects themselves. Thus a circle, having neither beginning nor end, was the symbol of eternity; a lion was the hieroglyphic of strength; a horse, of liberty. Egypt was the country where this kind of writing was most studied, and brought into a regular art. The Egyptians contrived to make their hieroglyphics both pictures and characters: in effecting this improvement they proceeded gradually, by first making the principal circumstance of the subject stand for the whole; thus they represented a battle of two armies in array, by two hands, one holding a shield, and the other, a bow: then putting the instrument representing the thing, whether real or metaphorical, for the thing itself; as an eye and sceptre to represent a monarch; a ship and pilot, the Governor of the universe; and finally, by making one thing stand for, and represent another, where they discovered or imagined any resemblance; thus the universe was designed by a serpent in a circle, whose variegated spots denoted the stars. The Egyptians, also, pitched upon animals to be the emblems of moral objects, according to the qualities with which they supposed them to be endowed: thus, imprudence was denoted by a fly; wisdom, or foresight, by an ant; and victory, by a hawk.

The Chinese writing was the next improvement in the use of hieroglyphics. The Egyptians joined characteristic marks to images, the Chinese threw out the images, and retained only the contracted marks; and from these marks proceeded letters, which they use to this day. They have no alphabet of letters or simple sounds, of which their words are composed, but every single character is expressive of an idea: it is a mark which signifies some one thing or object. The number of these characters is, of course, almost immense; seventy or eighty thousand have been enumerated, so that to become tolerably acquainted with them, is the business of a whole life, a circumstance that will readily account for the small progress that is made by the Chinese in literature and every kind of science. It is certain that the Chinese characters are of the same nature with hieroglyphics—they are the signs of things, and not of words; for the inhabitants of Japan, Tonquin, Korea, &c. who speak different languages from each other, and also from the Chinese, employ the same written characters with them, and thus correspond intelligibly with one another in writing, though they are ignorant of the language spoken in the respective countries. The figures that we use in arithmetic, afford an exemplification of this sort of writing. They have no dependence on words, each figure represents the number for which it stands, and consequently is equally understood by all nations who have agreed in the use of figures.

To remedy the imperfections which attached themselves to each of the methods of communication above referred to, was the invention of signs, which should stand, not directly for things, but words, by which things were distinguished from one another; hence it is probable an alphabet of syllables was invented previously to an alphabet of letters. Such is even said to be retained, at this day, in Ethiopia, and some countries of the East. This, on account of the number of characters wanted, would have rendered reading and writing very complex and laborious; and it, at length, gave way to the grand discovery of letters. To whom we are indebted for this sublime invention, we know not. They were, unquestionably, brought into Greece, by a person denominated in history, Cadmus, but who this Cadmus was, is not so easily determined. According to Blair, he was a Phœnician, and arrived in Greece about 1500 years before the Christian era, bringing with him sixteen letters, the others being added by Palamedes and Simonides, viz. four by each.

Those who have investigated this subject, admit that much difficulty is attached to it; but they say, that the similarity in name and figure, of the Phœnician, Hebrew, Greek, and Roman alphabets, is a decisive proof that they were originally derived from the same source.

To Cadmus also we are indebted for the first establishment of schools; he is said, likewise, to have taught the mysteries of trade and navigation to the Grecians; and from him was derived the epithet Cadmean, as applicable to brass, he being the inventor of this species of metal, and introduced the use of it into Greece.

Although Dr. Blair dates the arrival of Cadmus from the year 1493, B. C., yet this event is, by Sir Isaac Newton, referred to a much later period, viz. 1045 years before the birth of Christ. Sir Isaac Newton imagines that the emigration of the Phœnicians and Syrians, was occasioned by the conquests of David. "These people," he says, "fleeing from Zidon and from David, came, under the conduct of Cadmus and other captains, into Asia Minor, Crete, Greece, and Lybia, and introduced letters, music, poetry, metals and their fabrication, and the other arts, sciences, and customs of the Phœnicians. This happened about one hundred and forty years before the Trojan war, and it was about the sixteenth year of David's reign, that Cadmus fled from Zidon."

The ancient order of writing was from the right hand to the left: afterwards, the Greeks used to write their lines alternately from right to left, and from the left to the right. This continued to the time of Solon, and, at length, the motion from the left hand to the right being found more natural and convenient, it was adopted throughout all the nations of Europe.

Writing was first exhibited on pillars and tables of stone, afterwards upon metals: as it became practised more extensively, the leaves and bark of trees were used in some countries; and in others, tablets of wood, covered with a thin coat of soft wax, on which the impression was made with a stylus of iron. Parchment, manufactured from the hides of animals, was an early invention; but paper, the great discovery of modern times, was not made till the fourteenth century.

Having thus considered the origin of the elements of language, we may pass on to its structure: this comprehends the nature and arrangement of the different parts of speech, which will be considered at large in the succeeding chapters devoted to Grammar, observing, however, that grammatical rules have not sufficient authority to control the established usage of language; established custom, both in speaking and writing, is the standard to which we must at last resort for determining every controverted point in language and style. Grammatical rules are, however, not to be regarded as useless. In every language that has been cultivated, there prevails a certain structure and analogy of parts, which is understood to be the foundation of the commonly received modes of speech, and which, in all cases of doubt, possesses considerable authority.

Usage and custom, with respect to language, are entirely independent of reason; and on these, as a just foundation, commences grammar, a plan of which supposes a language already introduced by use, and, without pretending to alter or amend a tittle, only furnishes reflections, called rules, to which the manner of speaking, adopted in that language, may be reduced; which reflections, or rules, make up the *grammar* of that language.

CHAP. III.

ON GRAMMAR.

Arrangement of Words—The Noun—Abstract Nouns—Number—Gender—Adnoun—Pronoun.

THE Grammar of any language, as we have seen, is a set of rules and observations, directing to the proper use of the sorts of words composing that language. These rules are founded upon the general usage of good writers; and after this is ascertained, it is customary for those who are desirous of speaking and writing correctly, to be uniformly guided by it.

The Art of Grammar is sometimes divided into four parts: Orthography, Etymology, Syntax, and Prosody. The first and last of these have nothing to do with grammar, except so far as they relate to the grammatical changes made on different sorts of words. Etymology refers to the arrangements of the sorts of words, and to the various changes which are made upon them. Syntax directs the employment of those changes, and the situation of different sorts of words in a sentence.

Considered as a science, Grammar has for its object, those principles on which its rules are founded. Scientific Grammar discusses the grounds of the classification of words, and investigates the reasons of those procedures which the art of grammar lays down for our observance.

Grammar, as an art, refers only to particular languages; because it would be impossible to lay down any system of rules which would apply to two languages. We may point out in what respects the grammars of two languages agree; but we cannot form a common grammar for both. To a certain extent, the principles of scientific grammar are general, and some of them may be said to be universal. The laws of the human mind are the same in all ages, and in all nations; and of those causes which have called forth its energies, many have operated universally. Whatever have been the variety of terms, and of the modification and arrangement of them, the grand objects of men, in the formation and extension of language, have been the same,—to communicate their sensations, their judgments, their reasonings,—to express the objects of their thoughts, and the changes and connexions observed among them,—and to do this with dispatch. This has produced great uniformity in the general principles of language. But the connexion between words and thoughts is arbitrary, as well as the mode of connecting words themselves. Hence, with much uniformity, we meet with much variety; and hence, universal or even general grammar, must be confined within very narrow limits, till the phenomena of a variety of languages have been examined, and their correspondence with each other, as well as their diversities, ascertained. We shall here content ourselves with making the philosophy of our own language our principal object, though we shall occasionally be led to state the more general principles of grammar, and derive some of our illustrations from other languages. Such a mode of procedure may contribute to render the practical use of our own language more clear and certain.

Of the Arrangement of Words. The first object of Scientific Grammar is, to form an arrangement of the sorts of words (or parts of speech) composing a language. In languages which admit of various changes in the form of words, to denote changes of meaning, the arrangement, in a great degree, is pointed out for the grammarian; and a technical classification will, in such cases, have a decided superiority over one founded purely upon scientific principles. In languages like our own, we are less shackled by the contrivances of art; yet our arrangements ought to have practical convenience in view.

The true principle of classification seems to be, not essential differences in the origin or signification of words, but the mode in which they are employed. It should, however, be steadily kept in view, that all distinctions among the sorts of words, have gradually arisen out of the circumstances in which language has been formed, and has proceeded towards maturity; and that such distinctions are by no means to be extended beyond the present employment of words. It is necessary, for convenience and dispatch, that we arrange; but arrangement must not supersede further examination. The fact is, that originally there could have been but one sort of words, the *names* of the objects of our sensations and ideas. From these, all others must have sprung; but, without words expressing *affirmation*, language must have moved very slowly, and often have been very ambiguous; and therefore we may reasonably suppose, that the ever active principles of association would soon transform *nouns* into *verbs*, by making them, in certain situations, expressive of affirmation. From these two classes all the rest have sprung.

The objects of sense and intellect are, in reality, nothing more than properties, or collections of properties. The mind, however, resorts to a support for those properties; something by which they are connected; in which they exist: and this we call *substance*. As far, however, as this word has any definite meaning, it signifies nothing more than *a collection of properties existing*, or *capable of existing, independently of other properties*. These properties may be considered *collectively*; or they may be thought and spoken of, though they cannot exist, *separately*. We can think of no material substance, which does not possess at least two properties; no visible object, for instance, can be without colour and extension: but we can think of extension and of colour separately, that is, we can direct the attention of the mind to each of them, exclusively of the other properties with which it may be connected. This separate or exclusive attention of the mind, is called *abstraction*. It is a very simple, though a very difficult operation of the mind.

The *names of substances* are called *Substantives;* the *names of properties* without direct reference to the substances of which they form a part, are called *Abstract Nouns*. To every *name* comprehended under these two classes, the term NOUN is applied. A noun is said to be increased or diminished in *comprehension,* when the *number of ideas* denoted by it is increased or diminished; and in *extension,* when the *number of objects,* to which it can be applied, is increased or diminished. Those single words, which are added to nouns to vary their comprehension, or to vary or determine their extension, may be called ADNOUNS. From these similar, yet generally distinct objects of different adnouns, arise two grand classes, *Adjectives and Restrictives:* the former varying the *comprehension* of the conjoined nouns; the latter varying, sometimes determining, the *extension* of them. In one mode of the application of the term, adjectives are nouns; for they are the names of properties; and originally they were nouns; but since they are not employed *alone* (like substantives and abstract nouns) to denote the objects of thought or discourse, it is preferable to class them with words whose use and employment is similar.

We constantly find it necessary to speak of ourselves, to address others, or to speak of others. If we wish to speak of ourselves, to address others, or to speak of others, we immediately find, that we must either mention the names of the individuals concerned, or use some words not belonging to ourselves or them, as individuals, but, as the persons speaking, spoken to, or spoken of. This would be effected, by using some short words of equivalent signification; such are

I, *thou*, and *he*. *I* has the same force as *the person speaking*; *thou*, as *the person spoken to*; and *he*, as *the person spoken of*; except that *I* and *thou* are limited to the individuals actually speaking or addressed, or supposed to be so speaking or addressed. These words are then, strictly speaking, *nouns*; but as they are used *for names* of persons, they are called PRONOUNS, that is, *for-nouns*. It is obvious, that the word *he*, not only supplies the place of the name, on which account it might be called a pronoun, but has a distinct reference to the *person having been before mentioned*. In a similar manner, *she* means the *female person spoken of*; and *it*, the *thing spoken of*. These words, with their plurals, are all called pronouns; and though they obviously either come under other sorts of words, or are abbreviations for one or more of them, yet they are at present so distinct and important in their use, that they require a separate class. PRONOUNS, then, are words used for the names of persons or things, connected with the idea, that they are either speaking, spoken to, or before spoken of.

We cannot advance one step in language, without leading our hearers or readers to the inference, that certain ideas are connected in our minds; or that we believe certain objects, properties, or events to be connected. The connecting link in language need not always be stated. In the infancy of language it could not exist; and in the language of childhood it does not exist. Words are joined together, and it is easily understood, that the corresponding ideas are connected in the mind. 'Mother, milk, good,' would surely be understood by any one; and, in similar cases, depending upon the ease of inference, the ancient writers left it to the mind of the reader to form it for himself. But how slowly and how ambiguously communication would proceed, without some appropriated link of connexion, any one may be convinced, by leaving out of a few sentences, those words, which, in our language, serve that purpose, and which, in all languages, are necessary to render an affirmation complete. The intelligent reader, to whatever other account of such words he may have been accustomed, will perceive that we refer to verbs. The essential quality of a VERB is, to express affirmation, when joined with the subject of the affirmation. Whenever a word expresses it, that word is a verb: if in any case it does not express it, it ceases to be a verb.

From verbs (or rather from the *noun-state* of verbs, in which they do not express affirmation) a new class of words is formed, partaking of the characteristics of the noun and the adjective, and agreeing with verbs in the accidental circumstance of requiring after them a peculiar form of pronouns. These words are called PARTICIPLES.

In the same manner as it is found needful, for the purpose of accurate and expeditious communication, to employ words to modify or restrict the signification of nouns, it is found at least convenient to appropriate other words to modify or restrict the signification of adnouns and verbs. These are called ADVERBS, which are to be regarded as a class of words formed from nouns or adnouns, and used to express some quality or circumstance respecting the action, quality, or circumstance denoted by verbs or adnouns. They are, therefore, convenient abbreviations, which may be supplied by the other sorts of words.

1. From nouns, adnouns, and verbs, another class of words have arisen, which, from the long disuse of the original forms of them, have lost their peculiar characteristics, and are now regarded as independent of them. They are now used to connect words, or sentences, or words with sentences; and, in general, point out some particular kind of connexion. From the employment of them, they may be termed CONNECTIVES; and under this class, we comprehend those words which are usually denominated Prepositions and Conjunctions. The distinction between these two sorts of connectives, is merely technical; the latter requiring after them a peculiar form of the pronoun, and also of the noun, in languages in which the noun admits of flexion.

We feel obliged, very much against our inclination, to admit, as an eighth class of words, some of those which are usually denominated INTERJECTIONS. Words of this sort are of very little importance, and by many are thought undeserving of the name of words. Some are *involuntary* expressions of grief, or joy, or surprise, or some other strong emotion; and some may be used with the *intention* of informing others what emotions are in the mind of the speaker or writer. The former set have no more right to be called words, than the sigh of sorrow, the groan of pain, the laugh of mirth, &c., which no one calls words; for words are voluntary vocal sounds, employed to express our ideas to others. The latter set are generally found to be parts of sentences, or single words of the before mentioned sorts. Our great philosophical etymologist, Mr. Horne Tooke, has traced the origin of the greater part of them; and the few that remain, will probably be hereafter traced by some of those grammarians who are treading in his steps.

We now proceed to a few remarks on each of these sorts of words.

I. OF THE NOUN.—Those words which are *names* of things, and which can stand alone, as the subjects of an affirmation, are called No*uns*. This class of words has two grand divisions; *substantives* and *abstract nouns*. *Substantives* are the names of substances. All names must originally have been names of individuals; the extension of the application of them must, however, have been immediate. The difficulty of producing a great number of distinguishable articulate sounds, and the operation of the associative power, first led to the application of the same word to different individuals; convenience, perhaps, we may justly say, necessity, led to the extension of it. When a number of things resemble each other in some striking particulars, we class them together in one species; and give to the species, a name which is applicable to every individual included in it. When several species agree in some common properties; we refer them to a higher class, which we call a genus; and to the genus, we give a name which is applicable to every species and every individual included in it. This classification we extend to the limits of human knowledge; and it is one of those admirable contrivances which are the result of necessity, or of casual circumstances, but which, being extended and perfected by science, contribute essentially to the progress and diffusion of Knowledge.—But though it is necessary, for the purposes of communication, that many names should be applicable to *classes* of individuals, it is also necessary that there should be others capable of denoting *individuals*, without the circuitous plan of naming the general term, and the distinguishing qualities of the individual: and, accordingly, we find in all languages, numerous words, which apply to an individual only, or, at least, are at once referred, both by speaker and hearer, to an individual. Those names which, when alone, apply to a number of individuals, are called *General Terms, Appellatives,* or *Common Nouns;* and those which, when alone, are used to denote particular individuals, are called *Proper Nouns.* Sometimes proper nouns are so applied, as to become common nouns, as when we say, the Cæsars, or the Ptolemies. These are instances of the commencement of generalization; but there is another mode of the use of proper nouns, which is more illustrative of the processes actually adopted, in employing terms originally denoting an individual, to denote classes of individuals who resemble him in some striking characteristics: thus, we say, "the Bacons, the Newtons, and the Lockes, of the present day," meaning, by these terms, all those individuals who resemble Bacon, Newton, or Locke, respectively, in the mode and success of their investigation.

Of Abstract Nouns.—Though it seems to be a very simple process, to form and appropriate names to denote properties separate from the other properties with which we see them connected in nature, the origin and appropriation of such names must have been very gradual; and the contrivances which, in the natural progress of language, have been adopted to denote separate properties, are among the most curious procedures of the art of mutual communication. Mr. H. Tooke, who has indisputably conducted us further towards an acquaintance with the causes of language than any other author on grammar, considers abstract terms as (generally speaking) "participles or adjectives used without any substantive to which they can be joined." "Such words," he observes, "compose the bulk of every language. In English, those which are borrowed from the Latin, French, and Italian, are easily recognised, because those languages are sufficiently familiar to us, and not so familiar as our own: those from the Greek are more striking; because more unusual: but those which are original in our own language have been almost wholly overlooked, and are quite unsuspected." A large proportion of the nouns which he thus traces, are certainly not to be considered as abstract terms, according to what appears to be the customary meaning of that appellation, (such as *view*, the past participle of *voir*, something *seen*; *tent*, the past participle from *tendo*, something *stretched*:) and others, require more explanation than he has given; (for instance, *providence*, *prudence*, *innocence*, and all the rest of the tribe of qualities in *ence* and *ance*, which he represents as the neuter plurals of the present participles of the Latin verbs *videre*, *nocere*, &c. without shewing us why *things foreseeing*, or *things not hurting*, have acquired the force of the above words:) but a considerable number of his derivations are very satisfactory, and give great insight into the procedures of language. A few may be adduced as a specimen of his etymologies. *Skill* is the past participle of the Anglo-Saxon verb *skylan*, *to divide*, *to make a difference*, *to discern*; and it signifies that faculty by which things are properly *divided*, or *separated* one from another. *Sorrow* is the past participle of *syrwan*, *to vex*, *to cause mischief to*, and is the general name for any thing by which one is *vexed*, *grieved*, or *mischieved*. *Wrath* is the past participle of *writhan, to writhe. Heat* is the past participle of *heatan, to make hot. Doom* is the past participle of *deman, to judge, to decree.*

Another class of abstract nouns, *viz.* those ending in *th,* have been traced to a very probable origin by Horne Tooke: he considers them as the third persons singular of verbs. For instance; *truth* (anciently written *troweth, trowth, truth,* and *troth,)* means, what one *troweth, i. e.* thinketh, or firmly believeth: *warmth* means that which *warmeth: strength* is that which *stringeth,* or maketh one *strong.* While, however, we agree so far with Mr. Tooke, we cannot go with him, when he limits our acceptation of words to that in which they were first employed; and supposes that all the complicated, yet often definable associations, which the gradual progress of language and intellect has connected with words, are to be reduced to the standard of our forefathers. We cannot avoid expressing our belief, that he has either totally overlooked, or greatly neglected, the influence of the principle of association, both in the formation of ideas, and in the connecting of them with words. It does not follow, that because the ideas conneeted with abstract terms are not what Mr. Locke supposed, that there are no ideas connected with them, but that they are merely contrivances of language. Several classes of abstract nouns are altogether passed over by Mr. Tooke; and we regret it, because he was eminently qualified to trace the origin of those terminations, by which are formed the names of qualities, considered as separate from the substances in which they exist. One class is formed by the addition of *ness* to the adjective, such as *whiteness, goodness,* &c. *Ness* is the Anglo-Saxon *naes,* or *nese,* signifying *nose.* It is also used for *promontory;* as in *Sheer-ness, Orford-ness,* the *Naze,* &c. Joined to the name of a quality, it denotes that the quality is a distinguishing feature of an object; it consequently holds it up as an object of separate attention.

Of Number.—We now proceed to those changes which are

made in the form of nouns, to express a change of signification; and first, we shall attend to *Number*. In speaking of the objects of thought, we have constant occasion to speak of one or more of a kind; in every language therefore me may expect to find a variation in the form or adjuncts of nouns, to denote unity or plurality. To avoid the necessity of using such adjuncts, or rather, in consequence of the coalescence of them with the nouns, owing to the frequent use of them in connexion with the nouns, a change of form has taken place in most cultivated languages. The Hebrew plurals are generally formed by the addition of ם, *mem*, to the noun, probably because ם was the symbol of water, and denoted collection and plurality; and in that language the coalescence has actually taken place, and occasionally undergone some corruption. Among the Chinese, the plural adjunct has not yet coalesced with the noun; and they generally denote the plural by the addition of *min* to the singular. Supposing the coalescence of plural adjuncts to have been the origin of the changes on nouns to denote plurality of meaning, it does not necessarily follow that all plural changes were thus formed. The change of form produced by such coalescence in some cases, might suggest a corresponding change in others, though the change might not be exactly similar. Hence, could we trace some of the plural changes to art, as their earliest origin, it would weigh little against the general principle. We shall, however, almost universally find, that the extension of old procedures, rather than the invention of new ones, has been the cause of almost all even of the artificial changes in language. The reason is obvious: besides the greater ease to the innovator, it would be much more intelligible to those who are to adopt his innovation. Even the philosopher judges it more proper to follow the analogies of his language, than to deviate from them where he knows such deviation would be an improvement.

Except as far as is dictated by custom, and that convenience on which the custom has been founded, there is no reason why the same word, unchanged, should not be applicable both where *one* and where *more* are meant: why, for instance, we should not say *two man,* as well as *one man.* The plural form may be applied to two, or two hundred, or any indefinite number; now is there, in the nature of the thing, a more marked distinction between one and two, than between two and two hundred? In fact, were we always able to join to the noun a numeral, or some other adnoun denoting number, a plural form would be unnecessary; but it is frequently desirable to denote plurality where the number is indeterminate, or unnecessary to be specified. The Chinese drop their plural adjunct, when there is another word of plurality attached to the noun. We do not go upon the same principle; but there are cases in which we make no changes to denote plurality, as twenty *pound* of flour, thirty *sail* of ships, four *thousand,* &c. These instances, though contrary to the prevailing analogy of our language, certainly do not oppose the general principles of language; and though the neglect of the plural termination in such cases is ungrammatical, it probably savours less of vulgarity to go thus far with the multitude, than of pedantry to quit the beaten track. There are other instances, however, in which the use of the same word both in a singular and plural acceptation is perfectly legitimate; we say one, or twenty, *deer,* or *sheep.*

If there must be a form for unity as distinguished from plurality, why not forms to denote two things, three things, &c.? There is no reason but in their inferior utility. Some languages have a form for duality; and by the Greeks this form was carried through their nouns, adnouns, pronouns, verbs, and participles. They had, however, no scruple in using the plural form for two things, and in making their duals agree with plurals. The fact is, the distinction between one and more than one, is more useful than any farther distinction.

Of Case.—In every department of knowledge, we are concerned with individuals; and though, for the purposes of communication, general terms are not only convenient, but absolutely necessary, some contrivances are requisite to designate individuals, or less general classes of individuals. This is done either by means of adnouns, or by stating some connexion between what is denoted by the noun and some other substance or quality. The latter is accomplished by juxta-position, by prepositions, or by equivalent changes in the word connected. The last is called inflexion, and the word so changed is called a *case* of the noun. In English we have only one inflexion of the noun, and two of the pronoun. Persons who think that the processes of every language must be accommodated to the grammar of the Greek and Latin, strenuously contend for an equal number of cases with theirs. If *case* mean *a change in the word, to denote connexion with other words*, then the plan of our language cannot be accommodated to that of the Latin: if *of a man, to a man*, &c., be considered as cases, there is certainly no reason why the same appellation should not be given to every noun to which a preposition is prefixed, and then we shall have above thirty cases. It is fortunate for the speculator, that, in this and other instances, language will not bend to the contrivances of the technical grammarian: for his wish to reduce every process to an agreement with a standard which prejudice only can deem perfect, would, if successful, materially increase the difficulties of grammatical investigation.

The variation of our nouns is confined to mark one relation, that of *property* or *possession*; and it is therefore with great propriety called the *possessive case*. The appellation *genitive case* is sometimes applied to it; but the force of the Greek and Latin genitive is to denote relation in general, though capable of specific application, and is exactly equivalent to a noun preceded by *of*. The possessive case of a noun is not equivalent to the noun preceded by *of*, except where the latter has the specific force of belonging to. It may in all cases be represented by *of*, with the noun following; but the latter mode of expression cannot in many instances be represented by the possessive case.

The French, Spanish, and Italian languages have no cases

of nouns: the German has changes to express what we denote by *of* and *to*; but these changes are not carried through all the nouns. The Latin and Greek languages have still more variations, which they carry through all their variable parts of speech, except the verbs. The arrangement of these variations is the work of art: and the appellations of *case*, (or *falling*,) and *declension*, (or *bending from*,) appear to have gone upon the following principle: the word from which the cases are formed, was represented by a perpendicular line, and the cases by lines declining or falling from it. For the sake of convenience, the nominative and vocative are denominated cases; and from the above contrivance, the nominative was termed the *upright* case, and the other cases were termed oblique. The *nominative* is the name itself. The *vocative*, or case of calling, has its origin in those changes in the pronunciation which arise from the mode of utterance in calling to a person: it is a corruption, or an abbreviation of the nominative. We have already spoken of the force of the *genitive*; we shall only add here, that we have in English one procedure exactly corresponding to it in force, though not so universally applied, *viz.* juxtaposition. This is a very simple and intelligible process. To connect the terms is a satisfactory expression of the connexion of the things signified: and in this procedure, as in the genitive, the kind of connexion is left to be inferred; as in the expressions *iron chain*, *China orange*, *house door*, &c. The theoretical distinction between the *dative* and *accusative* does not appear to be clearly marked; but the general force of the former is to denote *acquisition*, and of the latter to designate the word as the *object* of the action of verbs and their derivatives. As to the *ablative*, there is scarcely room for doubt that it is merely a variation of the dative form, where indeed it has a form distinct from it. Probably in consequence of the ellipsis of a preposition, this form has by degrees come to denote the cause, manner, or instrument of an action; and this is now the primary force of the case when unattended by prepositions.

The changes which are made to denote connexion, have been formed by prefixing or affixing letters to the words themselves; and they might have been arbitrary, or gradually produced by the coalescence of words or abbreviations of words. The latter hypothesis is in every respect so very probable, that nothing seems requisite to prove it to have been the general procedure of language; but to shew that it has actually occurred in some instances. It has been for some time the prevailing opinion among philosophical philologists, and it has acquired great support from the discoveries of Tooke. He states it without any limit in the following manner: "All those *common* terminations, in any language, of which all nouns or verbs in that language equally partake (under the notion of *declension* or *conjugation*) are themselves separate words, with distinct meanings; which are therefore added to the different nouns of verbs, because those additional meanings are intended to be added occasionally to all those nouns or verbs. These terminations are all explicable, and ought to be explained." In fact, the progress of the coalescence has been detected in some of the most refined instances of it; and in many cases to which system has not reached, the coalescence is universally allowed. In the two principal cases of the Greek noun, in some at least of its forms of inflexion, the origin of the change has been traced; and all the cases of the Hebrew noun, are obviously formed by prefixing (instead of affixing, as in the Greek,) significant words. The grammarian does not indeed allow that the changes of the Hebrew noun are cases; but such arbitrary distinctions serve only to render obscurity more obscure. In the French, *au* and *du* are indisputably abbreviations of *à le* and *de le:* we can trace their corruption, and we are not obliged to suppose greater corruptions in more disputable instances. What is the origin of the possessive termination of our nouns is very uncertain.

Of Gender.—*Gender* is distinction of substantives, as denoting males, or females, or neither. The names of males are said to be of the masculine gender; the names of females of the feminine gender; and all other names are said to be of the neuter, that is, of neither gender. The purposes even of accurate communication, do not, in all cases, require any denotement of gender, and accordingly we find many words which are common to both sexes. The English and the pure Persian, appear to be the only languages which observe the natural distinction in the division of nouns. We denote difference of sex, either by a change of appellation, or by a change in the word itself, or by a significant adjunct; as, *horse, mare; lion, lioness; he-goat, she-goat*. In addition to its greater philosophical accuracy, the procedure of our language enables us to mark with greater perspicuity and force the personification of inanimate substances or abstract qualities.

In the earliest languages, there is no distinction of gender, further than into masculine and feminine, and the reason is obvious; for the principle of animation appears to the uncultivated mind to pervade all nature. In the more cultivated languages in which a third class is admitted, the arrangement seems to have been the work of art. The foundation was laid in the natural distinction of sex: by degrees those terminations which most frequently occurred in the respective divisions, were made the characteristics of those divisions; and nouns of similar terminations, were arranged under them, without respect to the original ground of distinction. We must not be surprised to find, that languages derived from those, in which the distinctions of nature had given way to the divisions of art, should leave nature altogether; and we accordingly find, that in those modern European languages which are derived from the Latin, gender is little more than a mere grammatical distinction of nouns into two classes, called masculine and feminine.

II. Of the adnoun.—We apply the term *Adnoun* to those single words which are added to nouns to vary their comprehension, or to vary or determine their extension. Those which effect the former object are called *adjectives;* those which effect the latter, we call *restrictives.* It is not, perhaps, in all cases, easy to say to which of these classes an adnoun should be referred, because the two objects are not always distinguishable, but, in general, those which denote *qualities* are adjectives, and those which denote *situation, possession,* or *number,* are restrictives.

Of Adjectives.—The adjective is exactly equivalent to a noun connected with another noun by means of juxtaposition, or of a preposition, or of corresponding flexion: *E. g. A golden cup,* is the same with a *gold* cup, or a cup *of gold*; a *prudent* man is the same as a man *of prudence,* or vir *prudentiæ.* It has been already observed, that the Greek and Latin genitive, our preposition *of,* and juxtaposition, are all equivalent procedures, though custom has produced a variety in the mode of their application: we now add, that the adjective is another equivalent; and further, that the connexion denoted by the adjective is equally indefinite with the others: *E. g.* A *healthy* colour is a colour *caused by* health; a *healthy* exercise is exercise *causing* health. And the use of all these procedures is the same, to particularize the general term, by connecting with the qualities which are included under it, some quality which the general term does not include. In many instances, to denote that the name of a quality is used thus in connexion with some other name, (that is, in fact, that it is used as an adjective,) certain terminations are employed which are significant of such connexion; and Horne Tooke informs us, that those by which the simple adjectives are formed, *viz. en, ed,* and *ig,* (our modern *y,*) convey, all three, the designation that the names to which they are annexed are to be joined to some other names; and this by their own intrinsic meaning, for they signify *give, add, join.* " So the adjectives *wooden,* and *woollen,*" he continues, " convey precisely the same ideas, are the names of the same things, denote the same substances, as the substantives *wood* and *wool;* and the termination *en* only puts them in a condition to be joined to some other substances, or rather gives us notice to expect some other substances to which they are to be joined."

Most languages which admit of inflexion, carry it through their adjectives as well as nouns. In some, the adjective is varied to express difference in the gender, number, and case, of the connected noun. Where great liberty of inversion is desirable, these variations are convenient; because they point out with what noun the adjective is connected: where juxtaposition ascertains this, they are unnecessary; since they make no change in the signification of the adjective. The signification of the adjective *wise*, is unchanged, whether it be applied to one man or woman, or to twenty men or women; whether its substantive be stated singly, or conjoined with others, as the names of the parents, place of abode, &c., of those to whom it is applied. The French always place the adjective close to its noun; yet they make changes on it to denote the gender of the connected noun. This is always unnecessary; but sometimes it contributes to elegance, by preventing an awkward circumlocution.

Of Comparison.—The qualities denoted by adjectives, may, in general, vary in degree: some, as dimensions and weight, may be measured with accuracy; and the comparative degree of some other qualities, at least of heat and cold, can be ascertained with precision. Many, however, are incapable of exact measurement; and the cases in which the exact degree of the quality cannot be ascertained, are few in comparison with those in which it is unnecessary.—When we use terms to express a greater or less degree of a quality, we may either make a direct and particular reference to the degree in which it is possessed by other objects, or use them without such reference. In the former case, we are said to *compare* the qualities and variations of the adjective, to express this comparison, are called *degrees of comparison*. The difference between the comparative and superlative in our language consists in the manner of construction merely, and not in the degree of the quality: thus, Solomon was *wiser* than any other king of Israel, is the same as, 'Solomon was the *wisest* of the kings of Israel.' The *comparative* is used, when we speak of an object as distinct from those with which we compare it; the *superlative*, when it is spoken of as one of those with which we compare it: *e. g.* Man is the noblest of animals, but not the noblest of the brute creation, otherwise he must be one of the brute creation; man is nobler than the brutes, but not than all animals, or he must be nobler than himself. The custom of our language makes one distinction between the comparative and superlative, which does not coincide with this grand distinction. We use the comparative with the force of the superlative, when we speak of two; as, he is the *wiser* of the two, and the *wisest* of any greater number. This is not an unjustifiable usage; but it has no particular foundation in the respective force of the comparative and superlative. Such nice distinctions, where well-founded, give language greater precision; in the present case, the distinction would not deserve much attention, were it not sanctioned by the usage of the most correct writers.

Few of the modern European languages vary the words themselves to express comparison. The French, e. *g.* express by *plus* and *le plus*, what we express by *more* and *most*, or (what is obviously equivalent, though custom limits their use to particular cases,) by the terminations *er* and *est*. What is the meaning of these terminations? is a natural question: the answer is not so easy. It appears, however, very probable, that *er* is nothing more or less than the word which we still use in the form *ere*, signifying *before*; and, that *wiser* signifies *wise before*. Now, as has been well remarked by Mr. Dalton, *then* and *than* are the same in origin and signification: hence, *wiser than I*, is exactly represented by, *wise before, than I*, *i. e.* wise before, then (that is, next in order) *I*. This derivation, if correct, explains the ground of the peculiarity above-stated, in the use of the comparative: he is the *wiser* of the two, means simply, he is wise before (the other) of the two. It might be conjectured, that the superlative termination *est*, is an abbreviation of *most*, annexed to an adjective, in the same manner as in *topmost*, *undermost*, &c.; but Horne Tooke has shewn, that *more* is merely *mo-er*, and *most*, *mo-est*, which leaves the origin of the terminations *er* and *est* as it was found.

Of Restrictives.—Those adnouns which, without expressing qualities, vary or determine the extent of the signification of the nouns to which they belong, we call *Restrictives.* Some restrictives are, by the custom of our language, applicable to singular nouns only; as *one*, *a* or *an*, *another*, *this*, *that*, *each*, *every*, &c.: others to plural nouns only; as *two*, *three*, *these*, *those*, *other*, *few*, *all*, &c.; but most restrictives, like all adjectives, are applicable to both singular and plural nouns.

Of the restrictives, two are called *Articles*, *the* and *an*, which last is abbreviated into *a* before consonants, *h* when pronounced (unless the second syllable of the word be accented) before *one*, and *u* long as in *use*. *An* is simply another form of the numeral *one*, still used in North Britain under the form *ane*; and in the French, the numeral and the article corresponding to *one*, are the same. But though *an* and *one* have the same origin and primary signification, there is occasionally an obvious difference in the mode of their employment. This difference is well expressed by Dr. Crombie, "If, instead of saying 'A horse, a horse, a kingdom for a horse,' I should say, 'One horse, one horse, one kingdom for one horse,' the sentiment, I conceive, would not be strictly the same. In both expressions, the species is named, and in both, one of that species is demanded; but with this difference, that in the former, the name of the species is the emphatic word, and it opposes that species to every other; in the latter, unity of object seems the leading idea." *An* is called the *indefinite* article, because it leaves undetermined what one individual is meant; *the* determines the application of the noun to some particular individual, and hence it is termed, the *definite* article. It has the same primary signification with *that;* but they vary in the mode of their employment, the former never being employed without a noun, the latter having its noun frequently understood; and farther, *that* is more emphatic than *the:* these, however, are the refinements of language, and have no foundation in the origin of words. Horne Tooke considers *that* as the past participle, and *the* as the imperative mood, of the verb *thean, to get, to take, to assume:* and *the,* he observes, may very well supply the place of the corresponding Anglo-Saxon article *se,* which is the imperative of *seon to see;* for it answers the same purpose in discourse to say, *see* man, or *take* man. We really like the import of our forefathers' article so much better than that of our own, that we shall cheerfully give up *the* for *se,* unless it should appear, that *the* and *that* have their origin in some verb signifying *to point at.*

Of that large class of restrictives called *numerals,* the origin of some may be traced; and as we wish to give our readers an insight into the labours of Mr. H. Tooke, we shall mention his derivation of words in this class. It is in the highest degree probable, that all numeration was originally performed by the fingers, the actual resort of the ignorant; for the number of the fingers is still the utmost extent of numeration.* The hands doubled, closed, or shut in, may therefore well be denominated *ten* (the past participle of *tynan, to enclose, to shut in),* for therein you have closed all numeration; and if you want more, you must begin again, *ten* and one, *ten* and two, &c., *twain-tens, twenty,* when you must begin again as before. *Score* is the past participle of the verb to shear, to separate; and means *separated* parcels or talleys. The ordinal numbers, as they are called, are formed like the abstract

* The Kamschatkans, however, take in the toes; and go as far as twenty; but this is the limit of their numeration. The Mexicans reckoned by twenties; probably from the same cause.

nouns in *eth; fifth, sixth, tenth,* &c. is the unit which *fiv-eth, six-eth, ten-eth, i. e.* makes up the number *five, six, ten,* &c.

III. Of the Pronoun.—So much has already been said respecting the force of the Pronoun, that it is unnecessary to enlarge upon it here. Horne Tooke's derivation of *it* must however be stated, as it shews what have been the actual procedures of language in the formation of one of our pronouns, and gives an insight into the probable origin of the rest. *It,* formerly written *hit* and *het,* is the past participle of the Gothic verb *haitan, to name,* and, therefore, means the person or persons, thing or things *named,* or afore-*said:* and accordingly was applied by all our old writers indifferently to singular and plural nouns. We do not know whether a similar opinion, as the origin of pronouns, had been previously laid before the public, but the philosophical Greek professor of Glasgow, (who, in his very interesting and important investigations, has often anticipated Mr. Tooke,) long ago delivered it as his opinion, that some, at least, of the pronouns are participles; and if we mistake not, traced the origin of εγω, and *ipse,* as follows. Εγω, in the more ancient dialect of Greece, was εγων, which is an obvious abbreviation or corruption of λεγων; so that εγω (whence the Latin and other languages have their first person,) signifies the *speaking* person. *Ipse* is the Latin past participle from ἱπω; and though this verb is not to be found in Latin writers, those who know how much the Latin is a dialect of the Greek, will not feel this a material difficulty: on this derivation, *ipse* signifies the *said* person, &c. These speculations might be advantageously extended, would our limits permit; but sufficient has been said to show, that these words are not of that unintelligible nature which has been usually supposed.

Respecting the inflexion of pronouns, the same general principles are applicable, as respecting that of nouns. *His* is obviously *he's;* and whatever be the origin of the possessive termination of the noun, it has the same origin here. *Mine*, *thine*, and *hern* and *theirn* still retained in some of our dialects, have apparently the same origin as *wooden*, *woollen*, &c. The objective form is merely a grammatical appropriation of one of the forms of the pronouns, to a particular purpose; and we still find that *her*, among the vulgar, is commonly employed as the subject of verbs, instead of *she*.

Of the Relatives.—Though we see no reason to give the appellation of *Pronoun* to those words which are called *Adjective Pronouns*, (and accordingly we class them as restrictives), yet there is one word of peculiar importance, which seems properly a pronoun, and to which some attention is necessary, *viz.* the *Relative*. We have already observed several of the contrivances of language to particularize general terms; another is, to restrict or explain the general term, by means of a dependent sentence connected with it by a relative. We will first consider what the relative performs, and then how it performs it. Take the following examples: every man, who loves truth, abhors falsehood; and John, who loves truth, hates falsehood. If the relative clause had been omitted in the former sentence, the remaining assertion would have been false; here then it is restrictive; in the second it is merely explanatory; and in such cases, so far from being necessary, may even destroy the unity and force of the sentence. To explain the subject of discourse, and to restrict its signification, are the two offices of the relative. If the custom of language allowed it, precisely the same purpose might be answered by an adjective or participle connected with the term, as, every man loving truth, &c. and it might seem useless to introduce a new procedure; but the utility of the present plan is obvious, when we consider the immense number of new words which must be introduced to supply the place of the relative, and further, that it enables us to state a greater variety of circumstances in connexion with the antecedent, and occasionally to state them more forcibly.

The relative is equivalent to a personal pronoun with a connective of general signification. We do not mean to affirm that, in the original signification, that connective will be found; but that such is the present force. The dependent clause may be joined to the principal, either by simple juxtaposition, or by means of a connecting particle, or lastly by a word including the force of a connective particle. Instances of the first, are, The ship he commanded was wrecked; and, The man that (i. e. that man) loves wisdom, shall find her: in both of which, the dependent clause is connected in that natural manner which is frequently adopted in our simple language, to express connexion in ideas; and in the same manner, the early Greek writers employ their definite article for their relative. As an instance of the second kind, we may adduce this mode of expression: A man if he do not love truth cannot be virtuous: in which, the dependent clause is joined by a connective, though of a less general kind than what is implied in the relative. This last mode is the most general, and on the whole the most useful, because most general and least ambiguous. Without venturing to assert that *who* essentially differs in its original signification from *that*, it certainly does now include more signification; and that additional signification we think to be what is expressed by *and:* so that, Every man who loves truth, hates falsehood, means, Every man *and he* loves truth, hates falsehood, *i. e.* as Mr. H. Tooke has shewn us, Every man *add* (this circumstance) *he* loves truth, &c,

CHAP. IV.

GRAMMAR, *Continued.*

The Verb—Participle—Adverb—Connective—Directions for the Study of Grammar.

IV. OF THE VERB. As we do not profess to consider the theory of grammar in general, we have not much occasion to enlarge respecting this important sort of words; for our language, simple in most of its procedures, is here almost at the verge of simplicity. Some languages have a great variety of changes in the form of the verb to denote the subject of affirmation, and the mode and time in which the affirmation is to be taken: we have only four, and of those, three are, to say the least, in no way necessary. We have already said enough respecting the nature of the verb, to render it unnecessary to recur again to that point, and we shall here direct the attention of our readers to the modes of signification assumed by the English verb: only repeating, that the *Verb* is a word which, when preceded by a noun or pronoun, or by what may be represented by it, expresses affirmation. In English, and in other languages, words appropriated to express affirmation are often used without any such force: in such cases it might, in some respects, be more scientific to cease to give them the appellation of verbs; but it would be inconvenient in practice, and we prefer speaking of them as in the *noun-state* of the verb; so in the expressions, 'Eat this,' and 'He dares not eat it,' *eat* is in the noun-state.

To denote that a name was appropriated to be used as a verb, our ancestors added a distinguishing termination, like all other common terminations, almost certainly significant in its original state. Why that was dropped does not appear: but the verb, in many instances, now ceases to have any thing in its form to distinguish it from the noun, and in a great variety of instances, it is used exactly as a noun. It is true, it is generally, when in the noun-state, preceded by the particle *to;* but, in most instances, *to* is used in its most customary sense; and in the few instances in which it seems to have merely the force of the Anglo-Saxon termination, it has a sense equally accordant with the original force of the word. Horne Tooke has shewn that *to* (as well as *do*, which is certainly the same word), is a particle of a Gothic substantive signifying *act*, *effect*, and, we presume, *object;* now, when we say, 'I am going to walk,' *to* shows that *walk* (which is still the *name* of an action) is the object of my going: but when we say, 'To walk is healthful,' *to* designates the word following as the name of an action, and the expression means, the *act (viz.) walk* is healthful. We must, however, admit, that the *use* of *to* before the noun-state of verbs, does not seem to be, in every case, consistent with its meaning; but such cases may fairly be referred to the general tendency there is to lose sight of the original force of words, in the stress laid on them in particular cases, or in the mode of their employment in particular cases; and hence, by degrees, to extend the employment of them to similar cases, without reference to their primary signification.

The *infinitive* mood, as it is commonly called, is the verb, divested of its peculiar force, *viz.* of affirmation, and uncompounded with those words which render it expressive of person, number, &c. and, in the modern languages, of time; but it seems erroneous to consider this as the fundamental form of the verb, where it has any distinguishing termination;

it is then the noun-state of the word with a termination added to it, to show that it is to be employed as a verb. Thus, in the Anglo-Saxon ðean, ðe is the fundamental form of the verb, and AN is the verbalizing adjunct. Now, as the *imperative* form of the verb, is nothing more or less than the simple verbal name, unattended with the inference of affirmation, this may be considered as the fundamental form; and in the Latin, in particular, the variations of flexion are traced with the greatest advantage from this source. But without enlarging on this point, with which our language in the present state of it, has no concern, we must repeat, that the imperative form of the verb is merely the noun-state, or verbal name; and that command, entreaty, &c. supposed to be conveyed by it, are merely the inference of custom. If I say to a servant, Bread, it is understood that I wish him to bring me bread, but it is not said: if I say, Bring some bread, in like manner it is understood, that I wish him to bring me bread, but all that is expressed, is the name of the action, and the object of the action. It has, indeed, been supposed, that an affirmation is understood, as, I desire you to bring some bread; but this supposition is rather with a view to show, that *bring*, &c., in such situations, are verbs, than to show the actual procedure. The fact is, full as much is done by inference, as by actual expression, in every branch of language, and even as it is, thought is too quick for words. Admitting the justness of this account of the imperative mood, we need not be surprised at the plan adopted by the Greek writers, of using the infinitive instead of it; nor need we resort to an ellipsis, in order to show the ground of this use, or to complete the grammatical construction.

When the verbal energy is referred to past time, a change is made in the form of nearly all our English verbs: the greater proportion of them add *ed* to the noun state. Whether this alteration was originally intended to refer the meaning of the verb to past time, or that the change had a different object, and the reference has been gradually formed, in consequence of an appropriation similar to what we spoke of respecting the objective form of pronouns, we have yet to learn; but there seems little room to doubt, but that all the common changes which have taken place in the verbs of all languages, whether to denote time, person, number, or mode of signification, have been formed in consequence of the coalescence of words of appropriate signification; and though the gradual refinements of language may have greatly varied the associations of words from what they originally possessed, yet that these changes were originally found sufficient to answer their respective purposes. In some cases the contrivances adopted, can be traced even yet; and from the new turn which has lately been given to etymological investigation, we may expect other discoveries respecting the causes or origin of particular flexions. The future of the French verb, is nothing more than the infinitive of the verb, with the present tense of *avoir* following it; thus, *blâmer-ai* is *ai blâmer*, and *je blâmerai* means *I have to blame*, which mode of expression is in our own language used with a future force. The leading distinction between the past and future tense of the Hebrew verb is, that in the former, the verb is placed *before* the fragment of the pronoun forming the person, and in the latter *after* it, as one would suppose, to indicate that the verbal denotement is in one case *past*, in the other case *future*.

Similar observations may be made, respecting the persons of verbs. In the Hebrew, they are formed, as one would expect, by the coalescence of syllables, which are still acknowledged as pronouns: the same plan has doubtless been adopted in the Latin and Greek verbs, and in some few cases it can be traced with much probability. In our own language there are additions made to the verb, in both the past and present form, when *thou* is the subject of affirmation, and in the present, when any singular word, excepting *I* and *thou* is the subject. We are not aware of any advantage derived from these changes, (and the same remark may be applied to the French verb;) for they do not supersede the necessity of expressing the subject of affirmation, as in the case of the Latin and Greek verbs; but probably in their original import they contained in them the subject of affirmation, unless indeed they were different dialects of the verb, which by degrees were appropriated to particular subjects.

The variations in the Greek and Latin verbs, which denote time and manner of signification, are supplied in English by other verbs, which, from their employment, are called *auxiliary*, or helping verbs: these are, *be, do, have, shall, will, may*, and *can*, which admit of the variations of other verbs, and *must* and *let*, which are unvaried. *Do* in its present use is merely emphatic; and assists in producing a discrimination which cannot be denoted in other languages; but from its general resemblance to the other auxiliaries we have mentioned it among them. It is obviously the same word, both in appearance and in force, with the word *do*, when not employed as an auxiliary. *Shall* signifies *owe*, and was formerly used as a simple verb. *Will*, we use at present as a simple verb. These two words are employed as the principal denotements of future time; and though their original signification has in some degree yielded to that with which custom has invested them, the former is usually to be traced. *May* signifies to be *able*. *Can* signifies to *know*, to *ken*, and thence to be *able*. These words are all employed as auxiliaries, in their past as well as present tenses. *Must* signifies to be *obliged*. *Let* is the noun-state imperative of to *let*, signifying to *permit*. *Have*, as an auxiliary, has the same force with the simple verb; it means to possess. How this meaning is preserved in the complex expression *I have loved*, or similar cases, we shall see in what will be said respecting the participle.

We have an abbreviated mode of expression in English, which has given some trouble to the grammarian, but is now pretty well understood, the *subjunctive mode*, or *future contingent form*. This arises from the omission of the future auxiliary, *shall* or *will*, after words which render the affirmation contingent: thus, instead of saying, *If thou shalt or shouldst love,* we may say, *If thou love.* In all other cases in which affirmation is made, we say the verb is in the *indicative* mood. On this mood we have only to make one remark, respecting the interrogative employment of it. In interrogations we may simply state the thing, or the assertion respecting which we require information, leaving our wishes to be inferred by the reader from the connexion, or some word or mark of interrogation, or by the hearer from a variation in our tone; or which is certainly preferable, we may make such a change in the order of the words, as may leave our meaning out of doubt. This is effected in our own language by putting the subject after the verb; but this is not to be considered as making any change on the mode of its signification, but merely as indicating to the eye or ear the wish of the speaker to gain information respecting the affirmation.

We shall here subjoin a specimen of the manner in which we would conjugate the English verb, agreeably to the foregoing principles.

NOUN-STATE.

Infinitive. Call, *or,* to call.
Imperative. Call, *or,* call thou, *or,* call you *or* ye.

PARTICIPLES.

Present. Calling.
Perfect. Called.

INDICATIVE.

Present Tense.

Sing. 1.	I call.	2. Thou callest.	3. He calleth *or* calls.
Plur. 1.	We call.	2. Ye *or* you call.	3. They call.

Preterite Tense.

Sing. 1.	I called.	2. Thou calledst.	3. He called.
Plur. 1.	We called.	2. Ye *or* you called.	3. They called.

Conditional.

Sing. 1.	I call.	2. Thou call.	3. He call.
Plur. 1.	We call.	2. Ye *or* you call.	3. They call.

Ye, is always plural; but *you* is continually employed, in modern colloquial language, instead of *thou.* When this is done, the verb is used in the same manner as though *you* were used with the plural force.

The verb *to be* is very irregular; and it possesses a form which is altogether peculiar to it, and is used exclusively after contingent words: this may be called the Preterite Tense of the conditional Mood. It is as follows:

Sing. 1. I were. 2. Thou wert. 3. He were. &c.

We imagine there is little room to doubt, that this form is merely a variation of the indicative form of the preterite tense; gradually appropriated to its present use, but having no distinction originally from that form. Such appropriations are often of great service in aiding accuracy of discrimination; but they are to be regarded as the refinements of language, not as making a part of its original structure.

V. Of the Participle. Participles are formed from verbs, generally by the addition of terminations, originally without doubt expressive, but now ceasing to have, in themselves considered, any force. Those participles which are formed by the addition of *ing* to the noun-state of the verb, express a *continued state* of the verbal denotement; and as it is frequently implied, that what is meant by the verb is *being* continued at some time referred to, they are called *present* participles. Those which are formed by the addition of *ed* or *en* to the noun-state, or by some change in the characteristic letters of the verb, usually denote the *completed state* of what is meant by the verb: hence they are called *perfect* participles, or sometimes, with less propriety, *past* or *passive* participles. There does not seem to be any material difficulty attending the employment of these words, except in the case where a perfect participle is employed after the verb *have*, as, I *have learned* my lesson. It has been supposed that this means, *I possess the finished act of learning my lesson:* we think it more probable that it means, *I possess my lesson in that state which is called learned;* in which case it is exactly equivalent to the Latin *habere*, followed by a participle in agreement with a noun.

We readily admit that by, *I have learned it,* there is an inference brought into view which is not by, *I have it learned;* but it seems to be merely the inference of custom, not resulting from any essential difference in the mode of expression.

VI. Of the Adverb. We have already given a general account of the class of words called *verbs.* Those to which our definition will apply, and to which alone the term should be appropriated, are principally adnouns with or without nouns connected with them; others are prepositions with nouns following them; and the remainder are participles. The chief class of adverbs are those which end in *ly;* which termination is an abbreviation of the adnoun spelt *like,* which is still frequently used in North Britain as we use *ly*; thus, for *wisely,* they say *wiselike.* Of this class, a large proportion are formed by adding *ly* to *adnouns;* another set by adding the termination to *nouns,* as *manly, early,* (from æꞃ morning) &c.; and these last are also used as adnouns. *Abed, aboard, ashore,* &c., and *perchance, perhaps,* are prepositions with nouns; *a* signifying *on, in,* or *at,* and *per* being the Latin preposition. *Why, how,* &c. seem to be restrictives, their nouns being understood; *why* signifying *what, cause,* or *reason* being understood; *how* signifying *which, way* or *manner* being understood. Several adverbs besides those before-mentioned ending in *ly,* are used either as adnouns or adverbs; such as *well, ill, much, worse, better,* &c.; in all such cases it must be remembered that not the manner of signification, but merely the manner of employment, is changed. On the origin of most of those adverbs which are less obviously formed from other sorts of words, Horne Tooke has thrown great light; and some of his derivations we shall briefly state. The following are past participles of Anglo-Saxon verbs: *ago* signifying *gone* (time); *adrift* signifies *driven; asunder* means *separated; fain, rejoiced; lief, beloved; astray, strayed* or *scattered. Needs* is *need-is,* used parenthetically. *Belike* is *by lykke, by chance. Aloft* is *on* or *in lyft, i. e.* the air, clouds, &c. *Much* is from *mo,* (a heap) and is merely the diminutive of this word, passing through the gradual changes of *mokel, mykel, mochil, muchel* (still used in Scotland), *moche, much.* *Rather* is the comparative of *rath, swift.* *Quickly* is *quicklike,* being a past participle signifying *enlivened;* and it means in a *lifelike* or *lively* manner. *Very* is merely the French adjective *vrai,* anciently *veray,* from the Latin *verus.* Some words usually classed with adverbs, seem to have no common link of union with the genuine adverb; such are *yes, aye, yéa,* and *no:* indeed Mr. H. Tooke speaks of this class of words as the common sink and repository of all heterogeneous, unknown corruptions. *Aye,* or *yeu,* is the imperative of a verb of northern extraction, and means *have it;* and *yes* is *ay-es,* have that. *Not* (a genuine adverb) and *no,* its derivative, have their origin in the word from which arise the Dutch *noode, node, no,* meaning *averse, unwilling.*

VII. Of the Connective.—The precise nature of the words usually denominated *Conjunctions* and *Prepositions,* was very little known, and not generally even suspected, till the publication of the "Diversions of Purley:" since that time, though philologists do not seem willing to admit, in all cases, the correctness of Mr. Tooke's derivations, yet his general principle is, we suppose, universally considered as completely established. Before his discoveries, it was the common opinion respecting the conjunction, that it is "a part of speech void of signification itself, but so formed as to help signification, by making two or more significant sentences to be one significant sentence;" and respecting the preposition, that it is "a part of speech, devoid itself of signification, but so formed as to unite two words that are significant, and that refuse to coalesce or unite of themselves." We cannot enter here into the arguments against these definitions, and the doctrine on which they are founded; nor indeed is it necessary; for, like the doctrine of instincts in mental philosophy, this solely depends on an appeal to ignorance, and falls to the ground when a probable account is given of those procedures which it is invented to explain. The distinction between prepositions and conjunctions we consider as merely technical, referring to the grammatical usage of employing the objective form of pronouns after the former, and not after the latter, unless there be some word understood which requires it; for it will be obvious to any one, that some conjunctions are still used "to unite words" as well as sentences; and that some prepositions are still used to unite sentences. The general principle before referred to is, "that all those words which are usually termed conjunctions or prepositions, are the abbreviations or corruptions of nouns or verbs, and are still employed with a sense (directly) referable to that which they bore when in the acknowledged form of nouns or verbs." We believe this to be a correct statement of Mr. Tooke's theory; to adapt it to our own arrangements, we must include our adjectives under the term nouns, and our participles under the term verbs: and in addition to this remark, which is merely verbal, we must add, that in some instances this great philologist appears to have too much overlooked a procedure which meets us in various stages of language, *viz.* that among the ideas connected with a word, that which was originally of primary importance, becomes by accidental circumstances in the mode of application, secondary only, and sometimes by degrees is altogether lost from the view of the mind, giving place to others with which, from some cause or other, the word has been associated.

We now proceed to lay before our readers some specimens of the derivations and explanations given by Mr. H. Tooke. *That* is frequently termed a conjunction; it is sometimes termed a pronoun; we class it with the restrictives: but under whatever name it is known, its use and signification is the same. The differences supposed to be perceived in them, arise simply from unnoticed ellipses or abbreviations of construction. If it be remembered that *that* was originally applicable to nouns of both numbers, no difficulty will be found by any intelligent reader in analyzing sentences in which it occurs as a pronoun: in cases where it is used as a conjunction, the following analyses will serve as a sufficient clue. "I wish you to believe that I would not hurt a fly." Resolution; I would not hurt a fly, I wish you to believe that (assertion.) "Thieves rise by night that they may cut men's throats." Resolution; Thieves may cut men's throats, (for) that (purpose) they rise by night.—*If* (formerly written *gif*) is merely the imperative of the Gothic and Anglo Saxon verb *gifan*, to give. In Scotland and the northern counties of England, *gin* is used in place of *if*; and *gin* is merely the past participle *given* abbreviated. Hence "I will read, *if* (or *gin*) you will listen," means, *give* (or this *given*) that you will listen, I will read: and it cannot be unknown to the classical reader that the imperative *da* is used in exactly the same manner.—*An*, now nearly obsolete, is the imperative of *anan*, to grant.—*Unless* (formerly sometimes written *onles*) is the imperative of *onlesan*, to send away. From *alesan* comes the imperative *else*; and from *lesan* the past participle *lest*; both verbs meaning the same with *onlesan*. From the same source come *less* and *least*, the privative termination *less*, the verbs *loosen*, *lose*, *lessen*, &c.—*Yet* is the imperative of *getan*, to get; and *still*, of *stillan*, to put.—*Though* (in some counties still pronounced *thaf*, *thof*,) is the imperative of *thafian*, to allow or grant.—*But* is now corruptly employed for two words, *bot* and *but*: *bot* is the imperative of *botan*, to *boot*, to add, in order to supply a deficiency; *but*, of *beon-utan*, to be-out, and has the same signification as *without*. *But* properly requires a negative in construction with it, as I saw none but him; but it is often omitted, as, I saw but two plants.—*Without* is the imperative of *wyrthan-utan*, to be-out.—*And* is the imperative of *anan-ad*, to heap, or add.—Formerly four different sets of words were used where now *since* is used, and it is now taken four ways: 1. For *siththan*, *sithence*, or *seen and thenceforwards*; as, It has not been done since the reign of John. 2. For *syne*, *sene*, *or seen*; as, Did George II. live before or since that example. 3. For *seand, seeing, seeing as*, or *seeing that*; as, I should labour for truth, since no effort is lost. 4. For *siththe, sith, seen-as*, or *seen-that*; as, Since death in the end takes from all. *Sithence* and *sith* were in good use till the time of the Stuarts.—*So* and *as* are articles meaning the same as *it, that* or *which*. *As* he sows, *so* he will reap, with the ellipses supplied is, (In) what (manner) he sows, (in) that he will reap, or even without supplying them, What he sows, that he will reap.

Prepositions, to use the ideas of Mr. Tooke, are necessary in language, because it is impossible to have a distinct complex term for each different collection of ideas which we have occasion to put together in discourse. By the aid of prepositions, complex terms are prevented from being indefinitely numerous; and are used only for those collections of ideas which we have most occasion to use. This end is thus answered: we either take that complex term which includes the greatest number, though not *all* of the ideas we would communicate, or else that which includes *all* and the fewest *more*; and then by the help of the preposition, we either make up the deficiency in the one case, or retrench the superfluity in the other: so, a house *with* a party-wall; a house *without* a roof. Other relations are declared by prepositions; but they have all meanings of their own, and are constantly used according to those meanings. *With* is the imperative of *withan*, to join: sometimes of *wyrthan*, to be; in which case it is exactly the same with *by*. *Through* or *thorough* is the Gothic substantive *dauro*, or the Teutonic *thuruh*, and like them means door, gate, passage: so, *through* the air, is, *passage* the air, or the air being the *passage* or *medium*. *From* is the Anglo-Saxon noun *frum*, beginning, source, author. Of this word, Harris produces three examples, which he considers as proving that it is used in three different relations, *viz*. detached relation, quiescence, and motion, the last two being contradictory: these figs come *from* Turkey; the lamp hangs *from* the ceiling; the lamp falls *from* the ceiling. Now *came* is a complex term for one species of motion; *falls*, for another; *hangs*, for a species of attachment. Have we occasion to mention the *beginning* or *commencement* of these motions and this attachment, and the place where they begin or commence? What more natural or more simple than to add the signs of these ideas, *viz.* the word *beginning* (which always remains the same,) and the name of the place (which will perpetually vary)? Figs came *beginning* Turkey; lamp $\left\{\begin{matrix}\text{hangs}\\ \text{falls}\end{matrix}\right\}$ *beginning* ceiling: *i. e.* Turkey, the *place* of *beginning* to come; ceiling the *place* of *beginning* to $\left\{\begin{matrix}\text{hang.}\\ \text{fall.}\end{matrix}\right\}$—*To* is the Gothic substantive *taui*, act, effect, end, or result, which is itself the past participle of *taugan*, to do. *While* is an Anglo-Saxon substantive, signifying *time; till*, is *to-while*, to the time; *until*, is on to the time. *Of* is probably a fragment of the Anglo-Saxon substantive *afora*, offspring, &c. and always means cousequence, offspring, succession, follower, &c. In all the instances produced in the dictionaries, *cause* may be substituted for *for*, without injury to the sense, though sometimes awkwardly. It is probably the Gothic substantive *fairina*, cause. *By* is the imperative of *beon*, to be; frequently, but not always, used with an abbreviation of construction, *instrument, cause, agent*, &c. being understood. *Among* is the past participle of *gamængan*, to mingle. *After* is the comparative of *aft*. *About* is from *boda*, the first outward boundary or extremity of any thing; hence *onboda, onbuta, abuta, about*. *In, out, on, off*, and *at*, Mr. Tooke does not profess to trace to an origin; we feel little doubt that *on* is simply one of the several forms of the numeral *one*; and the same process of thought has occurred in the Greek, where εις and εν (and perhaps also συν) are almost indisputably the corresponding numeral. We should have thought it probable that the English *in* has the same origin, as *on*, if Mr. H. Tooke had not produced the

Gothic substantive *inna*, the interior part of the body (used also for cave or cell). *Out*, he thinks, not improbably, originally meant skin.

Of the Interjection.—We have very little to say in addition to what we have said respecting this small and insignificant class of words. *Oh*, or O, is almost the only word for which it is necessary. A few other words may be mentioned as being usually classed with it. *Farewell* is the imperative of *faran*, to go, and the adverb *well*. *Halt* is the imperative of *healden*, to hold. *Lo* is the imperative of look. *Fie* is the imperative of *fian*, to hate. *Welcome* means, it is *well* that you are come. *Adieu*, used so often without a moment's thought as to its serions import, is the French *à Dieu*, *to God*, meaning, I commend you *to God*.

We shall now conclude with some directions for the study of Grammar. Though, in all probability, most of our readers will have learnt the *art* of grammar, as usually taught at schools, yet our remarks may be of service to them, either in their farther attention to the subject with a view to their own improvement, or in communicating instruction to others.

We know no better elementary work on grammar, than Lindley Murray's. He has, in some instances, burdened the learner with unnecessary additions to the simplicity of the English language; and, in our opinion, there is still room for improvement in his practical directions, and more especially in his arrangement or classification. We would have the English language taught as it is, not fettered with restraints derived from languages in which there is a great variety of flexion: and we wish to see *practical* grammars constructed upon correct *scientific* principles; though it may not be expedient to bring those principles too early in view. The young should have as little as possible to unlearn.*—Nevertheless,

* The writer of this article has for some years had by him, a brief Introductory Grammar, founded on what he regards as the real principles of our language. He has it in contemplation to print it, when his engagements afford him the opportunity of a revisal.

as a practical guide to the actual usages of our language, Mr. Murray's Grammar seems to stand unrivalled; and without paying too much attention to those parts which he classes under *Etymology*, his *Syntax* will afford a variety of very important and valuable observations, directing to the proper mode of writing and speaking. It will be found of the greatest advantage to those who may have neglected this branch of instruction, to write his Exercises on Syntax, carefully attending, as they go along, to the rules and observations on which they are founded: and if they have no competent assistance to enable them to ascertain the propriety of their corrections, the Key will generally prove an excellent guide. We would recommend them, however, never to consult the key, till they have themselves done their best, by the aid of the Grammar merely: they will thus make the employment very serviceable in the culture of the judgment, as well as more efficacious in acquiring a correct acquaintance with the rules of the language. At the end of the exercises on syntax, are some, which are very useful, on punctuation and the qualities of style. These may, with great benefit, be employed in the same way; but we can by no means recommend the use of his exercises on orthography. Their direct, and, we think, necessary tendeney, is to confuse the recollection of the visible appearance of words; and thereby to lessen, instead of increasing, the facility and accuracy of our spelling. To acquire correctness in orthography, the best way is to write, frequently from memory or from dictation, or to write translations from other languages; to employ a good dictionary (Walker's, for instance,) in all cases of doubt; and, which will be found very beneficial, to keep a register of all words wherein a difficulty is felt, and often to review those which have been entered. The mere transcribing of passages from manuscript or printed books, will also be found of great advantage; and it is assuredly much better to write from correctly spelt copies, than to correct what is spelt wrong. However, Mr. Murray's *Grammar* will furnish some useful directions in orthography.

To those who wish to study the rules of our language, with the greatest benefit to themselves, we also strongly recommend Dr. Crombie's work, on "Etymology and Syntax." Numerous very valuable observations will be found in it, calculated to aid the researches of the student in the department of scientific grammar; and the practical remarks it affords, are, in many places, excellent. We are not acquainted with any other work of the kind; and though we do not agree with the learned author, in all his philosophical or practical principles, we regard his book as a very useful one, and shall be glad if these remarks contribute to make it more known among those for whose use our volumes are primarily intended.

If the reader is desirous of pursuing the study of scientific grammar, he will scarcely need any directions from us; but he may find the following hints of use. Some valuable remarks occur in the general grammar of Messrs. de Port Royal, and in Mr. Dalton's English grammar. Harris's Hermes, which, in many respects, deserves the, sometimes unmerciful, ridicule of Horne Tooke, is, notwithstanding, entitled to a careful perusal. It is almost unnecessary to add, that Mr. Tooke's Epea Pteroenta, or Diversions of Purley, claim the very attentive examination of the student. He need not be alarmed at the size of the volumes, for the substance might be easily compressed into a moderate octavo; and, however much he may occasionally be wearied with the illustrative examples, he will find himself recompensed by the scintillations of wit and genius, which present themselves in every part; and from those examples, he may often derive great light as to the principles of language in general, and especially the progress and phenomena of our own. We cannot avoid mentioning, by way of caution, that he ought not to trust implicitly to the author's representations, respecting mental or moral philosophy. If Mr. Tooke had known more respecting the operations of the associative power, he would himself, in all probability, have gone farther than he has, and been a safer guide to others. To those who have access to the Encyclopedia Britannica, we recommend the perusal of the article grammar, in that work, as one from which we derived much benefit when we first attended to the subject. In the great French work, Encyclopedic Methodique, are many very valuable observations, in the portion on grammar, which will well repay the perusal of the student. He will, of course, if he have an opportunity, consult the article grammar, in Dr. Rees's Cyclopedia.

CHAP V.

ON THE STRUCTURE OF SENTENCES.

Of what a sentence is to consist—Rules for the construction of sentences—Properties of a good sentence—Precision exemplified in the use of adverbs, &c.—The Unity of sentences considered and exemplified.

A SENTENCE always implies at least one complete proposition, or enunciation of thought; but every sentence is not necessarily confined to a single proposition. It usually consists of component parts, which are called members; these may be few or many, and may be connected in different ways, so that the same thought or mental proposition, may frequently be compressed into one sentence, or distributed into two or three.

A proper construction of sentences is of great importance in every species of composition: it is the foundation of good writing, so that we cannot be too strict in our attention to it. In any subject, if the sentences be perplexed, clumsy, or feebly expressed, it will not only disgust the reader, but frequently destroy the effect which the writer intended to produce.

It is impossible to lay down rules, with regard to the precise length of sentences: a short period is lively and familiar, and likely to be remembered: but a long period, if clearly expressed, requiring more attention, is calculated to make a more grave and solemn impression. Without much attention, writers and speakers are liable to err in both these respects. By means of too many short sentences, the sense is divided and broken, the connexion of thought weakened, and the memory burdened. On the other hand, long sentences fatigue the reader's or hearer's attention. If a writer is fully master of his subject, he ought, and he will study a due mixture of long and short periods, which prevents an irksome uniformity, and entertains the mind with a variety of impression. Long sentences should never be placed at the beginning of discourses of any description: the reader's attention, and, if possible, his interest must be excited, before a person venture upon long sentences.

Lord Kames has given rules for the arrangement of words in a sentence, which are deserving of attention. His object is, that the arrangement of words in succession, should be such as to afford the greatest pleasure to the ear, a circumstance which, he says, depends on principles remote from view, and, therefore, he premises some general observations upon the appearance that objects make when placed in an increasing or decreasing series, which we shall transcribe.

"Where," says our author, "the objects vary by small differences, so as to have a mutual resemblance, we, in ascending, conceive the second object of no greater size than the first, the third of no greater size than the second, and so of the rest; which diminisheth in appearance, the size of every object except the first; but when beginning at the greatest object, we proceed gradually to the least, resemblance makes us imagine the second as great as the first, and the third as great as the second; which in appearance magnifies every object except the first. On the other hand, in a series varying by large differences, when contrast prevails, the effects are directly opposite; a great object succeeding a small one of the same kind, appears greater than usual; and a little object succeeding one that is great, appears less than usual. Hence a remarkable pleasure in viewing a series ascending by large differences, directly opposite to what we feel when the differences are small. The least object of a series, ascending by large differences, has the same effect upon the mind as if it stood singly without making part of the series: but the second object, by means of contrast, appears greater than when viewed singly and apart, and the same effect is perceived in ascending progressively, till we arrive at the last object. The opposite effect is produced in descending; for in this direction every object, except the first, appears less than when viewed separately and independent of the series. We may then assume, as a maxim, which will hold in the composition of language, as well as of other subjects, that a strong impulse succeeding a weak one, makes a double impression on the mind, and that a weak impulse succeeding a strong, makes scarcely any impression."

After establishing this maxim, he says, we can be at no loss about its application to the subject, and that in the arrangement of words in a sentence, we should not, in general, descend from the greater to the less, but, on the contrary, ascend from the less to the greater: thus, in the Latin, "Vir est optimus," reads much better than "Vir optimus est." This rule is also applicable to entire members of a period, which ought also to proceed from the less to the greater: and this arrangement of words, or members of a sentence, gradually increasing in length, may, as far as concerns the pleasure of sound, be denominated a *climax in sound.* To shew the importance of attending to this subject, Lord Kames says, by no other human means is it possible to present to the mind, such a number of objects, and in so swift succession, as by speaking or writing; and for that reason, variety ought to be more studied in these, than in any sort of composition. Hence the rule for arranging the members of different periods with relation to each other, is to avoid a tedious uniformity of sound and cadence: the cadence, and the length of the members, ought to be diversified as much as possible; and if the members of different periods be sufficiently diversified, the periods themselves will be equally so.

The properties, according to Blair, most essential to a perfect sentence, seem to be the four following: CLEARNESS and PRECISION:—UNITY:—STRENGTH; and HARMONY.

Every degree of ambiguity, arising from the want of *clearness* and *precision*, ought to be avoided with the greatest care: hence the necessity of observing exactly the rules of grammar, and in the arrangement of sentences, those words and members most nearly related should be placed in the sentence, as near each other as possible, so as to make their mutual relation clearly manifest.

1. In the position of adverbs, which are used to qualify the signification of something that precedes or follows them, there is often much nicety. This part of speech, as its name implies, is generally placed near the verb, which it affects or modifies:

Examples: "Theism can *only* be opposed to polytheism, or atheism." Lord Shaftsbury. By this arrangement of the word *only*, it should seem, the noble author meant that, theism is capable of nothing else, except being opposed to polytheism or atheism. He intended, no doubt, to say, it could be *opposed* to nothing but atheism and polytheism, and to express this, he should have written, "Theism can be *opposed only* to atheism," &c. Here the adverb stands, as it often ought, close to the verb.

Swift, in his *Project for the advancement of religion*, says, "The Romans understood liberty, at least, as well as we." That is, the Romans, in whatever else they were deficient, understood the nature of *liberty* as well as we; or it may mean, according as the emphasis is laid, The Romans understood the nature of liberty as well or better than ourselves: the latter was probably the Dean's meaning, and the arrangement should have been "The Romans understood liberty, as well, at least, as we."

There are, in common use, certain phrases which are themselves equivocal, and are calculated to produce obscurity, as, *not the least*, *nothing less*, &c. Thus, "He aimed at *nothing less* than the crown;" which may imply, that he was far from *aiming at*, or it may signify, that nothing less would satisfy him.

In common conversation, the tone and emphasis made use of in pronouncing such adverbs as *only*, *wholly*, *at least*, shew the meaning at once; and on this account we often acquire a habit of throwing them in, without due attention in the course of a period. But in written discourses, which address the eye, and not the ear, greater accuracy is requisite; and they should be so connected with the words they are intended to qualify, as to prevent every appearance of ambiguity.

2. Words, expressive of things connected in thought, should be placed as near as possible; because, when objects are arranged according to their connexion, we have a sense of order: when they are placed, as it were, by chance, we have a sense of disorder. This rule is very important, since it is chiefly by the connective parts of sentences, that the train of thought, and the course of reasoning in continued discourse, is laid open.

Examples. "The English are naturally fanciful, and very often disposed, by that gloominess and melancholy of temper, which is so frequent in our nation, to many wild notions and visions, to which others are not so liable." Spectator. In this sentence, the verb *disposed* is separated unnecessarily from the subject to which it refers. The sentence should run thus:—

"The English are naturally fanciful; and, by that gloominess and melancholy of temper, which is so frequent in our nation, are often disposed to many wild notions," &c.

"Our English is, among those dialects, one that I think more capable of improvement than any other." Monboddo on Language. It would be better: "Our English is one, among those dialects, that I think," &c.

3. Great attention is required in the proper disposition of the relative pronouns *who*, *which*, *what*, and *whose*, and of those particles which express the connexion of the parts of

speech with one another; because all reasoning depends on these; and a small error in this respect, may render a whole sentence obscure, and almost unintelligible.

Examples: In one of Dr. Sherlock's sermons, is the following passage, "It is folly to pretend to arm ourselves against the accidents of life, by heaping up treasures, which nothing can protect us against, but the good providence of our heavenly Father." According to the rules of grammar, the word *which* refers to *treasures;* this would, however, make nonsense of the whole period; and the sentence should run thus: "It is folly to pretend, by heaping up treasures, to arm ourselves against the accidents of life; which nothing can protect us against, but the good providence of our heavenly Father."

"Solomon, the son of David, *who* built the temple," &c.; and "Solomon, the son of David, *who* was persecuted," &c. The relative, in the first sentence, refers to Solomon, and in the second to David; and yet it is similarly situated.

"Many act so directly contrary to this method, that, from a habit of saving time and paper, which they acquired at the university, they write in so diminutive a manner, that they can hardly read what they have written." Swift. This should have run thus: "From a habit, which many have acquired at the university, of saving time and paper, they write," &c.

"I allude to the article *Blind*, in the Encyclopedia Britannica, published at Edinburgh, in the year 1783, which was written by him." Mackenzie's Life of Blacklock. By this arrangement of the sentence, Blacklock might be considered as the sole author of the Encyclopedia; whereas the writer of his life meant to say he was author of the article *Blind* only; and, therefore, the sentence would have been better, "I allude to the article *Blind*, which was written by him, and published at Edinburgh, in the year 1783, in the Encyclopedia Britannica."

Other instances might be enumerated; but these are sufficient to make the rule understood, that, in the construction of sentences, one of the first things to be attended to is, the marshalling of the words in such order, as shall most clearly mark the relation of the several parts of the sentence to one another; particularly, that adverbs always be made to adhere closely to the words which they are intended to qualify: to which may be added, that in cases in which a circumstance is thrown in, it shall never hang loose in the midst of a period, but be determined by its place to one or other member of it; and that every relative should instantly present its antecedent to the reader, without the smallest obscurity.

It may be further added, that obscurity frequently arises from the too frequent repetition of relatives, particularly of the words, *who, they, them,* and *theirs.*

Examples: "And *they* did all eat, and were filled, and *they* took up of the fragments that remained twelve baskets full." The last *they* is not obvious: it may refer to the multitude, or to the disciples.

"*They* were summoned, occasionally, by *their* kings, when compelled by *their* wants, and by *their* fears, to have recourse to *their* aid." When the personal pronouns crowd in too fast upon us, there is often no other method left, but to change entirely the whole form of the sentence.

All languages are liable to ambiguities; but Quintilian says, that a sentence is always to be deemed faulty, when the arrangement of the words is ambiguous, though the sense may be easily discovered. In the following sentences, the true meaning cannot be ascertained, without attending to the connexion in which they are found: "Statuam auream bastam tenentem:" upon this it became a dispute at law, whether the whole statue, or the spear only, was to be made of gold:—"Chrementem audivi percussisse Demeam," from this mode of construction, it cannot be known whether Chremes or Demea struck the blow.

"This work, in its full extent, being now afflicted with an asthma, and finding the powers of life gradually declining, he had no longer courage to undertake." Johnson's Life of Savage.

From this we may imagine. that it was the work, and not the author, that was afflicted with the asthma. It should stand thus: " Being now afflicted with an asthma, and finding the powers of life gradually declining, he had no longer courage to undertake this work in its full extent."

" The minister, who grows less by his elevation, like a little statue placed on a mighty pedestal, will always have his jealousy strong about him." This would be much better: " The minister, who, like a little statue placed on a mighty pedestal, grows less by his elevation, will always have his jealousy strong about him."

The relation of every word and member of a sentence should be marked in the most proper and distinct manner; which will give not only clearness, but grace and beauty to a sentence; making the mind pass smoothly and agreeably along all the parts of it.

The *Unity* of a sentence is next to be considered. There must always be some leading principle to form a chain of connexion between the component parts of every composition, and there must be the same connecting principle among the parts. In a single sentence, above all, the strictest unity is required; for the very nature of a sentence implies one proposition to be expressed. It may consist of parts; but these parts ought to be so closely bound together, as to make an impression upon the mind of one object, not of many.

To preserve unity in a sentence, the following rules have been laid down by Dr. Blair.

1. The scene, the subject, and the person, should be changed as little as possible. There is commonly, in every sentence, some person or thing which is the governing word. This should, if the case admit of it, be continued from the beginning to the end of it. The following sentences are violations of this rule.

Examples: " Cicero was oppressed by a new and cruel affliction, the death of his beloved daughter, Tullia, which happened soon after her divorce from Dolabella, whose manners and humours were entirely disagreeable to her." Middleton's Life of Cicero.

The chief object in this sentence, is the death of Tullia, the cause of Cicero's affliction. The time in which it happened was quite proper; but the introduction of Dolabella's character destroys the unity of the period, by presenting to the reader a new picture.

"After we came to anchor, they put me on shore, where I was welcomed by all my friends, who received me with the greatest kindness." Here, by shifting so often the *place*, and the *persons*, *we*, *they*, *I*, and *who*, the feeling of connexion and unity is nearly lost. It would have been better thus: "Having come to an anchor, I was put on shore, where I was welcomed by all my friends, and received with the greatest kindness."

2. We should never crowd into one sentence, things that have so little connexion, that they could bear to be divided into two or more sentences.

Examples: Archbishop Tillotson, speaking of a person lately deceased, says, "He was exceedingly beloved both by King William and Queen Mary, who nominated Dr. Tennison, bishop of Lincoln, to succeed him." In this sentence, there is no connexion whatever between the latter part and the former: it would have been more natural to have given some proof of the fact, that he had been the object of their majesties' affection, than to have spoken of his successor.

Plutarch, speaking of an army, says, "Their march was through an uncultivated country, whose savage inhabitants fared hardly, having no other riches than a breed of sheep, whose flesh was rank and unsavoury, by reason of their continual feeding upon sea-fish." In this sentence there is a sad jumble of objects, but very slightly related to each other, which cannot be comprehended under one view:—the march of the Greeks:—the description of the inhabitants of the country through which they passed:—an account of their sheep, and the reason of the ill taste of their flesh.

Authors, who are fond of long periods, are apt to fall into errors of this kind, of which we have a multitude of instances in Burnet and Clarendon; and though punctuation may sometimes remedy the evil, yet commas, colons, &c. cannot make the proper divisions of thought; they only serve to mark those which arise from the mode of the author's expression; and they are proper or not, as they correspond to the natural division of the sense.

3. Parentheses ought not to be introduced in the middle of sentences. On some occasions, a parenthesis may be fitly introduced, when prompted by a certain vivacity of thought, which can glance aside as it is going along; but, in general, their effect is extremely bad, and should be avoided, being, as it were, wheels within wheels, or separate sentences within other sentences.

Examples: "When the parliament sat down (for it deserves our particular observation, that both houses were full of zeal for the present government, and of resentment against the late usurpations), there was but one party in parliament; and no other party could raise its head in the nation." Bolingbroke.

The same author says, "It seems to me, that, in order to maintain the system of the world, at a certain point, far below that of ideal perfection (for we are made capable of conceiving what we are incapable of attaining) but, however sufficient upon the whole to constitute a state easy and happy, or at the worst tolerable; I say, it seems to me, that the Author of nature, has thought fit to mingle from time to time, among societies of men, a few, and but a few, of those on whom He is graciously pleased to bestow a larger proportion of the ethereal spirit, than is given in the ordinary course of his providence to the sons of men."

Into this sentence, by means of the parenthesis, and other circumstances thrown in, the author has so involved so many things, that he is obliged as it were, to begin again, with the words *I say*, which, whenever they occur, may be assumed as a sure mark of a clumsy and ill-constructed sentence, unpardonable in any one who pretends to neatness in style.

The best modern writers avoid all parentheses, as keeping the mind in suspense, and rendering the composition less clear, uniform, and agreeable. Long and frequent parentheses are intolerable, as rendering the discourse dull and languid. The proper characteristic of a parenthesis is, that it may be taken in or left out, without injuring either the sense or grammar. In speaking, the words in a parenthesis are pronounced in a different tone of voice; and in writing, they are enclosed between brackets, or between two commas.

4. Sentences ought never to be extended beyond their natural close. Every thing that is one, should have a beginning, a middle, and an end. An unfinished or imperfect sentence is no sentence at all. But some sentences are too full, and when we have arrived at what we supposed would be the conclusion, unexpectedly some circumstance occurs, which ought to have been omitted, but which is left dragging behind. Such additions tend very much to destroy the beauty, and to diminish the strength of a period.

Examples. Swift, in speaking of the writings of Cicero, says, " With these writings, young divines are more conversant, than with those of Demosthenes, who, by many degrees, excelled the other, at least as an orator." The natural close of the sentence is at the word *other:* the sense was complete, and the succeeding clause was quite unnecessary.

CHAP. VI.

ON THE STRUCTURE OF SENTENCES,
Continued.

Strength—A necessary quality of a good sentence—Obtained by divesting it of redundant words—By the moderate use of copulatives, relatives, &c. —By the proper disposition of the capital words—By the arrangement— By not concluding with an adverb, or other inconsiderable words—and by making the language correspond to the things described.

PERSPICUITY and unity, though of the most importance in the construction of sentences, are not the only things necessary; we must make such a disposition of the words and members, as will render the impression, which the period is designed to make, most full and complete, and give every word, and every member, their due weight and force. In this consists the *strength* of a sentence. To attain to this perfection in writing, the following rules should be attended to.

1. A sentence ought to be divested of all redundant words, because these are never consistent with strength. All words that do not add some importance to the meaning of a sentence, always injure it.

Examples: "*Being* content with deserving a triumph, he refused the honour of it." Bolingbroke.

"Never did Atticus succeed better in gaining the *universal* love and esteem of *all* men." The word *being*, in the first sentence, may advantageously be omitted; and in the second, one of the words in italics must be left out, because the same idea is included in *universal* and *all.*

"How many are there, by whom these *tidings* of *good news* were never heard?" This is tautology; it would be much better, "by whom these *good tidings* were never heard."

"I returned, full of *a great many* serious reflections." The words in italics should be omitted. Hence, says Dr. Blair, "I consider it, therefore, as one of the most useful exercises of correction, upon reviewing what we have written or composed, to contract that round-about method of expression, and to lop off those useless excrescences which are commonly found in a first draught. Here a severe eye should be employed; and we shall always find our sentences acquire more vigour and energy when thus retrenched, provided we do not run into the extreme of pruning so very close as to give a hardness and dryness to style."

As sentences should be free from redundant words, so also of redundant members. Every member should contain a new thought; and should not be a mere echo of the former, or the repetition of it in a different form. Mr. Addison says, "It is impossible for us to behold the divine works with coldness or indifference; or to survey so many beauties, without a secret satisfaction and complacency." The second member of the sentence adds but little to the first.

"Neither is any condition of life more honourable in the sight of God than another; otherwise He would be a respecter of persons, which He assures us He is not." Swift.

The last clause weakens the thought, as it implies, that without the assurance of God to the contrary, we should conclude that he sustained a character different from what was given by the preacher.

2. In constructing a sentence, particular attention is to be paid to the use of copulatives, relatives, &c. These little words are frequently the most important of any; they are the joints or hinges on which all sentences turn, and of course much, both of the gracefulness and strength, must depend upon such par-

ticles. The varieties in using them are, indeed, so numerous, that no particular rules respecting them can be given. The best way of attaining to accuracy is, to study writers who excel in neatness and elegance of style, and to observe, with critical attention, the effects produced by a different usage of those particles. The following observations may be of use to young people.

The splitting of particles, or separating a preposition from a noun which it governs, is always to be avoided.

Example: "Though virtue borrows no assistance *from*, yet it may often be accompanied by, the advantages of fortune." Here we are put to a stand in thought, being obliged to rest a little on the preposition *from*, by itself, which has no significancy, till joined to its proper noun.

We should not needlessly multiply demonstrative and relative particles, by the use of phrases like this: "There is nothing *which* disgusts us sooner than the empty pomp of language." This may be proper, when it is introductory to an important observation; but, in common cases, it is better to say, "Nothing disgusts us sooner than the empty pomp of language." It is not only shorter, but more simple.

We should not omit the relative; as in the following

Examples: "The man I love:"—"The dominions we possessed:"—"The soldiers in the camp were prepared for the part they were to act."

Though this elliptical style be intelligible, and is allowable in conversation and epistolary writing, yet it is not to be tolerated in grave and dignified compositions: in these, relatives must be used: "The man *whom* I love." "The dominions *which* we possessed." "The part *which* they were to act."

With regard to the copulative particle *and*, it may be observed, that an unnecessary repetition of it enfeebles the style. It has a similar effect in writing, as the frequent use of the phrase *and* so, in telling a story in common conversation. It is, however, worthy of observation, that though the natural use of the conjunction *and* be, to join objects together, and thereby to make their connexion more close; yet, in fact, by dropping the conjunction, we often mark a quicker succession of objects, than when it is inserted between them, of which an example is found in the famous expression "Veni, vidi, vici," "I came, I saw, I conquered." Another example of the same kind is taken from Xenophon: "Closing their shields, they were impelled, they fought, they slew, and were slain." By this means, sentences, artfully divested of conjunctions, drop smoothly down, and the periods are poured along in such a manner, that they seem to outstrip the very thought of the speaker. Voltaire, in the Henriade, has endeavoured to shew the hurry and confusion of a battle in this same way, by omitting all copulatives,

> François, Anglois, Lorrains, que la fureur assemble,
> Avançoient, combattoient, frappoient, mouroient ensemble.

The eagerness of Dido, at the idea of Eneas's departure, is shewn in the precipitate manner in which she commands her servants to endeavour to stop him:

> ——————————————Ite
> Ferte citi flammas, date vela, impellite remos.

> Haste, haul my gallies out; pursue the foe;
> Bring flaming brands, set sail, and quickly row.
>
> DRYDEN.

There are cases, in which copulatives may be multiplied with peculiar advantage and grace, as when we are making an enumeration, in which we wish that the objects should appear as distinct from each other as possible, and that the mind should rest for a moment on each object by itself; thus: Lord Bolingbroke says, "Such a man might fall a victim to power; but truth, and reason, and liberty, would fall with him."

An attention to the several cases, when it is proper to omit, and when to redouble the copulative, is of considerable importance to all who would write well, or become judges of good composition. It is a remarkable peculiarity in language, that the *omission* of a connecting particle should sometimes serve to make objects appear more closely connected; and that the *repetition* of it should distinguish and separate them, in some measure, from each other. On this account, the omission denotes rapidity; and the repetition of it is designed to retard. The reason seems to be, that, in the former case, the mind is supposed to be hurried so fast through a succession of objects, that it has not leisure to point out their connexion; it drops the copulatives in its hurry, and crowds the whole series together, as it were but one object. Whereas, when we enumerate, with a view to retard, the mind is supposed to proceed with a more slow and solemn pace: it marks the relation of each object to that which succeeds it; and, by joining them together with several copulatives, leads one to imagine that the objects, though connected, are yet in themselves distinct; that they are several, not one. As an illustration of this reasoning, Dr. Blair gives the enumeration of the apostle Paul, to shew what additional weight and distinctness is given to each particular, by the mere repetition of a conjunction: "I am persuaded, that neither death, nor life, nor angels, nor principalities, nor powers, nor things present, nor things to come, nor height, nor depth, nor any other creature, shall be able to separate us from the love of God."

3. Another rule for promoting the strength of a sentence is, to dispose of the capital word or words, in that place of the sentence, where they will make the fullest impression; this place will, however, vary with the nature of the sentence. In all cases, *perspicuity* is principally to be attended to; but generally, perhaps, the important words are placed in the beginning of the sentence, thus: "The pleasures of the imagination, taken in their full extent, are not so gross as those of the sense, nor so refined as those of the understanding:" It seems the most plain and natural order, to place that in the front, which is the chief object of the proposition to be laid down. Sometimes effect is given to a sentence, by suspending the meaning a little. Thus, in Pope's preface to Homer, we

have the following sentence, which is illustrative of the position: "On whatever side we contemplate Homer, what principally strikes us is, his wonderful invention."

By some English writers, inversion is practised with success; but, in general, those who have had frequent recourse to it, have become harsh and obscure. By inversion, Lord Shaftesbury's style is characterized for strength, dignity, and varied harmony; but Mr. Addison's sentences are constructed in a quite different manner; he always proceeds in the most natural and obvious order of language, and if, according to the observation of Dr. Blair, by this means he has less pomp and majesty than Lord Shaftesbury, he has more nature, more ease and simplicity—which are beauties of a higher order. "But," says our author, "whether we practise inversion or not, and in whatever part of the sentence we dispose of the capital words, it is always a point of great moment, that these capital words shall stand clear and disentangled from any other words that would clog them. Thus, when there are any circumstances of time, place, or other limitations, which the principal object of our sentence requires to have connected with it, we must take special care to dispose of them so as not to cloud that principal object, nor to bury it under a load of circumstances. This will be made clearer by an example. Observe the arrangement of the following sentence, in Lord Shaftesbury's Advice to an Author. He is speaking of modern poets as compared with the ancient: "If, while they profess only to please, they secretly advise, and give instruction, they may, now, perhaps, as well as formerly, be esteemed, with justice, the best and most honourable among authors." This is a well constructed sentence. It contains a great many circumstances and adverbs, necessary to qualify the meaning; *only, secretly, as well, perhaps, now, with justice, formerly;* yet these are placed with so much art, as neither to embarrass nor weaken the sentence; while that which is the capital object in it, viz. "Poets being justly esteemed the best and most honourable among authors," comes out in the conclusion clear and detached, and possesses its proper place.

4. The next rule to be attended to in the construction of sentences is, to make the members of them go on rising and growing in their importance one above another. This is called a *climax,* such as that of Cicero, addressed to Catiline: "Nihil agis, nihil moliris, nihil cogitas, quod ego non audiam, quod etiam non videam, planeque sentiam."

The following is an instance taken from Lord Bolingbroke: "This decency, this grace, this propriety of manners to character, is so essential to princes in particular, that, whenever it is neglected, their virtues lose a great degree of lustre, and their detects acquire much aggravation." Quintilian directs, that a weaker expression should never follow one of more strength, as if, after sacrilege, we were to introduce simple theft.

A *climax* has been defined, a figure, in which the word or expression that ends the first member of a period begins the second, and so on; so that every member will make a distinct sentence, taking its rise from the preceding, till the period be finished, as in the following gradation of Tillotson: "After we have practised good actions awhile, they become easy; and when they are easy, we begin to take pleasure in them; and when they please us, we do them frequently; and by the frequency of acts, a thing grows into a habit; and confirmed habit is second nature; and so far as any thing is natural, so far it is necessary, and we can hardly do otherwise; nay, we do it many times, when we do not think of it!"

5. The fifth rule for the strength of sentences is, to avoid concluding them with an adverb, preposition, or any other inconsiderable word. Agreeably to this rule, we should avoid concluding with any of those particles which mark the cases of nouns. For, besides the want of dignity which arises from those monosyllables being placed at the close, the mind cannot avoid resting a little upon the word that concludes the sen-

tence; and as these prepositions have no import of their own, but merely serve to point out the relation of other words, it is disagreeable thus to be left pausing on a word, which of itself cannot produce any idea, or present any picture to the fancy.

The pronoun *it* ought not to close a sentence; and nothing can be well worse, than to allow this same word *it* to conclude two successive periods; yet we find examples of the kind occur, occasionally, in our first-rate writers. Thus Mr. Burke: "In like manner, if a person in broad day-light were falling asleep, to introduce a sudden darkness, would prevent his sleep for that time, though silence and darkness in themselves, and not suddenly introduced, are very favourable to *it*. This I knew only by conjecture on the analogy of the senses, when I first digested these observations; but I have since experienced *it*."

6. In the members of a sentence, where two objects are either compared or contrasted, some resemblance in the language and construction should be preserved. We are disappointed when it is otherwise; and the comparison, or contrast, appears more imperfect.

"The wise man is happy, when he gains his own approbation; the fool, when he recommends himself to the applause of those about him." Spectator. The sentence would read much better, "The wise man is happy, when he gains his own approbation; the fool, when he gains that of others."

"After all," says Dr. Blair, "The fundamental rule of the construction of sentences, and into which all others might be resolved, undoubtedly is, to communicate in the clearest and most natural order, the ideas which we mean to transfuse into the minds of others. Every arrangement that does most justice to the sense, and expresses it to most advantage, strikes us as beautiful. To this point have tended all the rules I have given. And, indeed, did men always think clearly, and were they, at the same time, fully masters of the language in which they write, there would be occasion for few rules. Their sentences would then, of course, acquire all those properties of

Precision, Unity, and Strength, which I have recommended. For we may rest assured, that whenever we express ourselves ill, there is, besides the mismanagement of language, for the most part, some mistake in our manner of conceiving the subject. Embarrassed, obscure, and feeble sentences are generally, if not always, the result of embarrassed, obscure, and feeble thought. Thought and language act and re-act upon each other mutually. Logic and rhetoric have here, as in many other cases, a strict connexion; and he that is learning to arrange his sentences with accuracy and order, is learning, at the same time, to think with accuracy and order."

CHAP. VII.

ON THE STRUCTURE OF SENTENCES,
Continued.

The Harmony of a sentence depends on the choice and arrangement of the words—Ancient languages more susceptible of music than the modern—The current of sound to be adapted to the tenor of the discourse—Sounds may be employed to represent other sounds—Motion—The passions of the mind.

ALTHOUGH sound is a quality of much less importance than sense, yet it must not be entirely neglected by those who would draw attention to themselves, either as speakers or writers; inasmuch as there is always a connexion between the idea which is conveyed, and the sound by which it is conveyed. It was a maxim of Quintilian, that nothing could enter the affections which stumbles at the threshold, by offending the ear. Music, naturally, has a great power over men, in facilitating certain emotions, so that there are hardly any dispositions that persons, conversant with the human mind, wish to excite in others, but that they can find certain sounds tending to produce or promote them. Language may, in a less or greater degree, be rendered capable of this power of music, a circumstance that cannot fail to heighten our idea of it as a very wonderful invention. It is not only capable of simply interpreting our ideas to others, but of exciting in them those ideas, enforced by corresponding sounds;

and to the pleasure of communicating thought, it can add the new and separate pleasure of melody.

The musical cadence of a sentence will depend upon the *choice* of words;—and the *arrangement* of them. Those words will be most agreeable to the ear, which are composed of smooth and liquid sounds, and in which there is a proper intermixture of vowels and consonants, without too many harsh consonants clashing with each other, or too many open vowels in succession, to cause a disagreeable aperture of the mouth. Whatever sounds are difficult in pronunciation, are in the same proportion, harsh and painful to the ear. Vowels add softness; consonants, strength to the sound of words: the melody of language requires a just proportion of each, and will be rendered either grating or effeminate by an excess. Long words are commonly more agreeable to the ear than monosyllables; and among words of any length, those are most musical, which do not run wholly either upon long or short syllables, but are composed of an intermixture of both.

With respect to the harmony which results from a proper arrangement of the words and members of a sentence, it may be observed, that, however well chosen the words themselves may be, yet if they be ill-disposed, the music of the sentence is utterly destroyed. In the harmonious arrangement of his periods, no writer, ancient or modern, can be compared with Cicero. Instances in proof of this might be selected from almost every page of his works. "In English," says Dr. Blair, "we may take as an instance of a musical sentence, the following from Milton, in his Treatise on Education: 'We shall conduct you to a hill-side, laborious, indeed, at the first ascent; but else, so smooth, so green, so full of goodly prospects,—and melodious sounds on every side,—that the harp of Orpheus was not more charming.' Every thing in this sentence conspires to produce the harmony. The words are happily chosen; full of liquids and soft sounds: *laborious, smooth, green, goodly, melodious, charming:* and these words so artfully arranged, that, were we to alter the collocation of any one of them, we should presently be sensible of the melody suffering. For, let us observe how finely the members of the period swell one above another. 'So smooth, so green, —so full of goodly prospects,—and melodious sounds on every side,'—till the ear, prepared by this gradual rise, is conducted to that full close on which it rests with pleasure;—'that the harp of Orpheus was not more charming.'"

The structure of periods being susceptible of a very sensible melody, the next inquiry is, how the melodious structure is formed, what are the principles of it, and by what laws it is regulated. In this, we cannot, owing to the nature of our language, and other circumstances, follow the ancients. They, in treating upon the structure of sentences, always make the music of them the principal object. The other qualities of precision, unity, and strength, which we consider as of chief importance, they touch on but slightly. Dionysius of Halicarnassus, in his treatise on the "Composition of words in a sentence," refers only to their musical effect. He makes the excellency of a sentence to consist in the sweetness of single sounds:—in the composition of sounds, that is, the numbers or feet:—in change or variety of sound;—and in sound suited to sense.

Among the moderns, the subject of the musical structure of discourse has been less studied, and for the following reasons can be less subjected to rule.

1. The ancient languages were more susceptible than ours of the powers of melody. The quantities of their syllables were more fixed and determined, their words were longer, and more sonorous; their method of varying the terminations of nouns and verbs, freed them from that multiplicity of little auxiliary words, which we are obliged to employ; and what is of still more importance, the inversions which their languages allowed, gave them the power of placing their words in whatever order was most suited to a musical arrangement.

2. The Greeks and Romans were much more musical nations than we are, which is a reason of their paying more at-

tention to that construction of sentences, which might best suit their pronunciation. And

3. The musical arrangement of sentences did produce a greater effect in public speaking among them, than it would among us. But though this musical arrangement cannot be reduced into a system, yet it is a quality that ought not to be neglected in composition. There are two things on which the music of a sentence chiefly depends. These are, the proper distribution of the several members of it, and the close or cadence of the whole.

In the distribution of the several members of a sentence, it is of importance to observe, that, whatever is easy and agreeable to the organs of speech, always sounds grateful to the ear. While a period is going on, the termination of each of its members forms a rest or pause in the pronouncing, and these pauses should be so distributed, as to make the breathing easy, and at the same time should fall at such distances as to bear a certain musical proportion to each other: but the rests should not be too numerous, or placed at intervals too measured and regular, lest the style savour of affectation.

The following sentence, from Sir William Temple, has been given by writers on the subject, to exemplify this rule; he is speaking of man in an ironical style, "But, God be thanked, his pride is greater than his ignorance; and what he wants in knowledge, he supplies by sufficiency. When he has looked about him, as far as he can, he concludes, there is no more to be seen; when he is at the end of his line, he is at the bottom of the ocean; when he has shot his best, he is sure none ever did, or ever can, shoot better, or beyond it. His own reason he holds to be the certain measure of truth; and his own knowledge, of what is possible in nature." Here every thing is, at once, easy to the breath, and grateful to the ear; and it is this sort of flowing measure which renders the style of Sir William Temple always agreeable.

The close or cadence of the whole sentence demands the greatest care, because on this the mind pauses and rests. Here, every hearer and reader expects to be gratified: here, his applause breaks forth. The rule to be observed is, that when we aim at dignity or elevation, the sound should be made to grow to the last; the longest member of the period, and the fullest and most sonorous words, should be reserved to the conclusion. The following sentence from Mr. Addison is constructed upon this rule:

" It fills the mind with the largest variety of ideas, converses with its objects at the greatest distance, and continues the longest in action, without being tired or satiated with its proper enjoyments." " Every reader," says Dr. Blair, " must be sensible of a beauty here, both in the proper division of the members and the pauses, and the manner in which the sentence is rounded, and conducted to a full and harmonious close."

The same holds in melody, that takes place with respect to significancy, a falling off is always unpleasant, and offends the ear. Hence particles, pronouns, and little words are ungracious to the ear, and it is probable, that the sense and the sound have, in this respect a mutual influence on each other. That which hurts the ear, seems to mar the strength of the meaning. In general, a musical close, in our language, requires either the last syllable, or the last but one, to be a long syllable. But it should be observed, that sentences so constructed as to make the sound always swell and grow towards the end, give the discourse a tone of declamation, which soon becomes unpleasant to the ear. The measures should be frequently varied, and short sentences should be intermixed with long and swelling ones, to render discourse agreeable and impressive.

Though the music of sentences demands a very considerable degree of attention, yet it must be kept within bounds: there must be no affectation of harmony, especially if the love of it betray a person to sacrifice perspicuity, precision, or strength of sentiment to sound. All unmeaning words, introduced merely to round a period, or complete the melody, are considerable blemishes in writing.

It now remains to treat of the sound as adapted to the sense: which admits of two distinct considerations:

1. The current of sound may be adapted to the tenor of a discourse, in every language that admits of poetry; and the characteristic is found in every author, whose fancy enables him to impress images strongly on his own mind, and whose choice of language readily supplies him with just representations. On many occasions, we produce the music which we imagine ourselves to hear. In common life, it is not easy to deliver a pleasing message, in an unpleasing manner, and we readily associate beauty and deformity with those whom we have reason to love or hate. Hence no one tenor, supposing it to produce no bad effect from satiety, will answer to all sorts of compositions; nor even to all parts of the same composition. The same language cannot be used in writing a panegyric and an invective. In the common translation of the Bible, there is a multitude of instances, in which the language has been happily adapted to the subject. The very first verses in the book of Genesis, have been quoted as a good illustration of the rule:

"In the beginning, God created the heavens and the earth; and the earth was without form, and void, and darkness was upon the face of the deep; and the spirit of God moved upon the face of the waters."

2. Besides the general correspondence of the current of sound with the current of thought, there may be a more particular expression attempted of certain objects, by means of resembling sounds. The accomplishment of this is not often possible in prose compositions; but in poetry, where the inversions and liberties of style, give a greater command of sound, it is naturally looked for.

The sounds of words may be employed for representing three classes of objects, viz. other sounds:—motion;—and the passions of the mind.

In the common structure of language, the names of many particular sounds are so formed, as to carry some affinity to the sound which they signify: thus, as we have already observed, we speak of the *whistling* and *roaring* of the wind: of the *hissing* of serpents: of the *buzz* and *hum* of insects: of the *rustling* of trees and thickets: of the *crash* attending upon the fall of buildings. The following passages from Milton may be given as examples of this kind of beauty; they are descriptive of the sound made, in the *one*, by the opening of the gates of Hell; in the *other*, by the opening of those of Heaven:

———————On a sudden, open fly
With impetuous recoil, and jarring sound,
Th' infernal doors; and on their hinges grate
Harsh thunder. *Paradise Lost*, Book I.

————————Heaven opened wide
Her ever during gates, harmonious sound!
On golden hinges turning. Book II.

The motion of an arrow, and the sound of a bow, are excellently described by Pope in the following lines:

The impetuous arrow *whizzes* on the wing.

—————————The string let fly,
Twanged short and sharp, like the shrill swallow's cry.

To these, another example may be added from the same author:

Loud sounds the axe, redoubling strokes on strokes,
On all sides round the forest hurls her oaks
Headlong. Deep echoing, groan the thickets brown,
Then *rustling*, *crackling*, *crashing*, thunder down.

2. Another class of objects, which the sound of words is often employed to imitate, is *motion*, as it is swift or slow, violent or gentle, equable or interrupted, easy or accompanied with effort.

Long syllables naturally give the impression of *slow* motion: but *swift* motion is imitated by a succession of short syllables.

The description of a sudden calm on the seas, in Dyer's Fleece, can scarcely be exceeded:

——————with easy course
The vessels glide; unless their speed be stopped
By dead calms, that oft lie on these smooth seas,
When every zephyr sleeps; then the shrouds drop;
The downy feather, on the cordage hung,
Moves not; the flat sea shines like yellow gold
Fus'd in the fire; or like the marble floor
Of some old temple wide,

A line composed of monosyllables, by the frequency of its pauses, makes an impression similar to what is made by laborious interrupted motion. The following are examples:

First march the heavy mules, securely slow:
O'er hills, o'er dales, o'er crags, o'er rocks they go. POPE.

With many a weary step, and many a groan,
Up the high hill, he heaves a huge round stone. BROOME.

Slow and prolonged motion is well expressed by an Alexandrine verse:

A needless Alexandrine ends the song,
That, like a wounded snake, drags its slow length along. POPE.

From the same author, we select an example of forcible and prolonged motion:

The waves behind impel the waves before,
Wide-rolling, foaming high, and tumbling on the shore.

3. In the third set of objects, the sounds of words are capable of representing the passions and emotions of the mind: thus we have sorrow and complaint finely expressed in the pathetic soliloquy of Cardinal Wolsey on his fall:

Farewell! a long farewell! to all my greatness!
This is the state of man! to day he puts forth
The tender leaves of hope; to morrow, blossoms,
And bears his blushing honours thick upon him;

The third day comes a frost, a killing frost!
And when he thinks, good easy man, full surely
His greatness is a ripening, nips his root,
And then he falls, as I do.

Another fine example of this kind is in the part of Andromache, in the Distressed Mother:

I'll go, and, in the anguish of my heart,
Weep o'er my child.———If he must die, my life
Is wrapt in his, I shall not long survive.

Fear expresses itself in a low, hesitating, and abject sound. The speech of Lady Macbeth, while her husband is about to murder Duncan, and his groans, exhibit her affrighted even with the sound of her own voice:

Alas! I am afraid they have awak'd,
And 'tis not done; th' attempt, and not the deed
Confounds us—Hark! I laid the daggers ready,
He could not miss them.—Had he not resembled
My father as he slept, I had done it.

Melancholy and gloomy subjects naturally express themselves in slow measures and long words:

In those deep solitudes and awful cells,
Where heavenly pensive Contemplation dwells,
And ever musing Melancholy reigns. POPE.

Courage assumes a different tone:

Here satiate all your fury:—
Let Fortune empty her whole quiver on me,
I have a soul that, like an ample shield,
Can take in all, and verge enough for more.

Pleasure is displayed in a luxurious, mild, tender, and joyous modulation; as in the following lines:

Lavinia!—O there's music in the name,
That, soft'ning me to infant tenderness,
Makes my heart spring like the first leaps of life.

From these instances, and a great number of others, equally striking, might have been produced, we have shewn, that in good writing, an attention must be paid to the harmony of sentences; or, as it is described by the poet:

'Tis not enough, no harshness gives offence—
The sound must seem an echo to the sense.
Soft is the strain when Zephyr gently blows,
And the smooth stream in smoother numbers flows;
But, when loud surges lash the sounding shore,
The hoarse rough verse should like the torrent roar.
When Ajax strives some rock's vast weight to throw,
The line too labours, and the words move slow;
Not so, when swift Camilla scours the plain,
Flies o'er th' unbending corn, and skims along the main.

CHAP VIII.

TASTE.

Ornamental writing—Taste, origin of—How improved—Characters of—Qualities necessary to a good writer, illustrated with respect to narration—in argumentative discourse, and in historical composition—more attention to be paid to thoughts than words.

ANOTHER part of the Belles Lettres comprehends whatever is ornamental in a discourse or composition. The bare materials, and even the disposition of them in a discourse, are adapted to do little more than make an impression upon those persons, who, of themselves, either from a regard to the nature of the subject, or from its importance, will give their attention to it, but when the composition is ornamented, it is then calculated to attract and engage the attention, by the grace and harmony of the style, the turn of thought, or the striking or pleasing manner in which the sentiments are introduced and expressed. In considering the nature of grammar, and the arrangement and structure of sentences, we have only, as it has been expressed, examined what may be called the bones, muscles, and nerves of a composition; but now, to carry on the figure, we come to the covering of this body, to describe its external lineaments, its colour, its complexion, and graceful attitude.

Whatever contributes to adorn a discourse, must either give

life and beauty to sentiment, or harmony to the diction. By ornament of thoughts, is meant that manner of introducing and presenting them to the mind, which will give them the most favourable appearance. This, therefore, comprehends all the pleasures which may be said to be perceived by the mind; whereas, in treating of the ornaments of diction, language may be considered as affecting the ear only. Whatever it be, in the sentiment or ideas, that causes a discourse to be read with pleasure, must either be interesting, by exciting the passions, or must awaken those more delicate sensations, which are usually denominated the pleasures of the imagination. An exquisite feeling of the latter, may be said to constitute a fine taste, but no person can be a complete judge of the merit of a composition, unless he perfectly understand the subject of it, so as both clearly to distinguish the character of the design, and also to judge how far the execution is adapted to the undertaking.

Taste has been defined, "The power of receiving pleasure from the beauties of nature and art." It cannot, therefore, be resolvable into any operation of the mere rational faculties, because it is not by the discovery of the understanding, or by a deduction of argument, that the mind receives pleasure from a beautiful prospect or a fine poem: these often afford the same sort of pleasure to the philosopher and the peasant, the child and the man. The faculty, therefore, by which we relish such beauties, appears more nearly allied to the feeling of sense, than to the process of the understanding; but there is no doubt it may be improved in its operations by reason.

Judgment is universally admitted to be altogether acquired, and that Taste, too, or the capacity of perceiving the pleasures of the imagination, may be acquired to a great degree, is evident, from the actual acquirement of a variety of similar tastes, even late in life. Instances of this kind may be given in tastes for flowers, for gardening, and for architecture, which are hardly ever possessed at very early periods. It is scarcely possible, that any person who never attempted to sketch out an object himself, should have a high relish for the beauties of painting; but let him be instructed in the art of drawing and designing;—let him be employed in viewing and examining a great variety of pictures, let him associate with painters and connoisseurs in the fine arts, and he would, no doubt, not only acquire judgment in the productions of that art, and be able to distinguish a fine design and execution, but that he would have a relish for it; that what he approved, he would admire, and that the view of it would affect him with sensible pleasure. The same may be said of music, poetry and the other branches of the fine arts.

It may also be assumed, that all the *principles of taste* in works of genius, the sources from whence these pleasures are derived, are within the reach of all persons, and that there is hardly an individual who passes much of his time in cultivated society, where the fine arts flourish, without acquiring, in a greater or less degree, a taste for some or other of them.

The inequality of Taste among men, similarly situated, is owing, without doubt, to the different frame of their natures; to more delicate organs and finer internal powers, with which some are endowed beyond others. But since all emotions, excited by works of genius, consist of such ideas and sensations, as are capable of being associated with the perception of such works, nothing can be requisite to the acquisition of Taste, but exposing the mind to a situation in which those associated ideas will be frequently presented to it. Taste then may be considered as an improvable faculty, which is still farther evident, if we reflect on that immense superiority which education and improvement give to civilized, above barbarous nations, in refinement of Taste. "The difference is so great," says Dr. Blair, "that there is perhaps no one particular, in which these two classes of men are so far removed from each other, as in respect of the powers and pleasures of Taste: and assuredly for this difference, no other general cause can be assigned, but culture and education."

Exercise, indeed, is the chief source of improvement in all

our faculties. This holds both in our bodily and mental powers, and even in our external senses. How acute do the senses of those persons become, whose occupation leads them to nice *exertions!* Touch, for instance, becomes infinitely more exquisite in men whose employment requires them to examine the polish of bodies, than it is in others. Those who accustom themselves to microscopical observations, acquire a vast accuracy of sight in discerning the minutest objects. Practice in attending to different flavours and tastes in teas, spirituous liquors, &c. increases the power of distinguishing them, and of tracing their component parts. "Placing internal taste, therefore, on the footing of a simple sense, it cannot be doubted, that frequent exercise and curious attention to its proper objects, must greatly heighten its power. Of this we have clear proof in that part of Taste which is called an ear for Music. At first, only the simplest and plainest compositions are relished; use and practice extend our pleasure; teach us to relish finer melody, and by degrees enable us to enter into the intricate and compounded pleasures of harmony. So an eye for the beauties of painting is never all at once acquired; it is gradually formed by being conversant with pictures, and studying the works of the best masters. In the same manner, with respect to the beauty of composition and discourse, attention to the most approved models, study of the best authors, comparisons of lower and higher degrees of the same beauties, operate towards the refinement of Taste. When a person is only beginning his acquaintance with works of genius, the sentiments which attend them is obscure and confused. He can, perhaps, only tell whether he is or is not pleased, without assigning reasons for his decision. But allow him experience in works of this kind, and his Taste becomes by degrees more exact and enlightened. He now not only understands the character of the whole, but perceives the beauties and defects of each part, and is able to describe the qualities that afford pleasure or dissatisfaction. "The mist is dissipated which seemed formerly to hang over the object; and he can at length pronounce firmly, and without hesitation, concerning it. Thus in matters of Taste, as mere sensibility, exercise opens a great source of improvement." But if Taste be founded on sensibility, Reason and good sense have a most extensive influence on the operations and decisions of Taste; so that it may be considered as a power compounded of natural sensibility and improved understanding. It may be farther observed, that from the frequent exercise of Taste, and from the application of good sense and reason to the objects of Taste, it, as a power of the mind, receives its improvement. In its perfect state, it is unquestionably the result both of nature and of art. It supposes our natural sense of beauty to be refined by frequent attention to the most beautiful objects, and at the same time to be guided and improved by the light of the understanding.

Dr. Blair assumes, that not only a sound head, but a good heart, is requisite to just Taste. The characters of Taste, he says, when brought to its most improved state, are reducible to *Delicacy* and *Correctness*. The former respects principally the perfection of that natural sensibility on which Taste is founded; and it implies those finer organs or powers which enable us to discover beauties that lie hidden from a vulgar eye. The latter respects the improvement which that faculty receives through its connexion with the understanding. "A man of correct Taste is one who is never imposed upon by counterfeit beauties; who carries always in his mind that standard of good sense, which he employs in judging of every thing. He estimates with propriety the comparative merit of the several beauties which he meets with in any work of genius; refers them to their proper classes, assigns the principles, as far as they can be traced, whence their power of pleasing flows, and is pleased himself precisely in that degree in which he ought, and no more."

"Attempts," says Dr. Aikin, "have been often made in the walks both of literature and the fine arts, to establish such a criterion, and to reduce to precise rules, the determinations of what is called *taste;* but the wide differences still subsisting among those who lay claim to this quality, sufficiently prove the ill success of these efforts.". The diversities of original conformation, and early associations, must ever prevent mankind from feeling exactly alike, with respect to the objects presented to them. Hence the difference of opinion respecting the authors who have chiefly excelled in the style of their writings. Our object is not so much the comparison of the works of others, as to lay down such general rules, as may assist young persons, as well in judging of the merits of the compositions of their countrymen, as to enable them also to excel in the same career.

The most obvious purpose of writing, is to communicate with force and precision the ideas of the writer to the reader. To write well then, a person must study to acquire a clear idea of the subject on which he writes. For, unless he perfectly understand it, he can never expect to make another comprehend it. He is to reflect upon all parts of the subject, and when he has attained a clear view of it, the words will come of course. But it must be admitted, that this supposes in the writer, a perfect knowledge of the value and import of all the words which he uses, as well singly, as in combination. It supposes him master of the art of combining clauses and sentences, according to the rules already laid down, and also in such a way as to exhibit the dependence of ideas one upon another, and the train or succession in which the process of argumentation consists. It requires him to have, at his call, a sufficient store of expressions, and yet to be possessed of judgment sufficient to prevent him from running into prolixity. He should know *how* and *when* he can dwell upon an idea with advantage, and when to stop. To attain this, he must habituate himself to composition, for no rules, however excellent or well attended to, will form a correct and fluent writer without that sort of exercise which induces habit. For this purpose, it is not necessary to compose *much,* but to write *frequently,* and with great care. *Fast* writing is apt to produce a faulty style, not easily cured, but to compose frequently, and to subject the composition to strict and rigid revisions, will do more to the attainment of perfection than any rules which can be suggested.

Many of the qualities of good writing, depend on the powers of conception in the mind whence the ideas proceed, and to know how we have succeeded, we must frequently compare what we have written, with what we intended to write, and inquire what effect it is likely to produce on the minds of others, by reflecting upon the impression which such sort of writing, would, under different circumstances, have excited in ourselves.

In some cases there is not the smallest difficulty in pronouncing concerning the success of our efforts. The enunciation of a truth, and the statement of a plain argument, are complete with respect to conception and expression, when all that is wanted, and no more, is communicated to the reader, in its most precise and intelligible form. Clear notions, in subjects of this kind, readily clothe themselves in proper language; and he must be a very fastidious, and unreasonable person, who, while he receives the whole instruction he seeks for, should express a want of any thing more perfect. Demonstrations in mathematics and natural philosophy are of this kind, and in these, if the writer be methodical, clear, and as concise as the nature of the subject will admit of, he has done all that can be required of him.

The narration of a matter of fact is not quite so simple: circumstances strike different persons so differently, that scarcely any two will be found to agree in their account of the same transaction. There seems to be a propensity in man to alter and exaggerate, besides, if the transaction be at all complicate, or combine a variety of particulars, the selection of incidents must vary in different people who give an account of it. Some dwell upon circumstances important, which to others are wholly neglected as frivolous, or at least uninteresting. Some, in recording a fact, assign to each actor his own peculiar language, others relate the whole in their own words. "In general," says the author already quoted, "he is the most perfect narrator, who puts his reader most completely in the state of the spectator; who transports him to the very spot, marks out to him all the personages by their characteristic features, and fills the scene with manners and action. For success in such an attempt, nothing is so necessary as an imagination capable of receiving and retaining strong impressions." Where this exists, and the subject to be described be an interesting one, no artifice of language is wanted to produce a complete effect. The history of Joseph and his brethren in the book of Genesis, is written without the least art or effort, yet a more affecting one is not to be met with, and every attempt to embellish it by art and ornament has failed to produce an equal degree of interest. All that seems requisite in this kind of writing is, that the narrator should abstain from affected phraseology, unseasonable digressions, and impertinent remarks and observations.

The next in order of simplicity, is argumentative discourse. In this, great precision in the use of words, and a clear arrangement of the members of a sentence, are absolutely necessary. To these must be added closeness of method, strength and conciseness of expression, but free from obscurity, and grace and amenity of language: by these, the effect of conviction may be promoted by leading on the reader pleasantly through a subject which may, perhaps, be naturally dry and unalluring. Cicero and Hume have been cited as examples of this union of the agreeable, with discussions purely philosophical; and, if the manner of Cicero, in his argumentative works, be compared with that of his popular pieces and his orations, a good idea may be formed of the progress, from an address to the reason alone, to an attempt to persuade by addressing the affections.

The perfection of historical composition demands a still greater assemblage of literary qualifications. The historian must be able to give a lucid arrangement and skilful developement of facts, often involved and perplexed with contradictions. He should have sagacity to trace the connexion of causes and effects, and penetration to detect the motives and true characters of men, however disguised by artifice; to these should be added a philosophical spirit, and freedom from prejudice, which entitle him to assume the office of an instructor. If he be possessed of these requisites, the historian may be allowed considerable latitude in his style, and may enrich his language with every figure that can give it force or beauty.

Of the nature of figurative language we shall shortly treat, but it may be observed here, that a writer of real taste will never be anxious to embellish his compositions in this way: he will never study to find out comparisons or metaphors for the mere purpose of adorning his discourse. Figurative language, when good, and properly applied, comes spontaneously from a lively imagination, or from a mind well stored by the perusal of the best authors. To profit as much as possible in reading works of taste, we should mark every thing peculiar in their manners, so as to know how, afterwards, either to adopt or avoid it. At the same time, every thing like a servile imitation of others must be carefully avoided.

We must adapt the style to the subject; for nothing can be more ridiculous than to clothe grave subjects in a gaudy dress; or to attempt embellishing dry reasoning, which must convince only by strength of argument.

After all, more attention must be paid to our thoughts or conceptions than to our words: these should be consonant to nature, clearly conceived, agreeably diversified, regularly connected, and adapted to some good end.

Conformity to nature is essential to good writing, without which, whatever other excellence it may possess, it cannot obtain the approbation of good sense. An author may rise above the usual appearances of nature, by combining things which are not commonly associated, but he must not admit any thing that contradicts common sense and experience. The conception must be perfect and distinct: this is the basis of perspicuity. He who does not himself clearly understand his own meaning, can have no right to expect that his reader will. We must accustom ourselves to separate our ideas from one another before we attempt to clothe them in language. Variety of conception must be added to perspicuity. "It is this which raises a writer of true genius above one of moderate abilities. The field of nature lies open to all men, but it is only the man whose powers are vigorous and commanding, that can combine ideas with the diversity which is necessary to produce a strong impression upon the imagination. To discern, not only the obvious properties of things, but their more hidden qualities and relations; to perceive resemblances which are not commonly perceived; to combine images, or sentiments which are not commonly combined; to exhibit, in description, persons and things with all the interesting varieties of form or action, of which they are capable, are offices of genius: and it is only in the degree in which these marks of genius appear in any literary production, that it can be pronounced excellent."

In every good composition, there must be unity of design: some leading object, to which every part should have a relation. Whatever has no tendency to illustrate the subject, weakens the general effect; and to every other excellence must be added that of utility. This is the chief end of every literary effort, but it must be taken in an enlarged and liberal view; and it must be remembered, that whatever is calculated to afford innocent and rational amusement, as well as that which tends to enlighten the understanding, and improve the heart and morals, may be pronounced useful.

Next to the thoughts themselves, is the arrangement in which they are to be disposed. This requires the exercise of much attention and accurate judgment. The first conceptions which accidental association may raise in the mind, are not likely to proceed spontaneously in that order which is most natural, and best adapted to form a regular piece. It will, therefore, frequently be an author's inquiry, as he advances in the progress of his work, whether the method and plan that he has adopted, are the best suited to attain the end he has in view, and whether all the sentiments contained in it are not only just, but pertinent, and in their proper place.

With regard to *expression*, the first quality is *purity*, which consists in such words, and such a grammatical construction of sentences, as are agreeable to the analogy of the language, and to the general usage of accurate writers. The second kind of excellence is *perspicuity*, which, as we have seen, requires precision in the use of terms, and accuracy in the structure of sentences: it requires not only that what is written may be understood, but that it cannot possibly be misunderstood. An author's style, is the manner in which he writes, in the same way as a painter's style, is the manner in which he paints; in both, conception and expression are equally concerned. No one can write well, who has not learned to think well, to arrange his thoughts methodically, and to express them with propriety. See Aikin's Letters to his Son; and "An Essay on Reading Works of Taste," prefixed to Enfield's Speaker.

CHAP. IX.

ON FIGURATIVE LANGUAGE.

Figures, the most simple form of speech—Divided into classes—The tropes of the ancients—Comparisons—Similies—Metaphors.

A STRONG and vivid imagination is not, either in speaking or writing, satisfied with bringing before the hearer's or reader's mind, all the circumstances immediately connected with the principal subject, and placing them in a striking point of view: it borrows colours and forms from other objects, to embellish and adorn the picture: this is done by means of figurative language. It is called figurative, because the author's meaning is expressed, not by direct phraseology, but under the image of something else. The assertion, that "A good man enjoys satisfaction and hope in the midst of affliction," is an observation expressed in the simplest manner possible; but when it is said, "That, to the upright there ariseth light in darkness," the same idea is expressed in figurative language; that is, *light* is put in the place of satisfaction and hope, and *darkness* is used to suggest the idea of adversity. The Psalmist also, in his description of the virtuous character, makes use of highly figurative language: "He shall be like a tree planted by the rivers of water, that bringeth forth his fruit in his season; his leaf also shall not wither."

Though figures imply a deviation from what may be reckoned the most simple form of speech, yet they are so far from being uncommon, that on very many occasions they are the most natural, and the most common method of uttering our sentiments. It is impossible to compose a discourse of any length without using them very frequently: they occur even in didactic subjects. The origin of figures has, by some, been referred to the poverty of language; but by others, either to the sport of fancy, or to the expression of passion or enthusiasm. At any rate, and upon any theory, figures must be regarded as an important part of that language which nature seems to dictate to man. They are not the result of long study; nor the invention of schools: the most illiterate speak in figures, as often as the most learned. Imagery, especially from natural objects, is employed by the rudest and most savage nations, not from necessity, but as a matter of choice. Specimens of this kind abound in the speeches of the Indian chiefs in North America, and among the earliest productions of the Arabians. The oldest writings with which we are acquainted, namely, those of the Hebrew Scriptures, are full of figures; these are derived from those objects with which, from the time and situation of the country and nation they were most familiar.

Figures have been described to be language that is prompted either by the imagination or passions. They are divided into two great classes, viz. figures of *words* and figures of *thoughts*. The former are called *tropes*, a Greek term that signifies the *turning* of a word from its original meaning, and they consist in a word's being employed to signify something that is different from its original and primitive meaning; so that if the word be changed, the figure is destroyed: thus in the passage already quoted, "Light ariseth to the upright in darkness," the trope consisteth in the words *Light* and *Darkness* being substituted, the one for satisfaction and hope, and the other for affliction, on account of some analogy which they are supposed to bear to these conditions of life. Figures of *thought*, suppose the words to be used in their proper and literal meaning; and the figure consists in the turn of thought, as is the case in exclamations, interrogations, apostrophes, and comparisons. This distinction is of no great use, nor is it of much importance, whether we assign to any particular mode of expression the name of trope or figure, provided we remember, that figurative language imports some colouring of the imagination, or some emotion of passion.

Ancient writers classed as *tropes*, the metaphor, metonymy, synecdoche, and irony: with them, *figures* were almost innumerable. It is not necessary to follow rhetoricians in all their several distinctions; we shall very briefly proceed to treat of those forms of expression which are suggested by the relations of resemblance, contiguity, and cause and effect. From the relation of resemblance proceed the comparison or simile, the metaphor, the allegory, and the allusion.

The COMPARISON is the first and most natural of all rhetorical figures. Comparisons serve two purposes: when addressed to the understanding, their object is to instruct; when to the heart, their purpose is to please. Objects of different senses cannot be compared together; because such objects being entirely separated from each other, have no circumstance in common to admit either resemblance or contrast. Objects of hearing may be compared, and so also of the other senses; but the chief sources of comparison are objects of sight, as being more distinct and lively than those of any other sense. Similies are not the natural language of passion; they will not serve to express the vehement emotions of the mind; for if, at that time, the imagination is disposed to be excursive, it will drop the words expressing the resemblance, and adopt the metaphor. Hence the difference between a simile and metaphor: in the former, the resemblance is brought before the reader's view, by comparing the ideas together, and by words expressing a likeness; a metaphor is a comparison, without the words expressing resemblance. A distinction may likewise be established between *comparisons* and *similies:* the *one* is the general word, comprehending the whole class, or, at least, is appropriated to the most perfect of the kind; the other is chiefly used in poetry, and implies, perhaps, a slighter and more fanciful resemblance. The comparisons in the Scriptures of the Old Testament are bold, and remarkably beautiful; but, like those of the Orientalists in general, the resemblance is frequently too fanciful and remote. They are frequently very short, and the resemblance usually turns upon a single circumstance, which is explained in few words, without the introduction of any matter foreign to the purpose. Classical writers are more sparing in their similies; but there is too great a sameness in those of Virgil and Homer. In their descriptions of battles, the imagery of a lion, bull, an eagle, &c. occurs so often, as to render them tedious rather than attractive. Modern writers enjoy greater advantages in this respect, and to these they have not been inattentive. The superior knowledge which they possess of the arts and sciences, and of the history of nature in particular, has opened to them a wider and more varied field in poetical imagery. It will of course follow, that the author who possesses the greatest scope of knowledge, *ceteris paribus,* will have the greatest command of imagery, and will produce the boldest and most varied comparisons. They are often to be met with in our gravest productions; thus, in a sermon on slander, we have the following beautiful comparison: "Censure is in season so very seldom, that it may be compared to that bitter plant which hardly comes to maturity in the life of a man, and is said to flower but once in a hundred years."

The several rules which have been given with respect to the use of comparisons are as follow: (1.) They should not be taken from common or vulgar objects. (2.) They ought not to be trite, such as comparing a violent passion to a tempest. (3.) They ought to be founded on a likeness, neither too obvions nor too remote: if the likeness is too obvious, it disgusts; if too remote, it perplexes; and, instead of assisting, strains the fancy to comprehend them. (4.) Comparisons should never be drawn from an unknown object, or one of which few people can form clear ideas. Therefore, in works of general reading, or in discourses addressed to popular assemblies, comparisons founded on philosophical discoveries, or on any thing with which persons of a certain trade only, or a particular profession, are conversant, cannot produce their proper effect. They should, in general, be taken from those illustrious, noted objects, which most readers either have seen, or can strongly conceive. Thus Homer compares Achilles, shining in armour, to the sun in its ascent to the meridian. Milton, also, has taken the sun, moon, and other heavenly bodies, as noted objects, with which he forms some of his noblest similies:

——————— as when the sun, new risen,
Looks through the horizontal misty air,
Shorn of his beams, or from behind the moon
In dim eclipse disastrous twilight sheds
On half the nations, darken'd so, yet shone
Above them all, th' Archangel. PAR. LOST. B. I.

In this fine simile, the resemblance consists not only in sensible properties, but in character. Thus it is not only the form of Satan, still retaining its brightness, though obscured, which is compared to that of the sun behind a mist; but his malignant character is also expressed by the ominous nature of an eclipse, according to the superstitious notions then so generally admitted concerning that phenomenon.

Homer likens the shield of Achilles to the moon, and Milton does the same with respect to the shield of Satan:

And next he raised his ample, ponderous shield,
Whence beam'd from far a lustre, like the moon's. ILL. xix.

——————— his ponderous shield,
Ethereal temper, massy, large, and round,
Behind him cast, the broad circumference
Hung on his shoulders like the moon, &c.

Comparisons are not proper on all occasions: the mind must

be disposed for them to render them acceptable; and in general, when by any animating passion, whether pleasant or painful, an impulse is given to the imagination, we are in a condition to admit figurative expressions, especially comparisons: thus, in Shakespeare, the *dread* of misfortune, always involving some doubt and uncertainty, agitates the mind, excites the imagination, and fits it for Wolsey's soliloquy—

> ——————— Nay, then, farewell!
> I've touch'd the highest point of all my greatness,
> And from that full meridian of my glory
> I haste now to my setting. I shall fall,
> Like a bright exhalation in the evening,
> And no man see me more. HENRY VIII.

Happy as the poet often is in his similies, he sometimes introduces them very improperly. As they are not the language of a man in his ordinary state of mind, dispatching his usual employment, the speech of the gardener, therefore, to his servants, in his Richard II., is very improper:

> Go, bind thou up yon dangling apricots,
> Which, like unruly children, make their sire
> Stoop with oppression of their prodigal weight:—
> Give some supportance to the bending twigs.

As comparison is founded on the *resemblance*, so ANTITHESIS depends on the contrast or opposition of two objects. Contrast has always this effect: it makes each of the contrasted objects appear in the stronger light. Antithesis may, therefore, on many occasions, be employed to advantage, in order to strengthen the impression which we intend that any object should make. On this account, Cicero makes considerable use of it in his orations; as in the second against Catiline: "On one side stands modesty, on the other impudence; on the one, fidelity, on the other deceit; here piety, there sacrilege; here continency, there lust," &c. Such is also that of Augustus, to certain seditious young men: "Audite juvenes seuem, quem juvenem senes audivêre;" and this of Virgil:—

Flectere si nequeo superos, Acheronta movebo.

From similies we proceed to METAPHORS, which are the most common of all figures of speech; so much so, that when we say a thing is spoken figuratively, we refer to the metaphor. The metaphor is a short simile, or, as it has been called by Cicero, a similitude reduced to a single word, and it differs from it only in this; that the former is compared to the thing we design to express, and the latter is put for it. The principal advantage which the metaphor possesses over the simile, is, that the former carries the mind nearer the reality than the latter: as when it is said of Achilles, that "he rushed like a lion," we have the idea of a man going on furiously to battle; but when it is said, "the lion rushed on," the image is more vivid. So also when Virgil calls the Scipio's the thunder-bolts of war, the idea is much more animated than if he had compared them to thunder-bolts. By means of a metaphor, the rudder of a ship is called its reins; for, what reins are to the horse, that the rudder is to a ship in guiding and directing it. When Christ called Herod a *fox*, it was by the use of the metaphor: in the same way, a great minister, as the illustrious Earl of Chatham, was aptly denominated the "pillar of the state."

As the metaphor is intended to set things before the eyes, it becomes so much the more perfect, as it shews them the more vividly by representing them in motion and action. The metaphor is described by Cicero as the most florid manner of expression, and the brightest ornament of language that consists in single words.

A metaphor should have nothing in it coarse or shocking, or that may raise it above the simplicity of nature, so as to be forced or harsh; it should never be carried too far, for in that case it is apt to degenerate into puerility. Metaphors should always be followed in the same kind, otherwise they become mixed, unnatural, and unpleasing. We cannot, for instance, say, that a place was besieged by a deluge of troubles; because the two images of a *siege* and *deluge* have no sort of relation. A very striking metaphor from Lord Bolingbroke's "Remarks on the History of England" has been noticed by writers on Rhetoric. Speaking of the behaviour of Charles I. to his last parliament, he says, "About a month after their meeting, he dissolved them; and as soon as he had dissolved them, he repented; but he repented too late, of his rashness. Well might he repent, for the vessel was now full, and this last drop made the waters of bitterness to flow. Here," the historian adds, "we draw the curtain, and put an end to our remarks." The *vessel* is put for the state or temper of the nation, already *full*, that is, provoked to the highest by former oppressions and wrongs: *this last drop* stands for the provocation recently received by the abrupt dissolution of the parliament; and the overflowing of the waters of bitterness, beautifully expresses all the effects of resentment let loose by an exasperated people. There is nothing in which young writers are more faulty, than in the indiscreet use of metaphors: they who understand them the best, use them with the greatest caution and reserve. Mr. Addison proposes it as a rule, for writers to imagine their metaphors actually painted before them, and to view and examine the justness of their application and assemblage under those circumstances; throwing every thing out of the writing but what might be retained in the picture.

A metaphor is not always confined to a single word; it may extend to a whole sentence, as is the case in the following animated figure:

"The swarm of monks that arose from the Nile, overspread and darkened the face of the Christian world." Gibbon. Some metaphors, particularly those comprized in a single word, have become so common, that they are scarcely to be considered as figurative. Thus we speak of an *arm* of the sea; the *foot* of a mountain, &c. without thinking of figurative language.

The uses of metaphor are, that they render the style more animated and striking, by introducing a new idea, in which for the moment the original seems to be lost:— they diversify and vary a style, and relieve it from that tedious uniformity, which would be the result of a style, in which every word was used in the literal sense:—they serve to enlarge and elevate our subject, and bestow dignity on composition. Thus the expression, "Death spares neither the rich nor the poor," is low, when compared with the beautiful lines of Horace, expressive of the same idea:

> Pallida mors æquo pulsat pede pauperum tabernas,
> Regumque turres.

In English,—

> With equal pace, impartial fate
> Knocks at the palace, as the cottage gate.

The rules laid down with regard to metaphors are as follow: They should be suited to the nature of the subject of which we treat:—they should be neither too many, nor too gay, nor too elevated:—they should not be calculated to raise in the mind disagreeable, mean, vulgar, or dirty ideas:—the resemblance, which is the foundation of the metaphor, should be clear and perspicuous, not far-fetched, nor difficult of discovery: two different metaphors should never be made to meet on the same object. This is what is called a mixed metaphor, and is a wretched abuse of the figure. Such is Shakespeare's expression, to "take arms against a sea of troubles:" such, also, is the metaphor in Mr. Addison's letter from Italy—

> I *bridle* in my struggling Muse in vain,
> That longs to *launch* into a bolder strain.

It is highly improper to change the *muse* from a *horse* to a *ship*.

Lastly, metaphors ought not to be crowded or heaped one upon another, nor should they be pursued too far. It is true, that, under circumstances of great agitation, a flow of metaphors may be allowed; of this we have an instance in Macbeth, against which the most fastidious reader will scarcely object:

> Can'st thou not minister to a mind diseased?
> Pluck from the memory a rooted sorrow?
> Rase out the living tablets of the brain;
> And, with some sweet oblivious antidote
> Cleanse the foul bosom of that perilous stuff,
> That weighs upon the heart?

CHAP. X.

FIGURATIVE LANGUAGE,

Continued.

Allegory—Catachresis—Metonymy—Synecdoche—Periphrasis—Prosopopœia, or Personification—Rules for the management of: Apostrophe—Hyperbole—Irony—Paraleipsis—Interrogation—Exclamation; and Repetition.

AN ALLEGORY is, properly, a continued metaphor, or perhaps more correctly, a series of metaphors in one or more sentences; such is that contained in the 14th Ode of the First Book of Horace:—

> O navis, referent in mare te novi
> Fluctus? O! quid agis? fortiter occupa
> Portum, &c.

In which, the ship is usually held to stand for the Republic; waves, for civil war; port, for peace and concord; oars, for soldiers; and mariners, for magistrates. In Prior's Henry and Emma, the latter describes her constancy to Henry in the following allegorical manner:

> Did I but purpose to embark with thee
> On the smooth surface of a summer's sea,
> While gentle zephyrs play with prosperous gales,
> And fortune's favour fills the swelling sails;
> But would forsake the ship, and make the shore,
> When the winds whistle, and the tempests roar?

A fine example of an allegory is to be found in the 80th Psalm, in which the people of Israel are represented under the image of a vine, and the figure is supported throughout with great correctness and beauty.

Bishop Lowth has, in his "De Sacra Poesi Hebræorum," specified three forms of allegory that occur in sacred poetry. The first is, that which rhetoricians call a continued metaphor; an example of this kind occurs in the beginning of the twelfth chapter of the book of Ecclesiastes, in which old age is so admirably depicted. A second kind of allegory is that which, in a proper and more restricted sense, may be called a *parable*, and consists of a continued narration of some fictitious event, accommodated by way of similitude to the illustration of certain important truths. Allegories of this kind are called by the Greeks, apologues; by the Latins, fables. Such are the fables of Æsop, and Pilpay, the Indian sage; and such are the narratives of Christ, conveyed under the name of parables. Such, in later times, is Spenser's Fairy Queen, which consists of a series of these allegories; and the very popular work of John Bunyan, "The Pilgrim's Progress." The third species of allegory, which often occurs in prophetic poetry, is that in which a double meaning is couched under the same words; or when the same discourse, differently interpreted, designates different events, dissimilar in their nature, and remote as to time.

The first of these kinds of allegory differs only in length from the simple metaphor; and it may be observed, that no figure is more delicate or difficult in the hands of a young writer. If the great difficulty in the use of a metaphor, is to preserve the allusion in all its parts, it must be increased, by applying a series of metaphors, to illustrate the same subject. Accordingly we perpetually find even good writers forgetting the figurative, and resorting to the literal sense.

The following are given by Dr. Gregory, as excellent (the first, however, is not altogether faultless) allegorical compositions:

This is the state of man: to-day, he puts forth
The tender leaves of hope; to-morrow, blossoms,
And bears his blushing honours thick upon him:
The third day comes a frost, a killing frost!
And when he thinks, good easy man, full surely
His greatness is a ripening—nips his root,
And then he falls, &c. HENRY VIII.

In the fifth line, the literal is, in a measure, confounded with the figurative meaning; but, as a whole, it is very beautiful, and the third line is finely descriptive; but it cannot be concealed, that it is unnatural, as coming from Wolsey after his fall; for we cannot imagine such an exuberance of allegory and metaphor, as we meet with in this speech, ever fell from the lips of a man overwhelmed in distress and grief.

The next is taken from Gibbon's Roman History. The author, in speaking of the speculative dissensions which existed in the Christian church at the period he is describing, says, "It will not be expected, it would not, perhaps, be endured, that I should swell this theological discussion, by a minute examination of eighteen creeds, the authors of which, for the most part, disclaimed the odious name of their parent, Arius. It is amusing enough to delineate the form, and to trace the vegetation of this singular plant; but the tedious detail of leaves without flowers, and of branches without fruit, would soon exhaust the patience, and disappoint the curiosity of the laborious student."

The CATACHRESIS is a figure, which signifies, according to the true meaning of the Greek term, an *abuse* of words; that is, when the words are too far wrested from their native signification, as a voice *beautiful* to the ear. The catachresis, in oratory, is very likely to occur, when, in the eagerness and warmth inspired by true eloquence, a man, for want of a word proper to express a thought, uses, or, as the term καταχραομαι expresses, abuses a word that comes near it: as when we call a person who has killed his mother, his master, or his sovereign, a *parricide*, a term which can, in strictness of language, only be applied to one who has murdered his father. The Latin phrase *vir gregis ipse caper*, is also a catachresis. This figure, though not justifiable according to the principles of rhetoric, is often employed by poets for the sake of novelty, and to enforce expression, when the proper word does not seem strong enough. Thus, Milton adopts the catachresis, when he describes Raphael's descent from heaven,.

> ————Down thither prone in *flight*
> He speeds, and through the vast ethereal sky
> *Sails* between worlds and worlds.

Here the novelty of the word enlivens the image much more than if he had said flies. This trope is used occasionally by the gravest authors, and is to be found in the Scriptures. Thus, we read of the "blood of the grape;" and in the book of Proverbs, "The horse-leech hath two daughters." In these instances, the trope is, perhaps, a metaphor; but when St. John, in the book of Revelations says, "I turned to see the voice that spake to me," it is a *metonymy*, the *voice* being put for the person who uttered it. St. Matthew mentions "Simon, the leper," not that he was then a leper, but had been so, and was cured; which is a *synecdoche*. When a criminal is said to "have had his reward," that is, his punishment, it is *irony*. But to return to the catachresis: the vivid imagination of Mr. Burke, together with the violence of his temper, led him frequently to the use of this figure: thus, he describes the revolutionists of France, "Architects of ruin."

METONYMY, to which we have already alluded, consists in a transmutation, or change of names; or putting the effect for the cause, or the subject for the adjunct. There are four kinds of metonymy chiefly used: in the *first*, the external cause is put for the effect, which may be said to occur when the inventor's name is used for the thing invented; thus Mars is put for *War*: *Ceres*, for *Corn*; and *Bacchus*, for *Wine*: hence Virgil says,

> Implentur veteris *Bacchi* pinquisque farinæ.

Agreeably to this figure, the author's name is employed to designate his works: thus we say, that we have read Homer, Virgil, or Milton, that is, the works of these authors. The *second* metonymy puts the effect for the cause, whether the agent, or only the means and instrument, thus Virgil calls the two Scipio's the destruction of Libya, but they were the agents who effected it. Horace speaks of Pale Death, Pallida Mors, instead of Death that makes or causes paleness: the same author compliments Mæcenas,

O, et præsidium, et dulce decus meum,

in which, the titles of his guard and honour are put for guardian and vindicator of his honour. By the *third* figure of metonymy, the adjunct is used for the subject, as when we speak of the *fasces* for the magistrate: thus also Cicero says, in the time of battle the *laws*, that is, the *judges*, are silent. The *fourth* kind of metonymy is when the subject is put for the adjunct, that is, when we speak of statues or pictures, as the persons whom they represent. By this figure of metonymy, one name is often put for another, for which it may be allowed to stand, on account of some striking relation between the two: thus we call a very mild and humane prince, a Titus: a cruel one, a Nero; and a great conqueror, Alexander.

Another rhetorical figure is called *synecdoche*, which puts the whole for a part, or a part for the whole, a genus for a species, or a species for a genus, thus a man is said to get his *bread* by his *labour*, that is, his *whole subsistence*. If we say, he obtains his *bread* by the *sweat of his brow*, there are two figures; the bread is put for the subsistence, and by the phrase, "the *sweat of the brow*" the effect is put for the cause, viz. labour.

The PERIPHRASIS is a metonymy in which more words are employed than are necessary, or usual, which is much affected by orators to give variety to their mode of expression: thus we may speak of the Duke of Wellington as the "Immortal liberator of the Peninsula," and no person would mistake the man. It is often a mark of politeness to suppress the names of persons spoken of, who happen to be present, and only to point them out by their characteristic. In parliament, the name is never used, but instead of it, the person who would point out another, says, the noble Lord, or the honourable member on the right, or left, or who has just spoken, &c.

One of the most animated figures in rhetoric, when properly managed, is the PROSOPOPŒIA, or personification. It has some alliance with the metaphor; but still more with metonymy; and in fact it seems, in most cases, to be to the latter, what the allegory is to the metaphor. In some cases it is not easy to determine whether the figure be a metonymy or a prosopopœia, as in the phrase "Youth and beauty are laid in the dust." Dr. Gregory quotes a fine specimen of this figure from Miss Seward's Monody on Major André, who, according to the laws of civilized war, as they are called, was *executed*; but, in the eye of reason, *murdered* by the Americans,

Loud howls the storm, the vex'd Atlantic roars,
Thy *Genius*, Britain, *wanders* on its shores!
Hears cries of horror wafted from afar,
The groans of anguish 'mid the shrieks of war!
Hears the deep curses of the great and brave,
Sigh in the wind, and murmur in the wave!
O'er his damp brow the sable crape *he binds*,
And *throws* his victor garland to the winds.

Another beautiful figure is taken by the same author, from Hayley's Essay on History:

Humility herself, divinely mild,
Sublime Religion's meek and modest child,
Like the dumb son of Crœsus, in the strife,
When force assail'd his father's sacred life,
Breaks silence, and with filial duty warm,
Bids thee revere her parent's hallowed form.

Although personification is particularly adapted to poetry, yet this figure serves frequently to adorn the works of the best prose writers: thus in Tacitus; "After the slaughter of so many distinguished men, Nero meditated, at length, the extirpation of *virtue herself*, by the murder of Thrasea."

The mind, agitated by certain passions, is prone to bestow sensibility upon things inanimate, hence Antony, mourning over the body of Cæsar murdered in the Senate, supposes the dead corpse listening to him,

> O, pardon me, thou bleeding piece of earth,
> That I am meek and gentle with these butchers, &c.

Shakespeare makes Richard exclaim, upon landing from his Irish expedition,

> ——————I weep for joy
> To stand upon my kingdom once again.
> Dear earth, I do salute thee with my hand,
> Though rebels wound thee with their horses' hoofs.

The same poet personifies death in a fanciful, but striking manner:

> ——————Within the hollow crown,
> That rounds the mortal temples of a king,
> Keeps Death his court; and there the antic sits,
> Scoffing his state, and grinning at his pomp;
> Allowing him a breath, a little scene,
> To monarchize, be feared, and kill with looks;
> Infusing him with self and vain conceit,
> As if this flesh, which walls about our life,
> Were brass impregnable: and, humour'd thus,
> Comes at the last, and with a little pin
> Bores through his castle-wall, and, farewell! king.
>
> RICHARD II.

Shakespeare's personification of *sleep* is as well known as it is highly celebrated:

> ——————O gentle *Sleep*,
> Nature's soft nurse, how have I frighted thee!
> That thou no more wilt weigh my eye-lids down,
> And steep my senses in forgetfulness, &c.

Dr. Blair observes, that one of the greatest pleasures which we receive from poetry, is, to find ourselves always in the midst of our fellows, and to see every thing thinking, feeling, and acting as we ourselves do: this, perhaps, is the principal charm of the figure personification. It introduces us into society with all nature, and interests us, even in inanimate objects, by forming a connexion between them and us, through that sensibility which it ascribes to them. Our author gives some passages in illustration of this theory, of which we shall transcribe a part:

But, yonder comes the powerful king of day,
Rejoicing in the east. The lessening cloud,
The kindling azure, and the mountain's brow
Tipt with ethereal gold, his near approach
Betoken glad. THOMSON'S SUMMER.

————————To the nuptial bower,
I led her, blushing like the morn. All heaven,
And happy constellations, on that hour
Shed their selectest influence. The earth
Gave signs of gratulation, and each hill:
Joyous the birds; fresh gales and gentle airs
Whisper'd it to the woods, &c. MILTON.

This figure has uncommon force and expression, as it is used by Hebrew writers. What can be considered more apt, more beautiful, or more sublime, than that personification of Wisdom, which is so frequently introduced by Solomon? Prov. iii. viii. ix. &c. How admirable is that celebrated personification of the divine attributes by the Psalmist!—Psalms, lxxxv. 2. Such also is that in Habakkuk, chap. iii. 5, of the pestilence marching before Jehovah, when He comes to vengeance; that, in Job, chap. xxviii. 22. in which Destruction and Death affirm of Wisdom, that her fame only had come to their ears; and that tremendous image, in Isaiah, of Hades, extending her throat, and opening her insatiable and immeasurable jaws, chap. v. 14. There is another beautiful species of personification, which originates from a well-known Hebrew idiom; or that form of expression by which the subject, attribute, accident, or effect of any thing, is denominated the son. Isaiah, pronounced by Dr. Lowth, to be the sublimest of poets, furnishes, in one short poem, examples of almost every form of the prosopopœia; and, indeed, of all that constitutes the sublime in composition. See Is. xiv. 4—27. After a critique upon this sublime ode of Isaiah, the learned writer concludes in the following manner: "How forcible is this imagery, how diversified, how sublime!—how elevated the diction, the figures, the sentiments! The Jewish nation, the cedars of Lebanon, the ghosts of departed kings, the Babylonish monarch, the travellers who find his corpse, and, the last of all, Jehovah himself, are the characters which support this beautiful lyric drama. One continued action is kept up, or rather a series of interesting actions are connected together in an incomparable whole: this, indeed, is the principal and distinguished excellence of the sublimer ode, and is displayed in its utmost perfection in this poem of Isaiah, which may be considered as one of the most ancient, and certainly the most finished specimen of that species of composition, which has been transmitted to us. The personifications here are frequent, yet not confused; bold, yet not improbable; a free, elevated, and truly divine spirit pervades the whole; nor is there any thing wanting in this ode to defeat its claim to the character of perfect beauty and sublimity."—Lowth's Lectures.

Three rules are to be observed for the management of personification: (1.) It should rarely be attempted, unless when prompted by strong passion; nor continued when the passion begins to flag. (2.) We must never personify any object, but such as has some dignity in itself, and can make a proper figure in the elevation to which we raise it. (3.) Whenever it is introduced, the picture it presents should be complete in itself, which shews the meanness of the following attempt:

> Invidious *grave*, how dost thou *rend in sunder*
> Whom love has knit, and sympathy made one!

A person must have a very fertile, or very strong imagination, to form a picture of a *grave rending in sunder.*

The APOSTROPHE is a more animated personification, in which the object personified is addressed in the second person. A real personage may, however, be addressed in an apostrophe, but he must be supposed either dead or absent. In the Old Testament we have many remarkable instances of this figure, as in the prophet Jeremiah, "O thou *sword* of the Lord! how long will it be ere thou be quiet? put thyself up into the scabbard, rest, and be still!"

The apostrophe was never more properly introduced than in Lear's address to the *elements,* when discarded and turned out by Regan,

——————Spit, fire! spout, rain!
Nor rain, wind, thunder, fire, are my daughters.
I tax not you, ye elements, with unkindness,
I never gave you a kingdom, called you, children,
You owe me no subscription, &c.

The following is also a fine example, put into the mouth of Eve, by Milton,

O unexpected stroke, worse than of death!
Must I leave thee, *Paradise!* thus leave
Thee, native soil, these happy walks and shades,
Fit haunts of Gods? Where I had hoped to spend,
Quiet, though sad, the respite of that day
That must be mortal to us both. O *flowers,*
That never will in other climate grow,
My early visitation, and my last
At even; which I bred up with tender hand,
From the first opening bud, and gave you names;
Who now shall rear ye to the sun, or rank
Your tribes? &c.

The HYPERBOLE is nothing more than an excess of figurative language, the effect, when it is natural, of passion. All passions are inclined to magnify their objects. Injuries seem greater than they really are, to those who have sustained them; and dangers are magnified to those who are in apprehension of them:

Victors and vanquish'd join promiscuous cries,
And shrilling shouts, and dying groans arise;

With streaming blood, the slipp'ry fields are dy'd,
And slaughter'd heroes swell the dreadful tide.

HOMER'S ILIAD.

The hyperbole should never be introduced in the description of any thing ordinary or familiar, for in such case it is unnatural, being destitute of surprise, which is its only foundation. The hyperbole can never suit a dispiriting passion: and it should never be strained beyond due bounds. Longinus compares such a one to a bow-string, which relaxes by overstraining, and produces an effect directly opposite to what is intended. Finally, the hyperbole ought to be comprehended in the fewest words possible.

IRONY, according to some writers, has been classed as a figure of rhetoric, but others do not allow it that rank. All irony, says Dr. Priestley, is humour, but all humour is not irony; it generally consists in giving undeserved praise, implying censure on the object; or conveying censure under the appearance of praise: the former is the most common. When Frederic II. published his poem on the art of war, he omitted to notice the Duke of Marlborough. On that circumstance the Monthly Reviewers remarked, "that they presumed his Majesty had omitted the name of Marlborough, in the catalogue of distinguished commanders, because he might be deficient in one branch of his profession, having never, on any occasion, evinced his skill in conducting a retreat."

The PARALEIPSIS borders on irony, it implies an affectation of omission, as when an orator exclaims, "I refrain from mentioning the rapacity, the venality, the exceeding corruption of the person I accuse," &c. Cicero, in his orations, makes much use of this figure, but it requires powerful talents, and an ardent manner, to do justice to it.

Of the INTERROGATION, there are many fine instances in the poetical and prophetical parts of Scripture, "God is not a man, that He should lie, nor the son of man, that He should repent. Hath He said, and shall He not do it?"

EXCLAMATION is a stronger figure than the former, and

must be but rarely used, as it will appear ridiculous, unless where the passions are inflamed. When it is used by an orator, it requires the voice to be raised, as in the exclamation of Cicero, "O tempora! O mores! Senatus hæc intelligit, consul vidit: hic vivit; vivit? imo vero etiam in Senatum venit." The same author uses this figure to express a variety of passions; as indignation, resentment, contempt, grief, and admiration. It has its use in ridicule and irony, thus the orator exclaims, in his oration for Balbus, deriding the accuser, "O excellent interpreter of the law! master of antiquity, corrector and amender of our constitution!" St. Paul makes use of the exclamation in exultation and triumph, "O death, where is thy sting! O grave, where is thy victory!" It is frequently used with an interrogation, and serves to prepare the mind by exciting attention.

Another figure of speech, called by Blair and other critics, VISION, is adapted also to warm and animated composition, by which we describe a thing that is past or absent, as if actually passing before our eye, thus Cicero says, "Videor enim mihi hanc urbem videre, lucem orbis terrarum atque arcem omnium gentium, subito uno incendio concidentem, &c." "I seem to myself to behold this city, the ornament of the earth, and the capital of all nations, suddenly involved in one conflagration. I see before me the slaughtered heaps of citizens lying unburied in the midst of their ruined country. The furious countenance of Cethegus rises to my view, while, with a savage joy, he is triumphing in your miseries." This manner of description supposes a sort of enthusiasm which carries the speaker or writer in some measure out of himself, and if well executed, impresses the hearer or reader strongly, by the force of the sympathy.

REPETITION is another animated figure, by which the most material words of a sentence are repeated, in order to make the impression the stronger: one of the finest instances of this figure is in St. Paul's second Epistle to the Corinthians, "Are they Hebrews? So am I.—Are they Israelites? So am I.

Are they the seed of Abraham? So am I.—Are they ministers of Christ? (I speak as a fool) I am more; in labours more abundant, in stripes above measure, in prisons more frequent, in deaths oft."

Such are the principal figures of rhetoric, many others are enumerated and described by rhetoricians, all of which, says Dr. Blair, are beautiful or not, in proportion as they are native expressions of the sentiment, or passion intended to be heightened by them. Let nature and passion always speak their own language, and they will suggest figures in abundance. But if we seek to counterfeit a warmth which we do not feel, no figures will either supply the defect, or conceal the imposture.

CHAP. XI.

OF PROSE COMPOSITION.

Rules for didactic composition—For deliberative, and judicial eloquence —Of what regular orations must consist—Of the exordium—Proposition —Narration—Arguments; and Peroration.

ALL kinds of composition may be classed under two divisions, *prose* and *poetry*. Prose compositions, the subject of this chapter, may be arranged in the following classes: (1.) Didactic and argumentative; (2.) Oratorical; (3.) Narrative and descriptive. The *first* comprehends whatever relates to moral, political, or natural philosophy; all treatises on the arts and sciences, and all discussions and controversies, which do not come under the second division. This *second* division, includes not only the three great branches of oratory, the senate, the bar and the pulpit, but likewise much of controversy, and every thing that assumes a declamatory form. The third and last division extends to real and fictitious history, memoirs, books of travels; and essays, of which most are either narratives or descriptions. The three kinds are often found blended in one work, as in Thucydides, and Livy, in which will be found as much of oratory as of mere narrative.

In didactic or argumentative compositions, a figurative

style is improperly introduced, yet, in what are called moral essays, figures are often very appropriate. Productions of this kind, partake more or less of the nature of poetry or oratory, and being, in a measure, works of imagination, the ornaments of fancy are not improperly bestowed upon them. There are few productions of the narrative kind which will not admit of ornament, but description is more open to it than narrative; oratory, however, admits of the greatest variety of ornament. This, occasionally, has recourse to almost all the figures which are appropriated to poetry, and to some peculiar to itself; and it is to this branch of composition, that the art of rhetoric particularly applies.

This art, like all others, is the result of observations made by men of enlightened minds and enlarged understandings. After a great variety of attempts, those principles were at length discovered, which distinguish between the good and the bad; between the faulty and the perfect. These principles, when reduced to method and well arranged, save succeeding inquirers much pains and trouble, considerably shorten the road to knowledge, and materially assist in the formation of a correct judgment. Though, as in poetry, accurate rules of criticism will not bestow genius, they will be the means of checking redundancy and bombast, and of detecting errors, so also with regard to the precepts of rhetoric, it may be asserted, that though they will not generate that energy of mind, which rises to the highest flights of eloquence, they will warn the orator against incongruity in the disposition of his matter, absurdity in argument, and the false glitter of ornament, which amuses instead of convincing; or those injudicious attempts to interest the feelings, which excite ridicule rather than sympathy.

The foundation of eloquence is right reason, and its exercise implies the possession of that faculty, both in the speaker and hearer; hence, rhetoric is nearly allied to logic. Quintilian, in treating of the utility of the art of rhetoric, says, "If in any thing the Creator has distinguished us from the rest of the animals, it is by the gift of speech. They surpass us in strength, in size, in swiftness, in patience, and, especially, in independence of foreign aid. Guided by instinct, they soon learn by its instructions to walk, to feed themselves, and to swim. Their protection against the cold, and their weapons of defence, are provided for them by nature. But what pains and labour does it cost man to procure all these things. Reason is our inheritance, and this seems to associate us to immortal beings. But how feeble would reason be, were it not for the faculty of expressing our thoughts by speech, which is the faithful interpreter of reason! This is what is wanting in inferior animals much more than understanding, of which it cannot be justly said that they are absolutely destitute. If then, we have received nothing from the Deity better than the use of speech, what is there which we ought to cultivate with greater industry! What object is more worthy our ambition, than rising above other men by that faculty, which alone raises them above the level of brutes!"

A still greater dignity, says a modern writer, will attach to the acquirement of eloquence, and consequently to the science of rhetoric, if it be considered that eloquence and freedom go hand in hand. It is only in free states, and under popular governments, that oratory can flourish. When the people are appealed to on the subject of state-affairs; when political measures are to be enforced, either by the enlightening their judgment, or by the excitement of their passions, the greatest talents are exercised in studying the art of persuasion, and the result is found in the most wonderful efforts of human ability. But when brute force predominates, and the people bow beneath the yoke of tyranny, the voice of reason is stilled, and eloquence is mute. The ancient rhetoricians divide oratorical composition into three species, viz. the demonstrative, the deliberative, and the judicial. The *demonstrative* is chiefly conversant in bestowing praise or blame, and comprehends the panegyric, and the funeral eulogy: such are Isocrates' Panegyric on Evagoras, King of Salamis; Cicero's

Oration on the pardoning of Marcellus, his Phillippics against Mark Anthony, his orations against Catiline, and Pliny's Panegyric on Trajan: such also are the funeral orations composed by Thucydides and Plato, to commemorate the virtue of the Athenians, who fell at the commencement of the Peloponnesian war. In modern times, we have the funeral discourses of many celebrated French and English preachers; the *éloges* pronounced upon eminent men, before the French academy, and the occasional commendatory or vituperative speeches, which have been delivered in the British senate, by a Chatham, a Fox, a Burke, a Pitt, and many others, as well in the upper as in the lower house of Parliament. Most of these have, within the last twenty years, been collected and published in separate works, and afford rich subjects of study to those who wish to become acquainted with the principles of demonstrative eloquence.

Deliberative eloquence embraces, as its object, the whole extent of public affairs, and has never been exercised in a higher style, than in the senate of our own country. It includes all discussions relating to war and peace: all political negociations, foreign alliances, regulations of trade and commerce, and, in general, all matters connected with legislation and government. This species of eloquence cannot be cultivated in any other than a free state. The will of an arbitrary monarch supersedes its use, or terrifies it into silence. It is, therefore, to the best states of Athens and Rome, that we must look for its energies as exhibited in ancient times, and in the works of Demosthenes and Cicero are to be found its noblest memorials. In modern times, it has, by the operation of political causes, been almost exclusively confined to the limits of our own island.

Judicial eloquence comprehends every thing relating to the business of the courts of law, both civil and criminal; that is, to the attack and defence of persons and property. In ancient times, the business of judicial pleading was not confined to a particular class of men. The Roman orator was at all times ready to impeach a state criminal, or to plead in defence of the life, the honour, or the fortune of his friend. This was the period when the first characters of the republic displayed their abilities at the bar; when Cicero and Hortensius gave full scope to their superlative talents; and, in the proceedings of the British courts of justice, there have, for a long series of years, been exhibited proofs of the most searching sagacity, the soundest judgment, and the most ready wit.

In regular orations of every species, there will generally be found the *exordium*, or introduction; the *statement* of the subject; the *narrative*, or explanation; the *reasoning*, or argument; the *pathetic* part; and, lastly, the *peroration*, or conclusion. On each of these heads we shall say a few words, referring to other and more elaborate works for a fuller illustration, with examples.

The object of the *exordium* is to conciliate the good-will of the hearers, to awaken their attention, and to render them open to persuasion. Cicero defines an exordium to be a part of an oration, by which the minds of the audience are duly prepared for what remains to be said. The exordium is a part of chief importance, and is to be laboured with extraordinary care; hence it has been called "difficillima pars orationis." The topics by which the purposes of an exordium are best effected, will generally suggest themselves to the good sense of the speaker or writer: they arise from the particular situation of the speaker himself, or of his cause, or client; or from the character and behaviour of his antagonist, contrasted with his own; on other occasions, from the nature of the subject, as closely connected with the interest of the hearers; and, in general, from the modesty and good intention with which the speaker enters upon his subject; to engage the attention of the hearers, some hints may be thrown out respecting the importance, dignity, and novelty of the subject; and to render them docile, or open to persuasion, the speaker should endeavour to remove any particular prepossessions or prejudice against the cause, or side of the argument which he espouses.

The exordium requires *propriety* of address, that it may appear easy and natural; and become of a piece with the whole discourse, and match it as a part does the whole. It was the rule of Cicero to make the exordium last; and he says, "when I have planned and digested all the materials of my discourse, it is my custom to think, in the last place, of the introduction with which I am to begin. For if, at any time, I have endeavoured to invent an introduction first, nothing has ever occurred to me for that purpose, but what was trifling, nugatory, and vulgar." *Modesty* is another requisite in the exordium of a discourse; it should discover itself not only in the expressions of the orator, in the beginning, but in his whole manner, in his looks, in his gestures, and in the tone of his voice. It should, however, be observed, that the modesty of an introduction should never betray any thing mean or abject. The orator, while he exhibits real modesty and diffidence, should manifest a becoming sense of dignity, arising from a persuasion of the justice or importance of the subject of which he is about to speak. Besides the qualities of propriety and modesty, the exordium should be distinguished by its *brevity*, by the easiness of the *style*, and by the *calmness* of the manner.

In the *proposition* of the subject, the qualities chiefly to be aimed at, are clearness and distinctness. These qualities are of the most essential importance, and the attainment of them is well worthy the utmost care and pains. In debates of every kind, that speaker is listened to with the greatest pleasure, who is able briefly and plainly to give the most accurate account of the points in question.

As the *narrative*, or explanation of facts, is to be the ground-work of all future reasonings of the orator, it is obviously his duty to recount them in such a manner as may be most favourable to his cause; to place in the most striking light every circumstance which is to his advantage; and to soften or palliate such as make against him. He should exercise consummate judgment, so that his narrative may be at once concise and full, copious and distinct. A perfect narration is one, from which nothing can be taken without rendering it obscure, and to which nothing can be added without weakening its force.

In his *arguments,* a speaker should possess logic as a philosopher, and employ it as an orator. He should follow the lucid order of nature in their disposition, and express them in such a style and manner as to give them full force. He should take care not to multiply them to too great an extent, and to bring into a conspicuous point of view those which are most weighty and cogent.

In the *pathetic* part of his discourse, which generally introduces and pervades the peroration, the ancient orator collected all his talents to strike a finishing stroke. But Quintilian, with his usual judgment, warns the orator against dwelling too long upon this topic. "Time," he says, "soon calms real griefs; how much more easily must it dissipate the illusory impressions which act only upon the imagination! Let not, then, the pathetic strain be too long continued. If this precept be not well observed, the auditor is fatigued, he resumes his tranquillity, and recovering from the transitory emotion, he returns under the influence of reason. We ought not, then, to suffer his feelings to cool; but when we have carried them as far as they can go, we ought to stop, and not imagine that the mind will for any long space of time be sensible to emotions which are foreign to it."

The precise nature of the peroration, or conclusion of any discourse, must be determined, in a great measure, by the nature and the circumstances under which it is delivered. It is frequently expedient in this part of the discourse to compress a repetition of the substance of a long train of antecedent argument. The peroration, therefore, may generally be said to consist of two parts; first, a *recapitulation,* in which the substance of what is gone before, is collected briefly and cursorily, and summed up with new force and weight: secondly, the *moving of the passions*. The qualities required in a peroration are, that it be vehement and passionate, and that it be short. Cicero particularly excelled in the peroration. In this part of his discourse, that great orator not only set his judges and auditors on fire, but even seemed to burn himself; especially when he was to raise pity and commiseration towards the accused. The great rule of a conclusion, is to place that last, in which we think the strength of the cause should rest. Sermons commonly conclude with inferences: these should rise naturally, and so much agree with the strain of sentiment throughout the whole discourse, as not to break the unity of the sermon. Dr. Blair, in treating on this subject, says, "it is a matter of importance to bring our discourse just to a *point*, neither ending abruptly and unexpectedly, nor disappointing the hearers when they look for the close, and continuing to hover round the conclusion, till they become heartily tired of us. We should endeavour to go off with a good grace; not to end with a languishing and drawling sentence; but to close with dignity and spirit, that we may leave the minds of the hearers warm, and dismiss them with a favourable impression of the subject and of the speaker."

The conclusion of Mr. Burke's address to the electors of Bristol, when he was about to quit the hustings, at the election of 1780, has been given as a fine instance of peroration: "It has been usual for a candidate who declines, to take leave by a letter to the sheriffs; but I received your trust in the face of day, and in the face of day I accept your dismission. I am not—I am not at all ashamed to look upon you; nor can my presence discompose the order of business here. I humbly and respectfully take my leave of the sheriffs, the candidates, and the electors, wishing heartily that the choice may be for the best, at a time which calls, if ever time did call, for the service that is not nominal. It is no play-thing you are about. I tremble when I consider the trust I have presumed to ask. I confided, perhaps, too much in my intentions. They were really fair and upright; and I am bold to say, that I ask no ill thing for you, when, on parting from this place, I pray, that whoever you choose to succeed me, may resemble me exactly in all things, excepting my abilities to serve, and my fortune to please you."

CHAP XII.

OF POETRY.

Poetry, in what first used—Its excellencies pointed out—Poetic representation, how effected—Of ancient poetry—Classical poetry: Homer; Lyrical composition; the heroic ode; Dramatic poetry—Roman poets; Ennius, Virgil, Ovid, Tibullus, &c.

POETRY is unquestionably the oldest, and the most excellent of the fine arts. It was the first fixed form of language; the earliest perpetuation of thought; it existed before prose in history, before music in melody, and before painting in description. At a very early period of the world it was employed to celebrate the praises of the Almighty, to communicate lessons of wisdom, and to extol the achievements of valour: music was invented to accompany, and painting, to illustrate it. Poetry transcends all other literary compositions, in harmony, beauty and splendour of style, imagery and thought, as well as in the permanency and vivacity of its influence on the mind, for its language and sentiments are so intimately connected, that they are remembered together:—it excels music in the passion and pathos of its movements; and being progressive, it is superior to painting, which is stationary in its powers of description. The energies of painting are more confined to those objects that can be represented by colour and figure. Poetry can express these objects, though in an inferior degree; but the deficiency is compensated by the extensive range of the poet's excursions. He dives into the human breast, developes the windings of the heart, pourtrays the workings of the passions, gives form and body to the most abstract ideas, and, by the language which he puts into the mouths of his characters, unlocks the secrets of their mind. Another grand advantage, to which we have alluded, and which the poet possesses over the painter, is that the latter is confined to transactions that happen in an instant of time, while the former presents to the view a long series of events. "An interesting picture," says a writer on this subject, "might, no doubt, be drawn of the pious agony with which Æneas witnessed the obstinacy of his father, in refusing to save himself from the sword of the Greeks, by quitting his ancient and long-loved abode. But what a varied pleasure do we experience in reading of the circumstances that preceded and that followed this event; in tracing the steps of the duteous son from the palace of Priam to his father's mansion; and in beholding him at length bearing his parent beyond the reach of the foe. Since every finished composition should have a beginning, a middle, and an end, so the mind feels a superior degree of satisfaction, when the rise, the circumstances, and the consequences of events are displayed before it in artful order. Poetry can effect this; but, in painting, the present only exists; the past and the future are wanting."

Moreover, poetic representation is effected not merely by words, but by words metrically, or, at least, melodiously arranged: this is the exterior distinction; but too many writers seem to assign to it a place of eminence, to which it is by no means entitled. Poetry, if it deserve the title, must include something more than the "mere measuring of syllables, and the tagging of a verse." If the heart do not glow with the flame of genius, the mechanism of art will be unavailing. No one can excite strong feelings in others, who is not himself strongly excited; no one can raise vivid images in the mind of his reader, who is not himself illumined by the sportive light of fancy.

The poet should never forget, that the end of poetry is to amuse the fancy and powerfully excite the feelings, which will be best effected by impressing the mind with the most vivid pictures. "The primary aim of the poet," says Dr. Blair, "is to please and to move; and, therefore, it is to the imagination and the passions that he speaks. He may, and he ought to have it in his view, to instruct and to inform; but it is indirectly, and by pleasing and moving, that he accomplishes this end. His mind is supposed to be animated by some interesting object, which fires the imagination, or engages his passions; and which, of course, communicates to his style a peculiar elevation, suited to his ideas, very different from that mode of expression, which is natural to the mind in its calm and ordinary state."

As, then, the chief end of poetry is to make a lively impression on the feelings, we may in some measure estimate the vastness of its powers; and in this respect facts will correspond with pre-conceived theory. In consequence of the efficacy of poetry upon the human feelings, the maxims of early wisdom, the first records of history, and even the dictates of law, were delivered in a poetic dress. "In the infancy of states, poetry is a method equally captivating and powerful in forming the dispositions of the people, and kindling in their hearts that love of glory, which is their country's safeguard in the day of peril. Whether we look to the cold regions of Scandinavia, or the delicious clime of Greece; whether we contemplate the North American Indian, or the wild Arab of the desert; it will be found that, when mankind have made a certain progress in society, they are strongly influenced by the love of song, and listen with raptured attention to the strains that record the tale of other times, and the deeds of heroes of old. They listen till they imbibe the enthusiasm of warfare, and, in the day of battle, the hero's arm has not unfrequently been nerved by the rough energy of the early bard."

It is a well-known fact, that the Greeks were accustomed to march to the fight while singing in praise of Apollo; and that the songs written in honour of Harmodius and Aristogiton, by being habitually recited at their banquets and solemn festivals, tended in no inconsiderable degree to preserve among the Athenians an enthusiastic love of liberty. Nor is the power of the muses done away by the progress of civilization. Every nation, at every period of its existence, possesses some indigenous poetry, which nourishes the flame of patriotism. Such is the wonderful influence of poetical composition; and when directed to worthy objects, it is one of the most pleasant and most efficacious means of forming the youthful mind, and of exciting the emotions, and enforcing the principles of virtue.

Having said so much concerning poetry in general, we shall proceed to give an account of the different kinds of poetry, for which we shall be much indebted to an article in a very popular work.

Of ancient Poetry. That the higher order of poetry is attainable in an early stage of society, is a truth eminently illustrated by the example of the Hebrew people. It is evident that the bards of this nation composed their lofty songs for a primitive race, tenacious of its customs and opinions, unenlightened by science, uncorrected by taste, and as little acquainted with the arts, as the refinements of polished life. The simplicity and energy of the Hebrew language accorded happily with the sublime nature of sacred poetry; and to the peculiarities in its constitution it is perhaps owing, that the primitive character of its composition is tenaciously preserved to whatever language transferred, or with whatever idioms assimilated. The distinctive feature of Hebrew poetry was a symmetrical disposition of the sentences, which were cast into parallel verses of equal length, and correspondent in sense and sound; the sentiment expressed in the first distich, being repeated and amplified in the second, as in the following examples:—

The Lord rewardeth me according to my righteousness:
According to the cleanness of my hand he hath recompensed me.

The fear of the Lord is clean, enduring for ever:
The judgments of the Lord are pure and righteous altogether.

This practice, which was, perhaps, peculiar to the Hebrews, was derived from their rites of worship, in which the sacred hymns were chaunted by bands of singers, who alternately responded to each other. The Hebrew bards employ few epithets; but the brevity of their style renders its sublimity conspicuous: their imagery is bold and energetic; their imagination is ever rich and exuberant; and to them, metaphors spontaneously arise on every subject, in inexhaustible beauty and fertility. Although Hebrew poetry presents nothing that can properly be classed with epic or dramatic composition, it affords innumerable examples of the lyric, the elegiac, and the didactic style. In the prophecies, the favourite figure is allegory: the Hebrews, in common with other Oriental nations, had a decided predilection for the parabolic species of writing; their images are highly natural, and, on minute examination, they will be found to have harmonized with scenes and manners familiar to their observation and experience.

The figure, however, which elevates beyond all others the poetical style of the Scriptures, is the prosopopœia, or personification; and it is certain, that the personifications of the sacred writings exceed in boldness and sublimity every thing that can be found in other poems. This is especially the case when any appearance or operation of the Almighty is concerned, as the following examples will prove: "Before Him went the pestilence.—The waters saw Thee, O God, and were afraid.—The mountains saw Thee, and they trembled.—The deep uttered his voice, and lifted up his hands on high." Of the sacred Poets, the most eminent are, the author of the Book of Job, David, and the Prophet Isaiah. In the different compositions of David, there is a great variety of style and manner. He excels in the soft and tender; but there are likewise many lofty passages in the Book of Psalms. In strength of description, he yields to Job; and, in sublimity, he is inferior to Isaiah. The most sublime of all poets, without exception, is Isaiah, whom Dr. Lowth compares to

Homer; Jeremiah, he compares to Simonides; and Ezekiel, to Æschylus. Among the minor prophets, Hosea, Joel, Micah, Habakkuk, and more particularly Nahum, are eminent for poetical spirit. The Book of Job is extremely ancient, but the author is uncertain. It is remarkable, that it has no sort of connexion with the affairs, or the manners of the Jews and Hebrews. Its poetry is highly descriptive. It abounds in a peculiar glow of fancy and metaphor. Whatever the author treats of, he renders visible. The scene is laid in the land of Uz, or Idumæa, which is a part of Arabia; and the imagery employed in it differs from that which is peculiar to the Hebrews.

The Arabs were not, like the Hebrews, a stationary people, and insulated from the rest of mankind: they engaged in commerce and war, and, in their intervals of leisure, were no less ambitious to obtain poetical distinction, than they had been to secure military fame. With them, poetry became a polite accomplishment; and as the copiousness of their language supplied all the aptitudes of numbers, it is not surprising that bards should be found even in their deserts. The distich, and some other forms of metrical composition, adapted to familiar occasions, were of Arabian invention; and it is thought by Sir William Jones, that rhymes were borrowed from Eastern literature by the poets of Spain and Portugal, through whose influence they were naturalized in Europe.

With the copiousness and flexibility of the Arabic, the Persian language is found to possess an amenity and an elegance, which render it eminently susceptible of poetical beauty. Its poets, like those of ancient Greece, have the power of rendering language subservient to their pleasure, and of clothing original conceptions in newly created words. Several of the Arabic and Persian poems are of the epic and dramatic cast; but the compositions most familiar to the European, are of an amatory, elegiac, and lyric character. In general, Oriental poetry deviates from the primitive simplicity so conspicuous in

Hebrew compositions, and often degenerates into affectation and bombast.

Of classical Poetry. It is not possible to ascertain, with any degree of precision, the causes which have given to ancient Greece a pre-eminence in this department of literature. From the susceptibility of his language, the poet was enabled to exhibit the same idea under a new aspect, and to give to every fluctuation of feeling a permanent expression. If the vivacity of his descriptions fascinated the imagination, his numbers dwelt with no less enchantment on the ear. The length and shortness of syllables in the Greek and Roman languages, which constituted their quantities, were determined by rules no less accurate than the notes in music; and on the proper distribution and adjustment of these quantities, the harmony of their metre depended. A stated interval of time was allowed to the pronunciation of every verse; and to facilitate the labour of composition, artificial combinations of syllables, by the name of feet, were invented; and by the numbers of these, and the quantities included in them, the character of the verse was ascertained. To these combinations various names were given; the most important were the *spondee,* composed of two long syllables; and the *dactyl,* formed by one long and two short syllables. These were employed in hexameter verse, of which an imitation has been vainly attempted in the English language.

It is not certain what species of poetry was first cultivated in Greece. Fables were undoubtedly of great antiquity; the ode formed a part of religious worship; and the pastoral must have been introduced in an age sufficiently refined to relish simplicity. The Iliad and the Odyssey of Homer were composed at an early epoch of Grecian literature, and transmitted by oral tradition to a more polished age. Homer, of all the poets, our own Shakespeare excepted, may be considered as the poet of nature. His very epithets are beautiful and expressive, and peculiarly appropriated to the character or objects which they describe; and they are so picturesqne, that they often exhibit more in a single word, than can be found elsewhere in a much larger description. His allusions to the sea are frequent, and the ferociousness of his warriors is often compared to that of wild beasts, which give peculiar force and variety to his descriptions. Vast, violent, and loud motions are best described by Homer; smooth, gentle, or graceful ones, by Virgil: while, therefore, the latter poet excels in grace and beauty, the other transcends in descriptions of terror and sublimity. Upon the whole, Homer is at once majestic and simple; various, dramatic, and full of incident; highly descriptive and picturesque, yet natural; master of the most commanding strokes of the pathetic, and dwelling upon them when occasion requires; always moral, though apparently without design. The Iliad, though, at first view, and, to an inattentive reader, it may appear a rhapsody of battles, high passions, and characters formed without due discrimination, is nevertheless a most regular piece, and there is no poem in the world constructed with greater art and judgment. When critically examined, its time of action will be found regularly conducted; every part of it is seen connected with another, in due succession: it begins with the anger of Achilles, and ends with the death of Hector, when that anger ceased. All the parts rise out of each other in a natural, but surprising gradation; and every action has a manifest tendency either to elucidate or enforce the subject of the poem, exalt the principal character, or promote the design of the whole.

It has been pretended, that the Iliad and Odyssey of Homer were composed at different æras, by various authors; and that these desultory tales of Troy were at length collected by some ingenious person, who might have been distinguished by the appellation of Homer. It is, however, generally admitted, that one excellence in which the poet is supposed to stand unrivalled, is the energy of his conceptions, which gives to his personages, his scenes, and his descriptions, a real and individual existence. So happily, indeed are his characters cast, that no reader of feeling can be at a loss to conceive how Achilles would look, or Nestor speak, or Ulysses act on any given occasion. This being admitted, and it may be asked, whether such harmony of design could have been the result of chance, or whether each book had its separate Homer, or whether they were not all planned and executed by the same mind.

In lyrical composition, the most popular was the heroic ode. The name of Pindar has come down to us with great honour; but the poems which inspired in his compatriots the most exalted enthusiasm, are very imperfectly understood by the moderns. The public recitation of the ode was accompanied by music and dancing; a circumstance to which its structure is obviously adapted. The two first stanzas, called the strophe and antistrophe, were of equal length. In the first part, the performers approached the altars of their god; in the latter, the dance being inverted, they measured back their steps to their former place, where they sung the epode. This form was peculiar to the heroic ode; but there were other lyrical compositions of a different cast. Sappho's poems breathe only the tender, impassioned sentiment; those of Anacreon are equally remote from the sublimity of Pindar, and the softness of Sappho.

The heroic ode is evidently of a dramatic character, and was the source from whence the regular drama was produced. Tragedy originated in the hymns sung in honour of Bacchus, and its name was derived from the goat, which was the victim consecrated to that deity. The invention of the dialogue and action belongs to Æschylus; the original ode was preserved in the chorus, which constituted the popular part of the entertainment. The chorus, like the band of a modern orchestra, was composed of several persons, who recited in a different manner from the other performers. Their business was to deduce from the passing scene some lesson of morality, or to inculcate on the spectator some religious precept.

Comedy, like tragedy, originally consisted of a chorus, which derived its name from the god Comus. The rudiments of the comic art may, it is thought, be detected in the satyrs, a sort of interlude annexed to tragedies, in which the scene was rural, and the personages, satyrs or sylvan deities. It was not till the time of Aristophanes, that living characters were introduced on the stage. This abuse a better taste corrected; and the comedies of Menander, which were afterwards imitated by Terence, exhibited interesting scenes of domestic life. The chorus was gradually changed into the prologue, a personage who carefully apprized the spectators of all they were to see on the stage.

The Roman writers were modelled on those of Greece, and it was long before they attempted to emulate their masters; but Ennius produced the satire. With equal originality, Lucretius wrote his metaphysical poem, in which are developed the philosophical systems of his age. It was not till the æra of Augustus that Horace transplanted all the lyric beauties to his odes, opened a rich vein of satiric poetry; and Virgil, having equalled Theocritus, aspired to emulate Homer. He frequently fell short of his master; his characters do not possess the same features of durability, and his scenes are not equally animated and dramatic. To atone, however, for these defects, he unites every charm that gives interest to narrative, or lends enchantment to description. He rises occasionally to the sublime; but the beautiful is his natural element; he can excite terror, but he is more prone to inspire tenderness and pity. In the Georgics, Virgil has left a model of didactic composition, ennobled by a strain of philosophical sentiment, pure, graceful, and persuasive.

Ovid adorned the fables of mythology with description, and illustrated in his epistles almost every romantic story of antiquity. The style of his elegies is not unlike that of his epistles: he paints to the eye, but he has often too much wit and fancy to affect the heart. Tibullus has exceeded every other elegiac writer in simplicity and tenderness. Lucan and Statius were also epic poets; but they are not often read. Lucan possessed a fine genius, but his subject was unfortunate. Among the latter poets of Rome were Juvenal and Persius, of whom the former was one of the most original writers she had produced.

CHAP. XIII.

POETRY,
Continued.

Origin of modern poetry—English versification.

THE Gothic nations which over-ran Rome, and the countries subjected to it, though ignorant of the polite arts, were not insensible to the charms of poetry. Their bards were no less venerated than their priests; and whatever instruction they received; whatever knowledge they possessed, was communicated in metre, and probably in rhyme. In the age of Charlemagne, the minstrels of Provence, or, as they were called, the Troubadours, introduced the metrical tales or ballads, which, from the dialect in which they were written, acquired the name of Romances. The poems were all composed in rhyme; but whether this practice was borrowed from the Arabs or the Goths is uncertain.

Mr. Ellis (see his introduction to "Specimens of early English Metrical Romances") has given an account of the rise and progress of the minstrels and their poetry. From which it appears, that Normandy was the cradle of minstrelsy. The Northmen, who wrested that province from the feeble successors of Charlemagne, had, like all other barbarous people, especially the Scandinavian tribes, their national poets. These, it is believed, were carried by Rollo into France, where they probably introduced a certain number of their native traditions, relating to their heroes, who were afterwards enlisted into the tales of chivalry. Being compelled to a frequent exercise of their talent in extemporaneous compositions, the minstrels were probably like the *improvisatori* of Italy, and became good judges of the public taste. By the progress of translation, they became the depositaries of nearly all the knowledge of the age, which was committed to their memory: it was natural, therefore, that they should form a variety of new combinations from the numerous materials in their possession; and many of our most popular romances were probably brought by their efforts to the state in which we now see them.

Facts in history prove, that the profession of a minstrel was held in great reverence among the Saxon tribes, as well as among their Danish brethren. Alfred, in 878, wishing to ascertain the true situation of the Danish army, which had invaded his realm, assumed the dress and character of a minstrel; and, under this character, though he could not but be known to be a Saxon, obtained an honourable reception. About sixty years after, a Danish king made use of the same disguise to explore the camp of our king Athelstan. The minstrel was, therefore, a privileged character with both these people. In the reign of Edward II. the minstrels were admitted into the royal presence, an instance of which is mentioned by Stow. In the fourth year of Richard II. John of Gaunt erected a court of minstrels, with full power to receive suit and service from the men of this profession, within five neighbouring counties, to enact laws and determine controversies, &c., for which they had a charter.

The first compositions of the minstrels appear to have been unadorned annals or histories, reduced to measure, for the convenience of the reciter, who was to retain them upon his memory. Their poems were all composed in rhyme; but whether this practice was borrowed from the Arabs or the Goths is uncertain. The Italian language, which, of all the corrupt dialects introduced by the barbarians, assimilated most with the Roman, soon acquired a tincture of elegance. Dante wrote in the middle ages; Ariosto followed; and Petrarch appeared among the first founders of modern literature. The passion for allegory, so long the characteristic of the Italian school, was by Chaucer rendered as prevalent in England as it had previously been on the continent. During several ages, Italy continued to be the Poet's land of Europe; and in that interval was produced the "Jerusalem Delivered," a poem of great merit, and which still maintains a high character in modern literature. In Spain, poetry was early cultivated, but without much attention to classical taste. In France, it did not emerge from barbarism till the reign of Francis the First, and it arrived at its highest perfection in the æra of Louis XIV. La Fontaine and Boileau, Corneille and Racine had, at this period, produced works destined to immortalize their names. The modern drama originated in the *Mysteries*, a sort of religious farce imported from the East: to the mysteries succeeded allegorical plays, denominated *Moralities*. These produced the *Mask*, which became the favourite amusement of the court in the time of Charles I., and is redeemed from oblivion by Milton's Comus. Till the commencement of the last century, the German language was almost a stranger to poetry. Klopstock invented hexameter verse; and from that period many fine writers have arisen in Germany, distinguished for poetic taste, genius, and real talents.

Of English versification. In our own language, versification does not depend on the quantities, or the length and shortness of the syllables, but on the modulation of the accents, and the disposition of the pauses; to which is generally, though not universally, added, the recurrence of rhyme. The *heroic* verse consists of ten syllables, and its harmony is produced by a certain proportionate distribution of accented and unaccented syllables. Its specific character, whether lively or solemn, soft or slow, is determined by their order and arrangement.

When the unaccented and accented syllables are regularly alternated, it is called Iambic verse, as

> A shepherd's boy, he seeks no higher name,
> Led forth his flock beside the silver Thame.

With regard to the place of these accents, some liberty is admitted, for the sake of variety. Sometimes the line begins with an unaccented syllable; and sometimes two unaccented syllables follow each other. In general, there are either five, or four accented syllables in each line. The number of syllables is ten, unless where an Alexandrian verse, or one of twelve syllables, is occasionally admitted. Dryden was too fond of introducing the Alexandrian line, to which Pope refers:

> A needless Alexandrine ends the song,
> Which, like a wounded snake, drags its slow length along.

Nevertheless, it often forms a noble termination, of which the following is an instance:

> Teach me to love and to forgive;
> Exact my own defects to scan,
> What others are to feel, and know myself a man.

When the unaccented is preceded by an accented syllable, it is called a *trochaic* verse; as,

> Ambition first sprung from the blest abodes:

The frequent intervention of the trochaic is apt to produce harshness, which is carefully to be avoided.

Another essential circumstance in the constitution of English Verse, is the cæsural pause which falls towards the middle of each line. It is by the freedom with which this pause is transferred from one syllable to another, that the monotony that might be expected to result from a succession of *Iambic* lines is obviated: a freedom which constitutes the charm, and produces all the variety of our Verse. The pause or cæsura is that interval of suspension which must naturally arise in every verse; it is in fact found in the Verse of most nations. Pains have been taken to point it out in the Latin Hexameter. In the French Heroic verse of twelve syllables it is very sensible, and falls in every line just after the sixth syllable, regularly and indispensably, dividing the line into two equal hemisticks, the one half always answering to the other, and the same chime returning incessantly on the ear without intermission or change, which is a defect in their verse. In our own, it is a distinguishing advantage, that it allows the pause to be varied through four different syllables in the line. The pause may fall after the fourth, the fifth, the sixth, or the seventh syllable; and according as it is placed after one or other of these syllables, the melody of the verse is much changed, and its air and cadence are diversified.

When the pause falls after the fourth syllable, which is generally the earliest part on which it can fall, the briskest melody is formed, and the most spirited air given to the line; of which the following are instances:

> Soft is the strain | when zephyr gently blows,
> And the smooth stream | in smoother numbers flows.
>
> On her white breast | a sparkling cross she wore,
> Which Jews might kiss, | and Infidels adore;
> Her lively looks, | a sprightly mind disclose,
> Quick as her eyes, | and as unfix'd as those.
> Favours to none, | to all she smiles extends,
> Oft she rejects | but never once offends.

When the pause falls after the fifth syllable, which divides the line into two equal portions, the verse loses that brisk and sprightly air, which it had with the former pause, and becomes more smooth, gentle, and flowing:

> Eternal sunshine | of the spotless mind,
> Each prayer accepted | and each wish resign'd.

When the pause follows the sixth syllable, the tenor of the music becomes solemn and grave, and the verse proceeds with a more slow and measured pace. But the grave and solemn cadence becomes still more sensible, when the pause falls after the seventh syllable, which is the nearest place to the end of the line that it can well occupy. This kind of verse occurs but seldom, and it produces that slow Alexandrian air, which is suited to a close. Notwithstanding what has been said, the pause may occasionally dwell on the first, the second, or even penultimate syllable. The following may be given as instances to elucidate these observations;

Me | let the tender office long engage,
To rock the cradle of declining age.

O friend! may each domestic bliss be thine,
Be no unpleasing melancholy | mine.

When the pause falls on the second syllable, the verse is frequently accelerated, as:

Not so | when swift Camilla scours the plain.

A second pause in the same line is sometimes happily introduced:

O ever beauteous | ever lovely! | tell
Is it in heaven, a crime to love too well!

Triplets often occur in heroic verse, particularly in the works of Dryden, but they are now generally avoided by correct writers.

In English verse, we have different kinds of stanzas, as well as different kinds of verses. The stanza of nine lines in imitation of the Italian was introduced by Spenser, and that of eight lines such as Spenser employs, was generally used in the reign of Elizabeth and her immediate successors, James and Charles. Waller was the first who brought couplets into use, and Dryden established the practice.

The most popular stanza is that appropriate to the ballad, which is composed of four lines, of which the rhymes are ranged alternately. Such is the measure of Goldsmith's beautiful tale of Edwin and Angelina:

Turn, gentle hermit of the dale,
  And guide my lonely way,
To where yon taper cheers the vale
  With hospitable ray.

Such, with the remission of rhyme in the first and third lines, is the measure of Chevy-Chase:

God prosper long our noble king,
  Our lives and safetyes all;
A woeful hunting once there did
  In Chevy-Chase befal.

The elegiac stanza, consisting of four alternately responsive lines of ten syllables each, is well adapted to short poems: the celebrated elegy of Gray, is an example of this kind of stanza:

The curfew tolls the knell of parting day,
The lowing herds wind slowly o'er the lea,
The ploughman homeward plods his weary way,
And leaves the world to darkness and to me.

In Hammond's elegies, this kind of stanza is displayed to great advantage:

Why should the lover quit his pleasing home,
In search of danger on some foreign ground?
Or from his weeping fair ungrateful roam,
And risk in every stroke a double wound?

The simplest and most fluent of all verse is the couplet of eight syllables. It is often appropriated to ludicrous poetry, as in some of Swift's pieces, and in Butler's Hudibras; the following lines give a good specimen:

When civil dudgeon first grew high,
And men fell out, they knew not why;
When hard words, jealousies and fears,
Set folks together by the ears;
And made them fight, like mad or drunk,
For dame Religion, as for punk;
Whose honesty they all durst swear for,
Though not a man of them knew wherefore.

This kind of verse is however used on more serious occasions, and seems well adapted to tender expression. The Allegro and Penseroso of Milton are written in this measure:

And may at length my weary age
Find out a peaceful hermitage;
The hairy gown and mossy cell,
Where I may sit, and rightly spell
Of every star that heaven doth shew,
And every herb that sips the dew,
Till old experience do attain
To something like prophetic strain.

The dactyl or anapæstic measure of eleven and twelve syllables, and some of less, is appropriated to humorous subjects, especially songs:

My time, O ye Muses, was happily spent,
When Phœbe was with me wherever I went.

This measure, when worked into a stanza, assumes a different character, as in the war-song of Burns:

'Tis night, and the landscape is lovely no more:
  I mourn, but, ye woodlands, I mourn not for you;
For morn is approaching, your charms to restore,
  Perfum'd with fresh fragrance, and glittering with dew.
Nor yet for the ravage of winter I mourn;
  Kind nature, the embryo blossom will save:
But when shall spring visit the mouldering urn?
  Oh! when shall it dawn on the night of the grave?

In the stanza employed by Cowper, constructed on similar principles, the syllables are less numerous, and the cadence is, in general, more harmonious:

I am monarch of all I survey,
  My right there is none to dispute;
From the centre, all round to the sea,
  I am lord of the fowl and the brute.

Of Blank verse. Our blank verse possesses great advantages, and may be reckoned a noble, bold, and disencumbered species of versification. The chief defect in rhyme is the full close which it forces upon the ear, at the end of every couplet. Blank verse is freed from this; and allows the lines to run into each other, with as great a liberty as occurs in the Latin hexameter. Hence it is adapted to subjects of dignity and force, which demand more free and manly numbers than can be obtained in rhyme. It is composed of lines of ten syllables, which flow into each other without the intervention of rhymes. Its metrical principle resides in its pauses, which should be so spread as never to suffer the rhyme to be missed. Of the few poets who have attempted and succeeded in this species of composition, Milton is unquestionably the first; and after him, Thomson, Armstrong, Akenside and Cowper, take the next rank, and are indeed preeminent. Milton's verse is unequalled, it dilates with the author's thoughts, it harmonizes with the reader's sentiment, and its varied cadence rolls with majesty, or falls in a mellifluent strain of melody on the delighted ear. The following is a fine specimen: it is Adam's address to Eve:

——————————Awake,
My fairest, my espous'd, my latest found,
Heaven's last best gift, my ever-new delight,
Awake! the morning shines, and the fresh field
Calls us: we lose the prime, to mark how spring
Our tended plants, how blows the citron grove,
What drops the myrrh, and what the balmy reed,
How nature paints her colours, how the bee
Sits on the bloom extracting liquid sweet. Book v.

Mr. Crowe, the public Orator of Oxford, has endeavoured to account for the excellence of Milton's verse, and he refers the principle of its exquisite mechanism, to the author's bold practice of distributing in separate lines, words that are so nearly connected, such as the preposition governing the noun, and the pronoun attached to the verb, as almost to appear indivisible. "That this practice," says another critic, "which Mr. Crowe calls *the breaking the natural joint of the sentence,* is favourable to the freedom of blank verse, cannot be disputed; but it may be questioned whether the poet was himself conscious of the mechanism which he employed, or that he was directed by any other principle than his own acute sensibility to harmony."

Whether rhyme or blank verse be entitled to pre-eminence, is a question not easily determined. In the choice of his measure the poet must be influenced by the nature of his subject. In all gay and airy excursions of fancy, or the lighter touches of feeling, rhyme will be found an auxiliary equally pleasing and important: likewise in such compositions as require a measure of spirited and vivacious movement. "To satire it adds poignancy, to humour it gives elegance; it imparts renovation to old ideas, and lends attraction to trivial sentiments; it renders familiar illustration graceful, and plain sense eloquent." Wherever much originality of thought exists, this metrical charm is unnecessary; and where imagination reigns in luxuriance, it may be well resigned to blank verse.

CHAP. XIV.

POETRY,
Continued.

Of the thoughts and language of poetry—Remarkable differences between prose and poetry—Pastorals—The Elegy—The Sonnet—Lyric Poetry—Didactic Poetry—Epic Poetry—The Drama—The Epigram—The Epitaph.

HAVING described the several sorts of verse, so as to give a general idea of metre, we shall proceed to the different forms of poetical productions. Previously to this, we may make some observations on the thoughts and language of poetry. Horace has given the requisites of a poet in the following lines:

> Ingenium cui sit, cui mens divinior atque os
> Magna soniturum, des nominis hujus honorem.
>
> HOR. *Sat.* 4. *Lib.* I.

> Is there a man, whom real genius fires,
> Whom an enthusiasm divine inspires;
> Who talks true greatness;—let him boldly claim
> The sacred honours of a Poet's name. FRANCIS.

The *Ingenium* of Horace, means that *invention;* and the *mens,* that Enthusiasm, which form the Epic, Tragic, or Lyric poet. Invention is the character of poetry in general: it is that which can form a fable, plot, or story, and ornament it with characters and circumstances; the poet can create imaginary beings, describe what he never saw, and add fancied and interesting embellishments to what he had seen.

The *os magna soniturum* regards the language alone, which is proper for the higher departments of poetry. A certain strength and nobleness of style is so essential a part, that a poem, which had both invention and enthusiasm in the highest degree, would be ridiculous, if the language were cold and feeble.

The highest exercise of invention, is in the choice and arrangement of the subject; but here judgment must come in aid of imagination, to ascertain what subject admits of poetical embellishments. Unless that is interesting, all the ornaments of poetry and language will be lavished in vain. But if the subject be well conceived, appropriate beauties will seem naturally to arise out of it, and the execution will be proportionally easy. Attempts have been made to translate the Bible into English verse; the most however that could be done in this way, would be to form it into rhymes, as the greater part of it is not poetical. Milton selected almost the only Scriptural subject that afforded scope for a brilliant imagination. The fall of Adam and Eve was of itself well adapted to the ornaments of poetry; and from an obscure passage in the Epistle of St. Jude, the vigorous fancy of the poet formed the sublime episode of a war in heaven. Admirable, however, as the poem is, it is calculated to do much mischief, by infusing into ignorant minds, false ideas respecting the Almighty. Multitudes, no doubt, believe that the whole of the Paradise Lost, is founded entirely upon facts recorded in the Holy Scriptures, instead of being the work of the Poet's creative imagination.

Poetry has been denominated an imitative art: it must not, however, be an imitation of nature in every particular, but of what is dignified and exalted, as far as the human imagination is capable of rising. The poet must be capable of amplification; the very soul of fine poetry is detail; and the strongest mark of a vigorous imagination is the power of displaying all the nice and discriminating features of the human character and passions. Shakespeare surpasses every other poet in this excellence; and in Milton, though the subject may seem unfavourable to such a display, the most striking passages are of this kind. With respect to the thoughts and ornaments, poetry draws her resources from every quarter: of course he that knows most, and has read most, will be the best poet. Milton's extensive knowledge serves perpetually to enrich his poem, and keep alive the attention of his reader, and Shakespeare's fertile imagination, derived embellishments from every thing existing in nature and art, by means of the slightest associations.

Although we do not pretend to give rules for the execution of a poetical composition, yet the following observations, taken chiefly from Dr. George Gregory's Letters on Literature, may be deserving the attention of young writers.

Every ornamental thought in poetry, should flow naturally out of the subject: it should not be pressed into the service, as if it were dragged in from a common-place book.—Trite and common thoughts and reflections, notwithstanding their moral tendency, should be rejected, because in poetry we expect novelty and ingenuity, both in thought and expression; at the same time, it must be remembered that too much caution cannot be exerted in avoiding conceit or affectation.

It must be remembered that the language of poetry is essentially different from that of prose: this every one knows, though but few persons can assign for it the just reasons. They seem to result partly from poetry being of a more durable character, and partly from the circumstance, that whatever is addressed more to the passions than to the reason, requires a higher colouring. The *first* remarkable difference between poetry and prose, is, that the former admits of the use of words and expressions, which in the latter would be accounted obsolete. This principally arises from the permanency or stationary character of poetry. Prose in some measure depends on the style of conversation, which is perpetually varying, but poetry survives these vicissitudes, and therefore many words in Shakespeare and Milton, which perhaps the age immediately succeeding would have regarded as low, are now consecrated by time.

2dly. Some poetical words take an additional syllable, as *dis*part, *en*chain, &c. while others are made shorter by a syllable, as *vale, trump, clime, morn, eve,* &c.

3dly. Certain abbreviations, and particularly the *cæsura,* by which a letter is cut off from the beginning and end of a syllable, are admissible in poetry, which are not allowable in prose, as

> T'was on a lofty vase's side.
>
> T' alarm th' eternal midnight of the grave.

4thly. Poetry admits of a bolder transposition than prose, which might be exemplified in many passages from Milton, but the following is to the point:

> Together both, ere the high lawns appear'd
> Under the opening eyelid of the morn,
> We drove afield, *Monody on Lycidas.*

5thly. Poetry transforms nouns and adjectives into verbs and participles, thus we have *to hymn, varying, pictur'd* walls, *cavern'd* roofs, &c.

6thly. The soul of poetry is particularizing and bringing to view minute circumstances, which give animation to the picture; and for the same reason, poetry often uses a periphrasis rather than a plain or simple description.

7thly. Poetry admits of more and stronger figures than prose, and particularly the prosopopœia; and it also admits of a greater abundance of epithets: even compound epithets are necessary adjuncts in poetry, such as *cloud-capt* towers, *many-twinkling,* &c.

After all, the distinguishing character of poetry, as far as regards the style, lies more in the rejection than in the adoption of particular phrases or forms of speech. Whatever is technical, common, or colloquial, should be avoided. Where dignity is expected, a phrase, though not low in itself, yet being common in prose writing or conversation, will commonly degrade. On this subject, Dr. Johnson says "There was, before the time of Dryden, no poetical diction, no system of words at once refined from the grossness of domestic use, and free from the harshness of terms appropriated to particular arts. Words too familiar, or too remote, defeat the purpose of the poet. From those sounds, which we hear on small or coarse occasions, we do not easily receive strong impressions or delightful images; and words, to which we are nearly strangers, whenever they occur, draw that attention to themselves which they should convey to things. Those happy combinations of words, which distinguish poetry from prose, had been rarely attempted; we had few elegancies or flowers of speech; the rose had not yet been plucked from the bramble, or different colours joined to enliven one another."

Of Pastoral Poetry. The pastoral is a very agreeable species of poetry, but it is limited in its object. When formed on the model presented to us by Theocritus and Virgil, it should be a description of rural scenes and natural feelings enriched with elegant language, and adorned by the most melodious numbers. It was probably not invented till men had begun to assemble in great cities, and the bustle of courts and large societies was known. From the tumult of a city life, men look back with complacency and a longing eye to the innocence of a country retirement. Theocritus wrote the first pastorals which have come down to us, in the court of King Ptolemy, and Virgil imitated him in the court of Augustus.

The pastoral recals objects which commonly delight in childhood and youth. It gives the image of life, to which we join the ideas of innocence, peace, virtue, and leisure. It contemplates objects favourable to poetry; such as rivers and mountains, meadows and hills, flocks, trees and shepherds. The pastoral poet paints the simplicity, the tranquillity and happiness of a country life, but conceals its rudeness and misery. His pictures are not those of real life: they merely resemble it. Most of our English pastorals represent scenes that are artificial, and sentiments that are factitious, because they are imitated from other poets, the natives of a luxuriant region, accustomed to the living tints and glowing azure of a cloudless sky.

To have a proper idea of pastoral poetry, we must consider the scenery, the characters, and the subjects which it exhibits. The scene must be in the country, and the allusions should be to natural objects. The poet must diversify the face of nature, but on all occasions the scenery must be adapted to the subject of the pastoral, so that nature may be shewn under the forms that most accurately correspond with the emotions and sentiments which he describes. As to the characters in pastorals, it is not sufficient that they are persons who reside constantly in the country, they must be shepherds, and wholly engaged in rural occupations. The shepherd must be plain and unaffected, without being dull and insipid. He must possess good sense, and even vivacity; and should display tender and delicate feelings. With respect to the subjects of pastorals, it is not enough that the poet should give shepherds discoursing together. Every good poem must have a topic that should be interesting in some way, and in this lies the difficulty of pastoral poetry. The active scenes of a country life are too barren of incidents, and the condition of a shepherd has few things in it that produce curiosity and surprize.

Of Theocritus and Virgil, the former is distinguished for the simplicity of his sentiments, the harmony of his numbers, and the richness of his scenery; but he occasionally descends into ideas that are mean, abusive and immodest. Virgil, on the contrary, has all the pastoral simplicity and grace, without any offensive rusticity.

Of all the moderns, Gesner, a poet of Switzerland, has been the most happy. His scenery is striking, and his descriptions are lively: he is pathetic and writes to the heart. Neither the pastorals of Mr. Pope, nor of Mr. Philips, are any acquisition to English poetry. But Mr. Shenstone's

"Pastoral Ballad," is one of the most elegant poems in the English language, and the "Gentle Shepherd" of Allan Ramsay will bear being brought into comparison with any composition of this kind, in any language. To this poem, it is a disadvantage, that it is written in the old rustic dialect of Scotland, which is almost obsolete; and another objection is, that it is so entirely formed on the rural manners of Scotland, that none but a native of that country can relish, or even understand it. On the other hand, it is full of natural description, and it excels in tenderness of sentiment. The characters are drawn with a skilful pencil, the incidents are affecting, and the scenery and manners are lively and just.

Of the Elegy. The name of Elegy was originally given to the funereal monody, but was afterwards attached to all plaintive strains. In the Latin language it was always written in hexameter and pentameter verse. By the moderns, an elegiac stanza was invented, assimilating as nearly as possible with those slow numbers. Many elegies, and these probably the best, are expressive of only soothing tenderness: such are those of Tibullus, so happily imitated by Hammond. The Jesse of Shenstone, which has, perhaps, never been surpassed, is all pathos. The celebrated elegy of Gray combines every charm of description and sentiment. The elegiac stanza, which soon becomes oppressive to the ear, is sometimes exchanged for a lighter strain, as in the Juan Fernandez already referred to:

I am monarch of all I survey,
  My right there is none to dispute;
From the centre, all round to the sea,
  I am lord of the fowl and the brute.
Oh solitude! where are the charms
  That sages have seen in thy face?—
Better dwell in the midst of alarms,
  Than reign in this horrible place! COWPER.

Of the Sonnet. The Sonnet represents the elegy in an

abridged form; the same slow stanza is assigned to each, and the sentiments suitable to the one are appropriate to the other. It is derived from the Italian school, and has, at different periods, been much cultivated in this country, but it is not well suited to the genius of our language. The original form was fourteen lines, viz. two stanzas of four lines each, and two of three, and this form is still preserved in what are esteemed true sonnets. The following by Milton is a fine specimen of the English sonnet;

O nightingale, that on yon leafy spray
Wast blest at eve, when all the woods are still!
Thou with fresh hopes the lover's heart dost fill,
When the jolly Hours lead on propitious May.
Thy liquid notes, that close the eye of Day,
First heard, before the shallow cuckoo's bill,
Portend success in love. Oh! if Jove's will
Have link'd that amorous power to thy soft lay,
Now timely sing, ere the rude bird of hate
Foretell my hopeless doom in some grove nigh.
As thou from year to year hast sung too late
For my relief, yet hadst no reason why,
Whether the muse, or Love call thee his mate,
Both them I serve, and of their train am I.

Of Lyric Poetry. The ode is, in Greek, equivalent with song or hymn, and lyric poetry implies that the verses are accompanied with a lyre, or with a musical instrument. It is versatile and miscellaneous, and admits almost every diversity of measure and subject. Love and heroism, friendship and devotional sentiment, the triumphs of beauty, and the praises of patriotism, are all appropriate to lyrical composition. The soul of enthusiasm, the spirit of philosophy, the voice of sympathy, may all breathe in the same ode. It is not necessary that the structure of the ode should be so perfectly exact and formal as a didactic poem; but in every work of genius there ought to be a whole, and this whole should consist of parts, which should have a bond of connexion. In the ode, the transitions from thought to thought may be brisk and rapid, but the connexion of ideas should be preserved.

Pindar, the father of Lyric poetry, has led his imitators into wildness and enthusiasm; but in Horace, every thing is correct, harmonious and happy. Grace and elegance are his characteristics. He supports a moral sentiment with dignity, touches a gay one with felicity, and has the happy art to trifle most agreeably. Of our own lyrical writers, Dryden is eminent; his ode on St. Cecilia's day is well known. Gray is distinguished by the majesty and delicacy of his expression, and the correctness of his style. Collins is not unfrequently animated by a portion of Pindaric spirit.

Among the minor lyrics are included Songs, of which the themes are in general amatory or convivial. Some, however, are patriotic and martial, and not a few of a humorous cast. Shakespeare, Jonson, and some other of their contemporaries have left behind them songs of great beauty. In the last century, the most popular Song-writer was Gay.

Of Didactic Poetry. The express intention of this is to convey instruction and knowledge on a particular subject. The highest species of didactic composition is a formal treatise on some philosophical or grave subject. Such is the poem of Lucretius "De Rerum Natura;" such also are the Georgics of Virgil, Pope's Essay on Criticism, Akenside's Pleasures of the Imagination, Armstrong's poem on Health, and the Art of Poetry by Horace, Vida, and Boileau. In all these works, instruction is the professed object, but the practical lessons must be enlivened with figures, incidents and poetical painting. Virgil, in his Georgics, has, more than any other writer, the art of beautifying the most common circumstances in the business of which he treats. He was happy in his subject, for a dissertation on rural employments and affairs affords a vast scope for beautiful and luxuriant description. The plan which he adopts is sufficiently regular for the conveying of all necessary instruction, while the poem is every where enlivened by animated description, splendid allusions, or interesting narrations. The reader who is, in the least, acquainted with the Georgics, cannot forget the description of the perpetual spring in Italy, nor that of the Scythian winter; with what interest does the poet describe the happiness of a country life, the prodigies that preceded the death of Cæsar, and the disease among the cattle, the fable of Aristeus, and the tale of Orpheus and Eurydice.

In all didactic works, such a method and order are requisite, as shall exhibit clearly a connected train of instruction; but considerable liberties may be taken with regard to episodes and embellishments, for in a poetical performance, a continued series of instruction, without entertaining embellishments, would fatigue and disgust rather than amuse.

Of didactic poetry, satires and epistles run into the most familiar style. The satire is supposed to be a relic of the ancient comedy, but it was Horace who brought it to the perfection in which it has come down to us. Satire appears in three different modes, in the writings of Horace, Juvenal and Persius. The satires of Horace are characterized by their ease and grace: they glance rather at the follies and weakness of mankind, than their vices. Juvenal is more declamatory and serious, and has greater strength and fire. Persius has distinguished himself by a noble and sublime morality. Poetical epistles, when employed in moral and critical topics, resemble satires in the strain of their poetry. But in the epistolary form, various other subjects may be treated. The ethical epistles of Pope are a model, and he exhibits in them the strength of his genius. His imitations of Horace are so happy, that it is difficult to say whether the original or the copy is the most to be admired.

The Night Thoughts of Dr. Young may be fairly classed among moral didactic poems. In this work there is great energy of expression, many pathetic passages, happy images, and moral reflections. The opening of the poem has been regarded as only second to the exquisite lines of the immortal Shakespeare on Sleep:

> Tir'd nature's sweet restorer, balmy Sleep,
> He, like the world, his ready visit pays
> Where fortune smiles; the wretched he forsakes,
> Swift on his downy pinions flies from woe,
> And lights on lids unsullied with a tear.

Of Epic Poetry. Epic poetry concentrates all that is sublime in action, description, or sentiment. In the structure of a regular poem of this order, criticism requires that the fable should be founded in fact, and that fiction may fill the picture of which the outline is traced by truth. The machinery should be subservient to the main design. The action should be simple and uniform. In Homer's Iliad, the action is limited to the destruction of Troy, which is to be effected by the conciliation of Achilles to the common cause. In the Odyssey, it is the establishment of Ulysses in Ithaca, an event which, after innumerable difficulties, he is finally enabled to accomplish. In Virgil's Æneid, the hero is destined to found a Trojan colony in Latium. In the Jerusalem Delivered, the object is the restoration of that city to the Christians. In the Lusiad of Camoens the subject is the discovery of India by Vasco de Gama. The characters are well drawn, but not so well supported. The subject is perhaps too recent, and the savage barbarities which the Portuguese committed, naturally prejudice us against it. It, however, affords an admirable scope for description, and for the introduction of very interesting scenes.

In Epic poems, Criticism requires that poetical justice should be dispensed to all parties, success being awarded to the virtuous, and punishment inflicted on the guilty. Homer, Virgil and Tasso have constructed their poems on this principle. The Paradise Lost, whether it be, or be not ranked in the class of Epic poems, is justly deemed one of the highest efforts of poetical genius. The author, in the conduct of the subject, has shewn a very wonderful stretch of imagination and invention, and has admirably sustained the various characters which he has introduced. But Milton's distinguishing excellence is his sublimity, in which he very far surpasses Virgil, and by some is thought to excel even Homer. By all it is admitted that Milton's sublimity is different from that of Homer. That of the latter is generally accompanied with fire and impetuosity, while Milton's possesses more of calm and amazing grandeur. Homer warms and hurries us along; Milton's is that of wonderful and stupendous objects. Milton unites with his sublimity much of the beautiful, the tender, and the pleasing: his language and versification possess very high merit. His style is full of majesty, and wonderfully adapted to his subject. His blank verse is harmonious and diversified, and affords the most complete example of elevation, which the English language is capable of attaining by the force of numbers.

Of the Drama.—The Drama was originally a metrical composition, and exhibited all the critical refinements of poetry. The title of poet is still given to every dramatic author, although he should write in prose, and have no talent whatever for poetry. The avowed object of the drama is to develope the passions, or to delineate the manners of mankind, tragedy effects the one, and comedy the other. In the English language there are many popular dramas of a mixed character, which are written in verse intermingled with prose, and which are called plays. The triple unities of time, place, and action, are seldom observed on the English stage, and it is admitted, that between the acts any change is admissible. In truth, this operation is performed without condition and restriction, and is allowed without censure, provided the cause and object of it is immediately comprehended by the audience. To the limitation of time more attention is paid. In many tragedies the action is included in one day. Unity of design is an obligation imposed by good sense, and Shakespeare, guided only by his feelings of propriety, is, in general, careful to exclude from his plays a divided interest. In constructing a dramatic fable, the author has to provide sources of constantly augmenting interest; to present characters, to suggest situations capable of extorting from the spectators an active participation in the scene; above all, to supply a series of natural incidents, the springs of dramatic action, by which all the life and motion of the piece are produced. The dramatic style should imbibe its character from that of the individuals presented in the scene, and transmit the impression of every feeling which is there pourtrayed. On this excellence is founded the superiority of Shakespeare to all other dramatists: from his pen, each passion receives its appropriate language. With a few masterly touches, he lays open the heart, exhibits its most secret movements, and excites in every bosom correspondent emotions.

Of the Epigram.—An epigram is a little poem, treating of one thing only, whose characteristics are brevity, beauty, and point. The word epigram signifies *inscription*, for epigrams derive their origin from those inscriptions placed by the ancients on their statues, temples, pillars, triumphal arches, &c. which, at first, were very short, being sometimes no more than a single word; but afterwards, increasing their length, they made them in verse, to be better retained by the memory. This short way of writing came at last to be used upon any occasion or subject, and hence the name of epigram has been given to almost any small copy of verses, without any regard to the original application of the term. The usual limits of an epigram are from two to twenty verses, though it often extends to fifty, but the shorter, the better it is, and the more perfect; because the epigram, being only a single thought, ought to be expressed in a little compass, or it loses its force and strength. It is principally the *point* that characterizes the epigram. It admits of a great variety of subjects; some are made to praise, and others to satirize; the last are the easiest, as ill-temper frequently serves in the place of wit. We have many excellent epigrams in our own language: those of Prior are highly esteemed; the following is a fine encomium on the performance of an excellent painter:—

VENUS MISTAKEN.

When Chloe's picture was to Venus shown;
Surprized, the goddess took it for her own.
And what, said she, does this bold painter mean?
When was I bathing thus, and naked seen?—
Pleas'd Cupid heard, and check'd his mother's pride;
And who's blind now, mamma? the urchin cry'd,
'Tis Chloe's eye, and cheek, and lip, and breast:
Friend Howard's genius fancy'd all the rest.

The epigram of the celebrated Dr. Doddridge, on the words *Dum vivimus, vivamus,* is well known:

Live while you live, the epicure would say,
And grasp the pleasures of the passing day:
Live while you live, the sacred preacher cries,
And give to God each moment as it flies:
Lord, in my view let both united be,
I live in pleasure, while I live to Thee.

Of the Epitaph.—The epitaph is nearly allied to the epigram, and has a similar derivation, meaning, as the term imports, an inscription on a tomb. In its original structure, it consisted of only a single line, or a few words intended to attract the notice of the passenger. Such is that on the tomb of Tasso:

Les os du Tasse.

In a good epitaph, the name, and something of the character of the person should be introduced; and the place in which epitaphs are usually inserted, ought never to be forgotten, and on this account every thing light and trifling should be avoided. The following epitaph of Dr. Johnson, on a celebrated musician, possesses all these characteristics:

Philips! whose touch, harmonious, could remove
The pangs of guilty power and hapless love,

Rest here, distrest by poverty no more!
Find here that calm thou gav'st so oft before;
Sleep undisturbed within this peaceful shrine,
Till angels wake thee with a note like thine!

That of the illustrious Newton is highly appropriate:

Isaacum Newton
Quem immortalem
Testantur Tempus, Natura, Cœlum,
Mortalem hoc marmor
Fatetur.

The difficulty of writing an epitaph, consists in giving a particular and appropriate praise, which, in most instances, is almost impossible, because the greater part of mankind have little that distinguishes them from others, and, therefore, nothing can be said of them, that will not apply to thousands more.

The elegance of an epitaph consists in a nervous and expressive brevity, and it is often closed with a sort of epigrammatic point:

Underneath this noble marble hearse
Lies the subject of all verse,
Sidney's sister, Pembroke's mother:
Death! ere thou hast killed another,
Fair, and learn'd, and good as she,
Time shall throw a dart at thee.

Wit seems much out of place in an epitaph; yet we have many epitaphs that are jocose and ludicrous, such is that on an old fiddler, who was remarkable for beating time to his own music:

Stephen and Time are now both even,
Stephen beat Time, now Time's beat Stephen.

CHAP. XV.

ON ELOCUTION.

Cicero's division of Oratory—Defects in ennunciation—In what an orator should excel—Articulation, the principal thing—Accent—Emphasis—Passions of the mind, how expressed—Cadence—Pauses—Gesture—Action—Practical Rules.

ELOCUTION is a branch of Oratory of great power and importance. In common language, the term signifies utterance, delivery, or pronunciation. Elocution was much cultivated by Cicero and Quintilian, and before their time, by Demosthenes. It is well known, that the latter being asked what was the first point in Oratory? answered, Pronunciation: being asked what was the second? replied, Pronunciation; and what was the third?—Pronunciation: shewing thereby, that, in his judgment, the whole art of oratory consisted in this.

Cicero divided Oratory into five parts: (1.) *Invention*, by which we are to provide ourselves with suitable and sufficient materials for a discourse. (2.) *Disposition*, by which the subject was divided into parts, according to the most natural order, and which included the proper distribution and arrangement of their ideas. (3.) *Elocution*, which consisted in suiting words to the ideas, and which constituted the style of the subject. (4.) *Memory*, or a faculty of clearly discerning and retaining our ideas, and of calling to mind the most proper words by which to express them. (5.) *Pronunciation*, or the art of managing the voice and gesture in speaking. The great design of pronunciation, to which this chapter of our work is devoted, is to make the sentiments appear to come from the heart, in order that they may excite the attention and interest of those who listen to them.

Previously to the laying down rules for a good pronunciation, we shall mention some faults, into which young persons are apt to fall.

The faults of a bad or defective pronunciation are, (1.) when the voice is too loud, which is as inconvenient to the speaker, as it is disagreeable to the hearers. (2.) Another fault equally bad is when the voice is too low. Every person's voice should fill the place in which he speaks. The art of governing the voice consists very much in avoiding these two extremes. As a general rule we should carefully preserve the *Key*, that is, the command of the voice, and at the same time adapt the elevation and strength of it to the number of the persons we speak to; and the nature of the place we speak in. (3.) Another fault in pronunciation is a thick, hasty, and inarticulate voice. This is sometimes occasioned by a defect in the organs of speech, but more frequently by inattention and bad habits. In the former case more may be required than mere personal exertion: the aid of a professional person should be sought, to direct to the use of proper methods for overcoming the defect. But if the fault originates in mere bad habit, then nothing more is wanting than constant efforts, till the defect is cured. It is recorded of Demosthenes, who became the greatest orator the world ever produced, that he had, in the outset of life, three natural impediments in pronunciation, all of which he conquered by invincible labour and perseverance: one was a weakness of voice, which he cured by frequently declaiming on the sea-shore, amidst the noise of the waves. Another was a shortness of breath, which he corrected by repeating speeches as he walked up a hill. The third was the fault of a thick way of speaking, of which he broke himself by declaiming with pebbles in his mouth. (4.) Speaking too quick and too slow are likewise faults in pronunciation. By speaking too rapidly, the hearer loses the benefit of half he listens to, and by a too slow utterance the speaker becomes tedious, which can only be compensated by the importance and excellence of the sentiments delivered. (5.) There are other faults to be avoided, such as are produced by a flat, dull, uniform tone of voice, without emphasis or cadence, or any regard to the sense or subject of what is read; and likewise reading with a tone.

Having pointed out the faults that shew themselves in a bad delivery, we shall proceed to point out in what manner an orator ought to excel. It is evident that the prime objects of every public speaker should be, *first*, to speak so as to be fully and easily understood by his hearers; and, *next*, to express himself with such grace and energy as to please and move them.

In order to be fully and easily understood, independently of a proper degree of loudness of voice, the requisites are, distinct articulation, slowness and propriety of pronunciation. A speaker must endeavour to fill with his voice the space occupied by the assembly, which depends on the proper pitch and management of the voice. It is not necessary that the highest pitch of the voice should be used in order to be well heard. To assert the contrary of this, is to confound two things materially different, viz. loudness, or strength of sound, with the key or note on which we speak. The voice may be rendered louder without altering the key; and a speaker will always be able to give most body, most persevering force or sound, to that pitch of voice, to which in conversation he is accustomed. But if he begin on the highest pitch of his voice, he will fatigue himself, and speak with pain, which must excite uneasy sensations in the audience. To be well heard, a speaker, before he begins, should fix his eye on some of the most distant persons in the assembly, and consider himself as speaking to them, because we naturally and mechanically express our words with such a degree of strength, as to be heard by the person or persons to whom we address ourselves, provided he or they be situated within the reach of our voice. This will be the case in public speaking, as well as in common conversation.

In order to be well and clearly understood, distinctness of articulation is of much more importance than mere loudness of sound. A good articulation consists in giving a clear and full utterance to the several simple and complex sounds. The nature of the sounds, therefore, ought to be well understood; and much pains should be taken to discover and correct those faults in articulation, which, though sometimes ascribed to a defect in the organs of speech, are generally the consequence of inattention. Some persons find it difficult to articulate the letter *l;* others, the simple sounds expressed by *r, s, th,* and *sh*; but the instance of defective articulation which is most common, and requires the most particular notice, is the omission of the aspirate *h,* an omission, which materially affects the energy of pronunciation; the expression of emotions and passions, often depending, in a great measure, upon the vehemence with which the aspirate is uttered. Other defects in articulation, consist in a confused and cluttering pronunciation of words. The best methods of overcoming this habit, are, to read aloud passages chosen for the purpose, particularly such as abound with long and unusual words, or in which many short syllables come together; and to read at certain stated times, much slower than the sense and a just mode of speaking would require. Persons, who have not studied the art of elocution, often have a habit of uttering their words so rapidly, that the exercise now recommended, ought generally to be made use of for a considerable time, at least till they can read distinctly and deliberately. The speaker must give every sound which he utters its due proportion, and make every syllable, and even every letter, be heard distinctly. Such a pronunciation adds weight and dignity to language: it assists the voice by the pauses and rests which it enables the speaker to make, and he thus acquires a command over himself which is essential to good oratory.

In our language, every word of more syllables than one, has, at least, one accented syllable, which should always be marked by a stronger and more forcible utterance than the rest. This variety of sound serves to distinguish, from each other, the words of which a sentence is composed. According to Mason, whose "Essay on Elocution" is the foundation of almost all that has been since written on the subject, when we distinguish any particular syllable in a word with a force of voice, it is called *accent;* when we thus distinguish any particular word in a sentence, it is called *emphasis,* and the word so distinguished, the *emphatical* word. The emphatical words in a sentence, are those which carry a weight or importance in themselves, or those on which the sense of the rest depends; and these must always be distinguished by a fuller and stronger sound of voice, wherever they are found, whether in the beginning, middle, or end of a sentence; thus:

——————Rèm, facias Rèm
Rècte, si possis, si non, quocùnque modo Rèm.

Get plàce and weàlth, if possible, with gràce;
If nót, by àny means, get weàlth and plàce.

In these lines, the emphatical words are accented, and, in general, the sense will point out which they are. Sometimes, however, sentences are to be met with so full and comprehensive, that almost every word is emphatical; such is the expostulation in the prophecy of Ezekiel: "Why will ye die!" in which every word is emphatical, and according to the particular word on which the emphasis is laid, a different sense is expressed. Some sentences are equivocal, that is, they contain in them more senses than one; and which the intended meaning is, can only be known by observing on what word the emphasis is laid. The following sentence is given as an instance: "Shall you ride to town to-day?" The question is capable of being taken in four different senses, according as the emphasis is laid. If it be on the word *you*, the answer may be, "No, but I shall send the servant." If on the word *ride*, the answer might be, "No, but I propose to walk." If on the word *town*, the question is varied, and the answer may be, "No, I shall ride into the *country*:" and if the emphasis be laid on the words *to-day*, the answer may be, "No, but I shall to-morrow." Such may be the importance of laying a right emphasis.

To acquire the proper management of the emphasis, the chief rule is, that the speaker study to acquire a just conception of the force and spirit of those sentiments which he is about to deliver. Although it is of importance to a speaker to find out and distinguish the emphatical words, yet he must be cautious against multiplying them too much. They only become striking when used with prudence and reserve. If they recur very frequently, they soon fail to excite the attention of an audience.

We may farther observe, that the different passions of the mind, are to be expressed by a different modulation of the voice: *love*, by a soft, smooth, languishing note; *anger*, by a strong, vehement, and hasty speech; *joy*, by a quick, sweet, and clear sound; *sorrow*, by a low, interrupted pronunciation; *fear*, by a dejected, tremulous, hesitating tone; *courage*, by a full, bold, and rather loud address. In distinct orations, the *exordium* should be delivered in a lower voice; the *narration* should be distinct; the *reasoning*, or argumentative part, clear and slow; and the *peroration*, strong, forcible, and animated.

The variation of emphasis must not only distinguish the various passions just enumerated, but must be carried to the several forms or figures of speech in which they are expressed. In *prosopopœia*, the voice must be changed from one's own to that of him who is supposed to be introduced. In the *antithesis*, one contrary must be pronounced rather louder than the other. In a *climax*, the voice should always rise with it. In *dialogues*, it should be altered with the parts. In *repetitions*, it should be loudest in the second place.

Cadence is opposite to *emphasis*, but not less important in just elocution. The latter, as we have seen, elevates the voice; by the former, the voice gradually falls, and, if rightly managed, it is extremely musical. Besides a cadence of voice, there is, in all correct writers, a cadence of style: that is, when the sense is nearly completed, the remaining words gradually glide away among themselves. If an author's language be elegant, the cadence of his style will naturally direct the cadence of the voice. Cadence generally takes place at the end of a sentence, unless it closes with an emphatical word. Every *parenthesis* is to be pronounced in cadence, that is, with a lower and a quicker voice than ordinary; that it may not take off the attention too much from the sense of the period which it interrupts. *Apostrophes* and *prosopopœias* are to be pronounced in *emphasis*.

Next to emphasis, pauses demand attention: these are of two kinds, (1) emphatical pauses; and (2) such as mark the distinctions of sense. An emphatical pause is made after something has been said of importance, to fix the hearer's attention; and, sometimes, a subject of interest is preceded by a pause of this nature. In pauses, as with regard to emphases, care must be taken that they are not too often repeated. For since they excite particular attention, and raise expectation, if this be not fully answered, they will occasion disappointment and disgust. But the chief use of pauses is to mark the divisions of the sense, and, at the same time, to permit the speaker to draw his breath; and the just and graceful management of such pauses, is one of the most delicate and difficult points to be accomplished in elocution.

To obtain a proper command of the breath, a speaker should be careful to provide a supply of it fully adequate for what he is about to utter. It is a mistake to imagine that the breath is only to be drawn in at the end of a period, when the voice is allowed to fall. It may, with a proper degree of attention, be easily inspired at the intervals of a sentence, when the voice suffers only a momentary suspension, and hence a sufficient supply may be obtained for carrying on the longest without improper interruptions.

Pauses, in public discourse, must be formed upon the manner in which we naturally express ourselves in common, sensible conversation, and not from the punctuation usually found in books, which is arbitrary, and frequently capricious and false. To make pauses graceful and expressive, they must not only fall in the right places, but be accompanied by a proper tone of voice, by which the nature of the pauses is intimated, much more than by the length.

In reading or reciting verses, there is more difficulty in making the pauses with propriety. There are two kinds of pauses, one at the end of the line, and the other in the middle of it. Rhyme always renders the former sensible, and obliges one to observe it in pronunciation. In blank verse it is less perceivable; and when there is no suspension in the sense, it has been doubted whether, in reading it, any regard should be paid to the close of a line: and it is certain, that the close of the line, where there is no pause in the meaning, should be marked only by such a slight suspension of sound, as may distinguish the passage from one line to another, without injuring the sense. The pause within the line, usually falls after the fourth, fifth, sixth, or seventh syllables, and when it coincides with the division of sense, the line is read with the utmost ease, as in the following lines of Pope's Messiah:

> Ye nymphs of Solyma! begin the song;
> To heavenly themes, sublimer strains belong.

But if it happen that words, which have such an intimate connexion as not to admit even of a momentary separation, be divided from each other by this pause in the middle of the verse, there will be a conflict between the sense and the sound, which renders it difficult to read the lines with grace. In such cases, the sound must be sacrificed to sense: the following instance is taken from Milton:

> ——————What in me is dark,
> Illumine: what is low, raise and support.

The sense shews that the pause must be after the word illumine, that is, after the third syllable; but if the melody were only to be regarded, there should be no pause till after the fourth or sixth syllable. In the following line of Pope,

> I sit, with sad civility I read.

the sense allows no other pause than after the second syllable, which is the only one to be observed, though a well disciplined ear would point out the pause as occurring after the word sad.

Above all things, in elocution, we must follow nature, that is, our own natural dispositions and affections; hence a man will deliver his own compositions with more propriety and more animation, than he can those of another person: to heighten the effect of the pronunciation, the natural warmth of the mind should be permitted to have its course. We must study the most natural way of expressing ourselves, as to the *tone* of voice, which is different from emphasis, cadence, and pauses. This is best learnt by observation on the common forms of conversation, where all is free, natural, and easy; and when we are only intent on making ourselves understood, and conveying our ideas, in a strong, plain, and lively manner, with the most natural language, elocution and action. The nearer our pronunciation in public, comes to the freedom and ease of that which we use in common discourse, provided we maintain the dignity of the subject, and preserve a propriety of expression, the more just, natural, and agreeable it will be.

The orator must attain a certain degree of confidence, in order that he may be collected and composed: for this purpose he should not only be entirely master of the subject on which he delivers himself, but he must be conscious that his matter merits the attention of his audience. He should endeavour to be wholly engaged in what he has to say, and if the sight of any of his hearers discompose him, he should cautiously keep his eyes from that part of the assembly in which they are.

We are now led to make some observations on gesture or action. The best rule is to recommend attention to the looks and gestures in which earnestness, indignation, compassion, or any other emotion, discovers itself to most advantage in the common intercourse of men, and these may be the model for imitation. A public speaker must, however, adopt that manner which is most natural to himself. His motions and gestures should exhibit that kind of expression which nature has dictated, for, unless this be the case, no study can prevent their appearing stiff and ungraceful. The study of action consists chiefly in guarding against awkward and disagreeable motions, and in learning to perform such as are natural to the speaker in the most graceful manner.

The parts of the body that are principally employed in oratorical action, are the *head*, the *face*, the *eyes*, the *hands*, and, in fact, the whole upper part of the body. The *head* should be, for the most part, erect, turning gently, sometimes on one side, and sometimes on the other, that the voice may be heard by the whole audience, and that a seeming attention may be paid to the several parts of it. Every passion uttered by the tongue should be painted in the *face*, and there is frequently more eloquence in a look, than any words can express. By this, an audience may be awed, incensed, softened, grieved, &c. according as it catches the fire of the speaker's passion from his countenance. The eyes should be carried from one part of the audience to another, with a modest and decent respect, which will tend to recal and fix their attention, and animate the speaker in his delivery. In the motions made with the *hands*, consists the principal part of gesture in speaking. The right hand should be more employed than the left, but very warm and animated emotions require the exercise of them both together. But whether a speaker gesticulates with one or with both hands, it is an important rule, that all his motions should be easy and unrestrained. Perpendicular movements, in a straight line up and down, which Shakespeare calls, "Sawing the air with the hand," are to be avoided. Oblique motions are the most pleasing and graceful. Sudden and rapid motions are rarely to be used. The posture of the *body* should be usually erect; not perpetually changing, nor always motionless. It should accompany the motion of the hands, head, and eyes, where they are directed to any particular part of the audience. A sawing motion of the whole body is not only very ungraceful, but tends to send the audience to sleep.

Every speaker should guard against all affectation, and the servile imitation of another person: his manner, as well as his discourse, should be his own. Whatever is native, though attended with defects, is likely to please, because it shows the man, and has the appearance of coming from the heart. To attain an extremely correct and graceful method of delivery, is not generally to be expected, but to acquire a forcible and persuasive manner, is within the power of almost any person who attempts to plead at the bar, or speak from the pulpit.

The following hints and rules, taken from Dr. Knox's Treatise on Liberal Education, may be found useful, not only to instructors of the young, but to others who are endeavouring to improve themselves in the art of elocution.

When a boy is so far advanced in the classics, as to be able to afford time and attention to other objects, he should enter on the art of speaking. Once a week, or oftener, he should rehearse, in the hearing of all the boys in the school, seated as auditors, some celebrated passage from Demosthenes, Plato, Homer, Cicero, Livy, Virgil, Milton, Shakespeare, Pope, or Addison. These original writers, or others of the same class, whose characters are established, are recommended, as being fully sufficient to form the taste, as well as to furnish matter for the practice of elocution in all its varieties: and it may be observed, that the learning by heart the most beautiful passages of the finest authors, is a very great collateral advantage attending the study of the art of speaking.

The first object is to habituate the scholar to speak slowly and distinctly, for boys are apt to fall into a careless and precipitate manner of articulating their words, and till this fault is removed, no improvement can be made in elegance or expression. A distinct enunciation in speaking, resembles perspicuity in writing. Without it, there can be no graceful elocution; as, without perspicuity, there can be no beauty of style. It may be necessary that many weeks, and even months, should be employed in obtaining this primary and important point, a slow and distinct utterance. This, however, is, of itself, a valuable attainment. An excellent method of introducing it, is the motion of an instructor's hand, resembling the beating of time in music, and directing the pauses of the learner, and the slower or quicker progress of his pronunciation. It is, likewise, very useful to insist, during the exercise, that every syllable, but especially the last, shall clearly, and almost separately, strike the ear, but without dwelling upon it; otherwise the slow and distinct manner will degenerate into the heavy and the sluggish. During this process, all monotony, and all disagreeable tones are to be carefully corrected.

When a slow and distinct utterance is obtained, and the

disagreeable tones corrected, the graces of elocution will claim the pupil's attention. Modesty is one of the most becoming graces of a young person. When he speaks in public, it is one of the finest rhetorical ornaments that can be used. The best writers on the subject of rhetoric, have prescribed the appearance of modesty even in men: but it must not be the result of affectation. The classical manner, as it may be denominated, must be found in every place attached to ancient learning; for there, if that kind of learning be properly understood, and its beauties felt, *taste* will prevail, and where that is the case, no mode of speaking can be encouraged which would not please an Attic audience.

Dr. Knox does not approve of young people making much use of action, because it is unbecoming if it be awkward, and it must be awkward if the subject spoken be not evidently felt by the speaker. "I have," says the Doctor, "been present on many public occasions when boys have spoken, and I have never yet observed above one or two who used action without exposing themselves to the derision of the audience." He is also averse from the practice of acting plays, and still more, from lads and young people attending spouting clubs and debating societies; and having rejected the forward and declamatory style, he explains what he means by the classical: that is, a clear and distinct, an emphatic and elegant utterance without affectation. To speak well, our author admits, depends more on corporal endowments, than almost any other accomplishment, for whatever learning and judgment the mind may have acquired, yet unless nature has formed the organs of speech in perfection, and given a considerable degree of bodily strength to the student, he will seldom become a distinguished speaker. Art and application will, however, assist him, and if they only enable him to speak slowly and distinctly, they will have done him much service.

"I will not," says Dr. Knox, "close this section without seriously advising all who are designed to fill that office which is instituted to instruct their fellow creatures in moral and religious truth, to pay great attention, in their youth, to the art of speaking. The neglect of it has brought the regularly educated professors of religion into contempt among the lower orders of the people; among those who, for want of other opportunities, stand most in need of instruction from the pulpit."

It must be farther observed, that, in the application of the Rules of Elocution to practice, in order to acquire a just and graceful elocution, it will be necessary to go through a regular course of exercises, beginning with such as are more easy, and proceeding, by degrees, to those that are more difficult. For this purpose we have divers helps, excellently adapted to the attainment of the object sought; among these, Dr. Enfield's "Speaker," and "Exercises in Elocution," take the lead. Next in order are the "Academical Speaker," and "Rhetorical Grammar," by Mr. John Walker, who was a master in this useful art. By the same author we have a small tract entitled, "The Melody of Speaking delineated, or Elocution taught like Music," &c.

These works will furnish the practitioner with an abundance of all kinds of examples in reading, but, at first, he should content himself with the most simple sentences; for unless he can read these, and easy narrative or didactic pieces, with distinct articulation, just emphasis, and proper modulation, it is impossible that he should do justice to the sublime descriptions of poetry, or the animated language of the passions.

CHAP. XVI.

ON THE METHOD OF STUDYING THE BELLES LETTRES.

Gregory's Letters—Blair's Lectures—Barrow's Lectures—Lord Kames's Elements of Criticism—Priestley's Lectures on Oratory and Criticism—Mason's Essays, &c. &c.

IN a work of limited extent, and which is to serve as a directory to the young on many, not to say the circle of sciences, it cannot be expected that we should be very full on any one subject. It is, however, presumed, that the foregoing chapters on the Belles Lettres, may be regarded as a concise introduction, or practical guide, to the arts of Composition and Criticism, which are the chief desiderata in polite learning. For those, however, who have imbibed a taste for English literature, our directions will not be deemed sufficiently extensive. If they have entered into, and feel the advantages likely to be derived from the pursuit, as described in the first chapter, which has been chiefly taken from the manuscript lectures of an elegant scholar, the late learned and excellent Dr. Kippis, they will be anxious to enlarge their acquaintance with a branch of knowledge, calculated at once to excite their interest, and yield the most solid instruction and improvement.

In recommending a plan of study on the Belles Lettres, we can do little more than refer the reader to those works, from which we ourselves have borrowed largely in the composition of this department of our work. One of the first books that we would put into the hands of a young person desirous of becoming acquainted with the general principles of polite literature, is the late Dr. George Gregory's "Letters on Literature, Taste, and Composition," which contain the result of various observations, made by a vigorous and cultivated mind, upon the different subjects under discussion.

Dr. Gregory commences his volumes with a philosophical but popular analysis of those principles of association, from which we derive the pleasure that is excited by the study of the fine arts. His remarks on this phenomenon of the mind, may be considered as illustrative of Dr. Stewart's speculations on the same point, to which we shall have occasion to refer. The doctor then endeavours to explain this principle, continuing his inquiry, by some judicious remarks on style, and the sources of fine composition. His letters on the Sublime, Pathetic, and Ludicrous, will amply repay a close attention: they are short, but full of interest and sound instruction. From these our author carries us to a more particular detail of the component parts of Eloquence, and an examination of the essentials of good writing. Under this branch of his subject he comes to the consideration of language, the perspicuity, purity, and harmony of sentences, and the graces of good composition. On these subjects, as well as on the different usages and figures of speech, we have conducted the reader to a certain distance; he will find them treated more at large by Dr. Gregory, and illustrated by a greater number of examples, than we had room to admit. He next advances to a more enlarged view of composition. The several methods of analysis and synthesis in a logical discourse, are well explained and appreciated: the different kinds of oratory, viz. that of the senate, the bar, and the pulpit, are neatly contrasted, and the rise and progress of eloquence are described with accuracy and spirit.

Dr. Gregory begins his second volume with a comparison

of the difficulties attending the perfect composition of an argumentative or oratorical discourse, with those which must be encountered by the historian. The narrative style he considers as the most difficult of attainment. His observations on this subject are so excellent and so practical, that we shall transcribe a part of them for the benefit of those who may not have an opportunity of perusing the work itself.

"Let any man of letters try to compose an argumentative, or even an oratorical discourse, and let him afterwards attempt a narrative, and he will soon find the latter by far the more difficult task. It is difficult to form and pursue a lucid order and arrangement; it is difficult, out of the number of circumstances which will crowd upon him, to select those only which are important and striking; to know where to be brief and where to be minute; to distinguish the lights and the shades; to see on what he ought to enlarge, and what he should cursorily pass over. It is exceedingly difficult to avoid a flat and monotonous tone; to give spirit, animation, and interest to a mere recital of facts; and that, when the writer composes not under the influence of passion, or the ardour of controversy, which in narrative is seldom the case. . . . .

"Perspicuity, it will be easily seen, is the first excellence of narrative. The impression must be clear and vivid. Whether the subject will admit of ornament or not, is a remote consideration, compared with this indispensable quality. On this account, the writer of even an extended history should take care to have a clear and comprehensive view of the subject in his mind, at least to a given period. He should see it as a picture or a drama before his eyes, previous to his beginning to compose. If he has this view of the subject before him, he will easily, if he has judgment and taste, distinguish the parts or circumstances which should be treated in detail, from those which should be transiently glanced at, or perhaps wholly omitted.

"To have a just and comprehensive view of his subject previously formed, (at least to a certain extent as to the order of time) will enable an author to write with vivacity, and to interest his readers, for he will describe within a shorter compass, and in a manner less dull and tedious than the person who transcribes every circumstance from a note book; and the fancy will have a more unbounded range, and be able to throw in more of ornament and eloquence.

"As in the style of narrative perspicuity is the first object, an author should be careful that every sentence may present a distinct image; for nothing confuses more than when several circumstances are blended or complicated one with another. Yet for the sake of harmony, and to avoid a monotonous tone, which is a very common vice of narration, the sentences must not be too short. . . . .

"The degree of ornament or figure to be employed, must depend, in a great measure, on the subject; but in general it is safer to attempt too little in the way of ornament than too much. Nothing tends more to confuse a narrative than a style too florid; though figurative language, sparingly and judiciously introduced, occasionally gives animation. The comparison is a figure too flat and formal to suit with narrative, and almost the only figure which may be freely employed is the metaphor. But even metaphors, when introduced, should be easy and natural, for recondite or remote allusions perplex the mind, and withdraw the attention from the subject. They must not be common-place neither, for nothing renders a style so frigid as common-place ornaments. But after all, the attentive and studious perusal of the best writers in this, as well as in every other department, will effect infinitely more than any abstract rules or observations whatever. Read carefully the most approved narrators; mark their manner of bringing events and circumstances before your view; observe their mode of connecting them; the compass and turn of their periods. You will see that there is nothing abrupt; nothing either defectively terminated, or violently or harshly introduced; or where there is a deviation from the thread or course of the story, the reader's mind is prepared by a short introduction or apology, so that the smoothness and simplicity of the narrative shall not be materially interrupted. As you will have to write in English, I would advise you to study the best models in your own language, for none has better writers of narrative. It will also be an improving exercise, if, after having read a long passage, and made yourself master of the facts, you close the book and try to narrate them yourself, when the comparison will shew you your own defects, and enable you to avoid them on a future occasion. For the grave kind of narration, examine the style of Robertson, Hume, Gibbon, Goldsmith,* and Dr. Hawkesworth's Voyages; for the lighter and more familiar kinds, the short narratives in the Spectator, especially those of Mr. Addison; some of a similar nature in the Rambler of Dr. Johnson; and the Adventurer of Dr. Hawkesworth, will afford you unexceptionable specimens."

The criticisms of Dr. Gregory on the ancient and modern Historians, from Herodotus to Gibbon; on the Annalists and Biographers of our own country, on the writers of Voyages and Travels, Fictitious Narrative, and Epistolary writing, are well adapted to inform the mind, strengthen the judgment, and improve the taste of young persons, and, as such, cannot be too strongly recommended to their attention. A brief but excellent account of poetry follows the subjects already noticed: its various descriptions are correctly classified; and the authors who have excelled in each, are ranked without prejudice or partiality, we conceive, according to their most legitimately acknowledged precedence.

If, therefore, a young person desirous of extending his knowledge in polite literature, be limited either in the time that he can expend in study, or in the means of possessing himself of a number of books, we have no scruple in recommending

* The History of England, in a series of Letters from a Nobleman to his Son, is an admirable specimen of historical language, sufficiently familiar, without any loss of dignity.

Dr. Gregory's Letters, as a work that will answer all common purposes.

Dr. Blair's Lectures on Rhetoric and Belles Lettres, well deserve a place in the library of the student in polite literature. They were originally published in two volumes, 4to. but have gone through a great number of editions in three volumes, 8vo. In recommending this work to the reader's attention, we need do little more than briefly enumerate the contents of the several volumes.

The first volume contains introductory dissertations on Taste, Genius, and Criticism:—on the sources of the pleasures of Taste, Sublimity, Beauty, Novelty, Imitation, and Description; and on the rise and progress of language and writing. In this part of the work, the principles of Universal Grammar are investigated, and these principles applied to the English tongue. From this, the author proceeds to style, which is treated of under the two heads of Perspicuity and Ornament. The *former* is considered, as it relates to the choice of single words and phrases; and under the *latter* are examined the origin and nature of figurative language.

In the second volume, the general characters of style are explained, and directions are given for forming a style. These are followed by critical analyses of the style of some papers of the Spectator, and of a passage from the writings of Swift, which abound with much useful criticism, and merit the attention of those who would understand the principles of good writing.

The author next treats of Eloquence, properly so called, or public speaking, in its different departments. In this part, the eloquence of the bar, that of the pulpit, and that of popular assemblies, are illustrated at considerable length, and will be extremely useful to those who are practically engaged in the learned professions. Dr. Blair has drawn with a masterly hand, the characters of several of the most distinguished English writers, viz. Swift, Tillotson, Addison, Shaftesbury and Bolingbroke. These in general are accurate and highly finished delineations. The predominant and characteristical manner of each author is happily seized on, and exhibited in striking colours. To illustrate Dr. Blair's manner, rather than to give proof of our assertions, we will transcribe his character of Lord Bolingbroke. He is speaking of the vehement style, which implies strength, but which is not inconsistent with simplicity. It is, he says, a glowing style, the language of a man whose imagination and passions are heated, and strongly affected by what he writes; who is therefore negligent of lesser graces, but pours himself forth with the rapidity and fullness of a torrent. It belongs to the higher kinds of oratory, and indeed is rather expected from a man who is speaking, than from one who is writing in his closet. The orations of Demosthenes furnish the full and perfect example of this species of style. Among English writers, the one who had most of this character, though mixed with several defects, is Lord Bolingbroke.

" Bolingbroke," he adds, " was formed by nature to be a factious leader; the demagogue of a popular assembly. Accordingly the style that runs through all his political writings, is that of one declaiming with heat, rather than writing with deliberation. He abounds with rhetorical figures; and pours forth with great impetuosity. He is copious to a fault; places the same thought before us in many different views, but generally with life and ardour. He is bold rather than correct; a torrent that flows strong but often muddy. His sentences are varied as to length and shortness; inclining, however, most to long periods, sometimes including parentheses, and frequently crowding and heaping a multitude of things upon one another, as naturally happens in the warmth of speaking. In the choice of words, there is great felicity and precision. In the exact construction of sentences, he is much inferior to Lord Shaftesbury, but greatly superior to him in life and ease."

In his third volume, Dr. Blair, after giving a comparative view of the merit of the ancients and moderns, and making some observations on the different styles of Historical, Philosophical and Epistolary writing, with remarks on Dialogue and Fictitious History, devotes himself entirely to Poetry, in which is included the Drama. This part of the work, which to many readers will appear most interesting, contains a critical examination of the most distinguished species of poetical compositions.

A work of similar import to that of Dr. Blair, is entitled "Lectures on Belles Lettres and Logic, by the late William Barron, professor of Belles Lettres and Logic in the University of St. Andrews" in two vols. 8vo. These lectures, as far as the Belles Lettres are concerned, treat: 1. Of the structure of language, and the properties of style. 2. Of spoken language, or eloquence, as proper for deliberative assemblies, courts of justice, and the pulpit. 3. Of written language, or the most eminent kinds of composition in prose and verse. The reader, if he have an opportunity of comparing the lectures of Mr. Barron with those of Dr. Blair, will find a great similarity in the subjects discussed; in those of Mr. Barron, the arrangement is often more clear and lucid, but the author is evidently indebted to his predecessor for much of what is excellent and valuable in his work, and unfortunately there is no acknowledgment made of the obligations due to him. In justification of Mr. Barron, it must be observed, that the lectures were published after his death, and before they had undergone his own revision, and preparation for the press. The omission complained of does not affect their value to the student; he is concerned only with the information which they are calculated to convey; and certainly Mr. Barron's Lectures may be studied with great advantage, either with or without the aid of other works on the same subject.

"Elements of Criticism," by Lord Kames, is a very valuable work connected with the study of Belles Lettres: it was published more than half a century ago, and maintains, at the present time, a high reputation among the learned. It was in truth the first considerable work on the subject of criticism in our language; and every subsequent writer, whether he acknowledge it or not, is greatly indebted to his Lordship for the number of examples which he collected, and for the value and profundity of his remarks and observations. He was well acquainted with the human mind, and applied his knowledge to the illustrations and investigation of the science which he undertook to establish on a solid foundation.

Lord Kames introduces his work with some curious observations concerning the impressions which we receive from the senses. He next traces the progress of our pleasures, among which the organic take the lead, though they are of short duration: when prolonged, he says, they lose their relish; when indulged to excess, they beget satiety and disgust. The pleasures of the eye and ear succeed, and prepare us for enjoying internal objects, where there cannot be an organic impression. He then proceeds to recommend the cultivation of those pleasures of the eye and ear especially, which require extraordinary culture, such as are inspired by poetry, painting, music, gardening and architecture. The principles of the fine arts, he observes, are evolved by studying the sensitive part of human nature, and by learning what objects are naturally agreeable, and what are naturally disagreeable. The man who aspires to be a critic in these arts, must pierce still deeper. He must clearly perceive what objects are lofty, what are low, what are proper or improper, what are manly, and what are mean or trivial. Hence a foundation for judging of taste, and for reasoning upon it. Where it is conformable to principles, we can pronounce with certainty that it is correct. Thus the fine arts, like morals, become a rational science, and like morals, may be cultivated to a high degree of refinement.

Manifold, says his lordship, are the advantages of criticism, when thus studied as a rational science. A thorough acquaintance with the principles of the fine arts redoubles the pleasure which we derive from them. To the man who resigns himself to feeling, without interposing any judgment, they become mere pastime, and will in time lose their power over the mind, and be neglected; but to those who deal in criticism, as a regular science, governed by just principles, and giving scope to judgment as well as to fancy, the fine arts are a favourite entertainment, and will in old age maintain that relish which they produce in the morning of life.

In the next place, a philosophic inquiry into the principles of the fine arts, inures the reflecting mind to the most enticing logic: the practice of reasoning upon subjects so agreeable, tends to a habit; and a habit strengthening the reasoning faculties, prepares the mind for entering into subjects more intricate and abstract. This branch of science, moreover, furnishes an inviting opportunity to exercise the judgment; we delight to reason upon subjects that are equally pleasant and familiar: we proceed gradually from the simpler to the more involved cases; and in a due course of discipline, custom, which improves all our faculties, bestows acuteness on that of reason, sufficient to unravel all the intricacies of philosophy.

Another advantage mentioned by our author, is, that the reasonings employed on the fine arts, are of the same kind with those which regulate our conduct. Rational criticism tends to improve the heart, no less than the understanding. It contributes to moderate the selfish affections, and is a strong antidote to the turbulence of passion. Delicacy of taste, obtained by rational criticism, tends likewise, his lordship assumes, to invigorate the social affections; and is, in fact, the great support of morality. "I insist upon it," says he, "with entire satisfaction, that no occupation attaches a man more to his duty, than that of cultivating a taste in the fine arts: a just relish of what is beautiful, proper, elegant and ornamental, is a fine preparation for the same just relish of these qualities in character and behaviour."

Having thus stated the advantages which Lord Kames considers as necessarily the result of the study recommended and enforced by the "Elements of Criticism," he goes on to unfold the plan of his work, and the method which he has taken to accomplish his object. "It is not," says he, "the author's intention to compose a regular treatise upon each of the fine arts; but only, in general, to exhibit their fundamental principles, drawn from human nature, the true source of criticism. The fine arts are intended to entertain us, by making pleasant impressions, and by that circumstance, are distinguished from the useful arts: but in order to make pleasant impressions, we ought to know what objects are naturally agreeable, and what naturally disagreeable. That subject is here attempted, as far as is necessary for unfolding the genuine principles of the fine arts; and the author assumes no merit from his performance, but that of evincing, perhaps more distinctly than hitherto has been done, that these principles, as well as every just rule of criticism, are founded upon the sensitive part of our nature. What the author hath discovered or collected upon that subject, he chooses to impart in the gay and agreeable form of criticism; imagining that this form will be more relished, and is, perhaps, no less instructive, than a regular and laboured disquisition. His plan is to ascend gradually to principles, from facts and experiments; instead of beginning with the former, handled abstractedly, and descending to the latter. But, though criticism is thus his only declared aim, he will not disown, that all along it has been his view to explain the nature of man, considered as a sensitive being, capable of pleasure or pain; and, though he flatters himself with having made some progress in that important science, he is, however, too sensible of its extent and difficulty, to undertake it professedly, or to avow it as the chief purpose of his present work."

We have been thus particular in describing Lord Kames's work, it being, as we have observed, the foundation on which the others have been built: it is not, however, to be taken as a first book on the subject, if the student has access to any of those which have been before mentioned. The "Elements of Criticism," being more philosophical, and less practical, than the works either of Gregory, Blair, or Barron, but, nevertheless, it is such as cannot fail of affording to the diligent and attentive student, much valuable knowledge in the fundamental principles of polite literature.

Dr. Priestley's Lectures on Oratory and Criticism, published in 1777, in 4to., will be found exceedingly useful in conjunction with the "Elements of Criticism," or as a supplement to the Belles Lettres department of this work, or the other elementary treatises which we have noticed. The Doctor brought forward his work, avowedly with a view to illustrate the doctrine of the association of ideas, to which there is a constant reference through the whole of it, in order to explain facts, relating to the influence of oratory, and the striking effect of excellence in composition, upon the genuine principles of human nature. The Doctor farther observes, that at the time when he published this volume, the most extensive work on the subject of criticism, was that of Lord Kames, "to whom," says he, "I am indebted for a very great number of my examples, especially those from the dramatic writers, and sometimes for the observations too; but with respect to this subject, on which so many able men have written, it is hardly possible to say to whom we are ultimately obliged for any very valuable remark."

Dr. Priestley likewise acknowledges his obligations to Dr. Ward's Lectures on Oratory, in two volumes 8vo., which we also recommend to such of our readers, into whose hands they may chance to fall. To these we must add, "Essays on Poetical and Prosaic numbers:"—"On the Power and Harmony of Prosaic Numbers;" and "On Elocution," by the late Rev. John Mason; and the article Poetry in Dr. Gregory's Cyclopedia: to all which we ourselves have been indebted. Dr. Crombie's work, already referred to in the chapter on Grammar; the rules for style, by Mr. Lindley Murray, and his Exercises; Mr. Irving's "Elements of English Composition;" and still more, Mr. Rippingham's "Rules for English Composition," will be found useful in the practice of the art, of which we are now treating.

If the youth, who is desirous of improvement in composition, be acquainted with the Latin or French, or any other language than his own, he cannot do better than occasionally translate passages from a classical author, into English, and when he has done his best, if he compare them with an existing translation, he will perceive in what his own defects consist, and be able to correct them. In this view, he might take Cicero's treatise De Amicitia, or De Senectute, and compare his own efforts with the version of Mr. Melmoth.

Another useful method will be, to read, or to hear read, narratives, or other compositions, in various styles, and then write down what is remembered, in the student's own language; and at first, without much regard to any thing except correctness of thought. Writing down at home recollections of sermons that are heard, without attempting to remember the preacher's expressions, and occasionally allowing the mind to follow its own train of ideas, has been recommended by persons who have themselves benefitted by the practice.

With regard to original compositions, which must not be omitted, the youth should, previously to his taking up his pen, fix in his mind distinctly what object he has in view, what subject he means to discuss, what fact he intends to illustrate, what moral he wishes to inforce, or what circumstances he has to narrate. When he has made up his mind on this, he will next consider the several ways by which his object may be attained, and having determined upon what appears to him the best, let him patiently pursue it without deviation. In his first essays, he will probably be short; but modes of amplification will, after some practice, readily occur. All he should chiefly regard in his earlier attempts, is correctness in the structure of his sentences; and the bearing of his argument to the business in hand. Young persons are often defective in breaking down their thoughts into sentences, but on-this we have already treated at large. To sit in judgment on their own compositions, when they have not the assistance of a guide, they will do well to lay aside for a few days what they have composed, and then examine them by such rules of criticism as they may be masters of. Of one thing they may be certain, if they do not themselves understand what they have written, other people cannot. Learning to correct, and not sparing their own compositions, are very important points, and cannot be recommended too strongly.

Schemes have been given by Walker and others for theme-writing, but we feel strong doubts as to the propriety of shackling the minds of young people with those kinds of forms. If they attempt to write on a subject of imagination, let the imagination have fair and full play for the exercise of its powers: no candid friend will throw cold water upon the rudest essays. In matters of reasoning, they should digest their plan, and minute down their leading divisions.

To conclude, young people will acquire a just taste for composition, by the frequent perusal of those moral Essays, which periodically appeared during the last century, and which have been collected into volumes, and are generally known under the denomination of British Classics. Such are the Spectator, the Rambler, the Guardian, Adventurer, &c. These will enrich the mind with a variety of choice sentiments, and will inspire the reader not only with a love of what is excellent, but with a readiness to imitate it. "Whoever wishes," says Dr. Johnson, "to attain an English style, familiar but not coarse, and elegant but not ostentatious, must give his days and nights to the volumes of Addison."

CHAP XVII.

ON HISTORY.

Utility, pleasures, and advantages attendant on the study of History; illustrated by Bp. Burnet—Cicero—Dionysius. Study of History favourable to freedom—to the attainment of practical experience—to a just dependance on a superintending providence—Sources of History; oral tradition—poetry—public festivals—erection of pillars—monumental inscriptions—existing laws—records of courts of justice—archives of the state—public treaties—manifestoes—negociations—progress of statistical science—family history.

THE study of History is universally popular. It is equally attractive to the unreflecting and to the philosophical mind. The former it interests by the agitation and stimulus of novelty—the latter by the usefulness of the deductions which may be drawn from the facts which it records. By some philosophers, who have affected a more than ordinary degree of penetration, or at least of research, into the constitution of the human mind, this general attachment to the study of History has been ascribed to the principle of self-love.* The utility of these refined speculations may be called into question: they are generally founded on visionary notions, and are almost uniformly unsatisfactory in their results. In this instance how-

* See the commencement of Bolingbroke's second Letter on the study of History.

ever, the metaphysician admits the fact of the high gratification which is derived from historical inquiries. This fact is indeed so universally acknowledged, that in the public estimation, a person, who is not tolerably well versed in historical knowledge, is precluded from a copious source of amusement, as well as lamentably deficient in the requisites of a liberal education. An individual of this description is incapable of entering upon the most frequent and the most common topics of enlightened converse. He cannot ever comprehend the nature, or discuss the tendency, of passing events. It has been well observed, by an ancient author, "*nescire quid acciderit antequam natus sis, est semper puerum esse.*"

Were the study of History considered in no other light than as an innocent and elegant amusement, it would be in no small degree commendable. Whatever enables man to beguile the weariness of the journey of life, without debasing the mind, or inflaming the passions, produces an accession to human felicity, and is proportionally valuable.

In this point of view, History, when considered merely as a source of amusement, is infinitely preferable to novels and romances, the perusal of which too frequently debilitates the intellect by inflaming the imagination, and insensibly corrupts the heart by the infusion of a most dangerous species of moral poison.

But the study of History is adapted to purposes of a higher and a more noble nature. It is calculated to enlighten the judgment upon those subjects which have a direct bearing not only upon individual utility and comfort, but also upon the welfare of the community at large. It leads to a knowledge of man in his social relations. It exhibits the various operation of different systems of polity upon human happiness. It points out the rocks and quicksands upon which states and empires have suffered shipwreck. It speaks with a warning voice to the oppressor, and infuses consolation and courage into the oppressed. Upon the high principle of religious motives, virtue has been roused to exertion, or has been strengthened to the endurance of remediless wrong, by a belief in a future state. Where this principle has been unfortunately wanting, hope has fondly anticipated, as the reward of illustrious deeds, the verdict of history.

Who is not affected by the glowing terms in which Cicero, after having saved the Roman republic from the treasonable pests of Catiline, intimates that he looks forward for his reward to the honour in which he should be held by posterity. "Quibus pro tantis rebus, Quirites, nullum ego à vobis præmium virtutis, nullum insigne honoris, nullum monumentum laudis postulo, præterquam hujus diei memoriam sempiternam. In animis ego vestris omnes triumphos meos, omnia ornamenta honoris, monumenta gloriæ, laudis insignia condi et collocari volo. Nihil me mutum potest delectare, nihil tacitum, nihil denique hujusmodi quod etiam minus digni assequi possint. Memoriâ vestrâ, Quirites, nostræ res alentur, sermonibus crescent, literarum monumentis inveterascent et corroborabuntur: eandemque diem intelligo, quam spero æternam fore, et ad salutem urbis, et ad memoriam consulatûs mei propagatam."—*In L. Catil. Orat.* III. *sub finem.*

In the season of adversity, Hope has looked forward with confidence to the period when the dazzling glare of spurious glory shall be absorbed in the superior brightness of the rays of truth; and when the historic Muse, pointing to the issues of things, and to the unfolding of the great drama of politics, shall vindicate the claims of justice; shall exhibit delinquency in its true colours, and shall bestow on integrity its due reward.*

In the transactions of life, it unfortunately happens that corruption and depravity are not discountenanced to that degree which reason and a regard to the public good require. Nay, they are too frequently hailed by the sycophancy of flatterers

* Tacitus in the third book of his Annals, thus tersely states his opinion as to this province of History, "Præcipuum munus Annalium reor, ne virtutes sileantur, utque pravis dictis factisque ex posteritate et infamiâ metus sit."

with obsequious approbation, and with high applause. They, that are "worn and hackneyed in the ways of men," affect to treat with scorn the dictates of political integrity. They despise the admonitions of those who wish to inculcate the doctrine, that the laws of justice cannot, even in political transactions and relations, be violated with impunity.—They hold up to the ridicule of the thoughtless and the profligate, those who maintain that it is the duty of every individual possessed of any degree of influence in the conduct or in the control of public affairs, to consult, above all things, for the welfare of his country, by devoting his talents from the purest and most disinterested motives to the promotion of the general good. To the ingenuous youth an attentive perusal of the pages of history may be properly recommended, as furnishing an antidote against the mischief which is likely to be occasioned by the selfish and heart-chilling maxims of these pernicious teachers. There he will see a striking exemplification of the fatal consequences of error and prejudice, of folly and vice. Then will he behold the deceiver entangled in the toils which he had laid for others, and the vindictive and the violent hurried to destruction by their own ungovernable impetuosity. There too he will find recorded the actions and the sayings of patriots of high principle; and by imbibing a sense of the dignity of their characters, he will be incited to an emulation of their virtues.

It may perhaps with truth be asserted, that few individuals ever intermixed in practical politics with purer views than Bishop Burnet. That celebrated author, towards the conclusion of the History of his own Times, when speaking of the degeneracy of the age in which he lived, intimates in the following terms, his opinion of the evil consequences resulting to those who occupied the higher stations in society, from the neglect of historical studies:—"Men, who have no principles, cannot be steady; now the greater part of the capital gentry seem to return again to a love of tyranny, provided they may be the under-tyrants themselves; and they seem to be even uneasy with a court, when it will not be as much a court as they would have it. This is a folly of so particular a nature, that really it wants a name. It is natural for poor men who have little to lose and much to hope for, to become the instruments of slavery; but it is an extravagance peculiar to an age, to see rich men grow as it were in love with slavery and arbitrary power. *The root of all this is, that our gentry are not in time possessed with a true measure of solid knowledge and sound religion, with a love to their country, a hatred of tyranny, and a zeal for liberty. Plutarch's lives, with the Greek and Roman history, ought to be early put in their hands; they ought to be acquainted with all history, more particularly that of our own nation; which they should not read in abridgments, but in the fullest and most copious collectors of it, that they may see to the bottom what is our constitution, and what are our laws; what are the methods bad princes have taken to enslave us, and by what conduct we have been preserved. Gentlemen ought to observe these things, and to entertain one another often upon these subjects, to raise in themselves and to spread around them to all others a noble ardour for law and liberty.*"*

Nor let it be imagined, that remarks such as these, though just in themselves are applicable only to the favoured few who sit at the helm of the state, and direct the course of public affairs. It may at least be safely asserted, that in a country which enjoys so great a portion of civil liberty as happily falls to the lot of the inhabitants of the British empire, almost every order of the community has its influence upon the mea-

* It was not merely with a view of gratifying the ear of his reader with the jingle of alliteration, that the good Bishop in this passage thus associated the terms "law and liberty."—He was well aware that the ideas represented by these terms can never be disunited—that as liberty can never be reckoned secure unless it be fenced and guarded by legal provisions—so the exercise of true liberty consists, not in the indulgence of a capricious will, but in a course of action which is sanctioned by law.

sures of the legislative and of the executive powers; and that therefore, upon the principles of Bishop Burnet, a knowledge of History should be diffused amongst our countrymen to as wide an extent as possible. For it is a self-evident proposition, that it is highly expedient that they who are called upon to deliberate on matters of the highest moment, should be possessed of the guide which is the most likely to lead them to a correct decision. And in the case in question, this guide is to be found in the study of History, which is calculated to form good citizens, and to ornament society with integrity. It was in this view that Cicero denominated History "*magistra vitæ*," the preceptress of the art of living well. To the same purpose, Dionysius Halicarnassus has, in a maxim which has been repeatedly quoted with high approbation, characterized History as "Philosophy teaching by examples." A familiar acquaintance with the history of their country was, in the best times of the Roman Republic, held to be essentially requisite to qualify ingenuous youth for the attainment of stations of dignity, power, and profit, in the administration of public affairs. Hence the bitterness of the sarcasm uttered by Marius, when he asserted, in the speech in which he claimed the chief command of the war against Jugurtha, that in his degenerate days, men of illustrious birth did not begin to read the History of their country till they were elevated to the highest office of the state—that is, as he said "they first obtained the employment, and then bethought themselves of the qualifications necessary for the proper discharge of it."

Political Freedom indeed gives additional efficacy; and imparts an additional value to individual virtue, and consequently to those lessons of virtue which are to be learned by the study of History. This study, when prosecuted under propitious circumstances, produces that expansion of mind which is incompatible with the benumbing and debasing condition of slavery. If a modern Greek reads the story of the gallant onset made by Thrasybulus upon the oppressors of his country, he reads it with the apathy of indifference, or with the sigh of despair:* but the example of Hampden is still fresh in the remembrance of Englishmen, to incite them to a determined and vigorous resistance against the first encroachments of arbitrary power.

It is the practical use which may be made of History, which constitutes one of its chief recommendations, as contrasted with the fabulousness of romance. " History, as Dr. Priestley well observes, " presents us with the same objects which we meet with in the business of life." Hence it affords to men of thoughtful mind, a happy subject for the exercise of the judgment, and an excellent means of acquiring a certain degree of experience, without incurring the hazards which are incident to an actual intercourse with the world at large. Hence too, it tends to mollify and to subdue the prejudices, which are too apt to cloud the intellect of those whose knowledge of past transactions is partial and confined. For as the connexions of events are in a manner infinite, the examining of them in their different relations at once gives strength to the understanding, and liberality to the principles of the free inquirer. It enables him to perceive, and duly to appreciate, what is valuable in the institutions of ancient times, and of foreign countries; and thus prepares him for a due estimate of the political regulations of his native land. To which may be added, that the accurate acquaintance with the springs of action, and with the consequences of political measures, which is to be gained by a discreet application of the general principles which are to be deduced from a knowledge of historical facts, will enable the student to form a correct judgment of the tendency of any course of political measures, which may happen to be the practical subject of immediate discussion in his own

* It should seem, however, that the remembrance of the glory of our ancestors, is not entirely extinct among the oppressed tribes, who now people the islands and the continent of Greece. When a celebrated modern traveller was sailing along the coast of the Troad, a Greek seaman, one of his boat's crew, pointing to a particular part of the shore, exclaimed " there lay *our* fleet." Under happy auspices, recollections of this nature may produce signal and salutary effects.

times. Thus may the study of History be regarded as promoting the improvement of society, by imparting to the existing generation, the lessons which are to be gathered from the experience of their predecessors.

Nor is it to be mentioned as a circumstance of minor importance, that the study of History tends to convince the man of reflecting mind of the superintendence of the divine will in the affairs of the world, and to inspire him with a cheerful acquiescence in the dispensations of the deity. When we behold the most important events brought about by the most seemingly insignificant causes—when we see the schemes of the intelligent and the prudent frustrated by circumstances, which they could not possibly have taken into their calculation of contingencies—when we find the devices of the powerful thwarted, and issuing in events, the very contrary to what they intended to bring about—and especially when we contemplate the most signal good produced from apprehended evil, we are irresistibly compelled to acknowledge the natural blindness and weakness of man. We are awed and humbled to submission, and we rejoice in the assurance that.

> There is a providence that shapes our ends,
> Rough-hew them as we will.

In this brief enumeration of the principal uses to be derived from the study of History, it is pre-supposed that historical facts are made the subjects of mature reflection. The reader who contents himself with merely storing his mind with a multiplicity of events, even though those events may be most accurately arranged in his memory, will derive little profit from a great expense of time and labour.

It seldom happens that persons who are remarkable for the extent of their memory in the recollection of dates and of other minutiæ, are distinguished by the solidity of their judgment. It is not, however, intended, by this observation, to depreciate the study of chronology, which is absolutely necessary to a thorough acquaintance with History, and a competent knowledge of which may, in early life, be acquired by an easy effort. One twentieth part of the time which is usually devoted in grammar-schools, and that very properly, to the instructing of pupils in the genders of Latin nouns, would be amply sufficient to enable them to store up in their memory all the chronological epochs, a knowledge of which is necessary or expedient. But after all, the chief object of a preceptor ought to be to teach his scholar to seize the points of importance in a historical narrative, and by the application of his reasoning powers, to judge of the tendencies of events.

Historical facts ought to be considered as materials for thinking. If properly estimated, they serve, not simply to amuse the imagination, but to exercise the nobler faculties of the human mind, to strengthen the understanding, and to amend the heart. To this topic may be justly applied the observation of President Montesquieu, "*Il ne s'agit de faire lire, mais de faire penser.*"

The origin of the sources of history is to be investigated by observing, in remote ages, the early progress of civil society. To say nothing of the pride of ambition, which engages human ingenuity, and employs it in transmitting to future times the memory of signal victories and of extensive conquests, in the rudest stages of society, internal arrangements are agreed upon by the members of infant communities; and treaties and covenants are entered into by independent tribes. It is obvious to the slightest consideration, that the desire entertained by the parties concerned, to secure the memory of these arrangements and covenants, would give rise to records, which may be considered as the main sources of history. In the imperfection of human knowledge, these records would, of necessity, be first retained and handed down by the medium of Oral Tradition. And as the genius of man in the ruder ages of society is naturally inclined to the cultivation of poetry; and as metrical compositions are best adapted to make a permanent impression upon the memory, it is highly probable that the first historical memorials assumed a poetical form. And this presumption is corroborated by numerous hints which occur in the Greek and Latin writers, and by observations which have been made upon the condition and the customs of uncivilized nations in modern times. In the poems of Homer, minstrels and heroes are represented as singing to the music of the harp, the deeds of mighty chieftains of old.* And in Ovalle's Historical Relation of Chili, we have the following curious account of the appearance of a traditionary historian of that country. "For proof of the care they take to keep the memory of remarkable passages, I must relate here what I learned from Father Diego Torres Bollo, a very extraordinary man both for holiness of life and skill in government. This great man, returning from Rome (whither he had been sent as procurator of the province of Peru) to found the province of Quito, he saw, in a place where four ways met, an Indian, who, to the sound of a drum, was singing a great many things all alone, in his own tongue; the father called one in his company, who understood it, and asked him, what that Indian meant by that action; who told the father that the Indian was, as it were, the register of that country, who, to keep up the memory of what had passed in it, from the deluge to that time, was bound every holiday to repeat it by the sound of a drum, and singing as he was then doing. He was, moreover, obliged to instruct others in the same way, that there might be a succession of men to do the same thing after he was gone."

Even in modern times, the remembrance of the minute circumstances of History, is kept alive in ballads and party poems, an extensive collection of which affords matter, not

* Thus, when Ulysses and Phœnix visited Achilles for the purpose of deprecating his wrath, they found him playing on his lyre:

Τῇ ὅγε θυμὸν ἔτερπεν ἄειδε, δ' ἄρα κλέα 'ανδρῶν—

and Tacitus, speaking of the German chieftain Arminius, says, (Annal. L. II. C. 88.) "septem et triginta annos vitæ, duodecim potentiæ explevit, caniturque adhuc barbaras apud gentes."

only of amusement, but also of accurate information, especially as to the feelings entertained by different classes of a community, on the occurrence of specific political events.

Another simple method of preserving the memory of past transactions, is the commemoration of them by the observance of stated days of public festivity, or humiliation. Thus the migration of the children of Israel from Egypt, is still celebrated amongst their descendants, by the festival of the Jewish Passover; and the generality of the British youth derive their earliest knowledge of two important events in the history of their country, from the custom of wearing oak branches on the 29th of May, and of lighting bon-fires on the 5th of November.

Another method of preserving the memory of illustrious personages, and of important events, apparently more effectual, but in reality less so than the former, is the erection of uninscribed pillars, and monuments of stone or earth. Whatever memorials of this kind have been erected before the invention of alphabetical characters, have stood in need of the aid of tradition to communicate a knowledge of the persons and the events which they were intended to celebrate. But the tradition may be lost, and that the more easily, in cousequence of the apparently greater durability of its substitute. In that case, the object of the memorial finishes. It is an awful admonition of the vanity of human pride, and at the same time, a signal instance of the superiority of written records over all other historical memorials, that though the pyramids of Egypt seem calculated to endure as long as the earth itself, the date of their construction, and the object of their erection, are absolutely unknown.

From these uninscribed monuments, the next step to the perpetuating of the remembrance of remarkable events would be registering them in monumental inscriptions, and on tables of brass, stone, or other durable materials, exposed to public view.* Hence the transition is, by just degrees, easy and

* Of this, an instance is afforded in the celebrated Arundelian marbles,

natural, to the most copious accumulation of materials for History, in the collecting and preserving written records or authentic accounts of public transactions, composed by the authority, and digested under the inspection, of persons holding the higher offices in the state. These would of necessity be at first but scanty, supplying little more than the dates and order of events, without any detail of the circumstances by which those events were accompanied, or of the causes from which they derived their origin. But they would encrease in number and importance with the progress of civilization; they would become more ample in proportion to the diffusion of literature; and being deposited in places of safe custody, they would constitute a rich mine of historic facts, authenticated by the best authority. To give a full enumeration of the various species, and to point out the peculiar utility of the different subdivisions of these records, would be an arduous task. It may on the present occasion suffice briefly to mention their principal classes.

Aud it is obvious to remark, that collections of the laws, ordinances and internal regulations, enacted and enforced in a state during any particular period of its history, are well calculated to give an accurate view of the circumstances and condition of its inhabitants at that period. They give to those who examine them with due attention, full intimation whether they who constitute the great mass of the community, were then exalted by liberty, or degraded by slavery; whether their natural rights were strictly guarded, or violently trampled upon. They also apprize the reader, what were the prevailing crimes and vices of the age in which they were passed, and what measure of punishment was deemed sufficient to expiate or to repress them. As records of taxation, and of fiscal regulations they furnish a view of a nation's resources and of the course and system of its commerce. The laws by which a country is

which exhibit the dates of the principal events of the Grecian history, till sixty years after the death of Alexander the Great; and the Capitoline marbles, which contain a list of the Roman Magistrates, and the most important occurrences in the Annals of the Roman Republic.

governed, reflect on the attentive mind an image of the genius of the people and their rulers. They supply the means of detecting the ignorance of barbarism, and mark the progress of refinement, and of mental culture. They exhibit distinct traces of the usurpations, or of the depression of monarchs, and of the power or the impotence of legislative bodies. In short, a reference to collections of the laws of a community is frequently necessary to correct the errors of mere chroniclers, and to rectify the false conceptions of political theorists; and, in all cases in which it can be made, tends to promote the prime object of the historian's researches, namely, the establishment of truth.

Many of the preceding observations may be applied to demonstrate the utility, which the historian may derive from the records of Courts of Law. These furnish a vast variety of historical facts most minutely investigated. In their pages may be traced the artful devices of injustice, and the amendment of judicial principles and practice. They serve as a warning against that worst species of tyranny; oppression under the forms of law—and exemplify the superior felicity enjoyed by nations, when the lives and liberties of their citizens are securely fenced by legal provisions against the encroachments of power.*

The public archives in which are preserved original grants of titles, estates, and immunities, contain documents which throw great light upon the internal history of states and kingdoms—nor will the student, who wishes fully to investigate many historical questions, refuse their due praise to heralds, genealogists, and antiquarians; whose labours, though frequently made the subjects of ridicule, are, nevertheless, on many occasions extremely useful to the historian.

The reports, made by the governors of distant provinces to

* It may be with truth affirmed that no one can form an adequate and correct idea of the gradual amendment effected in the institutions of our native country, and of the value of those constitutional principles, from which those amendments have been naturally derived, who has not read with attention the State Trials of England.

the seat of government in the mother country, detail the difficulties experienced in the infancy of colonization. They mark the gradual growth of emigrant communities. They afford important hints of warning and instruction. By their aid may be traced the rise and progress of ideas of independence, from the first impatient murmurs against restraint, to the bold and manly struggle to throw off the yoke of despotism.

The recording of treaties with foreign powers, is an obvious method of preserving the remembrance of the external relations of a country; and the dispatches of envoys and embassadors, especially the confidential communications made by diplomatic agents to the executive branches of their respective governments, lay open to view the most secret springs of political conduct. How clearly is the policy, or rather the impolicy, of our King Charles II. and of his unfortunate successor, to be traced in the official letters of Barillon, which have been laid before the public by Sir James Dalrymple and Mr. Fox; and what a striking picture do we behold of the difficulties incident to the administration of a free government, in the papers of Sir Robert Walpole and his associates in office, as published by Mr. Coxe in the appendix to his Life of Sir Robert Walpole. Though a degree of obscurity is thrown upon some parts of this work, in consequence of its author's not sufficiently opening the general history of the times of which he treats, it is, in the main, highly interesting and instructive; and, above all, it evinces, what is a quality of rare occurrence in a political biographer, a candid and unprejudiced mind. The appendix, which occupies ten volumes supplementary to the life, contains an abundance of documents which disclose the secret springs of many political transactions, and which will teach the young to regard with due scepticism the professions of public men; to which it may be added, that the collection of letters, of which the appendix principally consists, exhibits an interesting variety of style, rising in excellence through just degrees, from the clumsy coarseness of Chancellor Middleton, to the graceful ease of the profligate Bolingbroke.

It is impossible, in many cases, correctly to decide upon the merits or the demerits of commanders of fleets and armies, without an inspection of such returns of their forces, and of such details of their plans, and the reasons of their movements, as they are accustomed, from time to time, to submit to their superiors. A mere attention to dates will apprize the readers of gazettes, that General Washington, in the years 1775 and 1776, lay encamped before the town of Boston, at the head of a force far superior to that of the British, for the space of nine months, without striking a blow. The general's official correspondence with Congress, accounts for his seeming dilatoriness, by revealing the astonishing fact, that, during a great part of this time, he was so scantily provided with powder, that, had the British been aware of his situation, and marched to attack him, he would have been under the necessity of abandoning his position.*

Though the declarations and manifestoes which the rulers of states, in deference to public opinion, are in modern times accustomed to issue as a record of their mutual grievances, and as apologies for disturbing the general tranquillity by an appeal to arms, are usually drawn up with considerable artifice, and with an anxious desire to distort facts and to disguise the truth, to the discerning mind they not unfrequently afford a clue for the tracing of political mysteries; and are by no means to be neglected by him who would wish to be well versed in history.

The records which have been preserved of the instructions given to plenipotentiaries, and of the successful and the unsuccessful negociations which have, from time to time, taken place between belligerent powers for the restoration of peace, afford abundant matter of information and instruction to the student of History. They admit the reader, as it were, behind the curtain. They reveal the views and expectations of adverse powers; their sense of strength, or their consciousness of weakness; the real as well as the pretended foundation of

* See Washington's Official Letters, published in London in 1795, in two vols. octavo.

their demands, and the true as well as the alleged reason of their relinquishment of claims. They not unfrequently develope the whole system of the policy of a state, and while they afford specimens of the mutual exercise of consummate dissimulation, they may be classed among the most valuable documents which can be submitted to the examination of an historian.

Of no less value are all those records which afford authentic materials for statistical science; namely, accurate accounts of the population of different countries at several periods—of their revenues—their commerce, their naval, military, and religious establishments—of their civil constitution, and the condition of the various classes into which their inhabitants are subdivided.

In addition to the information which is to be derived from these public documents, much light is frequently thrown on national transactions by the papers of individuals. The management of state affairs has been well denominated "a craft." It is esteemed one of the chief requisites of a politician, to be able to put a fair seeming upon the schemes in which he is engaged, and he frequently adopts the most skilful artifices to disguise the motives of his actions, and to conceal from observation his ulterior views and designs. These, however, he, in all probability, reveals, either to his superiors and employers, or to his confidential friends. When communications of this kind come to light, they obviously tend to explain what is obscure in the conduct of political affairs, and to give a full view of the truth. Of these repositories of private confidence, the diligent and faithful historical inquirer will be anxious to avail himself. In many points, the orations of Cicero exhibit the outward appearance of public transactions in which that true lover of his country was engaged; but the real nature, quality, and purpose of some of the most important of these transactions, are clearly to be understood only by the perusal of his Epistles, in many of which he appears to have opened to his friends his most secret thoughts.

Tacitus, in the compiling, or rather in the composition of his Annals, consulted not only the public records of the times of which he treated, but also the private memoirs of such senators as had taken an active part in the conduct and management of the affairs of the Roman empire.*

In this respect, the historian of modern times enjoys great advantages over the writer who endeavours minutely to investigate the events of ancient history. There exists a rich abundance of private memoirs and letters of such statesmen as have, in later days, directed the affairs of almost every country in Europe. These documents disclose the hidden causes of many public proceedings which cannot, without their aid, be thoroughly understood. They evince the occasional embarrassments of the rulers of nations, and display, in all their deformity, the mean artifices of political intrigue, and the interested manœuvres of the crafty and dishonest, who have abused the delegation of power. A careful perusal of their pages will abate the ardour of political idolatry, and prepare the free inquirer to investigate the truth with candour and impartiality.

The foregoing are the principal sources and repositories of historical materials. Others, no doubt, may be enumerated. The diligent and sagacious inquirer will glean facts from quarters apparently the most unpromising and barren. What is lost upon a careless or an ignorant reader, may dispense a ray of light to the man who applies the powers of an active mind to the investigation of historic truth. He who proposes to himself this as his object, will not, when occasion requires it, shrink with disgust from the toil of turning over heaps of rubbish in search of a single pearl. Thus the intelligent and industrious Gibbon, speaking of the works of Jerome, Augustine, and Chrysostom, observes: "the smallest part of these writings is of the historical kind; yet the treatises which

* Thus, in recording the proposal to assassinate Arminius, made to the Roman government by Adgandestrius, referring to his authorities, he says, "Reperio apud scriptores, senatoresque eorundem temporum."

seem the least to invite the curiosity of the reader, frequently conceal very useful hints or very valuable facts. The polemic who involves himself and his antagonists in a cloud of argumentation, sometimes relates the origin and progress of the heresy which he confutes; and the preacher who declaims against the luxury, describes the manners of the age, and seasonably introduces the mention of some public calamity, that he may ascribe it to the justice of offended heaven." Thus extensive is the field of investigation which lies open to the historian; thus various are the sources to which he must apply in search of materials from which he may deduce the thread of his narrative.

CHAP XVIII.

ANCIENT HISTORY.

First Historians mere Chroniclers—Characteristics of a good Historian—Ancient History, importance of—General Histories and Compendiums, Tursellin's—Le Clerc's—Sleidan's—Bossuet's—Rollin's—Millot's.—Particular Histories, Gillies' History of Greece—Hooke's Roman History—Gibbon.—Course of Ancient History described.

AS the Arts and Sciences, in general, attain to maturity by slow degrees, so the science of History, in particular, continued, for a lengthened period, in a state of infancy. The first historians of every country were mere chroniclers of events, the evidence of which rested on the uncertainty of tradition and hearsay; or which were in some degree, but in general slightly, investigated by inquiries made in the course of foreign and domestic travel. Those simple narratives which are to this day read with so much interest in the pages of Herodotus and Froissart, were the fruits of many a long and painful journey. It was in consequence of the personal, still more than of the epistolary intercourse, which, during the barbarism of the middle ages, the clergy of distant provinces and of remote countries maintained with each other, that the mass of true and false reports was collected, which, from the recesses of monastic libraries, shed a dim light upon the period which intervenes between the seventh and the fourteenth centuries of the Christian æra. For the monasteries were then the principal, or rather the only refuge of literature. Within their gloomy walls genius occasionally broke the trammels of superstition, and studious industry beguiled the dull uniformity of the endless round of religious exercises. There chronicles were compiled, transcribed, and deposited in a custody which was respected by the semi-barbarous chieftain, and even by the lawless freebooter. In many of these compositions the marvellous, as might be expected, frequently supersedes the probable; miracles and prodigies are more abundant than the incidents of common life, and truth is obscured by fable. The traditionary errors thus recorded, for some time obtained implicit belief, and were handed down, by compiler after compiler, to the credulity of successive generations. But as knowledge was improved and extended, the scope of the historian was enlarged; his judgment became more discriminating, and his taste more fastidious. He rejected the fabulous, the uninteresting, and the trifling matter which he found in the writings of his precursors, or cited it only as a characteristic of the credulity of the age in which it was collected. He fixed his principal attention upon topics of inquiry, the discussion of which blended the entertaining with the useful. By just degrees his character was matured; till, by applying to historical investigations the principles of sound philosophy, he rose from the rank of a mere narrator to that of a guide in morals, and an instructor in politics.

The spirit of philosophical inquiry, is, indeed, absolutely necessary to enable the student to reap the full advantage which may be derived from historical researches. If destitute of the power of discrimination, he is liable to waste his time and to be led into error, by listening to the inconsistencies and the improbabilities of fiction; if devoid of the faculty of deducing useful consequences, the utmost extent of accomplishment to which he may be expected to attain, will be the making his memory a depository of barren incidents. To distinguish probability from improbability, to separate truth from falsehood in the undigested mass of the obscure records of ancient times, or amidst the misrepresentations of party zeal and factious malignity in more modern periods, requires the exercise of consummate sagacity. Voltaire has justly observed, that, in order to be qualified to seize the proper objects of history, a man must not be acquainted with books alone. He must have a minute knowledge of the human heart, and must be endowed with sufficient skill to enable him to analyze the prejudices and the passions of men. A reader of this description will give due weight to circumstances and situations. He will not, for instance, estimate the character of a despot by the panegyric of a courtier; and if a prince has resisted the claims of ecclesiastical encroachment, and restrained the power of the clergy, he will not pass sentence of condemnation on him, merely because his reputation happens to be vilified in the writings of a monk.

In order to complete the character of an Historian, to this soundness of the intellect should be added a strict integrity of principle and a feeling heart. His standard of moral and political excellence must be fixed at an elevated point. He must be endued with a sense of dignity, which will lead him to disdain to become the convenient apologist of folly or of vice. He must entertain a strong dislike of every species of injustice, and he ought to be armed with a boldness of spirit, which will prompt him, without regard to personal consequences, to represent the actions of men in their true lineaments. At the same time it is his duty to cherish a spirit of candour, and to chastise and subdue all those party feelings, and sectarian prejudices, which, presenting facts through a deceitful medium, distort their forms, and display them in colours not their own. He must beware of indulging the partiality of favouritism—of lavishing upon some honoured hero praises to which he is not justly entitled, and of ascribing to him glories to which he has no claim.* He must also divest himself of that attachment to system, the consequence of a propensity to generalize ideas, which is too often mistaken for genuine philosophy. He must carefully guard himself against this error, which causes so many investigators of past transactions, to overlook circumstances which controvert their respective theories, and induce them to undervalue and suppress such facts, as appear to be in any point of apprehended importance inconsistent with their preconceived conceptions. He must eradicate from his mind those visionary notions, which have led some writers to behold in the midst of that historical darkness when nothing is distinctly visible, the perfect form of a free constitution.† Nor will he be actuated by the views which have induced others to dwell with satisfaction upon those incidents alone, in the annals of their forefathers which

* "Quis nescit primam esse historiæ legem, ne quid falsi dicere audeat, ne quid veri non audeat, ne qua suspicio gratiæ sit in scribendo, ne qua simultatis." Cicero de Oratore, Lib. II. C. 15.

† "Disciple jusqu'alors de l'estimable auteur des *Observations sur l'Histoire de France*, j'étois persuadé que la Nation, libre sous la première race et sous les premiers successeurs de Pepin, n'étoit tombée dans la servitude que par la foiblesse des derniers descendans de Charlemagne. Je me représentois un peuple heureux, ne dependant sous un monarque que des loix qu'il se donnoit lui-même, et que le souverain confirmait. Je savois que le vertueux abbé de Mably étoit incapable de vouloir tromper ses lecteurs, et je ne soupçonnois pas qu'il eût été trompé lui-même par le désir de voir la liberté dans des temps où les ténebres de l'histoire permettent à peine de rien voir distinctement. J'étois seulement étonné de ne pouvoir comprendre comment, en moins d'un demi-siecle, un peuple libre et législateur étoit tombé dans les fers, sans que l'histoire, à cette époque, nous ait conservé le souvenir d'aucune révolution violente. J'entrepris de lire nos vieilles formules et nos anciens capitulaires, non pour y chercher des armes contre l'opinion de l'abbé de Mably, qui étoit devenue la mienne, mais pour trouver de nouveaux appuis à cette opinion. Quelle fût ma surprise de ne voir dans ces siecles où il a placé le trône de la liberté qu'un peuple serf comme celui de la Russie, de la Livonie, de la Pologne; un peuple qu'on vendoit avec la terre qu'il rendoit féconde; de ne voir d'hommes libres que la foible population des conquérans et un petit nombre de Gaulois admis à l'hommage du Souverain," &c. See the Preface to M. Levesque's Histoire de France sous les Cinq Premiers Valois.

afford the plausible plea of precedent for the exercise of arbitrary power.*

The foregoing enumeration of the qualities of an Historian, may serve as a guide to those who enter upon historical inquiries, without a view of submitting the result of their investigations to the scrutiny of the public eye. In every department of knowledge, and in every circumstance of life, truth should be the object of the inquirer—and truth is to be found only by diligent research, and by an unprejudiced exercise of the reasoning powers which have been communicated to man, by his all-wise Creator. The author and the reader of History, ought to be directed by similar rules, in the same manner as an enlightened spectator judges of the merit of a specimen of art, by the principles which guide the hand of the skilful artist.

In a regular course of historical studies, our attention is in the first place directed to Ancient History. Though the importance of this branch of enquiry was, perhaps, in the age of pedantry too much magnified, it has of late, by some authors of no mean repute, been too much decried. The destiny of mighty states and empires, is surely in itself a legitimate subject of attentive examination. At whatever period of the world these states and empires may have existed, the tracing of the causes of their rise and of their decline, cannot fail to impart lessons of wholesome instruction; and as the natural constitution of man is the same in all ages, a due consideration of the events and characters of elder times, will tend to correct false estimates of things, and to establish moral and political principles, upon the solid basis of experience. The minute inquirer into the events of Ancient History will find, that they have a much more direct analogy to the transactions of modern times, than is generally imagined. To this, it may be added, that classical literature is so strictly connected with historical investigation, that whilst the original writers of

* This fault is, in some degree, chargeable to Hume's History of England.

Greece and Rome, retain the degree of importance which they at present hold in the education of an English gentleman, Ancient History will claim, and will usefully occupy, a reasonable portion of his time and attention.

As it is supposed, that the student of History enters upon this enquiry at an early period of life, it follows as a necessary consequence, that he ought to be directed to the perusal of such authors as are easy of comprehension, and at once clear and succinct in their style, and in the disposition and arrangement of their matter. In pursuing his historical studies, he will find it expedient to trace back the course which has been delineated, of the progress of historical composition. In this course *general histories* and *compendiums*, are the last in order. But these are the first books, to which the historical student will be referred; and in proportion as his knowledge increases and his judgment ripens, he will be encouraged to apply himself to the examination of the older chronicles and original documents, and to the discussion of disputed points in History. It has been well observed by Dr. Priestley, in his Lectures on History, that this method of beginning by compendiums, "is like sketching an entire outline, before any part of a picture is finished; and learning the grand divisions of the earth, before the geography of particular countries." The advantages of this method are indeed sufficiently obvious. It at once directs the attention of the youthful mind to those grand and striking events in the annals of states and empires, which have produced the most important effects in their respective destinies. It distinctly shows the bearing upon each other, of transactions which took place in successive epochs; and points out the reciprocal influence of the conduct of different countries upon their mutual welfare. For a judicious compendium follows the "*summa fastigia rerum.*" It dwells upon circumstances of primary importance, the conspicuous results of a multiplicity of minute operations. It avoids debatable points, or states in a short compass the decision which is the result of laborious investigation; and thus bringing to view nothing but what is in a manner palpable and plain, it is well calculated to arrest the attention, and to impress the memory of the youthful student.

A variety of general epitomes, embracing of course an abridgment of Ancient History, have been written in the Latin tongue. Of these the most celebrated are Tursellin's and Le Clerc's. The former was long made use of, as a text book in foreign universities. The custom, now almost universally adopted, of giving lectures in the vernacular tongue of the respective countries of Europe, has diminished the popularity of these Latin compends. Nevertheless, the two works above mentioned, together with Sleidan's "*Introductio ad Historiam*," or a brief account of the Babylonian, the Persian, the Macedonian, and the Roman Monarchies, are by no means undeserving of perusal.

Bossuet's Discours sur l'Histoire Universelle, which, as it was brought down only to the time of Charlemagne, may be considered, as in the main, an epitome of Ancient History; at its first appearance it attained a reputation, hardly warranted by its merits. It is indeed a very elegant, and even an eloquent performance. But the mind of its author was, unfortunately, not a little tainted with bigotry. Hence he too frequently restrains the excursions of inquiry, and is at the same time, uncharitable and credulous. To which may be added, that in presenting a chronological series of events, without their details, he frequently becomes dry and uninteresting.

The most complete, and at the same time, the most interesting compendium of Ancient History is that of Rollin. This work is compiled with scrupulous fidelity, from the best Greek and Latin historical writers. In style it is fluent and elegant; and it evinces in its narrative and in its reflections, the pious and upright views of its author. In consequence of the judicious interposition of detailed anecdotes of the principal characters of antiquity, it produces a kind of dramatic effect, which is well calculated to awaken curiosity, and to implant good principles in the juvenile mind. M. Rollin has not perhaps been sufficiently attentive to discriminate between the marvellous and the probable, in his recital of events—but as a genuine and entertaining abstract of the representations, made by the original historians of antiquity, his work has not hitherto been excelled.

The ancient History of the Abbé Millot, which constitutes the first part of his *Histoire Générale*, is more brief than that of Mons. Rollin. It is also composed with a more acute spirit of criticism. Its arrangement is judicious, and its diction is compact and terse. In pursuance of the principles laid down in his preface, the learned author seizes those topics of historical developement, which present the greatest portion of utility. He gives a bold, but faithful sketch of events and characters, and enriches his pages with such an admixture of philosophical observations, as may, without disgusting the reader, who is eager in the pursuit of incident, conduce to the formation of an early habit of reflection.

The historical works, both of Rollin and of Millot, may be read by the youthful student with improvement and pleasure.

If leisure is wanting, for so extended a course of the elements of Ancient History, the latter is, upon the whole, to be preferred to the former.

With regard to Greek history, we have in the English language, two works of considerable merit—the Histories of Gillies and of Mitford. These works stand paralleled nearly in the same manner, as those of Rollin and Millot. The former is the more popular, the latter the more learned. The former is fluent in style, the latter abrupt. By the perusal of the one, the reader is more amused than instructed—by the study of the other, he is more instructed than amused.

Our language is also enriched by two works, which comprehend the general history of the Roman state, from the period of its foundation to that of its extinction. Hooke's Roman history, from its earliest periods to the settlement of the empire under Octavius, is comprised in four volumes, quarto. Hooke was a gentleman of considerable erudition, and was intimately acquainted with the original historians, from whom he derived the materials of his own narrative. In the detail of facts, he is copious, accurate, and precise; and in stating the balance of evidence, he generally displays considerable critical acumen. His prejudices against Dr. Middleton, who had offended his feelings as a Roman Catholic, by his celebrated Letter from Rome, have perhaps induced him to give a certain colouring to facts, relative to the conduct of Cicero,* but on the whole, he is candid and impartial. If his style is not remarkable for its brilliancy, it is even in its tenor, clear and perspicuous. In consequence of its prolixity, his work is not known in proportion to its merits. But it may be safely recommended, as containing a rich repository of facts, collected with industry, and arranged with judgment.

A most important series of events, supplying the principal links of the chain which connects ancient and modern history, is presented to the view of the student in Gibbon's history of the Decline and Fall of the Roman Empire. The merits of this celebrated work, it is difficult to appreciate. It requires no common degree of scholarship, to be duly aware of the immense mass of materials, which, in the course of its composition, its author was obliged to study and to arrange. The minuteness of his references, is a circumstance deserving high commendation. His patience and the sagacity of his judgment in the investigation of facts, insure him immortal honour. His language is elevated and dignified; but his desire to vary his phrases, and to say common things in an uncommon way, frequently betrays him into affectation. The unremitting pomp of his periods becomes fatiguing to the ear; and in the midst of luxuriancy of diction his reader often sighs for the simplicity of Addison.† These remarks on

* On this account the student will do well to check, as it were, this portion of Mr. Hooke's narrative by the perusal of Middleton's Life of Cicero, a work of great labour, and, though the accuracy of some of Dr. M.'s occasional translations from Cicero's writings, has been questioned by the critical delicacy of the late Mr. Fox—a work of high authority.

† For a brief, but masterly criticism, on Mr. Gibbon's style, the reader may

the style of Gibbon are, it is presumed, properly introduced into a sketch of a course of study designed for the guidance of youth. "*Decipit exemplar vitris imitabile*"—and the gorgeous apparatus of ambitious ornament, is too apt to dazzle and mislead the juvenile scholar. At a very early period of his life, Gibbon gave indications of an active and inquisitive mind. He had scarcely assumed the *toga virilis*, when he began to study polemic divinity; and was soon bewildered in the mazes of the controversy between the Roman catholic and the Protestant churches. In consequence of his abjuring the Protestant faith, he was sent by his father to Switzerland, where he pursued his studies under the direction of a clergyman of Lausanne. Extremes often meet; and by a transition by no means unprecedented, he soon bounded over the limits that separate Popery and Infidelity. Nor were his new principles inactive. In his history of the "Decline and Fall," whilst he professes the utmost plenitude of belief, he aims an artful thrust at the system of Christianity, by attempting to account for its progress merely from the influence of natural causes, independently of its truth and divine original; and by covertly endeavouring to discredit the evidence of the miraculous powers delegated to the apostles. By the disingenuous manner in which he has insinuated his animadversions upon the Christian religion, he has deservedly incurred a serious impeachment of his character.* Had he openly attacked the evidence of the Christian faith, the great body of his readers would have been

be referred to the Preface to the late Professor Porson's Letters to Archdeacon Travis, on the severity of which the historian, in the Memoirs of his Life, remarks with exemplary good humour—"the sweetness of his praise is tempered by a reasonable mixture of acid."

* The integrity of Mr. Gibbon's principles on the subject of religion, may be duly appreciated by the perusal of the following extract from his private Memoirs. "Had I believed that the majority of English readers, were so fondly attached even to the name and shadow of Christianity; had I foreseen that the pious, the timid and the prudent would feel, or affect to feel, with such exquisite sensibility, I might perhaps have softened the two invidious chapters, *which would create many enemies and conciliate few friends*."

aware of the necessity of weighing his arguments, and deciding on their intrinsic worth. But in his celebrated xvth and xvith chapters of the Decline and Fall, he has so skilfully intermixed correct statements of facts with conclusions, or rather hints of conclusions, which are generally esteemed unwarrantable and mischievous, that it will be proper for every one who peruses his work, to read some of the answers that have been written to that portion of it, which is most strongly tinctured with Infidelity. Of these answers the ablest is that of Bishop Watson. Some very judicious remarks on this subject will also be found in the first part of the general conclusion of Priestley's "History of the Corruptions of Christianity."

After allowing for every deduction, however, Mr. Gibbon's History must be acknowledged to be one of the most correct and elaborate works, which grace the annals of English literature. It commences with a view of the policy which swayed the Roman cabinet in the time of Augustus. Rapidly passing on to the age of the Antonines A. D. 180, it then begins to assume the form of a history in detail, which is brought down to the period of the total extinction of the Roman Empire in the West; and is afterwards continued to the taking of Constantinople by the Turks, A. D. 1453, and concludes at the establishment of the Papal power in the city of Rome and the adjacent territory.

Whilst the generality of readers are obliged to content themselves with Epitomes of Ancient History, or with works which have been compiled from the most authentic writers of antiquity, the student who is so fortunately circumstanced as to enjoy a greater portion of leisure, will not limit himself to these means of information; but will apply himself to the original depositories of facts. In order to do this with the greatest prospect of advantage, he will find it expedient to pursue in his reading the regular order of time; for which purpose he may take as his guide, the following sketch of a course of Ancient History as abridged from Wheare's Lectures on History published by Bohun.

In this sketch of a course of History, it is taken for granted that, according to ancient and laudable custom, the pupil is at an early age initiated in a knowledge of the historical books of the Old Testament. Independently of their value in a religious point of view, the Jewish Scriptures deservedly claim the attention of the enquirer into the early state of the world. It has been well observed by a very competent judge, that "the truth of the history contained in the Hebrew Scriptures has never been invalidated by any monument of antiquity, that can stand the test of sober investigation."

He will then commence with Herodotus, the earliest historian extant next to the authors of the historical books of the Old Testament, and whose works include the history of the Lydians, Ionians, Lycians, Egyptians, Persians, Greeks and Macedonians, from the year 713, to the year 479 before the birth of Christ. By way of illustration of various circumstances related by Herodotus, it will be advisable for him to peruse the first, second, third and seventh books of Justin, and the seventh book of Xenophon's Cyropœdia.

In reading Herodotus, it is sometimes difficult to distinguish truth from fable. But fable is rejected from the valuable work of the philosophic Thucydides, whose introductory summary of the History of Greece, takes up the thread of narration where it was dropped by Herodotus; and who continues the Grecian annals to the twenty-first year of the Peloponnesian war. Additional light will be thrown upon this period, by the perusal of the eleventh and twelfth books of Diodorus Siculus—the fourth and fifth books of Justin, and the first book of Orosius.

The first and second books of Xenophon's History of Greece, complete the account of the Peloponnesian war, which was left imperfect by Thucydides. After these the student will read with no less pleasure than profit Xenophon's interesting story of the Expedition of Cyrus, and the retreat of the ten thousand. He will then resume the same elegant author's History of Greece, which brings down the annals of the Greeks and Persians to the battle of Mantinea, B. C. 363. The fourth and fifth books of Justin treat of the same events; as also the fourteenth and part of the fifteenth books of Diodorus Siculus, the continuation of whose work contains the history of Greece and Persia down to the commencement of the reign of Alexander the Great.

The history of Alexander has been written by Arrian, Quintus Curtius and Plutarch. After these authors may be read the eighteenth, nineteenth and twentieth books of Diodorus Siculus, which, together with the thirteenth, fourteenth and fifteenth books of Justin, contain the History of Greece from the year 323 before Christ to the year 301.

At this period, the course of historical narration may be traced from the sixteenth to the thirtieth books of Justin, and all that follow, till the two last, which complete the history of Greece till it mingles with that of Rome.

The early annals of Rome, are illustrated by Dionysius of Halicarnassus, the fragment of whose history which has been saved from the wreck of time, extends to the dissolution of the Decemvirate in the year 341 before Christ.

To this period also extend the three first books of Livy, whose tenth book brings the history of Rome to the year 292 before the Christian æra.

The work of Livy has unfortunately come to the hands of the moderns in a very mutilated and imperfect state. A chasm occurs between the tenth and twentieth books which may, however be, in some measure, filled up by the perusal of the first and second books of Polybius—the seventeenth, eighteenth, twenty-second and twenty-third books of Justin, and fourteen chapters of the fourth book of Orosius—the second tome of the annals of Zonaras, and Appian's Punic and Illyrian Wars. After Appian, may be read the remainder of Livy, from the twenty-first book to the end, which brings the Roman history to the year before Christ 166, and the Epitome of Florus, which carries it down nearly to the termination of the reign of Augustus.

The war of Jugurtha, and the conspiracy of Catiline, which happened respectively, 100, and 62, years before Christ, have been narrated with energetic conciseness by Sallust.

Many of the varied transactions, in which Julius Cæsar was engaged, are best illustrated by his celebrated commentaries, and the supplement to that work, compiled by Hirtius and others. The secret history of this important period will be most clearly understood, from the perusal of Cicero's Epistles; and great light will be thrown upon the whole of this extensive course of ancient history, by occasional references to the lives of illustrious Greeks and Romans, as recorded by Plutarch and Cornelius Nepos. The fragments of the history of Dio Cassius, which have survived the wreck of time, contain a detail, but not a very interesting one, of the events that took place between the period when Lucullus flourished, and the death of the Emperor Claudius. In combination with Dio Cassius, may be read with advantage the elegant Compendium of Velleius Paterculus.

The lives of the twelve Cæsars, written by Suetonius, will prepare the way for the study of the works of Tacitus, who may justly be denominated the chief of philosophical historians. On the times of servility, which succeeded the period in which he lived, a dim light is shed by the works of Aurelius Victor, Herodian, the six compilers, who are commonly known by the name of the Scriptores Romani, Eutropius, Zosimus, Zonarus, Jomandes, Ammianus Marcellinus, Procopius, Aguthias, Nicetas Acomiatus, Nicephorus Gregorus, and Joannes Cantacuzenus, which may be read in the order in which they are here detailed.

Procopius, Zonarus, &c. are distinguished by the appellation of the Byzantine historians; and their works relate the history of the Greek, or Eastern Empire, to the period of its destruction by the Turks. A collection of these writers, was, at various intervals of time, published in thirty-six magnificent volumes in folio, from the Louvre press. They were likewise reprinted at Venice, in the year 1729.

CHAP. XIX.

MODERN HISTORY.

Modern History—Voltaire's Essai sur les Mœurs, &c.—Hist. Moderne par Millot—Russell's Modern Europe—Gibbon—Gaillard's Histoire de Charlemagne—Berington's Lives of Abeillard, &c.—Abbé Sadé's Mémoires de Petrarque—Shepherd's Life of Poggio—L'Enfant—Roscoe's Lorenzo and Leo X.—Robertson's Charles V. and History of America—Watson's Philip II. and III.—Harte's Life of Gustavus Adolphus—Schiller's History of the thirty years' war—Voltaire's Louis XIV.—Sketch of English History: Rapin—Hume—Macaulay—Henry—Andrews—Robertson—Warrington—Original writers—General History of England—Bishop Burnet's History of the Reformation—Neal's History of the Puritans—M'Crie's Life of Knox.

A GOOD general epitome of Modern History, adapted to the use of young students, was a work long wanting to the republic of letters. The Modern Universal History is too voluminous, and its various portions are executed with very unequal degrees of merit. Voltaire's *Essai sur les Mœurs et l'Esprit des Nations*, is, as indeed its title imports, rather a commentary upon facts, the knowledge of which is pre-supposed, than a detail of the facts themselves. The *Histoire Moderne* of the Abbé Millot is judicious as far as it goes; but though it is sufficiently accurate and impartial, it is too much compressed for the extent and importance of the topics which it embraces. A more valuable compendium will be found in Russell's History of Modern Europe. This publication has, indeed, a high claim to notice. It is divided into two parts, the first embracing the period from the rise of modern kingdoms, to the peace of Westphalia in 1648; and the second comprehending the events which influenced the fate of Europe, from the peace of Westphalia to the peace of Paris in 1763. This is the grand outline of Mr. Russell's work. The subdivision is ingeniously effected by a series of letters, in which, with great labour and considerable sagacity, the principal transactions of the leading European States are concatenated with as rigid an adherence to chronological order, as was consistent with the mixed and fluctuating interests of these States. A third part, bringing the history down from the peace of Paris to the treaty of Amiens, in 1802, has been supplied by Dr. Coote, who has strictly adhered to the plan, and in a great degree imbibed the liberal spirit of his accomplished original.

As a repository of facts, methodically arranged, and diligently authenticated, Mr. Russell's history is a work of considerable utility; but to recommend it merely as the work of a faithful, or even of an elegant compiler, would be to deprive its author of the praise to which he is eminently entitled, for the admirable manner in which he has executed the higher offices of the historian. The settlement and changes, as well as the connexion and dependance of the different nations of Europe, are traced and illustrated by him, in a way which must make them familiar to almost the humblest capacity, and this very interesting part of the work has been mainly executed, not only by the limitation of the history to admitted facts; but from the additional light thrown back upon these facts, by the clear exposition which Mr. Russell has given of the consequences which resulted from them. By an adherence to this connexion, the true light and harmony of history are preserved. But such advantages, however striking, are not the only ones which serve to recommend this admired work. It occurred to the penetrating mind of Mr. Russell, that many events derived an air of importance merely from the period at which they occurred, or the personages, who happened to be engaged in them. Such events he has wisely passed over, in order to make room for those of a more permanent interest; and thus, without any real sacrifice, the labours of the student have been materially abridged, and what is of still more importance, his progress towards a thorough knowledge of history has been freed from those frequent interruptions, which usually embarrass the efforts of an ordinary mind.

This work is also enriched and illustrated by the substance of those various treaties, by which the destinies of the different nations of Europe have been so powerfully influenced. The progress of society, from the rise of modern kingdoms down to the present time, exhibiting the manners of the people in their rudest state and in their highest polish, is given at stated intervals, and with much ability and research. The advances made in taste and science, and the influence of religion in the usurpations of the ecclesiastical, at the expense of the civil power, are all developed in the period to which they belong, and as connected with the progress of war, politics, and legislation, exhibit in clear and prominent characters the intellectual and moral improvement, or rather the moral and intellectual changes of man.

The style of this work is at once familiar and elegant, and the reflections with which it abounds, are invariably made subservient to the sacred principle of public and private justice. The moral pre-eminence, and the political superiority of England, are strictly connected with the pure administration of her laws, and the correct exertion of her power; and it is no small recommendation of this History of Modern Europe, that it is evidently the chief object of its author, to inspire his youthful reader with a constitutional dependance upon the laws and institutions of his country, and upon them alone.

Modern History opens to the philosopher and the politician

a spacious field of inquiry. It is a most copious subject of study, the full and minute investigation of which, would occupy the whole of that time, which those who are the most fortunately circumstanced, are enabled to dedicate to learned leisure. It is, therefore, obviously impossible, in the narrow limits necessarily assigned to this essay, to enumerate even the principal works on this subject, which demand the attention of the historical student. It is hoped, however, that the following series of modern historical reading will be found amply to reward the diligence of those who may be disposed to enter upon the prosecution of it.

It being presumed that the great outlines of the events of modern history are distinctly impressed upon the mind by the diligent perusal of Russell's, or of some other compendium, it may be observed that the origin of the barbarous tribes, whose chiefs, at different periods making themselves masters of the various subdivisions of the Roman Empire, laid the foundations of the modern kingdoms of Europe, is minutely traced by Gibbon in the latter volumes of his Decline and Fall, and that so extensive is the range of this work, that it furnishes almost a complete history of Europe and Asia, to the commencement of the sixteenth century.

Much valuable information, relative to one of the most important of the early periods of modern history, is to be derived from the elegant *Histoire de Charlemagne*, published by Mons. Gaillard, in the year 1782, in four volumes, 12mo.

The general state of Europe in the eleventh century, is described in an animated manner by Berington, in the second edition of his History of the Lives of Abeillard and Heloisa. This book is, indeed, highly creditable to its author. It is composed from authentic materials, and conveys a very accurate idea of the characters of which it treats. Though Mr. Berington may be deemed too partial in ascribing the ambitious aims of Pope Gregory, to his ardent desire to effect a reformation in the manners of the age in which he lived, the remarks which he makes in other parts of his volume on the futility of the temporal claims of the pontifical see, evince, that, with whatever partiality he may regard the proceedings of that pontiff, it is a partiality to the man rather than to his dignity. His passing insinuations against the Protestants may be forgiven as a sacrifice necessary to deprecate the wrath likely to be excited in the bigottedly orthodox among the Roman Catholics, by the general strain of liberality which pervades this work.

The Abbé Sade's *Memoires sur la Vie du Francois Petrarque,* in three vols. 4to., is a work of extraordinary research; and the very circumstance which constitutes its chief fault as a biographical composition, renders it the more interesting and useful to the student of general history. Its author frequently, and indeed systematically, indulges himself in details of circumstances, with which his hero has little or no connexion; and has thus contrived to interweave into the memoirs of an anchoret, a minute and elaborate account of the events which took place in Italy, in France, and other parts of Europe, during the greater part of the fourteenth century. The style of the Abbé Sade, is too frequently flippant and affected, and the loves of Petrarch are almost uniformly dull and tiresome. But the rich fund of general information which is contained in these volumes, will make ample amends for the occasional tediousness which is apt to weary the patience of their reader.

A succinct narration of general history is also to be found in Shepherd's Life of Poggio Bracciolini, which work, in relating the origin of that famous ecclesiastical feud, the schism of the west, almost touches the period of Petrarch, and traces the course of the principal occurrences which took place in Italy and Europe in general, to somewhat beyond the middle of the fifteenth century.

An impartial and elaborate account of the progress, and termination of the above-mentioned schism, and of the disputes which took place between Pope Eugenius IV. and the representatives of the church, and which for some years disturbed the peace of Christendom, may be found in L'Enfant's Histories of the Councils of Constance and of Basil.

During the decline, and after the fall of the Roman empire, Europe was for a considerable period involved in the gloom of ignorance and superstition. This gloom first began to be dispelled in the time of Petrarch, by the study of the ancient classic writers. In proportion as an acquaintance with the works of these writers was disseminated, the human intellect was expanded. Considerable advances were made in knowledge at the commencement of the fifteenth century; before the termination of which, literature and the arts displayed a blaze of glory, under the auspices of a Tuscan merchant, Lorenzo de Medici, who became the founder of a family, the ramifications of which have, in process of time, been extended to the principal sovereignties of Europe.

The life of this illustrious patron of literature, by Mr. Roscoe, was published in two volumes, 4to. in 1795. Few works of modern times have acquired greater reputation than this elegant piece of biography. Introducing his subjects by a slight sketch of the life and character of Cosmo de Medici, who was born A. D. 1389, Mr. Roscoe proceeds to narrate the progress of Lorenzo's education, and traces his history through the various vicissitudes of fortune, to the period of his death, which took place A. D. 1492. As Lorenzo's political connexions were very extensive, his history embraces the principal occurrences which happened in the more civilized portions of Europe during his life. But Mr. Roscoe is particularly happy in the delineation of his hero, in the character of an encourager of literature and the arts. The intimate friendship which subsisted between Lorenzo and the most eminent scholars of his time, gives occasion to the introduction of masterly criticisms on the labours of a variety of scholars and artists of illustrious name. The purity of Mr. Roscoe's taste is evinced by the elegant simplicity of his style;

and his occasional translations of the poetical pieces with which his work is interspersed, may be quoted as specimens of highly finished versification.

The succeeding period of general History is ably illustrated by the same author in his Life of Leo X. When the subject of a biographical memoir has acted a conspicuous part in public life, his private history is so intermixed with the general course of historical events, that a reference to the one is absolutely necessary to the developement and explanation of the other. Hence Mr. Roscoe was not only authorized, but in a manner compelled, in the work in question, to enter at large into the state of Italy and of Europe, which had so much influence upon the fortune of Leo, and which was also in no small degree modified by the actions of that pontiff. Even when the power of the papal see had begun to decline, the personal character of an individual pope had considerable weight in political transactions; and it is well known that Leo X. in particular constantly interposed, and frequently with decisive effect, in the contests which took place during his pontificate, between the European powers. The causes and the progress of these contests therefore it was the duty of his biographer to investigate; and this task Mr. Roscoe has executed with a degree of diligence and impartiality which entitles him to high encomium. In the life of Leo, as in the life of his father Lorenzo, Mr. Roscoe has given a copious history of the progress of literature and the fine arts.

So extensive were the territories which fell by inheritance to Charles V. of Spain, and to the dominion of which he was called, by his election to the dignity of Emperor of Germany, that his history occupies a vast space, in the general history of Europe. In this subject the late Dr. Robertson found ample scope for the display of his talents. His History of the Life of the Emperor Charles V. is extended through four volumes; and comprehends a vast variety of interesting transactions. The first volume contains a view of the progress of society in Europe, from the subversion of the Roman Empire, to the beginning of the sixteenth century, embracing the several heads of Government, Laws, and Manners—Military establishments, and the political constitution of the principal states in Europe, at the commencement of the sixteenth century. By many critics this dissertation is regarded as the most valuable—certainly it is the most elaborate part of Dr. Robertson's work. It is illustrated and enriched by various notes, and by numerous references to authentic documents. The history of Charles V. comprehends the eventful period, which occurred between the years 1500 and 1559; and his biographer is naturally led to relate the revolution by which the free constitution of Spain was overturned—the rivalship between Charles and Francis I. king of France, on the subject of the imperial crown—the long and bloody wars which took place between those monarchs, and which for a lengthened period desolated the finest provinces of Italy—and, lastly, the rise and progress of the Reformation in Germany. A single glance at these topics, will convince the historical student of the great importance of this work, which is highly commendable as evincing the candour of its author, his patience in research, the luminousness of his arrangement, and the neatness and perspicuity of his style.

Dr. Robertson has also conferred a signal obligation on those, who are interested in tracing the changes which take place in human society and manners, by the account of the grand revolution, which took place in the system of European commerce, in consequence of the discoveries of Columbus, de Gama, and other navigators, which is contained in his History of America.

When Dr. Robertson dropped the thread of history, it was taken up by Dr. Watson. Though it cannot be said that the latter author follows his learned predecessor "*passibus æquis,*" yet he has performed his task with no common ability; and his history of the Reign of Philip II. King of Spain, occupies a distinguished rank in the extensive collections of English literature. It has been observed that those portions of time which have been adorned by virtues, present not any interesting materials for the labours of the historian. If the converse of this proposition be true—if history most strongly arrests the attention when it is the register of enormous crimes, Dr. Watson has been fortunate in the period which he has chosen for the subject of historic illustration. It is truly "*atrox præliis, opimum casibus.*" A large portion of the globe depended for its happiness or misery upon the character and conduct of Philip II. His connexion with this country, in consequence of his marriage with Mary, will interest the English reader in his destiny. His unrelenting bigotry against the Protestants, breaking out into acts of cruelty and oppression, intermixes with his personal history that of the reformed religion. The struggles of the inhabitants of the Netherlands and the United Provinces, to throw off his detested yoke, present a most awful and important crisis, and the reader is gratified by the narrative of the rise of the Dutch republic, whose constitution was cemented by the blood of its founders.

The History of Philip II. brings the course of events down to the year 1598.

The Life of Philip III. begun by Dr. Watson, and after his death finished by his executor, Dr. Thompson, presents us with an account of the fruitless efforts of the Spanish monarch, to subdue the Northern Netherlands, now known by the name of the United Provinces, and the establishment of the independence of the Batavian republic. The expulsion of the Moors from Spain, and the account of their manners and customs, form an interesting subject of historic narrative. It may be observed in general, that the political alliances and the wars of Philip II. and Philip III. involve the interests of so many states, that their history displays the general topics of the history of Europe, during the period of the lives of those monarchs, the latter of whom died in the year 1621.

Soon after this period, the royal authority was established in France, on the ruins of the aristocracy, and of the party of the Huguenots, by the transcendent abilities of Cardinal Richelieu. In consequence of this consolidation of domestic power, the French monarchy attained to a very considerable degree of influence in the transactions of Europe, and of course its history begins to occupy a large portion of the attention of the student. This history is narrated with his usual brilliancy and spirit, by Voltaire in the 175th and subsequent chapter of his "Essai sur les Mœurs et l' Esprit des Nations" which may be read with considerable profit, as well as with much amusement.

The origin and progress of the religious troubles which at this epoch laid waste the provinces of Germany, are related with more fidelity than elegance by Harte in his Life of Gustavus Adolphus. A more popular narrative of these interesting events is to be found in Schiller's history of the thirty years' war.

Voltaire's Life of Louis XIV. will conduct the reader to the period when, in consequence of the alliances formed by the English nation, with various continental powers, the history of the world is strictly connected with that of our native land.*

It is indeed advisable that during the whole course of reading as referring to Modern History, a steady eye should be directed to the History of England. To this, as to a central point, the historical enquiries of an English gentleman should habitually tend. "Nature" as Mr. Gibbon justly observes "has implanted in our breasts a lively impulse to extend the narrow span of our existence, by the knowledge of the events that have happened on the soil which we inhabit, of the characters

* In the foregoing detailed course of Modern History, such works have been industriously selected, as may serve to exhibit besides the ordinary transactions of states and chieftains, the progress of the human mind in literature and the arts. These topics are too often neglected by general historians. They however claim the attention of him who would wish to become well acquainted with our common fortune—and the reader of well disciplined feelings will undoubtedly be pleased occasionally to retire from the spectacle of fields of carnage, to the contemplation of the calm and tranquil pursuits of the poet or the philosopher.

and actions of those men, from whom our descent as individuals or as a people is probably derived.* The same laudable emulation will prompt us to review and to enrich our common treasure of national glory: and those who are best entitled to the esteem of posterity are the most inclined to celebrate the merits of their ancestors." It would be presumptuous to endeavour to give any additional weight to the suffrage of a writer so eminently well qualified to appreciate the relative value of the different departments of historical study. The following sketch of a course of English History, is therefore introduced without any farther preliminary remarks.

It is somewhat singular that the most elaborate, and perhaps the most faithful general History of England should have been composed by a foreigner, Rapin de Thoyras, a French refugee, who was obliged to quit his native country, in consequence of the revocation of the edict of Nantz. His voluminous work is of great authority on account of his per-

* If it be true, as has been frequently remarked, that nature is uniform in her operations, the foregoing observation of Mr. Gibbon is more oratorical than strictly correct. According to the testimony of the Missionary Proyart, there has existed at least one nation, the inhabitants of which entertained no will to "extend the narrow span of their existence" by a reference to the transactions. Speaking of the natives of Loango, the good father says, "They are endowed with a happy memory. The missionaries saw some, who, within a month, have repeated God's commandments, which they had heard only once recited in a public place. They make no use, however, of this faculty, for transmitting to future ages what passes among them that is memorable, assuming as a principle, that they should confine themselves to what is strictly necessary, as well for knowledge as for the wants of life; they all live, with regard to history, in that indifference which characterizes the inhabitants of our country places, who know no more of what passed in France under Lewis the Great, than under Julius Cæsar. If you ask them why they do not preserve the remembrance of what has been done by their fathers, they answer, that it signifies little to know how the dead have lived; the main point is, that the living should be honest people. According to the same principle, they keep no account of their age: it would be, say they, loading one's memory with an useless reckoning, since it does not hinder us from dying, and gives us no insight into the term of one's life." *Proyart's Hist. of Loango Chap.* viii.

petual references to original documents, and the ample quotations which he frequently makes from important state-papers, confer upon it additional value. He has so copiously detailed the matters which were agitated in the turbulent, but prudent parliaments of Charles I. as to give a clear view of the rise of those parties which to this day divide the people of England. On the dark and horrible transactions of the reign of Charles II. he perhaps throws as much light as it is now possible to obtain. In reference to this important period, he has stated historical difficulties with candour, and in discussing the merits and demerits of parties, he has weighed evidence with laudable scrupulosity. It may however be discerned that the bias of his affections inclines to the Whigs. But such is the authenticity of his materials, and so impartial are the general conduct and results of his investigations, that his history to this day deservedly maintains a considerable degree of popularity.

The continuation of Rapin's history, which bears the name of Tindal, his translator, but which it is now understood was in reality written by Dr. Birch, is copious to prolixity; but it gives a clear view of the intrigues of party, and of the parliamentary manœuvres which have in modern times taken place, of the violent and mortal contests of the barons of old.

Hume's History of England affords a singular instance of a literary production at first unjustly depreciated, and afterwards gradually winning its way to a station of high eminence in general estimation. On the appearance of that portion of his work which he first submitted to the public inspection, viz. the history of the House of Stuart, Mr. Hume was assailed, as he himself informs us "by an universal cry of reproach and disapprobation."

The leaders of the public opinion, were at that time strenuous supporters of the Whig principles, which justified the claim of King William III. and consequently of the Hanover family, to the throne of these realms, and they received with indignation references to ancient authorities and coloured statements of facts, which tended to controvert many of their favourite maxims. At the same time Mr. Hume's sceptical notions on the subject of religion, were well known to the literary public; and his reputation was attacked by an union of orthodox zeal and political enthusiasm. His constitutional apathy, however, prevented him from being discouraged; and he proceeded by degrees to enlarge his plan, till his History was completed in its present form, embracing the period from the Invasion of Julius Cæsar, to the Revolution in 1688. In process of time, this history has been generally acknowledged to be a standard work; and its merits are certainly very considerable. In his selection of topics, its author is judicious—in his investigation of facts, he is in the main accurate and precise—in his delineations of character, he evinces a deep insight into human nature. Calm and dispassionate consideration and impartial enquiry have, it has been observed, tended to confirm rather than to controvert those views of the progress of the British constitution, which for a time rendered him so unpopular as an historian. It is now generally agreed that the liberties of Englishmen are not to be staked upon precedent—we may therefore read with patience even an industriously ample record of the despotic maxims which regulated the conduct of certain of our ancient monarchs; and while improvements in our civil polity can be peaceably effected by the regular forms prescribed by the constitution, we may listen without vexation to the minutest detail of the tyranny of the Tudors. The chief defect of Mr. Hume is however a want of that feeling of sympathy with the general body of the community, which fosters in the mind of man the generous principles of freedom. He views with little or no indignation, the violence and cruelty of despotism; and records with frigid apathy the glorious struggles of the assertors of liberty. He can bestow a sigh upon the sufferings of men exalted in rank and endued with power; but for plebeian sorrows he has no pity.

The continuations of Hume's history by Smollet and Belsham, are rather the essence of gazettes and party pamphlets than specimens of genuine historical composition.

If any tory poison lurk in that portion of Hume's History, which treats of the dynasty of the house of Stuart, the antidote is to be found, in "The History of England, from the accession of James I. to the elevation of the House of Hanover, by Catherine Macaulay." This work exhibits the view in which the most interesting period of English history is contemplated by the stern spirit of a female republican. Mrs. Macaulay had studied with fixed attention the voluminous writings in which the principles of civil and religious polity were freely discussed by the industrious scholars, who dignified the annals of English literature during the reign of James, and of the first and second Charles. From these writers, she has imbibed those maxims, which, in the course of her history, she has steadily maintained as the standard of political excellence An inspection of her references, and an examination of the curious and interesting notes, which she has appended to her narrative, will afford ample proof, that in the investigation of facts, she has had recourse to the most genuine sources of information.

When the student has, by the perusal of the works of Rapin and Hume, obtained a clear notion of the general course of events in the English History, he may read with advantage Henry's History, originally published in six volumes, quarto. In this work, the several topics of historical information, at certain defined periods, are discussed in separate chapters. By this novel plan, the course of historical narrative is necessarily interrupted; but in the work in question, this fault is compensated by the exhibition of a mass of minute and particular information, collected with great research, and which throws a much clearer light upon the literature, arts, and manners of the several periods of our history, than is to be obtained from the perusal of works, composed with the usual arrangement.

The History of Great Britain, connected with the Chronology of Europe, by James Petit Andrews, F.A.S., is also a publication singular in its design, but of no inconsiderable utility. Of the plan of this work, the following account is given in the preface. "The history of England is meant to be concisely told, yet not so briefly as to have any material circumstances omitted. The corresponding page of general chronology, is extended on the same system to comprehend the annals of every European state, and only wanders into the other quarters of the globe, when tempted by circumstances closely connected with the interests of Europe. The notes are intended to contain events of an inferior class which although not foreign to the text, are yet not necessary to be intruded on those, who read only for solid information. To each book are added two Appendixes. The one tells such incidents as could not properly be thrown into the notes; relates the life of every distinguished British writer; includes a specimen of his works, if poetical; and thus becomes a chronicle of British literature. The other presents an analysis of the times and their manners, under the respective heads of Religion, Government," &c.

In the two volumes, which he lived to publish, Mr. Andrews executed with diligence and success what he thus undertook to perform; and it is to be lamented that his labours were diverted to other objects, and at length prematurely closed by his death, when he had arrived at the period of the accession of Edward VI.

The early history of Scotland, like that of most other nations, is obscured by fables, which are detailed with every grace of style, in the History of Buchanan. But whoever wishes to become acquainted with the more important periods of the Scottish Annals, will do well to peruse with attention, Robertson's History of Scotland, during the reigns of Queen Mary, and King James VI. till his accession to the crown of England; and Laing's History of Scotland, from the Union of the Crowns, on the accession of James VI. to the throne of

England, to the Union of the Kingdoms, under the reign of Queen Anne. These are standard works, and are executed in so able a manner, as at once to instruct the inquisitive mind, and to gratify refined taste.

No work has hitherto superseded Leland's History of Ireland, which traces in a masterly manner, the transactions which took place in that country, from the Invasion of Henry II. to the treaty of Limerick, in the reign of William III.

In the History of Wales, by the Rev. Wm. Warrington, the reader will find collected all the facts, which can throw light upon the government, manners, and final subjugation of a people, still strongly marked by distinctive characteristics and peculiar customs.

It seems to be the consequence of the operation of a great law of our nature, that the stream of History should become more mixed and polluted, in proportion as it flows farther from its source. Secondary historians are apt to view facts through peculiar media; and from various motives, to give an erroneous representation of their nature and bearings. To which it may be added, that events and circumstances, which to one man appear of little or no moment, are regarded by another as extremely important. Hence the student of English history who has leisure, industry, and opportunity to encounter the laborious undertaking, will ascend to the original writers of our annals, and diligently peruse the statements which they have handed down to posterity. Of these writers, a catalogue, accompanied with copious critical remarks, is given in Nicholson's English historical Library, of which the following abridgment, may at least serve to evince what copious materials serve to throw light, on almost every period of our annals.

The earliest document of English history, now known to be extant, is Gildas's Epistola de Excidio Britanniæ, or account of the devastation of Britain, by the Caledonians and the Saxons.

Next in order, occurs the Venerable Bede's Historiæ Ecclesiasticæ gentis Anglorum Libri tres, which, though professedly a history of the church, throws some light on the civil affairs of the period of which it treats.

Nennius, a monk who flourished in the year 830, composed several works, of which the only one remaining, is his Historia Britonum.

The laws of Howel Dha, will convey to the philosophical reader many suggestions, as to the state of society and manners in the tenth century, at which period they were promulgated.

The romances of Geoffrey of Monmouth, and the unimportant annals of Caradocus, the monk of Lancarvan, will scarcely repay the trouble of a perusal; but the reader will derive some interesting information, from the Saxon chronicle, and the Life of Alfred, commenced by Asserius Menevensis, and completed by some of his learned contemporaries.

Ethelward Patricius lived in the year 1090, and compiled a chronicle of the Saxon kings to the time of Edgar.

Verstegan's Restitution of decayed Intelligence in Antiquities, though by no means devoid of error, treats somewhat at large on the language, religion, manners, and government of the Anglo-Saxons.

It is not less true than surprising, that light is thrown upon the remote periods of English history, from the twilight of Iceland. Aras Frode in his history of that island, gives an account of the affairs of Denmark, Norway, and England. The Norwegian histories of Theodoric, and of Snorro Sturlesonius, are also said to touch upon the exploits of our Danish kings.

Saxo Grammaticus, Sweno Agonis, and Olaus Wormius in their respective works, take cursory notice of the History and Antiquities of England.

After the Conquest, Ingulphus, Abbot of Croyland, wrote a history of his convent, in which he incidentally narrates the general occurrences, which took took place in England, during the period of which he treats, which commences A. D. 626, and terminates A. D. 1089.

Marianus Scotus, a monk of Mentz, wrote a general history of Europe, in which he traces the English History to the year 1083.

Of the history of Marianus, much use was made by Florentius Bravonius, a monk of Worcester, who, however made considerable additions to his narrative of events. The work of Florentins, which is carried to the year 1119, was continued fifty years farther by one of his brother monks.

Eadmerus, a monk of Canterbury, wrote the history of William I. and II. and of Henry I. with great judgment and impartiality.

High encomiums have been justly bestowed on the work of William of Malmesbury, De Gestis Anglorum, which contains a view of the English history, from the first arrival of the Saxons in this country, to the end of the reign of King Stephen.

The historical works of Simeon Dunelmensis, of Ealred, Abbot of Rievaulx, and of Henry, Archdeacon of Huntingdon, though they throw some light on the annals of the twelfth century, are but of minor importance.

Gervase, a monk of Canterbury, wrote much at large upon the British History; but the only portion of his work which has survived to modern times, commences with the year 1112, and ends with the death of Richard I.

Roger de Hoveden, a contemporary with the two former historians, has traced our history to the fourth year of the reign of King John.

Ralph de Diceto, Dean of London, who is much praised by the illustrious Selden, wrote two historical treatises, the latter of which terminates with the early years of the reign of John.

Matthew Paris, a monk of St. Albans, was endued with a degree of intellect and integrity, far superior to what might have been expected from the age in which he lived, and the profession to which he was devoted. His Historia Major, as continued by Rischanger, contains the history of our kings, from the beginning of the reign of William I. to the conclusion of that of Henry III. Though the Chronicle of the same author purports to be merely an abridgment of the above-mentioned work, it in point of fact contains several particulars, which are not therein mentioned.

The chronicle of Melross, which is brought down to the year 1270, though it was compiled in Scotland, treats principally of the affairs of England.

The history of Thomas Wikes, canon regular of Osney, near Oxford, begins at the conquest, and ends at the death of Henry I.

The Polychronicon Temporum of Roger Cestrieus, traces our history from the time of the Romans to the year 1330.

From the chronicles of John Brompton, Walter Hemmingford, and Ralph Higden, some useful information may be gleaned.

Matthew of Westminster, a monk of the Benedictine order, compiled a history which ends at the year 1307, and was continued by Adam Merimuth to the year 1380.

The chronicle of Henry Knighton touches slightly on the Saxon period of our history, but treats more at large of the posterior events to the year 1395.

The most interesting, and at the same time the most accurate account of the wars of Edward III. and of the disorderly reign of his successor, Richard II. is to be found in the chronicles of Sir John Froissart.

Thomas Walsingham, a Benedictine monk of St. Albans, took up the thread of our history where it was dropped by Matthew Paris, and continued it to the reign of Henry V.

Of the disasters which befel the English in France, at the commencement of the reign of Henry VI. a particular account is given in the chronicles of Monstrelet.

William Caxton, who was a menial servant to Margaret, Duchess of Burgundy, sister to Edward IV. wrote a history entitled *Fructus Temporum*, in the latter portion of which he narrates interesting transactions, the truth of which, from the situation that he held in the family of the Duchess, he had good means of ascertaining.

In the sixteenth century, Robert Fabian, a merchant of London, wrote his *Historiarum Concordantiæ*, which is held in particular esteem, on account of the minuteness with which he gives the local history of the Metropolis.

Polydore Virgil's history supplies a chasm of almost seventy years in our annals, including particularly the lives of Edward IV. and Edward V. His work also contains the view taken by a zealous Catholic of the transactions of the Reformation.

The history of the wars of the houses of York and Lancaster, was written by Edward Hall, whose work is, however, chiefly valued by such of our antiquaries as are curious concerning the changes of costume, which took place in England, in the times of which he treats.

The chronicle of Ralph Holinshed, continued to the year 1586 by John Hooper, alias Vowel, is a work deservedly held in high estimation.

John Stowe, who died A. D. 1605, left behind him a historical work, the fruit of forty years' research ; in the revising and continuing of which, Edward Hows was employed for thirty years more. The result of this industry is an excellent arrangement of a great variety of valuable materials.

In the opinion of Mr. Nicholson, the author of the English Historical Library, the Chronicle of John Speed is the best work of the kind now extant. It commences with the earliest period of our history, and is continued to the union of the two kingdoms under James I.

The chronicle of Richard Baker contains the history of our kings, from the time of the Romans to the end of the reign of James I. It was brought down to the Restoration by Edward Philip. This work is not, however, regarded as by any means equal, in interest and authority, with that of Speed.*

From the period of the union of the crowns of England and Scotland, original records of our history are to be found in abundance in the proceedings of parliament and of our courts of law; in royal proclamations, manifestoes, and charters; in voluminous collections of state-papers made by Rushworth, Thurloe, Clarendon, Whitelocke, Dalrymple, and others, which it does not fall within the province of this Essay to enumerate. To this stock of documents, the curiosity of inquirers and the liberality of our nobility and gentry, are almost annually making important additions, so that with regard to the later annals of the British history, the student is rather in danger of being bewildered by the variety, than of being left in the dark by the want of historical materials.

Though nothing can be further removed from a spirit of strife and discord than the spirit of true religion, and those principles of genuine Christianity, the aim of which is to inculcate, above all things, the virtues of justice, benevolence, and mutual forbearance, it has unfortunately happened that, by the intermixture of human interests with matters purely spiritual, our holy faith has been perverted into an occasion of animosity; and religious disputes have even influenced the destiny of states and kingdoms. The struggles of the first Christians against the power of paganism; the rise and pro-

* Most of our ancient historians will be found in Sir Henry Saville's Quinque Scriptores Angliæ Historiæ, printed in 1652; in the Rerum Anglicanarum Scriptores, published at Oxford in 1684, and in two vols. of Dr. Gale, the first containing five, and the second, fifteen historical writers. There are separate editions of Marianus, of Florentius, of Eadmerus, of Matthew Paris, of Trivet, of Matthew of Westminster, of Froissart, of T. Walsingham, and of William Caxton.—Of Froissart and of Monstrelet, Thomas Johnes, Esq. of Hafod, in the county of Cardigan, has favoured the public with translations, which will long survive as memorials of his industry, and of his ability.

gress of theological sects and opinions; the gradual usurpations of the Bishops of Rome—and the rapid decline of their authority, at the period when the human mind was roused from the long sleep of ignorance—the various modifications of religious establishments—the oppression exercised, in different countries, by the professors of the dominant belief, and the resistance made against that oppression by sectaries—these are topics which cannot be neglected by him who would fully reap the best fruit of historical inquiries—an acquaintance with the progress of the human intellect. These topics, indeed, are so prominent in importance, that they continually present themselves to view in the details of the civil history of the world. But they well merit being considered as objects of primary consideration; and being thus considered, they constitute the subject of Ecclesiastical History. This thorny maze of inquiry has been explored by a multitude of writers, with various degrees of industry and discretion. But the views of the student of general history, will be most completely answered by the perusal of the work of Mosheim, whose learning and whose patience in investigation, are only to be equalled by his candour as a critic, and by his fidelity as a narrator of facts.

The general history of our native country, will give abundant proof of the good sense and vigour, from time to time evinced by our Roman Catholic ancestors, in resisting the extravagant claims and pretensions of the pontifical court. But the series of the events and transactions which finally liberated the subjects of these realms from the yoke of popery, are recorded with due particularity and minuteness by Bishop Burnet, in his History of the Reformation. In point of composition this work is not a model of elegance; but its matter is excellent, and the information which it contains is founded on the most authentic documents.

Whosoever wishes to trace the ramifications of Sectarianism in England, may be referred to Neale's History of the Puritans, a work of considerable merit, which, commencing at the rise of Non-conformity in the days of Elizabeth, traces the varying circumstances of the English Protestant Dissenters, to the triumph of the principles of equity in the passing of the Toleration Act, in the first year of the reign of William and Mary.

A spirited account of the rise and early progress of the Reformation in Scotland, is to be found in Dr. M'Crie's Life of John Knox; the favourable reception of which work is a happy indication of the encouragement at this day afforded, by the suffrage of the public, to industrious research, an honest representation of facts, and a rational attachment to the principles of religious liberty.

The subsequent annals of Scottish ecclesiastical affairs are given in sufficient detail in the latter part of the fifth, and in the sixth and seventh books of Spottiswood's History of the Church of Scotland—and it may be observed, that the struggles against the introduction of Episcopacy, which, from time to time, disturbed the tranquillity of Scotland, till by the Act of Union, the Presbyterian form of Church Government was firmly established in that country, are in no publication so ably narrated as in Mr. Laing's History, which has before been mentioned with due applause.

To the books which have been recommended as worthy of perusal in the foregoing course of History, it were an easy task to make considerable additions. But in a sketch of this nature, designed for the guidance of the young Academic, selection is obviously more desirable than variety—compactness, than diffusion. Though, therefore, many works of indisputable merit are omitted in the foregoing list, it is hoped that the series of which it is composed, will be found tolerably well connected, sufficiently complete, and, above all, selected with impartiality. In the perusal of these, as indeed of any historical works, the student must not neglect the requisite geographical investigations; nor must he turn with disgust from the dry arrangements of Chronology. It will, of course, then be expedient that he should provide himself with the best maps, both ancient and modern, and with the most copious and accurate historical and chronological tables, by frequent reference to which, his memory will be aided, and a more vivid representation of past transactions will be impressed upon his mind. But above all—for the precept cannot be too frequently or too anxiously inculcated—let him make historical facts the subjects of serious meditation. Let him consider them as exhibiting a picture of human life, and as tending to refine the moral sense, and to correct the evil passions of men, by exhibiting, in striking points of view, the dignity of virtue, and the deformity of vice.

CHAP. XX.

GEOGRAPHY.

The importance of Geography to history—Divisions of Geography—Ancient Geography—The Gnomon—Thales—Meton—First geographical observation—Excellent Roman custom—Roman Empire delineated—Ptolemy—Dionysius—Knowledge of the globe by the ancients—Middle ages—Iceland, discovery of—Columbus—Discovery of America—Vasco de Gama—Circumnavigations of the globe—Discoveries.

GEOGRAPHY, is, as its name imports, a description of the terrestrial globe, and particularly of the known and habitable part thereof, and hence we infer its great importance in connexion with the study of history. Without a competent knowledge of the situation and relative magnitudes of the several countries of the earth, no student of history can have clear and distinct ideas of what he reads. As history is divided into ancient and modern, so also must the science of geography be considered. Those who have been more particular in their descriptions, have considered history, and geography also, as naturally admitting of three divisions. (1) The *ancient* or classical, which describes the state of the earth, so far as it was known from the remotest antiquity, to the decline of the Roman empire. (2) That of the *middle* ages, which reaches to the restoration of learning in the beginning of the fifteenth century, when the discoveries of the Portuguese began to lay broader foundations of the science; and, (3) Modern geography, which embraces all the recent discoveries. We shall endeavour to trace the rise and progress of the science, and in so doing we shall borrow freely from a work by Dr. John Blair, that he published in 1784, to accompany and illustrate his excellent Chronological Tables, which will be described hereafter.

The geography of ancient writers scarcely went beyond the description of countries. Of this kind is that portion of it, which we find in the books of Moses, written, perhaps, about fourteen or fifteen hundred years before the birth of Christ. Of this kind also is the geography of Homer, in his Iliad and Odyssey, who flourished about nine centuries before the Christian æra. The geographical knowledge that we derive from Herodotus, who lived five hundred years after the time of Homer, is partial, imperfect, and not at all to be depended on. It relates chiefly to certain parts of Asia; to the northern and western parts of Europe, and also to part of Africa.

It should seem that those who made geography their pursuit in those early times, being destitute of mathematical instruments, and of course unable to make any accurate astronomical observations, began to determine the situation of places according to climates, which they probably fixed on, from the form and colour of certain animals that were to be found in the different countries. The appearance of negroes, called, at that time, Ethiopians, and of the larger sized animals, as the rhinoceros and elephant, suggested the line of division, where the limits of the torrid zone began towards the north, and terminated towards the south. This manner of dividing the surface of the earth into climates, must be considered as the earliest outline of geography in the first ages of the world.

The Chaldeans and Egyptians, who were distinguished by their skill in geometry and astronomy, were of course the first persons who paid any particular attention to geography, and it has been said that the earliest map was made by order of Sesostris I., who conquered Egypt. This prince having traversed a great part of the earth as it was then known, recorded his march in maps, and gave copies of those maps, not only to the Egyptians, but to the inhabitants of Scythia, or Tartary, to their great astonishment. The Jews likewise seem to have had geographers among them, and it has been thought, by able commentators on the Scriptures, that they possessed a map of Palestine, when they assigned different portions to the seven tribes at Shiloh: "Go", said Joshua, "and walk through the land, and *describe* it, and come again to me, that I may here cast lots for you." See Joshua, chap. xviii. and xix. In confirmation of this opinion, Josephus says, that when Joshua sent out people from the different tribes to measure the land, he gave them, as companions, persons well skilled in geometry, whose knowledge would prevent them from deviating far from the truth: hence it is inferred, and with a great shew of reason, that a geometrical survey was taken of the Holy Land.

Besides the method of dividing the surface of the globe by climates, it is certain that the Egyptians and Babylonians adopted another, which was that of determining the situation of places, or their distance from the equator, by observing the length of their longest and shortest days. This they performed by means of a gnomon,* erected upon a horizontal

* The simplicity of the gnomon for the purpose above alluded to, renders it very probable that it was the first instrument ever used for astronomical purposes. All the knowledge that the ancients had of the solar theory, seems to have been derived from the gnomon. The principle of this instrument is readily described: if the height of a vertical staff or pillar, be compared with its shadow on a perfectly horizontal plane, the altitude of the sun may be found by the most simple trigonometrical calculation, because the height of the pillar will be to the length of the projected shadow, as the *tangent* to *radius*, or as the sine to the co-sine of the altitude required. [See our chapter on trigonometry, where this is more fully explained.]

The ancient obelisks found in Egypt were probably, many of them, at plane, by which they were enabled to measure the shortness or length of the shadow in proportion to the height of the sun.

Thales, a celebrated philosopher, and one of the seven sages of Greece, who flourished about 600 years before the Christian æra, discovered the passage of the sun from tropic

least, instruments of this kind: this was their original purpose, and the figure of an obelisk being rather pleasing to the sight, it was adopted as an ornament to public places. As practical astronomy advanced towards perfection, the gnomon was discovered to be considerably defective. The shadow is generally ill-defined, so that its length cannot be very accurately measured, and to obviate this, the gnomon must be of greater height than is easily practicable. In modern times, therefore, the original gnomon has been abandoned, and a new one substituted in its place. The gnomons of Italy are usually constructed in large buildings, in the upper part of which an aperture is made to allow a luminous circular image of the sun to be formed on the pavement below, on which a meridian line is accurately traced. A plumb line is suspended from the aperture to the floor, so that the height of the aperture, and the distance of the solar image, from the point beneath it, is very accurately ascertained. There are on record some very ancient observations made with gnomons, particularly of Pythias, who observed the solstices at Marseilles, full three centuries before the birth of Christ. One still older is mentioned by Pliny, as erected by Augustus, which had been brought from Egypt, and was made originally by Sesostris nearly a thousand years before the Christian æra. It was used by Manlius for the same purpose for which it was originally destined, namely, to measure the height of the sun. The most famous gnomon of modern times, was constructed in 1575, by Ignatius Dante, a Dominican friar, and afterwards bishop of Alatri, in the church of St. Petronius at Bologna. It was originally only about seventy feet high, but was raised by Cassini in 1653, to the height of 90 feet; and it was with this that he made his solar observations. Almost all modern gnomons are accompanied by a meridian line, ornamented with the names of the month and the signs of the zodiac, so as to serve as a calendar. One of great note is in the Carthusian convent at Rome, built on the Ancient Thermæ of Dioclesian, by Bianchini. In the royal observatory at Paris, there is one erected by the celebrated Picard; and another in St. Sulpice at Paris, begun by Sully, a watchmaker, in 1727, but which has since been improved and highly ornamented. The reason why none of these gnomons are to be found in this country, is, that we do not regulate our clocks by solar, but by mean time; and another circumstance may be, that our climate is very unfavourable for solar observations. We shall have occasion to refer again to this subject.

to tropic, which enabled him to ascertain the four particular days when that body appeared to be in the equinoctial and solsticial points in the heavens. He was led to the division of the year into its four parts, and is said to have written treatises on the tropics and solstices; and, as we have no account of any other instrument being at that time known, by the use of which the discovery could have been made, it has been concluded, that Thales employed the gnomon in his observations, the use of which he had probably learnt in his travels into Egypt. It has been observed, as a proof of this, that calculations of the kind were familiar to him, that he first determined the height of the Egyptian pyramids by their shadows, at the moment when the shadow of an object is equal to its height, that is, when the sun is precisely 45 degrees above the horizon. To Thales also has been ascribed the division of the year into three hundred and sixty-five days; this, however, there is scarcely any doubt, he learnt at Egypt, and the discovery is, with great probability, traced to Trismegistus, who is supposed to have been a contemporary of Moses. Pliny asserts, that the addition of five days and a quarter added to three hundred and sixty days, into which the year was first divided, was made by observing when the shadow returned to its marks, a proof that either the gnomon, or some similar instrument was used; and hence it has been inferred that the Greeks derived their knowledge of the gnomon from the Egyptians, to whom it was known long before the dawn of Greek learning. See CHRONOLOGY.

From the time of Thales, and his immediate successors, geography seems to have received very little improvement for two hundred years, till the establishment of the famous school of Alexandria; although Pythagoras and his disciples were rightly informed with regard to the true system of the world, being satisfied that the sun was in the centre, and that the earth was globular, and had an annual motion round the sun, and a diurnal motion on its own imaginary axis.

During this period, we have an astronomical observation of

considerable importance to geography, and the first that is recorded, as made in Greece. It was taken by Meton and Euctemon, who observed the summer solstice at Athens, on a day that corresponded to our 27th of June, 432 B. C. This observation was probably applied by the two philosophers to the determining the latitude of Athens at the same time; for, as the length of the shadow of the gnomon was attentively watched at the moment of the solstice, the proportion of that to the gnomon's height was easily known, by which the sun's altitude would be given. There is reason to believe that Timotheus and Aristillus, who began to make observations about three centuries before the birth of Christ, were the first who introduced the manner of determining the position of the stars, according to their longitudes and latitudes, with respect to the equator. This is ascertained from the "Almagest" of Ptolemy: one of their observations gave rise to the discovery of the precession of the equinoxes, which will be explained in our chapter "On Astronomy." Hence Hipparchus was led to dispose the different parts of the earth according to latitude and longitude, this being a new application of that art which had been introduced in the arrangement of the constellations, and therefore equally proper to be adopted in tracing the meridians and parallels of the earth. Hipparchus, by thus uniting geography and astronomy, fixed the former on a solid and invariable foundation.

When the true principles of geography were thus pointed out by the invention of longitude and latitude, maps began to assume a new form of projection, essentially different from those in use prior to this period.

It was an universal custom among the Romans, after they had conquered and subdued any provinces, to have a map, or painted representation of them, carried in triumph; and in this way, those who were the conquerors, became the delineators of the world, and thus rendered the horrors of war subservient to the interests and extension of science. Every new war produced a new survey and itinerary of the countries where the scene of action occurred; thus the materials of geography were accumulated by every additional conquest. So attentive were the Romans to the accumulation of this kind of knowledge, that we find Julius Cæsar ordered a general survey to be made of the whole Roman empire, by a decree of the senate, selecting, for the purpose, persons who had been well instructed in every branch of science. The three surveyors were Zenodoxus, Theodotus, and Polyclitus, each of whom, with proper assistants, was appointed to survey a different division of the empire; and the survey is said to have occupied more than twenty-five years. There are Roman itineraries still extant, which shew with what accuracy their surveys were made in every province.

To shew, however, that geography was not at this period a new science in the world, we may observe, that before the Romans engaged in the business of depicting countries, Neco, king of Egypt, ordered the Phœnicians to make a survey of the whole coast of Africa, which they accomplished in three years. Darius procured the Ethiopic sea and the mouth of the Indus to be surveyed. Other instances might be produced, but these are sufficient to shew how much geography, as a science, was cultivated at the period of which we are speaking. In the time of Socrates, it is evident, that maps of some kind were not uncommon at Athens, for this philosopher is represented as mortifying the pride of Alcibiades, by desiring him to point out his territories in Attica in a map; and Pliny relates, that Alexander, in his expedition into Asia, took with him two geographers to measure and describe the roads, and that, from their itineraries, the writers of the following ages took many particulars. According to Strabo, a copy of Alexander's survey was given by Xenocles, his treasurer, to Patrocles, his geographer, who was also commander of the fleets of Seleucus and Antiochus. Patrocles was author of a work on geography, which is frequently quoted by Strabo and

Pliny, and it appears that he furnished Eratosthenes with the chief materials and authorities for constructing the oriental part of his map of the known world.

From the æra of Alexander's expedition and conquest, Geography began to assume a new form, and it went on improving till the time of Ptolemy, in the second century of the Christian æra, who contributed greatly to the improvement of this science, by a more accurate delineation of the terrestrial globe, than any that had then been given of it. He availed himself of all the observations of those who had gone before him, corrected the mistakes of some, and supplied the many defects of others; and, by reducing the distances of places on the earth to degrees and minutes, making use of the degrees of latitude and longitude, and settling the situation of places by astronomical observations, he reduced geography to a regular system; and, seventeen hundred years ago, actually laid a foundation for those farther discoveries and improvements, which resulted from the progressive, and, at present, advanced state of geography.

Some time after Ptolemy, Dionysius, the African, flourished, usually called the *Periegetic,* from the title of a work that he composed in verse, containing a description of the world, which is considered as one of the most correct systems of ancient geography. It was translated into Latin verse first by Priscian, and afterwards by Arienus, the latter of whom also wrote a description of the maritime coasts.

We come now to speak of the knowledge which the ancients possessed of the globe, and of which there have been various opinions; but, according to Montucla, whose authority may be safely depended on, they were well acquainted with the greater part of Europe, at least, all that portion of it which had been made subject to the Roman empire, as far as the banks of the Danube and the Rhine. They were familiar with Germany and Sarmatia, the latter including much of the northern parts of Europe and Asia. They had some knowledge of the Baltic, as a fleet had been sent by Augustus, which sailed as far as the modern Jutland, which was the Cimbrian Chersonesus of antiquity. They had acquired a knowledge of the island of Britain, from the expeditions of Julius Cæsar and Claudius; but the northern parts of the island, and the whole of Ireland, were to them nations of rude, uncivilized savages. The boundary of their knowledge of Europe to the north, was Iceland, supposed to be the same with what they denominated the "Ultima Thule."

With respect to Asia, they surveyed the country as far as the river Ganges, and the immense tract comprehended between the Indus and Ganges, was called by them India on this side the Ganges. Farther on, towards the north of China, in the neighbourhood of the mountains, where these rivers derive their source, they placed several nations of people; and, beyond these, still more to the east, the Seres, and upon the coast of the Gulf, which is now the bay of Cochin China, called by Ptolemy, the Great Bay, were situated the Sinæ. The Seres mentioned by the same geographer were probably the inhabitants of the northern parts of China, and the Sinæ those of the southern parts, who very early occupied what we now denominate Cochin China, Tonquin, &c. countries which, in process of time, they entirely subjugated. They maintained a commerce by land with the Seres, and their route is pointed out in one of the maps of Ptolemy.

The ancients, in their accounts, carried the eastern extremity of Asia much farther to the east than it is found to extend by modern geographers; for, according to them, the Seres and Sinæ were situated about the longitude of 180°, while the meridian of Pekin reaches no farther than 134°, reckoning the longitude from the most distant of the Canary islands, as was done by Ptolemy. To the north of the Indus, the ancient geographers placed the Scythians and Hyperboreans, that is, the Tartars and Samoides of modern date, and some other nations to an indefinite extent, who were supposed to form an insurmountable barrier, having behind them an ocean of ice, which was believed to communicate with the Caspian Sea. The boundary of Asia, assigned by the ancients to the south, was the Indian Ocean, and they were acquainted with its communication with the Red Sea by means of a strait, the figure of which is very ill expressed in their maps. This is also the case with the Persian Gulf, with which they were acquainted.

The situation of the island of Taprobana, referred to by Ptolemy, and so celebrated among the ancients, has never been ascertained; some suppose it was no other than the peninsula of India; others contend that it was the modern island of Ceylon; and there are some who refer it to Sumatra. The ancients were acquainted with the peninsula of Malacca, which they called the Golden Chersonesus, and they seem to have examined the gulf formed by that land, which is now known as the Gulf of Cochin China, or the Gulf of Tonquin. There is no reason for supposing that they were acquainted with Java, Borneo, and that numerous group of islands which form, in that part of the globe, probably, the greatest Archipelago in the world. It is not less surprizing that the Maldives had escaped the observation of these navigators; a circumstance that seems to prove they never ventured out into the open sea.

The ancients were acquainted only with those parts of Africa that lay along the coast, and to a very small distance inland, if we except Egypt, which they had explored as far as the cataracts of the Nile, and beyond them, to the island of Meröe, about the 20th degree of north latitude. Their knowledge of the coasts of Africa, on the side of the Red Sea, extended no farther than the shores of that sea, excepting the part which was dependent on Egypt; the interior of the country being inhabited by a wild and ferocious people. Nor were they at all acquainted with the countries which lay beyond the strait, and Ptolemy seems to have given no credit to the navigators who were said to have sailed round that part of the world, for he has left the continent of Africa imperfect towards the south. Strabo and Pomponius Mela were better acquainted with the subject; they decidedly asserted that Africa was a peninsula, and that it was joined to the continent only by a neck of land, which is now called the isthmus of Suez.

We may observe, that the coast of Africa, upon the Mediterranean, was once covered with towns, dependent upon the Roman Empire, flourishing and highly polished, which, at present, and for ages past, is, and has been, the harbour of pirates, whom the foolish jealousy of the great commercial nations supports to their own prejudice and disgrace. Proceeding from the straits of Cadiz or Gibraltar, they coasted along as far as a cape, which they called "Hesperion-Keras," probably the modern Cape de Verde. The Fortunate Islands, or Hesperides, at present the Canaries, seem to have been the boundaries of ancient geography to the west, as the Seres and Sinæ already referred to, were to the east.

Patteson, in his Atlas, says, "there is little doubt concerning the names by which most of the principal countries of Europe were known to the ancients; nor is there any difficulty in disposing the chief nations which ancient writers have enumerated in the south-west of Asia, or on the African coast of the Mediterranean; but, of the north and north-east parts of Europe, about two-thirds of Asia towards the same quarters, and nearly the same proportion of Africa to the south, they appear to have been wholly ignorant. Of America, they did not even suspect the existence; and if it ever happened, as some writers have imagined, that Phœnician merchant-ships were driven by storms across the Atlantic to the American shores, it does not appear that any of them ever returned to report the discovery.

"The names of provinces, sub-divisions, and petty tribes, mentioned by ancient authors, in those countries which were the scenes of Roman, Grecian, or Israelitish transactions, are almost as numerous as in a modern map of the same countries, and the situations of many of them can be very nearly assigned; but the limits of each, or indeed of the states and nations to which they belonged, can, in very few instances, be precisely fixed. Thus the southern boundaries of the Sarmatæ, in Europe, cannot be ascertained within a degree; and, in France, neither the limits of the people called the Belgæ, Celtæ, and Aquitani; nor those of the Roman divisions, viz. Belgica, Lugdunensis, &c. can be laid down but by conjecture.

During the middle ages, geography shared the fate of other arts and sciences, and went backward rather than advanced. The weakness of the Roman emperors, the relaxation of military discipline, the passion for luxury, which banished every desire of improvement, and every attempt at discovery, and the continual incursions of the barbarous nations, while they contributed to hasten the fall of the western empire, accelerated the ruin of the arts, and enveloped the world in profound and universal ignorance. The principal geographers, during the dark ages, were Arabians, who applied themselves chiefly to the study and translation of Ptolemy's works, and, as is not uncommon in versions from one language to another, increased, instead of diminishing, the number of his errors. The principal attempt which they made towards the improvement of geography was, that of measuring a degree of the meridian on the plain of Shinar, near Babylon, in the beginning of the ninth century; but, so far were they from the truth, that the result came out between fifty-six and fifty-seven Arabian miles, which was equal to sixty-five English miles: and the almost only geographical discovery, during the lapse of twelve or fourteen centuries, from the decline of the Roman empire, was that of Iceland. It was in 861 that a Norwegian navigator, in a voyage to the Feroe Islands, was driven upon the coast of an unknown country, to which he gave the name of Snio-land, or Snow-land, as characteristic of the mountains covered with snow. Another navigator from the same country, passed a winter on the northern shores of this island, and the immense shoals of ice that he met with, led him to bestow upon it the appellation by which it has ever since been known.

When the clouds of ignorance, which had overspread Europe for so many centuries, began to disperse, and science and commerce to assume their proper rank among the affairs of men, geographical improvements attained an extension, and a degree of correctness unknown to former ages. The discovery of the properties of the loadstone, and of its application, in the Mariner's Compass, to directing ships across the ocean, gave an astonishing facility to geography, and led to the most important results in every part of the globe. This discovery was announced about the year 1302, and in 1360, Nicholas Lynn, a friar and astronomer of Oxford, undertook a voyage to the northern islands of Europe, in order to prove the virtues of the magnet in the northern ocean. The Portuguese were also among the maritime adventurers of this period, and their discoveries towards the east began early in the 15th century. The island of Madeira was visited by them in 1419, and its fertility, and the salubrity of its climate, soon caused it to be colonized. Cape Bajador, on the western coast of Africa, was first passed by them in 1433: St. Mary, one of the Azores, having been visited in the preceding year. Cape de Verde and the islands opposite to it were known and explored in the year 1446, and farther discoveries were likewise made in the Azores about the same time. It was not till the year 1471 that the equator was crossed, and it was at or near this period that Bartholemew Diaz was sent for the purpose of making discoveries towards the south-east, when he descried the grand southern promontory of Africa; but the season was so tempestuous that he was prevented from passing it; and hence for a time it was denominated Cabo Tormentosa, or Cape of Tempests; but it afterwards obtained the appellation of the Cape of Good Hope.

While the Portuguese were thus pursuing their way to glory and wealth in the east, Spain was influenced by the vast projects of Christopher Columbus. He imagined that the eastern limits of India could not be very distant from the western shores of Spain, an error which probably induced him to undertake the enterprize that led to the discovery of the American continent. For a considerable time his plans were treated with contempt by the sovereigns to whom he proposed them. At length he obtained a patron in Isabella of Spain, and with three small and ill equipped vessels set sail for India, as he hoped; but after enduring many evils, necessarily attendant upon such an attempt, he arrived at a new world instead of the distant shores of the old one. He sailed from Spain on the 3d of August, 1492, and on the 12th of the following October, fell in with an American island, which he named San Salvador. Encouraged by this success, he persuaded the court of Spain to allow him to make three other voyages, in the course of which he discovered the continent, and many other islands; and in the year 1495, he founded a town at St. Domingo, which was the first European settlement in the western world. It obtained the name of America from Amerigo Vespucci, who published an account of the discoveries made by Columbus.

We must not omit to observe that some modern writers have claimed the honour of this most important discovery for a German, Martin Behem, or Boehm, a native of Nuremberg in Franconia. This person had, in early life, studied under the illustrious Regiomontanus, and in 1459-60, he established a colony at Fagal, one of the Azores, where he resided till 1484, when, by the patronage of John II. of Portugal, he undertook a voyage to the south-west, and discovered that part of America that is now called Brazil, and sailed through the straits of Magellan. This was eight years before the first voyage of Columbus. The advocates for the fame of Behem maintain that Columbus would not have thought of his expedition, had he not obtained some information on the subject from their hero, while in the island of Madeira. It may, however, be remarked, that Dr. Robertson, whose character as an historian deserves the highest respect, treats the history of Behem as a fiction, and as such we should not have introduced it in our work, had not his claims been lately revived by M. Otto in the Transactions of the American Society established at Philadelphia. In point of fact, to the *student* of geography, it is but of little moment to whom the honour of discovering the continent of America is due; he is concerned only with the fact of its existence, which he applies to the extensions of his geographical knowledge; and it will, to him, be matter, hereafter, of curious research to examine the claims of discoverers, or pretended discoverers, not only on this, but other subjects.

The success obtained in the western hemisphere, acted as a fresh stimulus to the same spirit in the east; another expedition sailed from Portugal, under the command of Vasco de Gama, who was more successful than Diaz had been, and passed the Cape of Good Hope in November, 1497. At first he employed himself in exploring the eastern shores of Africa, as far as Zanguebar, when he launched courageonsly to the East, and arrived in 1498 at Calicut on the coast of Malabar. Men of genius and talents applied the powers of their mind to the improvement of geography, by other means, than that of practical navigation; in the retirement of the closet, they devised methods of aiding those who were capable of bringing their theories to the test of experiment.

Duration and space, however different in nature, it was soon found, might be applied, in an astronomical or geographical sense, to the measure of each other, with great precision. For as one hour in time, corresponds to 15 degrees of longitude on the earth, or in other words, as a space on the earth, equal to 15 degrees, requires one hour to pass by a given point, longitude may be expressed by *time*, or *space*, with equal accuracy and clearness: thus we may say, a place is 15 or 30 degrees east or west longitude from London, or that it is one hour or two hours earlier or later time than that city; and we know on what meridian to look for it, hence it was inferred, that accurate and well going time-pieces would afford a method of ascertaining longitude.

Notwithstanding the vast additions that had been made to the previous stock of geographical knowledge, by the discoveries in both hemispheres, it is not certain that little more than a third of the earth's surface was as yet known. Although more than half the globe, from east to west, had been traversed, the northern and southern parts were still unexplored. The limits of Asia on the east, and of America on the west; and whether the two continents were joined, and thus, in fact formed only one, or whether they were separate were matters of mere conjecture; even the spherical figure of the earth rested almost entirely upon reasoning and theory, which, however, was confirmed pretty strongly by the curved line formed by the shadow on the sun and moon in solar and lunar eclipses. By many theorists at this period, and for three centuries after, it was believed there must be a southern continent somewhere as a balance to those chiefly in the northern hemisphere. Accordingly the hopes of interest and honour impelled individuals and nations, to fit out expeditions for the purpose of still further discovery. Hence arose the circumnavigation of the globe, which constitutes a memorable epocha in the history of geography, and by which the globular form of the earth was experimentally proved; and at length the idea of another continent has been completely banished from the mind.

Ferdinand Magellan, a Portuguese, was the first who bravely undertook the circumnavigation of the globe. He sailed from Seville, a port in Spain, on the 10th of August, 1519; and, on the 6th of November following, entered the strait which has ever since gone by the name, though the advocates for Behem give the honour to him. This strait, which is near the southern extremity of America, he navigated, and after a tedious voyage, found himself in the South-Sea. He then directed his course towards the north west, on that hitherto unknown ocean called from its tranquillity, the Pacific, for four months, without meeting with any thing of importance. He still proceeded on his voyage, and in March, 1521, discovered the Ladrone islands, from thence he went to others, probably the Philippines, on one of which he was unfortunately killed in a skirmish with the natives. After this, the ship, entrusted to the care of Jean Sebastian del Cano, passed by Borneo to the Moluccas, which had been visited before by the Portuguese. From these it proceeded to, and passed the Sumatran group of islands and the Cape of Good Hope, and returned to Seville, the port from whence it started, in September, 1522, after a voyage of three years and a month.*

* We shall set down in this note a brief account of the other most remarkable voyages that have been made round the globe, in a chronological order, beginning with our countryman,

Sir Francis Drake, a native of Tavistock, in Devonshire, who sailed from Plymouth on the 13th of December, 1577, fell in with the coast of Barbary on the 25th, and with Cape de Verde on the 29th; on the 13th of March, he passed the equinoctial; on the 5th of April, he made the coast of Brazil, at the 30th degree of South Latitude, and entered the river La Plata; on the 29th of May he entered the port of St. Juliens, and on the 20th of August, he entered the straits of Magellan, and passed through them on the 25th of September. On the 25th of November, he came to Macao, in the latitude of 30 degrees; thence he coasted along Chili and Peru, to the height of 48° N. Lat. here he landed and called the country New Albion, taking possession of it for Queen Elizabeth; from thence he sailed to the Moluccas, which he reached early in November: he next proceeded to the Celebes, and then to Java, from which island he came to the Cape of Good Hope on the 15th of June; and on the 12th of July, he passed the line, reached the coast of Guinea on the 16th. On the 11th of September, he made the island of Tercera, and entered the harbour of Plymouth. See Stockdale's edition of Campbell's Admirals, Vol. I.

Sir Thomas Cavendish sailed from Plymouth, having two small ships, under his command; on the 1st of August, 1586, he passed through the straits of Magellan, took many rich prizes along the coasts of Chili and Peru, and completely circumnavigated the globe, returning by the Cape of Good Hope on the 9th of September, 1588, having been out little more than two years and a month.

Simon Cordes and James Mahu, Dutchmen, sailed round the globe; the former finishing his voyage in 1596, at the time the latter set out. Pre-

Most of the American islands had been discovered, and the western and eastern shores of the continent explored, by Columbus, Cortes, the two Cabots, and others, in the latter end of the preceding century; but the Bermudas or Sommer's

viously to these, a native of Utrecht, viz. Oliver De Noort, had sailed round the earth in little more than three years.

George Spillenberger, a Fleming, set sail from the Texel the 6th of August, 1614, and having circumnavigated the globe, landed in Zealand the first of June, 1616. Le Maire and William Schouter, to whom we have referred in the text, made a successful voyage round the earth in two years and eighteen days, having left the Texel on the 14th of June, 1615, and returned to the same place on the 1st of July, 1617. James, the Hermit, sailed round the globe, during the years 1623, 4, 5, and 6.

Our countryman, Lord Anson, set sail in Sept. 1740, doubled Cape Horn, crossed the great Pacific Ocean, and returned by the Cape of Good Hope, in 1744. Commodore Byron sailed from the Downs, on the 21st of June, 1764, to make discoveries in the South Seas: he passed through the straits of Magellan, crossed the South Sea, and returned on the 9th of May, 1766; he first discovered and conversed with the Patagonians, a gigantic race of men in South America. In his course, he met with, and explored to a certain extant, Disappointment island, King George's island, Prince of Wales's island, Duke of York's island, and Byron's island. Captain Wallis made a like voyage in twenty-one months; but Captain Carteret, who set out with him, was unfortunately separated from his friend by adverse weather, and did not reach home till March, 1769. Wallis was the first who fell in with Whitsun island, Queen Charlotte's island, Egmont island, Glocester island, Prince William Henry's island, and Osnaburgh island. He also discovered Otaheite, Howe island, and many others. Carteret added Sandwich island, the Admiralty islands and Stephens island, to the stock of former discoveries.

Bougainville, a Frenchman, set sail from Nantz in November, 1766, and returned by the Cape of Good Hope to the port of St. Maloes in March, 1769. He discovered the Great Cyclades and the New Hebrides of Cook.

The immortal Cook, to whom geography, and every science connected with it, is so much indebted, sailed in the ship Endeavour, from Plymouth, August 26th, 1768, and after a most satisfactory voyage, returned on the 12th of June, 1771. We have not room to enumerate the great discoveries made in this and his two other voyages. After having circumnavigated the globe, and explored the utmost navigable limits of the ocean, he was cut off by the savage natives of Owhyhee, one of the Sandwich islands, Jan. 14, 1779.

M. J. F. G. de la Perouse went, in 1785, on a voyage of discovery, by order of Louis XVI. of France: he bent his course to the north-western coasts of America, which he explored from nearly 60° North Latitude to island was not known till John Bermudas, a Spanish captain, arrived at it, in 1527. In 1528, Papua, or New Guinea, was discovered by a Spaniard, whom Cortes had sent from America, to explore the Spice islands. The hope of finding a shorter course to the East Indies has occasioned the most perilous voyages to be undertaken. In 1553, Sir Hugh Willoughby sailed from England to the north-east of Europe, in search of this passage. He entered the White Sea, and opened a commercial intercourse with Russia and Archangel, but being prevented from prosecuting his voyage by the ice, he attempted to winter in Lapland, where both he and most of those who were with him, perished by the intensity of the frost. Solomon's island was discovered by a Spanish captain, Mendana, who sailed from Lima towards the west, in the year 1575.

Martin Frobisher, who sailed from England in 1578, with the view of obtaining a north-west passage to China, fell in with West Greenland. To the same cause, we are indebted for the knowledge of Davis' straits, Hudson's Bay, and Baffin's-bay, which were discovered by captains whose names they bear, in the years 1585, 1610, and 1662. The Falkland islands, at the southern extremity of America, were discovered by Sir Richard Hawkins, in 1594. In crossing the Pacific ocean, Mendana de Neyra, a Spanish captain, fell in with the Marquesas, Santa Cruz, and St. Bernardo. In 1616, Le Maire and Schouten sailed from the Texel, in search of the ideal

Montery-Bay in California, in about 37° N. L. From California he proceeded to Macao, in China, to Manilla, and thence, through the sea of Japan, and along the north-eastern coast of Tartary, and the islands in the sea of Jesso, to the harbour of St. Peter and St. Paul, in Kamtschatka. Of these and other places he remitted at different times accounts to his government After this, the commander, his two ships, the Boussole and the Astrolabe, and all their crews, were unfortunately lost, but how or where has never been discovered.

Captain George Vancouver's voyage of discovery to the North Pacific Ocean, and round the globe, was undertaken and performed in the years 1790, 1, 2, 3, 4, and 5, in the Discovery, a sloop of war.

southern continent, and explored the strait, since called Maire's strait, between the southern coast of Terra del Fuego and Staten island; and after the death of Maire, which happened very soon after they had passed the strait, his friend and companion, Schouten, made many other discoveries, and returned to Holland in 1617. Batavia, New Holland, and the Southern part of Van Diemen's Land, were discovered in the year 1616, by Dutch navigators. In 1642, the celebrated Abel Jansen Tasman, a Dutchman, sailed from Batavia, and during an absence of a year and ten months, he discovered among other islands, New Zealand, and the Friendly isles, and demonstrated that New Holland and New Zealand to be insular. The Carolines were first found out by the Spaniards; and New Britain and New Ireland, by our countryman, Dampier.

Easter-island, and several others of less note in the Pacific ocean, were discovered by Roggewin, a Dutch navigator, in his course round the globe, in 1722.

The Pelew islands first excited the attention of the English by the shipwreck of Captain Wilson on the coast, in 1783; but they had been discovered long before by the Spaniards, by whom they had been denominated the Palos islands, from the abundance of tall palm-trees.

CHAP. XXI.

ON GEOGRAPHY,
Continued.

Lines and Circles on the globe—Zones—Longitude and Latitude—Divisions of the Globe—Division of land—of water. Europe—Asia—Africa—America—Australasia—Polynesia.

IN studying geography, the pupil should have before him an artificial globe, or good maps. On these he will observe several lines and circles, of which the principal are as follow.

The *Equator*, which divides the earth equally into two parts, north and south. This line is likewise called the Equinoctial, because on the two days in each year, viz. in March and September, on which the sun is in the Equator, the length of the day and night is equal in all parts of the world.

The *Ecliptic* is the circle in the heavens, in which the sun appears to move, and it is marked on the terrestrial globe, and on maps, for the convenience of working problems.

The *tropics* are two lines drawn parallel to the equator, at the points where the Ecliptic is at the greatest distance, north and south, from the Equator, that is, at 23°½ from that circle.

They derive their name from a Greek word, signifying to *turn*, because when the sun by its apparent motion, has ascended thus high in the heavens, he appears to turn back and to descend. It must be observed, that the ascent and descent refer to his meridian height, that is, to the height every day at twelve at noon. The sun is in the tropics on the 21st of June and the 22nd of December: on the former, he attains to his greatest meridian height; and will be found, if his progress be watched at intervals of two or three weeks, at the same hour in the day, to be lower and lower in the heavens, till the 21st of December, when it will again ascend.

The *Polar* circles are drawn at the distance of $23°\frac{1}{2}$ from the poles.

Besides these circles, the surface of the earth has, by Geographers, been divided into five spaces, called zones, contained between the circles which we have described. Thus between the poles and polar circles, are the two *frigid* zones: between these and the tropics, are two *temperate* zones; and the space included between the two tropics is called the *torrid* zone. These all derive their names from the temperature experienced in them. Formerly it was believed, that the temperate zones were the only inhabitable parts of the globe; but the contrary has been long ascertained. Large nations, for instance, are found to exist in the torrid zone, in the continents of Africa, Asia, and America, independently of those who inhabit the almost innumerable islands in the Indian, Pacific, and Atlantic oceans, that are included in the torrid zone. Some parts of the north frigid zone, are likewise known to be inhabited, as Spitzbergen, Greenland, &c.

Longitude and *Latitude* are terms perpetually occurring in the science of Geography, and should be well understood. *Longitude* is the distance of any place from a given spot, generally the capital of the country, measured *east* or *west* from that capital, thus we say Lisbon 9° 4′ W. L. that is, nine degrees, four minutes west of London, and Pekin, in China, is 116° 22′ east of London. But Paris being 2° 25′ east of London, the Geographers of that city would say, the longitude of Lisbon was 11° 29′ west, and that of Pekin, 113° 57′ east; and so of any other places.

Latitude is the distance north or south from the Equator: thus London is 51° 31′ north latitude, and the island of

St. Helena is 15° 15′ south latitude: The line from which the latitude of places is measured being invariable, geographers of all nations refer to the same place, when speaking of any given degree of latitude, but the degrees of longitude will vary according to the place fixed on, as a boundary from which the measures commence.

The terms *Longitude* and *Latitude* are of ancient origin, meaning length and breadth; the former was probably so denominated and applied to the direction east and west, because more of the earth was known from the Straits of Gibraltar, to the Euphrates or Indus, than from the coast of Barbary to the Baltic sea, that is, from the south to the north. Even now the term length is usually applied to the greater, and breadth to the smaller dimension of a body or space. The ancients measured their longitude from Ferro, one of the Canary islands, west of the coast of Africa, and which is 18° 6′ west longitude of London. This meridian, or circle of longitude, is even now referred to in some works of science, as that from which the degrees are reckoned.

The map of the world, whether *in plano* or on a globe, is divided into two hemispheres, the one, or eastern hemisphere, contains the continents of Europe, Asia, and Africa, called also the Old World, as having been partially known to the ancients: the other, or western hemisphere, contains the two continents of North and South America, denominated the New World, having been discovered by Columbus, about the year 1493.

Till within a very few years, it has been customary to denominate Europe, Asia, Africa, and the two Americas as the four quarters of the world. This division was not more absurd than disproportionate, the relative extent of these *quarters* as they have been called, being nearly as the numbers 1, 4, 5, and 7: that is, Asia is about four times larger than Europe, Africa five times, and America seven times.

Modern geographers, among whom is Mr. Pinkerton, include the land of our globe under six great divisions, viz. Europe, Asia, Africa, and America, with the two recent denominations of Australasia and Polynesia: of the latter terms, the first is applied to New Holland and the adjacent isles; the second includes the numerous islands situated in the Pacific ocean, between Australasia and America.

The waters of the ocean occupy at least two thirds of the earth's surface. The depth of the ocean, is in many parts too great to be ascertained by any means that have been devised for the purpose, but the mean depth of the whole has been calculated at about 220 fathoms. The facts, however, on which this estimate has been made, are not sufficiently numerous to justify us in speaking upon the subject with any degree of certainty. Various ingenious hypotheses have been invented, to account for the saltness of the ocean, but the true theory is probably still enveloped in darkness. The greatest degree of saltness is in the waters between the tropics, and it gradually diminishes towards the poles.

The ocean is divided by geographers into various parts, which are limited by real or imaginary boundaries. Of these, the largest is (1.) the *Pacific* ocean, sometimes called the Great South Sea, which is situated between the eastern coasts of Asia, and the western borders of America. It contains a vast multitude of islands, which appear like the summits of immense mountains emerging from the deep: this ocean is divided by the Equator, into the North and South Pacific: and (2.) the Atlantic ocean, which separates Europe and Africa from America, and it derives its name from the mountains of Atlas, situated in the north-west of Africa. The northern, or frozen ocean surrounds the north pole, and is bounded towards the south by the northern limits of Europe, Asia, and America, with the Atlantic Ocean and Beering's Strait, by which last a communication is formed between it and the Pacific Ocean. The South Polar Sea encompasses the south pole in a similar manner, and is a continuation of the Atlantic, Pacific, and Indian oceans. The Indian Ocean washes the eastern coasts of Africa, the southern shores of Asia, and forms the western boundary of New Holland.

There is no doubt, from the experience of past ages, as recorded in well-authenticated histories, that the waters are constantly encroaching upon the land in some places, and receding from it in others. A considerable part of the eastern coast of Great Britain appears, at some remote period, to have been under the sea; and, in the reign of Henry I. the estates of the Earl Goodwin were overflowed by the sea, and formed what are now denominated the Goodwin Sands. It is not improbable that the island of Sicily was once united to Italy, and our island, with France.

EUROPE.

EUROPE is bounded on the north by the Frozen Ocean, on the west by the Atlantic, on the south by the Mediterranean, and on the east it is divided from Asia by an imaginary line drawn through the Archipelago, the Black Sea, the Sea of Azoph, continued along the rivers Don and Wolga, and thence to the Uralian mountains, from which it proceeds to the north sea under Nova Zembla. Within these limits are several kingdoms, as Norway, Sweden, Denmark, and Russia, in the north; then follow Prussia, Germany, Austria, and Turkey in Europe, Italy, and Switzerland; on the westerly side there are Holland, France, Portugal, and Spain. Between Switzerland and Italy, is the city of Geneva. The lower part of Italy is called the kingdom of Naples. At the top, to the west, is Genoa, above this, is Piedmont, in which is Turin, formerly the capital of the king of Sardinia's dominions. At the top of Italy, on the east, is Venice, from which the gulf of Venice, that separates Italy from Turkey in Europe, takes its name. Above the gulf of Venice is the Tyrol, Carinthia, Istria, and Carniola; and above Turkey in Europe are the dominions of the emperor of Austria, Hungary, and Bohemia. The lower part of Turkey in Europe is called Romelia: this was anciently the celebrated Greece, of which the lowest part, called the Morea, was the Peloponnesus. To the east of Germany, above Hungary, was formerly situated the kingdom of Poland, which the then sovereigns of Russia and Germany, with the king of Prussia, seized, and wickedly divided among themselves. That part of Russia which is contained between the Black Sea and the Sea of Azoph, is called the Crimea, or Little Tartary. To the north of Norway, Sweden, and Russia, is Lapland, divided into Danish, Swedish, and Russian Lapland, and between the gulfs of Bothnia and Finland, is that large tract of country denominated Finland. Norway has long been subject to the crown of Denmark; but, by a late treaty, it is to pass under the government of Sweden. Between the island of Zealand and the coast of Sweden, is the Sound, where a toll is claimed by the king of Denmark, from all ships which pass through it.

The chief of the European islands are Great Britain and Ireland, whose decided pre-eminence among the nations of the world, was never so signally displayed as within the last five or six years. Above these islands is Iceland; and, about midway between Europe and America, off the coast of Portugal, are the Azores, the most remote of the European islands. In the Mediterranean, off the coast of Spain, are Yvica, Majorca, and Minorca. Under Genoa are Corsica and Sardinia. At the foot of Sicily is the celebrated island of Malta. To these may be added to the east, Candia and Cyprus. Zealand is the principal island in the Baltic, in which is Copenhagen, the capital of Denmark.

ASIA.

ASIA is bounded on the north by the Arctic ocean, on the east by the Pacific, on the south by the Indian ocean, and on the west by Europe, the Mediterranean and Red Sea: by the latter it is separated from Africa.

Asiatic Turkey comprizes several states which have obtained conspicuous places in the ancient history of the world;

among these are Asia Minor, Syria, Mesopotamia, Armenia, Mingrelia. It is now divided into provinces, Natolia, or Anatolia, occupies the western part of Lesser Asia, and is followed on the south-east by Caramania. East of this is Roum, extending from the north-east shore of the Mediterranean to the southern coast of the Black Sea. Syria is the name still applied to a district on the eastern limits of the Mediterranean Sea; and Armenia, on the south-east extremity of the Black Sea, retains its ancient appellation. Algezira borders on the Arabian desert, and occupies the greatest part of the ancient Mesopotamia, situated between the Euphrates and Tigris.

To the south of Asiatic Turkey, and between the Arabian or Red Sea, and Persian Gulph, is Arabia, and on the East is Persia, below which is Hindostan, the ancient empire of the Great Mogul, lying between the rivers Indus and Ganges. In this part of Asia are the principal British and European settlements. On the west of Hindostan is the British settlement of Bombay, an island a little below the gulph of Cambay. Lower down on the western side is the coast of Malabar, and on the eastern, is the coast of Coromandel. On the coast of Malabar is the Mysore, and on the opposite is the Carnatic. The southern point of Hindostan, is called Cape Comorin. On the Coromandel coast is Pondicherry, long famous as the capital of the French settlements in the East Indies, but now possessed by the British, who are, in fact, the masters of India Proper. Above Pondicherry is Madras, and, at the mouth of the river Ganges is Bengal, of which the capital is Calcutta, the principal of the British settlements in India. South of Bengal is Orissa, and, to the north-west of it, is Bahar. Above Bahar is Oude, and to the north of Oude is Delhi; below Delhi is Agra. Eastward of the Ganges is the kingdom of Pegu, which, with Ava, constitutes the Birman empire. To the south of Pegu is Siam, and on the west of the gulph of Siam is Malaya, and on the east of the same gulph is Cambodia. On the north-east of this is Cochin-China, and more north is Tonquin. China extends from the gulph of Tonquin to the Yellow Sea. West of China is Thibet. North and north-west of China, is the region of Chinese, or Mogul Tartary. Still westward, towards the Caspian, is Calmuc and Usbec Tartary, and the space between the Black and Caspian Seas, is Russian Tartary. The whole of the upper part of Asia, beyond the provinces already described, is Siberia. Quite in the north-east, is Kamtschatka.

The principal Asiatic islands, are, Ceylon, to the south-east of Cape Comorin. Off the promontory of Malacca, are the Sumatran or Sunda Isles. East of Sumatra, and above Java, is the large island of Borneo, and north of Borneo, are the Philippines, called also the Manillas. East of Borneo, are the Celebezian Isles; north-east of the Celebes, are the Molucca or Banda Isles. East of these is New Guinea. Off the coast of China, lies the island of Hainan: to the east of Canton, is the island of Formosa; and, north of the coast of China, are the islands of Japan.

AFRICA.

Africa is an immense peninsula, connected with Asia by the isthmus of Suez, bounded on the north by the Mediterranean, which separates it from Europe, on the East by the above named isthmus, the Red Sea, and the Indian ocean, by which it is divided from Asia: its southern part runs into the Southern ocean, and the Atlantic flows on its western shores. It is probably more than thrice as large as Europe, but in the estimation of the politician and philosopher it is of vastly less importance than any of the other three grand divisions of the globe, nevertheless, if its relative situation be examined, it is better adapted to commerce than any other quarter of the globe. Its north coast, for a thousand miles, being opposite to, and at no great distance from Europe.. From Asia it is separated only by the Red or Arabian Sea: and its western coast, for two thousand miles, lies opposite to America. The people, however, are ignorant, and where there is little or no knowledge, the great spring to action is wanting, and from such a country, nothing good can be expected or hoped for.

In Africa, the first kingdom on the western side below the straits of Gibraltar, is Fez; proceeding eastward is Algiers, then Tunis, and Tripoli, beyond which is Barca, and still more eastward is Egypt. The coast from Fez to Tripoli inclusive, is called the Barbary coast, of which the governments are military, under a governor called a Dey or Bey, who is said to be subject to the Grand Signior; but who, in fact, is really independent, except on his own troops.

South of the Barbary coast is the Sahara, an immense and unexplored Desert; and below this, reaching from a little above Cape de Verde to the coast of Guinea, is the coast of Senegambia. On the south of this is the settlement of Sierra Leone, below which is the coast of Guinea, divided into the Grain, the Ivory, and Gold coasts. Below Guinea are the Portuguese settlements of Congo, Loango, and Angola. The southern point of Africa is called the Cape of Good Hope. Here is Caffraria, the country of the Hottentots. Ascending from the Cape along the eastern side of Africa, are the coasts of Natal, Sabia, Sofala, Mozambique, Querimba, Zanguebar, Azania, and Ajan. On the north point of Ajan, is Cape Guardana, west of which are the straits of Babelmandel, which lead into the Red or Arabian Sea. West of this sea is the kingdom of Abyssinia, above which is Nubia, comprizing Sennaar and Dongola, and, still higher up, is the long and far-famed Egypt. The remainder of Africa is but little known, notwithstanding the attempts that have been made to explore the country.

The islands to be enumerated with this quarter of the globe are the Madeiras. The Canaries, or Fortunate Islands, of which seven are inhabited. The chief of these is Teneriffe, celebrated for its mountain called the Peak of Teneriffe, an extinct volcano, twelve thousand feet above the level of the sea. South of the Canaries, are the ten Cape de Verde islands, of which St. Jago is the chief. In the gulph of Guinea, are

Prince's and St. Thomas's Islands. South of the latter is the island Annabon, far to the west of which are St. Matthew and Ascension islands; and, much to the south of St. Matthew, is the island of St. Helena. Off the coast of Mozambique is the island of Madagascar, one of the largest in the world, to the East of which are the islands of St. Mauritius and Bourbon.

AMERICA.

AMERICA, though usually denominated a quarter of the world, is, more properly speaking, a hemisphere, discovered as we have seen, by the immortal Columbus. On the 11th of October, 1492, this great man perceived a light in one of the Bahama islands, on which he landed the following morning, and gave it the name of San Salvador, though by the natives it was called Guanahani. Soon after, he landed at Cuba, and on the 6th of December, he arrived at the island of Hispaniola, since called St. Domingo. It was not till some years after, that he discovered the main land of South America; previously to which, North America had been visited by Giovanni Cabot, a Venetian, employed by Henry VII. of England.

Among the followers of Columbus, was Amerigo Vespucci, a Florentine, who, on his return, wrote a narrative of his adventures, with so much art as to make it appear, that he had the glory of having first discovered the continent of the New World. Amerigo's account was drawn up with elegance: it contained an amusing history of the voyage, and as it was the first description that was published, it circulated with amazing rapidity, and was read with admiration. The country of which Amerigo was supposed to be the discoverer, came gradually to be called by his name, and time has perpetuated the error. Notwithstanding attempts have been made to substitute the name of COLUMBIA for that of AMERICA, the latter is almost universally adopted as the designation of this newly discovered hemisphere. Thus the bold pretensions of a fortunate adventurer and impostor, have robbed the discoverer of the New World, of a distinction that belonged to him. The name of Amerigo has supplanted that of Columbus, and mankind may in vain regret an act of injustice, which, having received the sanction of ages, it is now too late to redress.

North America, with which we shall begin, is bounded on the east by the Atlantic, on the west by the great Pacific ocean, on the south by the isthmus of Panama, on the north, above Hudson's Bay, its boundaries are unknown. Travellers have, however, penetrated far into the Arctic circle. Davis's Strait, which leads into Baffin's Bay, may be said to separate North America from Greenland, which has been divided into West or New Greenland, and East or Old Greenland. A north-west passage, in these high latitudes, has been frequently attempted, but without success, and the project seems now to be completely abandoned.

The British possessions in North America, lie above lakes Ontario, Erie, Huron, Michigan, and Superior, which discharge themselves, through the river St. Lawrence, into the Atlantic ocean. At the mouth of St. Lawrence, and on the eastern side, is New Brunswick, and still farther east is Nova Scotia, almost surrounded by the Atlantic, but the part which separates this peninsula from New Brunswick, is called Fundy Bay, remarkable for its high and rapid tides, which frequently rise fifty or sixty feet in height.

The country, lying north-east of St. Lawrence, is called Lower Canada, that which is to the north of the lakes just enumerated, is Upper Canada. Labrador, or New Britain, is a very extensive tract of country north of Lower Canada, between Hudson's Bay and Davis's Straits. On the southern coast of Hudson's Bay, is New South Wales, and on the west, is New North Wales. The British territories are the two Canadas, Labrador, New Brunswick and Nova Scotia, besides the islands of Newfoundland, Cape Breton and St. John. The metropolis of the British American possessions is Quebec, situated on the river St. Lawrence: next to this is Montreal in the Lower, and York, the seat of government of the Upper Canada.

South of the river St. Lawrence and the lakes, are the United States of America, formerly provinces of Great Britain, but which, in 1782, after a seven years' war, obtained their independence. There were at first only thirteen of these confederated provinces, but they are now divided into seventeen; besides seven territorial governments. In books of Geography they are frequently arranged according to their situation, as the northern and southern, and the middle between the other two; but if they are enumerated according to their population, the following will be the order, as given in the late census:

Provinces.	*Population.*	*Provinces.*	*Population.*
Virginia —	— 965,079	Connecticut —	— 261,942
New York —	— 959,220	Tennassee —	— 261,727
Pennsylvania	— 810,163	Georgia — —	— 252,433
Massachusets and the Main	— 700,745	New Jersey —	— 245,562
		Ohio — —	— 230,760
North Carolina	— 563,526	Vermont —	— 217,913
South Carolina	— 414,935	New Hampshire	— 214,412
Kentucky —	— 406,511	Rhode Island	— 76,931
Maryland —	— 380,546	Delaware —	— 72,674

The territorial governments are,

Orleans — —	— 76,556	Louisiana —	— 20,845
Mississippi —	— 40,352	Illinois — —	— 12,282
Indiana — —	— 24,520	Michigan —	— 4,762
Columbia —	— 24,023		

It should be noticed that Louisiana is a subject still in dispute between Spain and America. The remainder of North America belongs to Spain, consisting of East and West Florida, New Mexico, and, still more westward, California. To the south of these is Mexico, or New Spain, divided into various provinces, at the lower part of which is Honduras, celebrated for its logwood, and, still more southward, is Panama, giving name to the isthmus which separates North from South

America. The western parts of North America are but little known.

We have already noticed the large and important island of Newfoundland: in the mid-way between this and the West Indies, are the Bermudas or Sommer's Islands. Off the coast of East Florida lie the Bahamas, and below are Cuba, Hispaniola, and Jamaica. Porto-Rico is east of Hispaniola, and to the south-west of this, are the Caribbee Islands, of which the chief are Barbadoes, Martinique, and Guadaloupe. Of the Caribbees, those south of 15° N. Lat. are called *Windward* islands: those more northerly, are denominated *Leeward* islands.

South America requires a very short description. The more northerly part is called the Spanish Main: east of the isthmus of Panama is the government of the Carraccas, to the east of which is Guiana, divided among the Spaniards, French, and Portuguese: on the west is New Granada. South-east of these is the immense province of Brasil, belonging to the Portuguese, at the back of which is Paraquay, attached to Spain. Below is Buenos Ayres, and below this, in the central parts of South America, are the Pampas, or immense plains between the Eastern coast and the Andes. At the most southern parts of the continent is Patagonia, on the western side above this is Chili. Above this is Peru, and above this is Granada, reaching up to the Isthmus of Darien.

The islands of South America, in the Pacific ocean, are the Gallipagoes, through which the Equator runs. Off the coast of Chili, is the island of Juan Fernandez. At the bottom of Chili, is the island of Chiloe. At the extremity of South America is a collection of small islands, called Terra del Fuego, or land of fire, from the volcanoes there. The extreme southern point of these is called Cape Horn. Terra del Fuego is separated from South America, by the straits of Magellan. North-east of these are the Falkland isles.

AUSTRALASIA, is a name employed by some modern geographers of eminence, to denote the territory of New Holland, and some other large islands situated on the south-east of the great Asiatic continent. This part of the globe includes, (1.) New Holland and the adjacent isles. (2.) Van Diemen's Land. (3.) Papua, or New Guinea. (4.) New Britain, New Ireland, and Solomon's Isles. (5.) New Caledonia, and the New Hebrides, and (6.) New Zealand.

POLYNESIA. The islands said to be included in this geographical division, are (1.) The Pelew Isles. (2.) The Ladrones. (3.) The Carolines. (4) The Sandwich Isles. (5.) The Marquesas. (6.) The Society Isles. (7.) The Friendly Isles,

CHAP. XXII.

GEOGRAPHY,

Continued.

Ancient Geography—Europe—Asia—Africa. Directions for studying Geography.

WE shall now give a brief sketch of ancient geography, which will be useful, as well in reading the classics, as to those who study ancient history. This will connect the modern with the ancient state of the world, and the reader will find his advantage in having before him a modern atlas, with D'Anville's maps of Ancient Geography, or a work entitled "Atlas Classica," published several years since, by Wilkinson of London. We shall set out with the southern part of

EUROPE.

HISPANIA, which answers to our Spain and Portugal, was divided into Citerior and Ulterior. The citerior, or nearer, was afterwards called Tarraconensis, and extended from the Pyrenees to the mouth of the Douro, comprehending all the north of Spain, together with the south, as far as a line drawn below Carthago Nova, or Carthagena, and continned obliquely to the Douro, above Salmantica, now Salamanca. Hispania Ulterior was divided into Bœtica, situated between the river Anas, or Guadiana, and Hispania Citerior; and Lusitania, which corresponds nearly to our Portugal.

Hispania was sometimes denominated Iberia, from the river Iberus, Ebro; and Hesperia, from its westerly situation. At the ancient Fretum Herculeum stood Calpe, or Gibraltar, one of the pillars of Hercules; the other was at Abila, on the African coast. These pillars were supposed to have been erected by Hercules, as the boundaries of the western world. The name Gibraltar, is derived from Gebel Tarik, the mountain of Tarik, a Moorish General, who first led the Moors into Spain. The Junonis promontorium on the Atlantic side of the straits, is the modern Trafalgar, which is Gades, now Cadiz. The modern Cape St. Vincent was denominated the *Sacrum* promontorium, because the ancients thought that this was the place, at which the Sun plunged his chariot into the sea. The isles of Majorca and Minorca, were the insulæ Baleares of the Romans, and the Gymnesiæ of the Greeks.

GALLIA was much more extensive than modern France, as it included parts of the United Provinces, the Netherlands, Switzerland, and Italy to the west of the Alps. It was originally divided among three great nations, viz. the Celtæ, the Belgæ, and the Aquitani. The Celtæ extended from the Sequana or Seine to the Garumna or Garonne: the Belgæ lay above the Celtæ, between the Seine and the Lower Rhine; and were intermixed with several of the Germanic tribes: the Aquitanæ lay between the Garonne and the Pyrenees, and were intermixed with the Spanish tribes.

About 126 years B.C. the Romans, at the request of the people of Marseilles, entered Gallia, and obtained possession of a district called Provincia, anciently called Gallia Braccata, from the braccæ, or breeches, worn by the inhabitants, hence the second division of Gallia consisted of Belgica, Celtica, Aquitania, and Provincia. In the year 27, B.C. Augustus made a new distribution of Gallia into the provinces, Aquitania, Belgica, Lugdunensis and Narbonensis.

BRITANNIA included England, Scotland, the Orkney, Shetland and Hebrides islands; also the isles of Man, Anglesea, Wight, and Thanet. But *Britannia* and Albion, were often especially applied to England and Scotland. HIBERNIA, sometimes denominated Britannia Minor, Scotia and Irne, was the modern Ireland. Vectis was the isle of Wight, and the modern Scilly islands were denominated the Cassiterides; Mona Taciti was the isle of Anglesea, and Mona Cæsaris, the isle of Man.

GERMANIA included part of the United Provinces, Denmark, or the Cimbrica Chersonesus of the ancients, Germany as far South as the Danube, including Bohemia; part of Prussia, Poland, to the West of the Vistula, and that part of Hungary contained between the Danube, the Morava, and the Gran. The remainder of Europe, East of Germania, and North of the Danube, went under the generic name of Sarmatia, the inhabitants being called Sarmatæ and Sauromatæ. In the same manner, the North of Asia, beyond the Euxine and Caspian seas, was known by the generic name of Scythia. In ancient Germany was an immense forest, called Hercynia Sylva, the whole extent of which was unknown; Cæsar was nine days in crossing it, and a longitudinal journey of sixty days, had been made without coming to its boundary. It contained part of Switzerland and Transylvania.

SCANDINAVIA included Norway, Sweden, and Lapland.

RHŒTIA included the country of the Grisons, part of the circle of Swabia, the greatest portion of Bavaria, and part of the circle of Austria.

NORICUM included that portion of the circle of Bavaria, which is east of the right branch of the Inn, and that part of the circle of Austria, which is south of the Danube, west of Vienna, north of the Save, and to the east of Wessenfels situate on the Save, near its source. Noricum once an independent government was reduced, during the reign of Augustus, to the subjection of the Romans.

PANNONIA, situated to the east of Noricum, consisted of

the territory included within the Drave and Danube, till their junction near Essek, and part of Croatia, Sclavonia, a small portion of Bosnia and Servia, and the eastern part of the circle of Austria. Pannonia was first reduced to a Roman province by Tiberius, after which it was divided into Superior and Inferior, the former occupying part of Hungary, the latter, Sclavonia. In Pannonia Superior was Vindebona, now Vienna; Acincum, now Buda, opposite to which was Pest. In Pannonia Inferior, between the Save and Drave, was Sirmium.

ILLYRICUM included the south-eastern part of the circle of Austria, part of Croatia, Dalmatia, the greater part of Bosnia, and Albanio north of Alesse. This country became a Roman province in the reign of Augustus, and the divisions were denominated Liburnia and Dalmatia.

ITALIA, so called from Italus, a prince of the country, included the whole extent of modern Italy, excepting that part of it which is included within the Alps, and which made one of the eastern boundaries of Gallia. This country was also called *Hesperia* by the Greeks, as being west of Greece; *Ausonia*, from a people of the country; *Œnotria*, from a prince named Œnotrus, the son of Lycaon; and it was called Saturnia, from its being supposed the residence of Saturn, after his expulsion from heaven by Jupiter. It was anciently divided into Gallia, Cisalpina, or Gaul on this side the Alps, and Gallia Propria; after this the southern part of Italia was denominated Græcia Magna, from the Grecian colonies which it contained, viz. Apulia, Calabria, Lucania, Brutium, &c.

SICILIA, CORSICA and SARDINIA, islands in the Mediterranean sea, attached to Italia, retain their ancient names.

GRECIA is that part of Turkey in Europe, which is bounded on the west by the Gulf of Venice and the Grecian Sea; on the south by the Mediterranean, and on the east by the Archipelago. It was divided into Macedonia on the north, Græcia in the middle, and Peloponnesus, or island of Pelops, on the south. The modern name for the Peloponnesus is

Morea, from the mulberry trees that grow there, having been introduced for supplying silkworms with food.

THRACIA included that part of Turkey in Europe, between the Black Sea, and the mountains Hæmi and Rhodopes. This country was conquered by the Romans during the reign of Claudius, and toward the end of the third century of the Christian æra, Thracia was divided into four provinces; Europa, Hæmimontus, Rhodope and Thracia.

MOESIA comprehended that part of Turkey, which included Bulgaria and Servia, deducting that part of it which belongs to Pannonia, and part of Romania. The extent of Moesia along the Ister, was divided into Moesia Superior and Inferior.

DACIA included the district of Bessarabia, Moldavia, Wallachia, Transylvania, Upper Hungary, and part of Lower Hungary.

SARMATIA EUROPÆA, comprehended Prussia and Poland, to the east of the Vistula; Courland, Lithuania, Crimæa, and Russia in Europe.

ASIA.

ASIA MINOR, a term never used by the ancients, comprizes the provinces between the Euxine and Mediterranean seas, and is now called Anatolia. Along the shores of the Euxine and the Propontis, is Bithynia, next to which is Paphlagonia, and on the east of this is Pontus. South of the Propontis is Mysia, and, still more southerly, are Lydia, Caria, and Lycia. South of the Hellespont, which leads from the Propontis to the Archipelago, is Troja or Troas, the scene of Homer's Iliad. North-east of Lycia is Pamphylia, Pisidia, and Phrygia, and east of Phrygia is Cappadocia. Cilicia and Isauria are on the south, the latter bordering on the Mediterranean.

SYRIA is below Cilicia, not far from the eastern coast of the Mediterranean; the coast itself is called Phœnicia, south of which is Palestina, or the Holy Land. The northern part of

Palestina was Galilæa, the middle, Samaria, and the lower or southern part, Judæa. Below Judæa, at the top of the Sinus Arabiens was Arabia Petræa, or Stony Arabia, lower down was Arabia Felix, or the Fruitful, and the rest of the plain between the Arabian and Persian gulphs was Arabia Deserta. East of Arabia, near the mouth of the Euphrates, at the top of the Persian gulph, is Chaldea, and, above it, Babylonia. Mesopotamia is situated between the rivers Euphrates and Tigris: on the east of the Tigris is Assyria, and still more easterly is Media, to the south of which is Persia. North of Mesopotamia is Armenia, above which, on the eastern coast of the Euxine, was Colchis, between this and the Caspian, were Iberia and Albania. Above was Sarmatia Asiatica. East of Persia was Caramania, and south of this latter was Gedrosia, which reaches almost to the Indus. The country between the Indus and the Ganges, was India intra Gangem, and that east of the Ganges, was India extra Gangem: south-east of which were the Sinæ, Cochin China. East of Media was Aria and Bactriana: north of Media at the southern extremity of the Caspian, were Hircania and Parthia, and north of Hircania were the Chorasmii, to the north-east of whom were the Massagetæ. All the country to the North was called Scythia, divided into Scythia intra Imaum, or Scythia within the mountain Imaus, and Scythia extra Imaum. North-east was Serica, which approached to the north-west of China.

AFRICA.

AFRICA was called Libya by the Greek and Roman poets, the name which moderns give to the whole continent being generally confined to a particular province now denominated Tunis. Little was known of this quarter of the globe excepting the parts adjacent to the coast of the Mediterranean. The first province of Africa on the western side below the Fretum Gaditanum, was Mauritania, now Morocco and Fez: east of it was Numidia, now Algiers, and east of Numidia was Africa Propria, now denominated Tunis, between this and

Tripolis were the Syrtes, minor and major, two dangerous quicksands. East of the Syrtis major, was Cyrenaica, now Barca. Proceeding still eastward, we come to the mouths of the Nile and Egypt, divided into the Inferior and Superior, the former or Lower Egypt, on the coast, the latter or Upper Egypt in the interior of the continent. Below Cyrenaica was Libya properly so called; below Egypt was Ethiopia.

As a course of general study in the science of Geography, we have no hesitation in saying, that the pupil should begin with Modern Geography; and, if he is not satisfied with the sketch given in the preceding chapters, and wish to treasure up in his mind the leading facts necessary to be known, he may commit them to memory by means of Goldsmith's "Easy Grammar of Geography." The maps and questions for examinations will afford him much aid; but he should, by all means, if the price is not an object to him, obtain maps on a larger scale, and which may have higher claims to accuracy than can be expected in a work of that form. "Geography for Children" has been much used; and in the later editions, the facts may be depended on. Its chief merit is, that it is adapted to save trouble to the teacher, who will have nothing more to do in using the work, than to ask his pupils the questions, and the answers regularly follow. To a person who performs the duty of a self-instructor, this plan does not seem so good as that of the work before-mentioned.

Turner's Geography has gone through many editions: it is a small volume, consisting of a series of letters, written with neatness, accuracy, and spirit. These will, by many persons, be preferred to works drawn up in a didactic style. The letters include a considerable portion of historical knowledge, well adapted to learners; and the questions formed upon each letter, and also on the maps, render the work of much value as an introduction to geography. The maps are, however, too small for the purpose; but the questions will apply to others on a larger scale, and which possess a higher authority.

From these, or any of them, or of others of the same kind, the student may proceed to Pinkerton's Modern Geography, in three volumes, 4to. of which the plan is as follows: the author *first* gives the historical, or progressive geography of each country: *secondly*, its political state, including most of the topics which are commonly denominated statistic: *thirdly*, the civil geography, comprising objects not so immediately connected with the government, as an account of the chief cities, towns, &c.; and, *fourthly*, the natural geography of the countries described. Mr. Pinkerton has arranged the countries according to their comparative importance, it being, he observes, proper, that the objects which deserve most attention, should be treated of at the greatest length, and claim the earliest attention of the student. An abridgment of this work, in a very large and closely printed octavo volume, was drawn up by Mr. Arthur Aikin, and an Introduction to it has been published by Mr. Williams, with outline maps, to be filled in by the learner, a plan which will be found of eminent service in fixing upon the learner's mind, a strong and correct impression of the relative situations of the countries with respect to the whole globe; and of the cities, towns, rivers, mountains, &c. with respect to each kingdom, country, or state.

We would not willingly pass over "A Compendious System of Modern Geography, Historical, Physical, Political, and Descriptive, by Thomas Myers," because it is a work of much merit, drawn up with great care, and, as far as we have been able to examine it, the details are accurate and highly interesting.

Of Geographical Grammars on a large scale, one of the most considerable is that by Salmon; and there is another by Guthrie; the latter has, in a great measure, superseded its predecessor, and contains a vast body of information; but the historical department has been enlarged beyond due bounds, for a work professedly devoted to geography.

There are several gazetteers which may be recommended as highly useful in historical and geographical studies. The one by Brookes is a work of much merit; this, and also one by the Rev. Clement Crutwell, profess to notice all the places in the known world; and, perhaps, in the last edition of Crutwell's Gazetteer, there are but few material omissions. It is extended to four large and closely printed octavo volumes, and contains, in an alphabetical arrangement, a description of all the empires, kingdoms, states, provinces, cities, towns, forts, seas, harbours, rivers, lakes, mountains, and capes, in the world; with accounts of the government, customs, manners, and religion, of the inhabitants. As a *vade mecum*, the "Compendions Dictionary, containing a Concise Description of the most remarkable places, ancient and modern, in Europe, Asia, Africa, and America," &c. may be recommended. This small volume has been several times reprinted, and in the second and subsequent editions, there is added a large chronological table.

In addition to the works already enumerated, as connected with teaching and illustrating modern geography, we may notice Goldsmith's larger work, entitled, "Geography on a Popular Plan," and Dr. Aikin's "Geographical Delineations;" the former was intended to follow the "Grammar" before referred to. In this, every country is treated of separately, and at the head of each article is an account of the situation, boundaries, latitude and longitude, of the country treated on, with other useful particulars. Then follow more minute accounts of the inhabitants, their dispositions, amusements, and customs; of their festivities, the climate of their country, the religion which they profess, and of their education. The volume concludes with a description of the curiosities of nature, a view of the universe, and instructions for projecting and drawing maps.

Dr. Aikin's "Delineations," in two volumes, differ materially as to their object, both from the elementary treatises, and the more complete systems of this branch of knowledge, and they may be considered as occupying a station whence young persons of both sexes may review the extent and bearing of their former studies. In arranging and proportioning the various information concerning each country, the author has adopted for his two leading considerations, the characters that are impressed upon it by nature, and those which it derives from its inhabitants.

Such may be mentioned as among the leading works in modern geography, many others of real merit might, no doubt, have been added, but we choose to refer to those concerning which we can speak from our own knowledge, rather than depend upon the authority of other persons.

To connect ancient with modern literature, Dr. Butler's "Sketch of Modern and Ancient Geography" may be recommended to the attention of young persons, as containing much information in a small compass, and put in a striking light; to this, and to a much smaller work by Mr. Richard Perkins, we have been indebted for assistance in the former part of the present chapter.

"Cellarii Geographia," in two volumes, quarto, is a work of considerable authority; as a school-book, there is a very useful abridgment of it. D'Anville's maps of modern and ancient geography, with his compendium of ancient geography, to which we have already referred, will be a valuable acquisition to the student. So also will Rennel's Geography of Herodotus, and his memoir of a map of Hindostan, and of the Peninsula of India. Chauchard's General Map of Germany, Holland, the Netherlands, &c. with a descriptive volume, in 4to. will be a very desirable addition to the Geographical library. The comparative view of ancient and modern geography in "Tytler's Elements of General History," will be very useful in the way of reference. The Geography of the New World will be best learnt from Dr. Morse's "American Geography."

In connexion with these, or any of them, recourse should be had to the facts and discoveries collected and related by modern travellers. These may be had separately, or in collections; of the latter, the work of Mr. Pinkerton, in seventeen volumes, 4to. is one of the last published; but there is a very good collection in twenty-six volumes, crown 8vo.

CHAP. XXIII.

ON CHRONOLOGY.

Importance; and principles of Chronology—Sir Isaac Newton's method, by generations—by the precession of the equinoxes—by eclipses. Divisions of time into days—months—years. Cycles—Lunar cycle—Julian year —Gregorian year, and new style—Solar cycle—Cycle of Roman indiction—Julian period.

CHRONOLOGY is the art of measuring time, distinguishing its several constituent parts, such as years, months, weeks, days, hours, &c. by appropriate marks; and of adjusting these parts to past transactions, by means of æras, epochs, and cycles, to the illustration of history.

The utility and importance of the knowledge of chronology, as it comprehends the distribution of time into its subordinate parts, and the arrangement of historical events, by means of these several divisions, in the order according to which they occurred, so that their respective dates may be accurately fixed, will be universally acknowledged. We can form but very confused notions of the intervals of time, of the rise and fall of empires, and of the successive establishment of states, without some general comprehension of the whole current of time, as may enable us to trace out distinctly the dependence of events, and distribute them into such periods and divisions, as shall lay the whole chain of past transactions in a just and orderly manner before us. This is what the science of chronology undertakes to teach, or, at least, to afford us very important aid in the attainment of.

Chronology derives much assistance from several other branches of knowledge, such as astronomy, geography, geometry, and arithmetic; and also from the observation of eclipses, from the testimony of credible authors, and from ancient medals, coins, and monuments.

Many ages undoubtedly elapsed before the mode of computing time, or of giving dates to important events, was brought into established use. The most ancient philosophers and historians, as we have seen, wrote in verse, and were unacquainted with chronology. From the works of Homer, it appears that there existed, at that early period of the world, no formal calendar of time, nor any well-authenticated register of events. Time was then measured by the revolutions of the sun and moon, by the changing seasons, or the successive returns of labour and rest. There was then, nor for ages afterwards, no political distribution of time into such parts as months, weeks, or hours, serving the purpose as guides to history, or as registers of facts; nor is there any reference to clocks, dials, clepsydræ, or other instruments, by which the perpetual flow of time was broken into parts. Several centuries intervened between the Olympic æra, and the first historians, and several more elapsed before the period in which the first chronologers appeared.

Sir Isaac Newton, to whose "Chronology of Ancient Kingdoms," we shall have occasion to refer, has shewn that all nations, before they began to keep exact accounts of time, have been prone to advance their antiquity. The priests of Egypt reckoned one period of their history, viz. from Menes to Sethon, at more than eleven thousand years. The Chaldeans boasted a still greater antiquity than even the Egyptians pretended to; and there were others, who made the kingdoms of Assyria, Media, and Damascus, much older than the truth.

According to the account of the illustrious Newton, the Greeks called the times before the reign of Ogyges, *unknown,* because they had no history of them: those between his flood and the beginning of the Olympiads, they denominated *fabulous*, because their history was very much blended with poetical fables; and those after the beginning of the Olympiads, *historical*, because their history was free from such fables. The fabulous age, however, was destitute of a chronology, so also was the historical, during the first sixty or seventy Olympiads. Hence it should seem, that the chronology of ancient kingdoms was involved in the greatest uncertainty; and it has been shewn, that the Europeans in particular had no chronology before the Persian empire, which began five hundred and thirty-eight years before Christ; and that the dates of events, which they now have of more ancient times, have been given as the result of reasoning and conjecture. After this time, several of the Greek historians introduced the computation by generations.

The chronology of the Latins was still more uncertain; their old records being burnt by the Gauls one hundred and twenty years after the expulsion of their kings, and about the year 388, B. C.

The chronologers of Gaul, Spain, Germany, Scythia, Sweden, Britain, and Ireland, are of a still later date. For Scythia, beyond the Danube, had no letters, till Ulphilas, their bishop, formed them, about the year 276 of the Christian æra. Germany had none, till it received them from the western empire of the Latins, about the year 400. The Huns had none in the days of Procopius, about the year 526, and Sweden and Norway were still later.

After a general account of the obscurity of the ancient chronology, Sir Isaac Newton observes, that, though many of the ancients computed by generations and successions, yet the Egyptians, Greeks, and Latins, reckoned the reigns of kings eqnal to generations of men, and three of these to a hundred, or a hundred and twenty years, which was the foundation of their technical chronology. He then proceeds to shew, from the ordinary course of nature, and a detail of historical facts, the difference between reigns and generations; and that, though the latter, from father to son, may, at an average, be reckoned at about thirty-three years, yet, when they are taken by the eldest sons, three of them cannot be computed at more than seventy-five or eighty years; and the reigns of kings are still shorter, so that eighteen or twenty years may be allowed as a just medium. He then fixes on four remarkable periods, viz. the return of the Heraclidæ into Peloponnesus, the taking of Troy, the Argonautic expedition, and the return of Sesostris into Egypt, after the wars in Thrace; and settles the epocha of each by the true value of a generation.

Our object in this place is, to give a view, by means of a single example, of the method which this illustrious philosopher makes use of in tracing the real dates of the most important events in history, from which, of course, others of minor importance, but more interesting to general readers, are settled on a sure foundation.

We take as our example, the Argonautic expedition, an event which is the grand hinge on which all the chronology of ancient Greece turns. Having fixed the return of the Heraclidæ to about the one hundred and fifty-ninth year after the death of Solomon, and the destruction of Troy to the seventy-sixth after the same epoch, Sir Isaac observes, that Hercules, the Argonaut, was the father of Hyllus, the father of Cleodus, the father of Aristomachus, the father of Temenus, Cresphontes, and Aristodemus, who led the Heraclidæ into Peloponnesus: hence their return was four generations later than the Argonautic expedition, and these generations were short ones, being by the chief of the family. Counting, therefore, eighty years backward from the return of the Heraclidæ to the Trojan war, and the taking of Troy, will be about seventy-six years after the death of Solomon, as has been observed above; and the Argonautic expedition, which was one generation earlier, will be forty-three years after it. From the taking of Troy to the return of the Heraclidæ, our author observes, "cou'd scarcely be more than eighty years, because Orestes, the son of Agamemnon, was a youth at the taking of Troy, and his sons lived till the return of the Heraclidæ."

Another method used by Sir Isaac Newton for fixing the date of the Argonautic expedition is purely astronomical, but nevertheless intelligible to those who have made but a small progress in the science. The sphere, it is known, was formed by Chiron and Musæus at the time, and for the use of the Argonautic expedition, and they placed the solsticial and equinoctial points in the 15th degree of the constellations Cancer, Libra, Capricorn, and Aries. Now Meton, in the year of Nabonassar, 316, or 431, B. C. observed that the summer solstice had then gone back seven degrees, and as it goes back one degree in seventy-two years, it must have taken five hundred and four years to have gone back seven degrees, but five hundred and four years added to the four hundred and thirty-one, B. C. just mentioned, gives nine hundred and thirty-five years, B. C.; and forty-three years added to this as found above, brings us to the period of the death of Solomon, or about the nine hundred and seventy-eighth year before the Christian æra. See Sir Isaac Newton's Short Chronicle.

The same author ascertains this, and several other capital events in the Grecian history, by the above, and many other independent arguments drawn from similar sources, which are so agreeable to the present course of nature, that there seems no reason why we should not place the fullest confidence in the facts drawn from them.

But the time of past events is likewise ascertained by means of celestial appearances, from which, on account of the regularity and constancy of the revolutions of the heavenly bodies, and because the laws of their motions are so exactly known to us, the most clear and undeniable conclusions may be drawn. In this respect, modern chronologers and historians are greatly indebted to the superstition with which the ancients regarded unusual appearances in the heavens. It was their supposed portentous nature that drew upon them the attention of mankind, who dreaded their unknown influences and effects; and, on this account only, they engaged the notice of historians. Fortunately for the historians and chronologers of modern times, the catalogue of ancient eclipses, not observed by philosophers, but gazed at by the superstitious vulgar, is pretty full.

With the history of many remarkable revolutions and critical situations in the history of states, the eclipses which preceded or accompanied them, are faithfully transmitted to us; and in cases where the time, the place, and the quantity of an eclipse are mentioned, though not with astronomical exactness, it is not difficult, by certain rules of calculation, to fix the very year, and often day, when the event happened. For, considering the great variety which the three circumstances of *time, place,* and *quantity,* occasion in the appearance of eclipses, there is no room to suspect that any two, happening within a moderate distance of one another, can be in the least danger of being confounded.

Dr. Playfair, Ferguson, and others, have given long lists of eclipses that occurred before the Christian æra, observed by astronomers, or recorded by historians: likewise of all the eclipses that have occurred, and that will happen between the birth of Christ, and the end of the present century, and have shewn how they may be applied to the verification of dates in history. The following example will point out in what manner this kind of knowledge is to be appreciated; and how the date of the events is ascertained by its help.

In Thucydides' history, an eclipse of the moon is thus recorded: "Upon the arrival of Gylippus to the assistance of the Syracusans, the Athenians, finding that they were no match for the united force of their enemies, repented that they had not quitted their situation before, and immediately came to the resolution to sail out of the harbour as secretly as possible. But when every thing was ready for sailing, the moon was eclipsed, for it was then full moon. Upon this most of the Athenians, alarmed at the omen, desired their commanders to proceed no farther; and Nicias, being himself a superstitious observer of such prodigies, declared that he would not come to any final resolution about quitting the place till they had staid three days longer, according to the advice of the soothsayers. This occasioned the Athenians to remain in the place, which they had never after an opportunity of leaving, and in which they almost to a man perished." This event is placed by historians in the year 413, B.C. To ascertain the truth of this fact, we refer to the astronomical tables, from which it appears that the moon was full about midnight at London, on the 27th of August* in that year, when the sun was so near the nodes, as to be within the limits of Lunar eclipses, and when of course there must have been a total eclipse of the moon, which would be visible, from beginning to end, to the Athenians, and may therefore reasonably be supposed to have produced the effect ascribed to it by the historian.

A history, which contains an account of a sufficient number of these phenomena, furnishes the surest test of its authenticity. It may be farther observed, that the truth of the Scripture history being unquestionable, and relating to times prior to the age, in which history began to be written by any other people than the Jews, it is the best guide to the knowledge of prophane antiquity. It was in pursuing this plan, that Sir Isaac Newton was led to correct the ancient chronology of the Greeks, by itself. The principles on which he reduces their accounts are, as we have seen, founded on nature; and independent of any arguments drawn from Scripture. But it is probable that believing (see his Chronology, p. 66-79.) Sesostris to have been the same person with Sesae, or Shisak, of whom an account is given in the history of Reboboam, in the second book of Chronicles, he first fixed the date of that expedition according to the Scriptures; and after-

* In Playfair's tables, the date of the year is 423, which is evidently a mistake of the printer, who inserted the 2 instead of 1.

wards from considering the subject in various points of light, he was led to the other arguments that have been referred to, by which he was able to confirm the Scriptural date of that event, and also the dates of the principal facts in the history of Greece connected with it, in a manner independent of the authorities on which he originally founded his opinion. Then, having by the joint assistance of Scripture and reason, rectified the chronology of the Greeks, he made use of it to adjust the contemporary affairs of the Egyptians, Assyrians, Babylonians, Medes and Persians, which are the subjects of the several chapters contained in his "Chronology of Ancient Kingdoms amended," &c.

Having briefly shewn in what way the astronomy of eclipses, and of the precession of the equinoxes; and the use of observations on the intervals between the generations of men, and succession of kings, are applied to ascertain the dates of past events, as recorded on the page of history, we shall proceed to notice and explain the several artificial divisions of time, which are of great importance to the student in history.

The divisions of time which are considered in chronology, relate either to the different methods of computing days, months and years, or the remarkable æras or epochas from which any year receives its name, and by means of which the date of any event is fixed.

The divisions of time which probably first attracted the notice of mankind, were those marked by the revolutions of the heavenly bodies, as days, lunar months, and years; and if these had exactly corresponded with each other, so that every lunation had consisted uniformly of the same number of days, and each year of a regular number of lunations, the business of chronology would have been comparatively easy. But as this is not the case, the embarrassments and difficulties attending the subject, have been owing to the methods that have been adopted to accommodate the three methods of computing time, viz. by days, months, and years, to one another, so as to make use of them all at the same time.

Besides these three natural divisions of time, there is another into weeks of seven days; which division, however, though used by Jews, Christians and Mahometans, and by almost all the people of Asia and Africa, was not observed by the ancient Greeks and Romans. We shall now proceed to give an account of the above named divisions of time, and point out the methods, as briefly as we can, of accommodating them to one another.

Of the day. It must be observed that days have been very differently begun, and divided by different people, in different ages: thus the ancient Babylonians, Persians and other eastern nations, began their day with the sun's rising. The ancient Athenians, Jews, and many German nations, the modern Italians, and Chinese, reckon from the sun's setting: the Arabians, &c. with modern astronomers, reckon from noon; and the Egyptians and Romans, with the modern English, French, Dutch, Germans, Spaniards, and Portuguese, from midnight.

The Jews, Romans, and most other ancient nations divided their day into twelve hours, and the night into watches. But the custom now generally prevails in the western part of the world, to divide the day into 24 equal portions: with a few of the nations, as the Italians, the Poles, and Bohemians, the twenty-four hours are counted on without interruption, but in general they are divided into twice twelve, to which our time-pieces are accommodated.

Of the month. There is scarcely any doubt, but that the division of time into months was originally suggested by the phases, or periodical changes of the moon, and that in ancient computations, the months were lunar. As a complete lunation consists of about 29½ days, and the changes of the moon are very visible, there was no great difficulty in accommodating them to each other, or in fixing what number of days should be allowed to a month. In general the ancients made them consist of 29 and 30 days alternately. When months came to be reckoned not by lunations, but were considered as the twelfth part of a year consisting of about 365¼ days, it became necessary to allow sometimes 30 and sometimes 31 days to a month, as in the Roman Calendar.* Whenever months are mentioned as divided into days in the Scriptures, they are supposed to consist of 30 days each, and in these cases 12 months, or 360 days, are reckoned in the year.

Of the year. Different nations have made their years begin at different times, and have used a variety of methods to give names to them, and distinguish them from each other. The *Jews,* for instance, began the year for *civil* purposes in the month called *Tizri,* which answers to our September; but, for ecclesiastical purposes, they began with *Nizan,* which answers to our April, at which time they kept the passover. The people of Athens began the year with the month which commenced with the first new moon after the summer solstice. The early Romans had only ten months in their year, but Numa Pompilius added two others, viz. January and February.

In modern Rome, there are two modes of reckoning: one begins the year at Christmas, on account of the nativity of our Saviour: this the notaries and public men make use of, by prefixing to their deeds *à nativitate:* by the other, the commencement is in March, which refers to the incarnation of Christ, hence the pope's bulls are dated, *anno incarnationis.*

In England, we had, till the year 1752, two beginnings of the year, one in January, and the other on the 25th March; but by act of Parliament, at the period alluded to, the first of January was appointed to be the beginning of the year for all purposes.

The eastern nations generally distinguish the year by the reigns of their princes. The Greeks named their years from the magistrates who presided over them, as in Athens,

* This Calendar, as it existed in the days of Julius Cæsar, may be found in Danet's Classical Dictionary 4to. 1700: it was copied into a very entertaining periodical work, entitled "Time's Telescope, for 1814."

from the Archons. The Romans likewise named the year by the consuls, and it was a long time before names were assigned to years, from any particular æra or remarkable event. At length the Greeks reckoned from the institution of the Olympic games, and the Romans from the building of their city. It was not till about the year 360, that Christians began to reckon from the birth of Christ, and hence the difficulty of ascertaining with precision, the true time of that important event.

Cycles. The chief difficulty in chronology, has been to accommodate the two methods of computing time, viz. by the course of the moon, and that of the sun, to each other; the nearest division of the year by months, being twelve, but twelve lunar months falling eleven days short of a complete year. This gave birth to many *cycles* in use among the ancients.

Cycles are fixed intervals of times, composed of the successive revolutions of a certain number of years. The Greeks for instance reckoned by *Olympiads*, or periods of *four* years: and the Romans by *Lustra*, or periods of five years. These, strictly speaking, may be denominated cycles, though the term is usually appropriated to larger intervals, connected with the periodical return of certain appearances.

As the twelve Lunar months did not agree with the number of days in a year, the Greeks were accustomed to add, or as it is technically called, *intercalate*, a month every other year, this was eight days too much, and was no doubt rectified by omitting the addition, when it was observed, by comparing the seasons with their annual festivals, that they ought so to do. This method would therefore never have deviated far from the truth, had not other circumstances occurred of a political nature, which baffled all regular computation. When, for instance, it was the interest of the chief magistrate to lengthen or shorten a year, for purposes of ambition, all other considerations were often sacrificed to it, and the greatest confusion was introduced. Hence they found themselves under the necessity of having some certain rule to compute by, and at first they added, or intercalated one month in every four years, but as four times 11 is 44, the error would be still 14 days in that cycle or period of time. They then intercalated three months or 90 days in 8 years, in this, there was an excess of about 2 days, which error being but trifling, the cycle continued in use a considerable time.

Lunar cycle. Meton, an Athenian Astronomer, invented the cycle of 19 years, in which 7 months were intercalated. This, which was called from the inventor, the Metonic cycle, brought the two methods to so near an agreement, that after the expiration of the period, the new and full moons return on the same days of the year, on which they were nineteen years before, hence it is called the Lunar cycle. This cycle, somewhat improved, was adopted by the Christians, A. D, 325, at the council of Nice, for the purpose of settling the time for Easter, and the other feasts, which depend upon it. This period, however, falling short of 19 years, almost an hour and half, the new and full moons in the heavens have anticipated the new and full moons in the calendar of the Common-Prayer book, at this time, 1815, by 117 hours, or nearly 5 days.* These last are called Calendar new moons, to distinguish them from the real new moons.

From the great utility of this cycle to the purposes abovementioned, the council of Nice caused the numbers of it to be written in golden characters, whence it obtained the name of the *golden* number. If the lunar cycle had been made, or supposed to commence with the Christian æra, the *golden* number for any year would have been the remainder found by dividing the given year by 19. But this consideration was neglected, and in reckoning back, it was found that the first year of our æra corresponded to the second year of the cycle of 19 years. Therefore the golden number is found for any year by adding 1 to the given year, and dividing by 19; and the remainder left after division is the number sought: thus

* 1815—325=1490 and this multiplied by $1\frac{1}{2}$ and divided by 19, gives 117 hours.

for the year 1815, we say $\frac{1816}{19}=95$ and 11 over, therefore the Golden number for the year is 11; if there be no remainder, then the Golden number is 19.

Julian year. Before we come to the Solar cycle, we must give some account of the method of adjusting the number of days to a year, in which there was considerable difficulty, inasmuch as the period that the earth takes in going round the sun, which is the length of the year, does not consist of any even number of days, but of 365 days 5 hours and 49 minutes.

The Egyptians, Chaldeans and Assyrians, reckoned at first 360 days to the year, and afterwards 365. The consequence of this was, that the beginning of their year, would go back through all the seasons, though slowly, viz. at the rate of 5 hours and 49 minutes every year. Of this form were the years which took their date from the reign of Nabonassar of Babylon, Yesdigerd of Persia, and the Seleucidæ of Syria, of which we shall soon have occasion to speak.

The inconvenience attending the form of the year above noticed was remedied by Julius Cæsar, who added one day to every fourth year, which, from its place of insertion, viz. the sixth of the calends of March, was called bissextile, or the sixth repeated, answers to our *leap* year. This form is, from its inventor, called the *Julian* year.

Gregorian year. The true length of the year being 11 minutes short of 365 days 6 hours, Pope Gregory XIII. introduced another amendment in the year 1582, by ordering a day to be taken out of the calendar once in 133 years, or what amounted to the same thing, that three days should be taken out of 400 years, in the following manner: viz. from and after the year 1600, every hundredth year, which according to the Julian form, should be bissextile, or leap year, was to be reckoned common, but every four hundredth year was to continue bissextile, as in the Julian account. When this pope undertook to rectify the calendar, the error which had crept in by the former method amounted to ten days; he, therefore, commanded the ten days between the 4th and 15th of October, in that year, to be suppressed, so that the 5th was called the 15th. This alteration took place, at the same time, through the greater part of Europe, and the year was afterwards called the Gregorian year, or *New Style*, which was not admitted into our calendar till 1752, when the error amounted to eleven days, which were taken from the month of September, by calling the 3d of that month the 14th. By act of parliament at the same time, New Year's day was changed from the 25th of March to the 1st of January. Of course the following months of January, February, and March, up to the 24th, inclusive, which would, by the old method, have been reckoned part of the year 1752, were accounted as the first three months of the year 1753. Hence in many books printed after that period, we read of such dates as 20th February, 1774,5, that is, by old style it would be 1774, but by the new it was 1775.

Solar Cycle. It has been of consequence to Christians to adjust the days of the week to the days of the month, and of the year, in order to get a rule for finding Sunday. Had there been no bissextile, as the year consists of fifty-two weeks and one day, all the varieties that could have happened, would have been comprised in seven years. But the bissextile returning every fourth year, the series is interrupted, and does not return in order, until after four times seven, or twenty-eight years, which is, therefore, called the *solar cycle*, serving as a rule to find Sunday, and of course the other days of the week. At the expiration of this period of twenty-eight years, the sun returns to the sign and degree of the ecliptic, which he had occupied at the conclusion of the preceding period, and the days of the week correspond to the same days of the month as at that time.

In finding what year of the solar cycle corresponds to any given year of the Christian æra, it must be remembered, that the first year of the Christian æra is supposed to correspond to the tenth of the solar cycle, and the rule is as follows:

To any given year add nine, and divide the sum by 28, the quotient gives the number of the revolutions of the cycle since its commencement, and the remainder will be the year of the cycle. If there be no remainder, the year of the cycle is called 28. The year of the solar cycle for the present year, 1815, is $\frac{1815+9}{28}=\frac{1824}{28}=65$ and the remainder, 4, is the number of the solar cycle.

In our calendars the days of the week are distinguished by the first seven letters in the alphabet, A, B, C, D, E, F, G. The letter A is always put for the first day of the year, B, for the second, and so on in succession to the seventh. If, for example, the first of January fall on a Sunday, the dominical, or Sunday letter, will be A, Monday, B, &c.; and as the number of letters is the same as that of the days of the week, A, will fall on every Sunday, B, on every Monday, C, on every Tuesday, &c., throughout the year. Had the year consisted of 364 days, making an exact number of weeks, A, would have been a perpetual Sunday letter, but as it contains one more, the dominical letter for the following year will be G, because, Sunday, being the first day of the preceding year, will also be the last, the first Sunday will fall on the seventh day, and will be marked by the seventh letter, or G. This retrocession of the letters will, from the same cause, continue every year, so as to make F, the dominical letter of the third year, E, of the fourth, and so on. In leap-years, for obvious reasons, the Sunday letter will, after the 28th of February, be thrown back two letters. Thus, in the year 1814, the dominical letter was B, in the present year it is thrown back a letter, and is A, and in January and February, 1816, it will be G, but in the other ten months, as a day is added to February, the Sunday letter will be F. If a table be constructed for the years of one of these solar cycles, it will answer for the corresponding years in every successive cycle.

Cycle of Roman Indiction. Besides the above mentioned periods of years, there is one called the cycle of Roman Indiction, a period of fifteen years, at the end of which, a certain tribute was paid by the provinces of the Roman empire, and by which the Roman Emperors ordered their public acts to be dated. The current year of the Roman Indiction is found by adding 3, and dividing by 15, the remainder, 3, is the number of the year sought, thus $\frac{1815+3}{15}=\frac{1818}{15}=121$ and 3 over.

Julian period. This, which has been called the most remarkable of all the periods in chronology, was invented by Joseph Scaliger, it takes its name from the years of which it consists being Julian years. The object of the inventor was to reduce to a certainty, the different methods of computing time, and fixing the dates of events by different chronologers. For this purpose, nothing was necessary but a series of years, some term of which was fixed, comprehending the whole extent of time. Since if all chronologers would apply that common measure to their several schemes, they would understand one another.

To attain this object, the author combined the three periods of the *sun*, the *moon*, and *indiction*, together, that is, multiplying the numbers 28, 19, and 15, into one another, which produces 7980; after which, all the three cycles will return in the same order, every year, being distinguished by the same number of each. To fix the beginning of this period, he took the cycles as he then found them settled in the Latin church, and tracing them back through their several combinations, he found that the year in which they would all begin together was the year before the Creation, 714, and that the first year of the Christian æra would be 4714 of this period. The year of the Julian period corresponding with any given year, before or since the commencement of the Christian æra, may be found by the following rule. If the year required be *since* the commencement of the Christian æra, *add* to it 4713, and the sum will be the year required. If it be *before* the Christian æra, then *subtract* the year B. C. from 4714, and the difference will be the result.

Christian æra. The period just mentioned is now seldom used, notwithstanding the high estimation in which it was formerly held, because, in truth, the very general adoption of the Christian æra, supersedes the want of any other standard of time than that. It is true there may be a difference of opinion respecting the time when Christ was born, but this is no inconvenience, since all chronologers agree in calling the present, and of course every other year, by the same name, and, therefore, they have the same idea of the interval between the present year, and any other year in the system. The real time of the birth of Christ cannot affect the use of this system, since, using the same system of dates, they may say Christ was born in the third, fourth, fifth, sixth, or seventh, or any other year before the Christian æra. Whenever, therefore, chronologers ceased to date events from the Creation, they had no occasion to have recourse to any such period as the Julian, since another, capable of answering the same purposes, was already in common use, supplying them with a language which they all equally understood.

CHAP. XXIV.

CHRONOLOGY,

Continued.

Epochas and Æras—Creation of the World—Deluge—Argonautic expedition—Destruction of Troy—Olympic Games—Roman Æra—Æra of Nabonassar—Æra of the Seleucidæ—Spanish Æra—Christian Æra—Mohammedan Æra—Memoria Technica.

WE shall now give some account of the Epochas and Æras which are most known in history, and which are of frequent recurrence, as well in chronology as in history. An *Epocha* or Epoch, relates to a certain point of time, which is generally determined by some remarkable event, from which subsequent events are reckoned, and the years reckoned from that period are denominated an *Æra:* thus the birth of Christ is considered as an epocha; but the series of years flowing from and after that event, are called the years of the Christian æra: hence we date the present year, Anno Domini, 1815.

In sacred chronology, the first and most remarkable epocha is that of the Creation of the world, but as learned men could not agree, as to the time when this event took place, they have long since ceased to reckon from it. Archbishop Usher, whose Scripture-chronology is adopted in our translation of the

Bible, fixes this event in the year 4004 before the birth of Christ; Dr. Playfair places it in the year B. C. 4007: but according to the Septuagint version, it is placed 5872, B. C. and by the Samaritan version, it is fixed to the year 4700.

The Universal Deluge forms another epoch, which, according to the reckoning of Usher, is placed in the year 2348, B. C. The two other chief epochas, founded on the Old Testament, are, the call of Abraham, in the year 1921; and the departure of the Israelites from Egypt, in 1491, B. C.

The æra of the Seleucidæ, or year of the *Contracts*, is reckoned from the establishment of Seleucus, one of Alexander's generals, after the death of his master, in the empire of Babylon, and is reckoned from the year B. C. 312.

The Greeks, as we have seen, for a long time had no epocha from which they reckoned, but afterwards they assumed the commencement of the Olympic Games as the foundation of their first æra, which were instituted in honour of Jupiter, and celebrated once in four years. The Olympic æra begins with the year 776, B. C. The chief epocha among the Romans, and to which there is a perpetual reference in their histories, is the building of the city, assumed to have taken place in the year 753, B. C.

The æra of Nabonassar is reckoned from the commencement of the reign of Nabonassar, the founder of the Babylonish monarchy, which is placed in the year 747, B. C. The year in this æra consisted of 12 months of 30 days each, and five intercalary years.

In profane history, the epocha of the Argonautic expedition is much celebrated, and has been, as we have observed, that which Sir Isaac Newton has adopted as the foundation of his system of chronology. This has been referred to the year 1225, B. C., but writers are not at all agreed as to the date. The destruction of Troy forms another remarkable epocha, and though much uncertainty prevails as to the exact time when this event actually took place, yet it is generally fixed by chronologers and by Dr. Playfair at 1183, B. C.

The Spanish æra, reckoned from the year 38, B. C. is founded on a division of the Roman provinces among the Triumviri, and was pretty general in Spain and Africa, and adopted in the dates of the principal councils and synods held in those countries. This gave way to

The Christian æra, which was invented about the year 526, by Dionysius Exiguus, a Roman Abbot, who reckoned the first year of it to correspond with the 4714 of the Julian period. Learned men differ very materially with regard to the exact time of the *birth* of Christ, from which this period is dated, and this uncertainty arises from the æra not having been adopted until the sixth century, so that it was impossible at that time to fix the date with accuracy. Dr. Playfair makes the

First year of the Christian æra correspond with the - - -	4008th year of the	World.
	1st ————	195th Olympiad.
	754th ————	Building of Rome.
	749th ————	Nabonassarean æra.
	313th ————	Seleucidæ.
	46th ————	Julius Cæsar.
	39th ————	Spanish æra.
	10th ————	Solar cycle.
	18th ————	Cycle of the moon.
	2d ————	Paschal cycle.
	4th ————	Roman Indiction.
	11th ————	Epact
	B as the Dominical letter.	

Previously to the establishment and adoption of the Christian æra, the Christians, (who had formerly computed from the building of Rome) had made use of the Dioclesian æra, which took its rise from the persecution by Dioclesian, in the year 284, after the birth of Christ.

The Hegira, or Mohammedan æra, is founded upon the flight of Mohammed from Mecca to Medina, to escape the persecution of his enemies, which is agreed by his followers to have been A. D. 622. It must be observed, with respect to all those methods of denominating time, that great care will be required that the year be reckoned according to the method of computation followed by the people who use it. Thus, in reckoning from the Hegira, or in accommodating any year of this æra, to one of the Christian æra, a person would be lead to a mistake, who should make those years correspond to Julian years, because the Mohammedans make their year consist of lunar months, without adapting it to the course of the sun; so that with them the beginning of each year goes backward, computed with true time, at the rate of eleven days every year. He must, therefore, deduct eleven days from every year, which has elapsed since the commencement of it. Thus, though the first year of this æra corresponded to the year 622 of Christ, and began on the 16th of July; the year 331 of the Hegira, does not correspond with A. D. 953, but with 942, and it began Sept. 15th, and the beginning of the year 1231, of the Hegira, answers to Dec. 2d. of the present year 1815.

By the following table, the year of the Hegira may always be readily reduced to its corresponding year of the Christian æra:

33— 1	429—13	825—25	1221—37
66— 2	462—14	858—26	1254—38
99— 3	495—15	891—27	1287—39
132— 4	528—16	924—28	1320—40
165— 5	561—17	957—29	1353—41
198— 6	594—18	990—30	1386—42
231— 7	627—19	1023—31	1419—43
264— 8	660—20	1056—32	1452—44
297— 9	693—21	1089—33	1485—45
330—10	726—22	1122—34	1518—46
363—11	759—23	1155—35	
396—12	792—24	1188—36	

In the use of this table, it must be remembered that 33 Arabic years, are shorter than the same number of Christian years by one year, 66 by 2 years, &c.

To reduce a year of the Hegira to a year of Christ, add 621, the Christian date of the commencement of the Hegira, to the given year, and then look for the date of the Hegira in the preceding table. If you do not find it, take the next lowest date, and subtract the number corresponding with it from the sum already obtained, and you have remaining the exact year of the Christian æra.

Example 1. To reduce the year 757 of the Hegira to its corresponding year in the Christian æra.

$$\begin{array}{r} 757 \\ 621 \\ \hline 1378 \end{array}$$

Look for the next number, not exceeding the date of the Hegira in the table, which will be found to be 726, the corresponding number of which is 22.

Therefore from	1378	
Subtract	22	
and you have	1356	the year sought.

Example 2. To reduce the year 1231 of the Hegira, to the year of Christ, which answers to it.

$$\begin{array}{r} 1231 \\ 621 \\ \hline 1852 \\ 37 \\ \hline 1815 \end{array}$$ the year sought.

Another method of finding what Julian year corresponds to a given year of the Hegira, is "to multiply the number of the given year by 354, and divide the product by 365: to the quotient add 622. Thus the year answering to 1231 of the Hegira, is $\frac{1231 \times 354}{365} + 622 = 1815$.

This compendium of chronology will, it is presumed, be sufficient for almost all the purposes of reading history. It remains, therefore, that we now give some account of what we esteem the best method of retaining the dates connected with facts recorded in history, which is that described by Dr. Grey, in his

Memoria Technica.

Of all things, there is the greatest difficulty in retaining numbers. They have been compared to grains of sand, which will not cohere in the order in which we place them; but, by transmuting figures into letters, which easily cohere, in every combination, we fix and retain numbers in the mind with the same ease and certainty with which we remember words. As this method is so easily learned, and may be of so much use in recollecting dates, when other methods are not at hand, particularly in conversation upon the subject of history, when dates are often wanted, Dr. Priestley says, "I think all persons of a liberal education inexcusable, who will not take the small pains that is necessary to make themselves masters of it, or who think any thing mean, or unworthy of their notice, which is so useful and convenient." We shall therefore explain Dr. Grey's method, and give, as an exemplification, two or three of the examples which will be found most useful to the student in history and chronology, and which will enable him to form others, *ad libitum*, for himself, in the course of his reading.

To remember any fact in history, a word is formed, the beginning of which being the first syllable or syllables of the thing sought, will, by frequent repetition, draw after it the latter part, which is so contrived as to give the answer. Thus, in history, the Deluge happened in the year before Christ 2348, which date is to remembered by the word Del*etok*, Del standing for Deluge, and *etok*, as will be now shewn, for the date, 2348.

In this art, letters stand for numbers; thus, the five vowels, *a e i o u*, stand for 1, 2, 3, 4, 5; these combined, make diphthongs, as *a u*, *o i*, *o u*, which represent the numbers 6, 7, and 9: *e i*, as the first letters of the word, stand for *eight*.

Consonants being required as well as vowels, we have *b*, *d*, standing for 1 and 2, as the first two consonants; *t*, *f*, *s*, *n*, for *three*, *four*, *six*, and *nine*; *l* stands for *five*, *p* for *seven*, *k* for *eight*, and *y* and *z* for a cypher, or 0.

The whole method is explained in the following table:

a	e	i	o	u	au	oi	ei	ou	y
1	2	3	4	5	6	7	8	9	0
b	d	t	f	l	s	p	k	n	z.

Here it is evident that *a* and *b* stand for 1; *e* and *d* for 2; *i* and *t* for 3; *o* and *f* for 4; *u* and *l* for 5; and so on.

Although the letters are arbitrarily assigned, we may observe, that *a u* stand naturally for 6, because *a* stands for one, and *u* for five, and $1 + 5 = 6$; for a similar reason, *o i* stand for 7; and *o u* for 9; *l* stands for 5, being, as Dr. Grey observes, the Roman letter for 50, p stands for 7, as being the emphatic letter in the word se*p*tem, seven; and, for a similar reason, *k* stands for 8, ὀκτὼ, the Greek for eight.

The foregoing table being committed to memory, with the explanations, the next thing to be done by the learner is, to obtain the habit of forming technical words to any combinations of figures.

Examples.

10	325	399	1921	6491	680	1810
az	*tel*	*toun*	*aneb*	*aufna*	*seiz*	*akby.**

* The *y* is pronounced broad to distinguish it from the *i*, and where it can be done conveniently, it is pronounced like the *w*, as *syd*, is pronounced *swid*, *typ*, *twip*, &c.

Suppose I wish to remember the date of the death of our great *Milton*, and know that it happened in the year 1674; I will make use of the first four letters of the name, and add to them the technical syllable *asoif* for the year, *a* being 1, s 6, *oi* 7, and *f* 4; thus the word is Milt*asoif*.

Where many cyphers come together, as 1000, 1,000,000, *g* stands for 100; *th* for 1000; *m* for 1,000,000; thus *u g* stands for 500; *e i t h* 8000; *u m* 5,000,000, five million; *a u g m* six hundred million.

The same date or number may be expressed by different words, according as vowels or consonants are used to represent the figures, or begin the words, thus:

tel	*buf*	*alf*	*ni ola*
325	154, or	154;	93,451.
idu	*blo*	*alo*	*out olb.*

This variety gives scope for choice in the formation of words; so that such terminations and combinations may be made use of, as by their singularity will be best remembered, or which may be most adapted to the thing by any accidental relation or allusion.

TABLE I.

General Epochas and Æras, Ecclesiastical and Civil.

	Bef. Christ.
THE Creation of the World [Cr *othf*] - - -	4004
The universal Deluge [Dél *etok* - - - - - -	2348
The Call of Abraham [Ab *aneb*] - - - -	1921
EXodus of the *Israelites* [Ex *áfna*] - - - - -	1491
The Foundation of *Solomon's* Temple [Tém *bybe*] -	1012
Cyrus, or the End of the Captivity [Cyr *uts*] - -	536
The Destruction of Troy [Tróy *abeit*] - - -	1183
The First Olympiad [Olym *pois*] - - - - - -	776
The Building of Rome [Rom *put*] - - - -	753

	Bef. Christ.
ÆRA of NABONASSAR [Æuabonáspop] - - - -	747
The PHILippick Æra, or the Death of *Alexander* [Phíl*ido*] - - - - - - - - - - - -	324
The Æra of CONTRACts, or of the *Seleucidæ*, called in the Book of *Maccabees*, the Æra of the Kingdom of the *Greeks* [Contráe *tad*] - - - - - -	312
	A. D.
The DIOCLESian Æra, or the Æra of Martyrs [Dio-clés *eko*] - - - - - - - - - - - - -	284
The Æra of the *Hegira*, or Flight of MAHOMet [Máhom *audd*] - - - - - - - - - - -	622
The Æra of YEzdegird, or the *Persian* Æra [Yéz *sid*]	632

The Memorial Lines.

Cr*othf* Dél*etok* Ab*aneb* Ex*áfna* Tém*bybe* Cyr*uts.*
Tróy*abeit* Olym*pois* Rom*put* & Æuabonás*pop.*
Phil*ido* Contrác*tad* + Dioclés*eko* Máhom*audd* Yéz*sid.*

TABLE II.

The Regal Table of England since the Conquest, *and some of the most remarkable Princes before it.*

	Bef. Christ.
CASIBELanus chosen chief Commander by the *Britains* against the Invasion of *Julius Cæsar* [Casibel*ud*] - - - - - - - - - - - - -	52
	Aft. Christ.
Queen BOADicea, the *British* Heroine, being abused by the *Romans*, raises an Army, and kills 7000 [Bóad*aup*] - - - - - - - - - - - - -	67
VORTIGern, who invited the *Saxons* to the Assistance of the *Britains* against the *Scots* and *Picts* [Vortig*fos*] - - - - - - - - - - - - -	446

	Aft. Christ.
HENGist, the *Saxon*, who erected the Kingdom of *Kent*, the first of the Heptarchy [Heng*ful*] - -	455
King ARTHur, famous for his powerful Resistance and Victories over the *Saxons* [Arth *laf*] - - -	514
EGBErt, who reduced the Heptarchy, and was first crowned sole Monarch of *England* [Egbe *kek*] -	828
ALFREd, who founded the University of *Oxford* [Alfré *kpe*] - - - - - - - - - -	872
CANute, the *Dane* [Can *bau*] - - - - -	1016
Edward, the CONFESsor [Coufés*fe*] - - - -	1042

WILliam the CONq. [Wil-con *sau*] - - -	*Oct.* 14.	1066
William RUFus [Ruf *koi*] - - - - -	*Sept.* 9.	1087
HENRy I. [Henr *ag*] - - - - - -	*Aug.* 2.	1100
STEPHen [Steph *bil*] - - - - - -	*Dec.* 2.	1135
HENry the sEcond [Henséc *buf*] - -	*Oct.* 25.	1154
RIchard I. [Ric *bein*] - - - - - -	*July* 6.	1189
John [J *ann*] - - - - - - - -	*April* 6.	1199
HEnry the THird [Heth *das*] - - -	*Oct.* 19.	1216
EDward I. [Ed *doid*] - - - - - -	*Nov.* 16.	1272
EDvardus sEcundus [Edse *typ*] - - -	*July* 7.	1307
EDvardus TERtius [Edter *tes*] . - - -	*Jan.* 25.	1326
RIchardus sEcundus [Rise *tóip*] - - -	*June* 21.	1377
HEnry the Fourth [Hefo *toun*] - - -	*Sept.* 20.	1399
HEnry the FIfth [Hefi *fúd*] - -	*March* 20.	1412
HENry the sIxth [Hénsi *fed*] - - -	*Aug.* 31.	1422
EDvardus QUARtus [Edquar *fauz*] - -	*March* 4.	1460
Edward the FIfth } [Efi-R *okt*] - - {	*April* 9.	1483
Richard III. }	*June* 22.	1483
HENricus sEPtimus [Henség *feil*] - -	*Aug.* 22.	1485
HENricus octav. [Henoc *lyn*] - - -	*April* 22.	1509
EDvardus sExtus [Edsex *los*] - - -	*Jan.* 28.	1546
MARY [Mary *lut*] - - - - - -	*July* 6.	1553
ELisabeth [Els *luk*] - - - - - -	*Nov.* 17.	1558
JAMes I. [Jam *syd*] - - - - -	*March* 24.	1602

CAROlus PRIMus [Caroprim *sel*]	*March* 27.	1625
CARolus SEcundus [Carsec *sok*] - -	*Jan.* 30.	1648
JAMes II. [Jam *seif*] - - - - - -	*Feb.* 6.	1684
WILliam and Mary [Wil *seik*] - - -	*Feb.* 13.	1688
ANne [An *pyb*] - - - - - - -	*March* 8.	1701
GEorge I. [Gëo *bo*] - - - - - -	*Aug.* 1.	1714
GEorge II. [Gëosec *doi*] - - - -	*June* 11.	1727
GEorge III. [Geoter *sy*] - - - -	*Oct.* 25.	1760

The Memorial Lines.

Casibe *lud* Bóad *aup* Vortig *fos* Heng *ful* & Arth *laf*.
Egbe *kek* Alfré *kpe* Can *bau* Confés *fe* Wilcon *sau*.
Ruf *koi* & Henr *ag*.———
Steph *bil* & Heusée *buf* Ric *bein* J *ann* Heth *das* & Ed-*doid*.
Edse *typ* Edter *tes* Rise *tóip* Hefo *toun* Hefi *fád*que.
Hénsi *fed* Edquar *fauz* Esi-R *okt* Henséр *feil* Henoc *lyn*.
Edsex *los* Mary *lut* Els *luk* Jam *syd* Caroprim *sel*.
Carsec *sok* Jam *seif* Wil *seik* An *pyb* Gëo *bo-doi-sy*.

N. B. After Canute inclusive, One Thousand is to be added to each. It was thought unnecessary to express it, it being a thing in which it is impossible that any one should mistake.

TABLE III.

Chronological Miscellanies since the Conquest.

	Aft. Christ.
Jerusalem regained from the *Turks*, and GODfrey of BULloigne made King of it [Godbul *nou*] - -	1099
The INQUIsition first erected against the *Albibigenses* [Inquis *ded*] - - - - - - - - - - -	1222
The Confirmation of Magna CHARTa by King *Henry* III. [Chart *eel*] - - - - - - - - - -	1225

Aft. Christ.

Wat TYLer's Rebellion suppressed [Tyl *ika*] - - 1381

Jack CADE's Rebellion suppressed [Cade *fly*] - - 1450

The Mariner's COMPass found out [Comp *atze*] - 1302

GUNPOWder invented in *Germany* by a Monk [Gunp *átfo*] - - - - - - - - - - - - 1344

The Invention of PRINting [Prin *afon*] - - - 1449

Christopher COLUMbus, a Native of *Genoa*, discovers *Cuba* and *Hispaniola* [Colum *bont*] - - - 1493

MARtin LUTHer begins to preach in *Germany* against Indulgencies, and other Errors of the Church of *Rome* [Mar-luth *lap*] - - - - - - - - 1517

The Name of PROTestants first began on Occasion of the Protestation the *Lutherans* made against a Decree of the Chamber of *Spire* against them [Prot-*alen*] - - - - - - - - - - - - 1529

The SMALCALdan League, or Agreement made between the Protestants of *Germany* for their mutual Defence at *Smalcald* [Smalcal *loz*] - - - - 1540

The Council of TRENT began DEC. 13. [Tren-dec-*at-alfu*] - - - - - - - - - - - - - 1545

The MAssacre of Protestants at PARis [Maspar *aloid*] 1572

The UNited provinces, under the Protection of *William*, Prince of *Orange*, throw off the *Spanish* Yoke [Un-p *loin*] - - - - - - - - - - 1579

The SPanish INvasion [Sp-inv *ukk*] - - - - - 1588

The GunPOWDer Treason [Powd *syl*] - - - 1605

The famous Rebellion at *Naples*, on Occasion of the grievous Excises, headed by MASSANELlo [Masanel *sop*] - - - - - - - - - - - - - 1647

Oliver CROMwell usurps the Government of *England*, under the name of Protector [Crom *sli*] - - - 1653

The Island JAMAIca in *America*, taken by the English [Jamaic *aull*] - - - - - - - - - 1655

CROMwelli MORs [Crom-mor *suk*] - - - - 1658

GIBRAltar taken by the *English* [Gibra *pzo*] - - 1704

The Memorial Lines.

God-bul *nou* Chart *eel* Inquis *ded* Tyl *ika* Cade *fly*.
Comp *atze* Gunp *atfo* Prin *afon* atque Colum *bont*.
Mar-luth *lap* Prot *alen* Smalcal *loz* Tren-dec *at-alfu*.
Mas-par *aloid* Un-p *lōin* Sp-in *leik* Powd *syl* Masanel *sop*.
Crom *sli* Jamaic *aull* Crom-mor *suk* capta Gibra *pzo*.

N.B. A Thousand is to be added, as above, where it is not expressed.

TABLE IV.

Grecian Lawgivers, Philosophers, and principal Poets.

	Bef. Christ.
LYcurgus born [Lyc *nes*] - - - - - -	926
DRAco [Drá *sdo*] - - - - - - - - - -	624
Solon died [So *lun*] - - - - - - - -	559
PYTHAGoras died, aged 80 [Pythág *lys*] - - -	506
EUCLid the Geomet. fl. [Eucl *izau*] - - - -	306
SOCRates died [Socr *inn*] - - - - - -	399
XENOPHon died [Xenóph *ilou*] - - - - -	359
PLAto died [Pla *tok*] - - - - - - - -	348
DIogenes died, aged 90 [Dio *tet*] - - - -	323
ARIstotle died, aged 63 [Aris *téd*] - - - -	322
EPICurus died, aged 72 [Epicu *dpa*] - - - -	271
ARCHImedes died [Archi *dad*] - - - - - -	212
LINus and Orpheus [Lin *adka*] - - - - -	1281
HOMer died [Hom *nad*] - - - - - - -	912
ARCHILOCHUS [Archilochu *skau*] - - - -	686
SAPPHO [Sapph *syd*] - - - - - - - -	602
ANACreon [Anác *loud*] - - - - - - - -	592
ÆSCHylus born [Æsch *lel*] - - - - - - -	525
PINDar died, aged 80 [Pind *fóz*] - - - - - -	440
SOPHOCLes born [Sophocl *ozoi*] - - - - -	407

The Memorial Lines.

Lyc *nes* Drá *sdo* So *lun* Pythág *lys* Eucl *izau* Socr *inn*.
Xenoph *ilou* Pla *tok* Dio *tet* Aris *ted* Epicu *dpa*.
Archi *dad* Lin *adka* Hom *nad* & Archilochu *skau*.
Sapph *syd* & Anác *loud* Æsch *lel*. Pind *foz* Sophocl *ozoi*.

CHAP. XXV.

CHRONOLOGY,

Continued.

Chronological Tables—Playfair's—Blair's—Tytler's—Lenglet du Fresnoy—Importance of Medallic Science to history—Antiquities.

ONE of the most obvious contrivances to reduce History into a short compass, and to make an entire course of it easy of apprehension, and at the same time to observe a proper distinction between the parts of it, has been by Chronological Tables. These would indeed be of great use, if they consisted of nothing more than an enumeration of the capital events in history, brought together promiscuously, as it were, without any distinction of kingdoms, regard being only had to the order of time in which the events happened, because we thereby see the principal things that history exhibits, and from the dates annexed to each article, can readily form an idea of the interval of time between each of them. Such is the Chronicle prefixed to Sir Isaac Newton's Chronology; and such also is the large table, or series of remarkable events in Dr. Playfair's Chronology. This table, which extends from the Creation of the world to the year 1782 inclusive, is by no means the most valuable part of the volume, which as a whole may be considered as a treasury of chronological knowledge, more ample and judicious than any that has even yet appeared. It unites the advantages of many different systems, and selects from them what is most valuable, while at the same time it combines them with so much skill, as justly to claim the praise of originality. The author is various without being perplexed, extensive without being superficial, and accurate without being tedious.

To return to chronological tables: besides a distinct view of the succession of events in different histories, it is an advantage to have in separate columns, an account of great men in arts, or arms, which each age has produced: and likewise in other columns, a *variety* of dates corresponding to the most important æras, to save the reader the trouble of reducing the different methods of computation to one another. These advantages are combined in Dr. John Blair's tables, which, however, differ according to the period of which they treat: to take, as an example, the fifth century before Christ:—the first four columns give the corresponding years of the Julian period, the æras of Nabonassar,—the Olympiads,—the building of Rome, and of the years before Christ: the next five columns point out the reigning kings of Persia, Macedon, and Lacedemon, and High Priests of the Jews: then follow columns containing the names and descriptions of illustrious men:—remarkable events—and the names of Statesmen, Warriors, &c.

Dr. Blair, in speaking of his own work, says, " The ancient Chronology has been digested in the tables, according to the Hebrew text, and agreeably to the system of Archbishop Usher; though it is proper to observe, that we do not assume the earlier dates of years, as if they could be demonstrated mathematically. For as we only prefer them, from their being more generally received than any other, amidst a vast uncertainty of no less than three hundred different opinions, about the exact year of the creation, we therefore choose to decline any controversy upon points, where the data are so few, and the range of hypothesis is so unlimited. And we may be the easier satisfied on this head, if we consider, that neither religion nor history, are fundamentally concerned, in precisely fixing the times of such remote antiquity.

The tables of Dr. Blair* reach to 1753 inclusive, and blank spaces are left, that the student may continue them to the beginning of the present century, and by the aid of another leaf, properly ruled, he may, and the exercise will be highly useful, bring them down to the present eventful period. The author has given three indices, *one* of the Emperors, Kings, High Priests, Caliphs, Popes, Men of Learning, Statesmen, Warriors, &c. in an alphabetical order, with references to the preceding plates: the other *two* are alphabetical indices to the remarkable events before and after the Christian æra, with constant references likewise to the plates.

As however the Chronology of Playfair, and the Tables of Blair, are scarce and expensive works, we can recommend as a succedaneum, the chronological table attached to the second volume of Tytler's Elements of General History. The plan of this table is as follows. In order to give a distinct view of the succession of princes in the chief empires or kingdoms, without employing different columns, the series of the sovereigns of the several nations is distinguished by their being printed in different typographical characters.

To the foregoing works in Chronology we may add a work which, in the course of our reading, we have found extremely useful, viz. "Tablettes Chronologiques de l'Histoire Universelle, &c. &c. Par M. L'Abbe Lenglet du Fresnoy," in two volumes; the first contains Ancient, and the second, Modern history. The edition which we have been accustomed to make use of, was corrected and revised by J. L. Barbeau de la Bruyere, in 1778. To the first volume are prefixed, (1) A preliminary discourse on the method of studying History—(2) A long list of books, necessary in the study of history, accompanied with judicious observations—(3) A sketch of Chronology and of the different modes of reckoning—(4) A chronological series of the eclipses mentioned by ancient authors.

Of Coins and Medals. There are few studies of more

importance to the study of history, than that of medals. The sole evidence we can have of the veracity of an historian, depends on such collateral documents as are evident to every body, and cannot be falsified. In modern times, these are found in public memoirs, instructions to ambassadors, and state papers, to which we have already referred in Chap. xvii. Such kind of memorials, are however, subject to various accidents, and being attached to the countries in which they were first published, cannot give to the world at large that perfect and entire satisfaction, which ought to be the result of genuine history, so that more durable and widely diffused monuments, are still to be wished for. Such in fact, are coins and medals: they are portable and infallible documents of the truth, capable of being diffused over all countries in the world, and of remaining through the latest ages. The materials of both are similar, and the events they record are single and remarkable. The small size of a coin does not admit of its being so circumstantial as a monument, and it is more liable to be lost; but on the other hand, it is more capable of being concealed, and is not exposed to the injuries of the weather; and as numbers are struck at the same time, they stand a fairer chance of being seen by posterity. Though we may be more liable to be imposed upon by pretended antiques, this does not affect the historian; for if the new ones be exact copies of ancient coins, they corrupt no history, and it cannot be worth a person's while to coin a piece, whose known existence has not acquired a considerable degree of reputation.

The original and primary use of coins, is not to be mentioned among the direct methods of recording events; for all the ancient coins, which have now obtained the denomination of medals, were nothing more than the stamped coins of ancient nations. The monumental use, however, of such portable pieces of metal, struck by the direction of the state, were so very obvious, as to lead, at an early period, to the double use of them. Of the impressions of the *Crœsi*, so called from Crœsus, the first prince whose money is mentioned by historians, we know little; but the Latins coined their first money with the head of Saturn on one side, and the figure of a ship on the other, in memory of his coming to Italy by sea; and upon every new and remarkable event, and upon the accession of a new magistrate in the Roman empire, the dies of their coins were changed, to take proper notice of that new circumstance.

So great a number of events have been recorded by ancient medals, and so great has been the attention and care of moderns, in collecting and preserving them, that they now give great light to history, in confirming such passages, as are true in old authors, in ascertaining what was before doubtful, and in recording such as were omitted.

It must be observed, that the Greek coins do not shew the dates of events, though they illustrate the chronology of the reigns. This defect is supplied by those of Rome, which commonly mark the date, giving on the reverse, the representation of some grand event. Medals therefore may be said to afford the most authentic documents of the Roman history, in particular, that could have been invented by man. The histories of Nerva and Trajan are much better elucidated by medals than by authors; for the history of Suetonius ends with Domitian, and the "Historiæ Augustæ Scriptores" begin with the reign of Adrian, so that the reigns of the two emperors just mentioned, are almost unknown.

The study of medals may therefore be regarded as of the greatest importance in the study of History. In some instances, as we have remarked, they furnish the principal proof of historic truth. Their evidence reaches to the most remote ages, and the most remote countries. It is remarkable, that history scarcely makes any mention of Balbec, or Palmyra, whose ruins are so famous, and we have little knowledge of them, but what is supplied by inscriptions. It is by this means that M. Vaillant has disentangled a history, that was lost to the world before his time. In his learned work, printed at Paris in 1681, he has fixed the dates, and arranged the order of events in ancient historians, by means of these infallible vouchers. Thus he was enabled to ascertain to a very great degree of accuracy, the chronology and progress of events of three of the most important kingdoms in the ancient world, viz. those of Egypt, Syria, and Parthia. Father Hardouin, Norris, and Bayer, have pursued the same plan, to which might be added many others.

All the principal events of the reign of Lewis XIV. have been recorded in a set of medals, avowedly struck for that purpose. But the inconvenience attending modern medals is, that not being used as the current coin of any state, and being made of costly materials, they are confined to the cabinets of a few persons.

Besides its service to history, the science of medals is of considerable use to geography and natural history, to the illustration of ancient writers, to architecture, and to the knowledge of ancient monuments, busts, statues, ceremonies, &c. in all which views its utility is well illustrated, by examples in Mr. Pinkerton's "Essay on Medals, or Introduction to the Knowledge of Ancient and Modern Coins and Medals." This author has also shewn the connexion of the study of medals with the fine arts of poetry, painting, sculpture, and architecture. But these are subjects not connected with this part of our work. It is sufficient therefore that we recommend the reader, if he wish to become acquainted with the science of medals generally, to study with care, the essay just referred to, in which he will either find every thing that he can require, or be directed to all the best works on the subject which are extant. To the mere English student, Clarke's "Connexion of the Roman, Saxon, and English coins," will be extremely useful. To which may be added, Snelling's "Views of English Money," and Folke's "Table of English Silver Coins, from the Conquest," &c. Ducarel's "Letters on Anglo-Gallic Coins" are interesting to all who are concerned in the ancient glory of this country. On the Scottish coins, the only books are those of Anderson and Snelling, and the Irish are described by Simon, in his "Historical Essay on Irish Coins," published at Dublin in 1749, to which, in 1767, a supplement was added by another hand.

Antiquities. This term implies all testimonies, or authentic accounts, that have come down to us, which illustrate either the particular or universal history of ancient nations. According to Lord Bacon, antiquities may be considered as the wrecks of history, collected from the various sources to which we have already referred, and in this view of the subject, the study of antiquities is not only closely allied to the study of history, but naturally leads one to ascertain the commencement and early epochas of all nations, whether ancient or modern. Many writers have thought it sufficient to inquire into, and investigate the ancient remains of Greece and Rome, but others have included in this department of science, the antiquities of the Jews, Egyptians, Phœnicians, Carthaginians, and other nations, mentioned in ancient history. We shall give an outline of the subject, taken chiefly from an article, compiled by the present writer some years ago, for another work. The most that can be aimed at in this place, is to excite the curiosity of young persons, and direct them to objects that may engage their attention, and to authors most likely to furnish information, under the several heads of inquiry and research.

The history and antiquities of nations and societies, have been objects of inquiry, as they enable the mind to separate truth from falsehood, and tradition from evidence, to establish what had probability for its basis, or to explode what rested only either in the vanity or prejudices of the inventors and propagators: of this we have a striking instance in the Chaldeans, who pretended to astronomical observations of 500,000 years standing. They mention the king who reigned over them at the time of the deluge, to whom they attribute several things which we ascribe to Noah; from whence it is assumed that the fundamental facts in their history, and in that of the Jews, are the same.

Moreover, the Chaldaic antiquities of Berosus are lost, except the fragments that have been collected by Joseph Scaliger, and Fabricius. To supply the chasm, Annius Viterbo, a Dominican monk, towards the close of the fifteenth century, forged the work of Berosus, which he published at Rome, in 1498. He was not satisfied with the first forgery, but produced a supplement to Berosus, supposed to have been written by Manetho, containing details of what had happened, from the time of Egyptus, king of Egypt, to the origin of the Roman state. The fraud was detected, and the monk disgraced.

The first traces of every history were rude and imperfect, which renders the office of the antiquarian of the utmost importance to the faithful and diligent historian. The history of the Old Testament is the most ancient well authenticated collection of facts, that has come down to the present times, These records go beyond the flood, which is a boundary to the annals of every other nation that lays a just claim to credit. The Jews, who are closely connected with this part of history, trace back their ancestry to the common parents of the human race. The antiquities of this wonderful nation, have been treated of by numerous writers. The history of their origin, ordinances, and vicissitudes previously to the Christian æra, is to be found in the Old Testament. Their subsequent ruin and dispersion, are predicted by Christ, in the New Testament, and treated of at large by Josephus, who flourished at Rome under Vespasian, Titus, and Domitian, and who published his great work on the Jewish Antiquities, during the life and reign of the latter. On the same subject, we have the Thesaurus of Ogolinus, in thirty-four volumes folio, published between the years 1744 to 1760, containing all the best works which previously to that time had appeared, on the manners, laws, rites, and institutions of the Hebrews, amounting in number to nearly five hundred distinct pieces, and many of them elaborate treatises. The most curious collection of Hebrew manuscripts in this country, which illustrate the literary antiquities of the Jews, may be found in the Bodleian library at Oxford. Few of them in point of age go beyond eight hundred years, and of these the most ancient are said to have been brought by Dr. Pocock from Constantinople. Of the taste and learning of the Jews, Dr. Lowth's Lectures contain the best view.

The antiquities of the Jews, are supposed to be much connected with those of Egypt, since Moses, their great lawgiver, was educated in the schools of Egyptian learning, and was without doubt deeply conversant in all their sciences. If therefore we could come to a faithful account of the antiquities of Egypt, we might hope to attain an illustration of many things belonging to the Jewish economy, both civil and sacred, which are still involved in darkness and mystery.

Of Egypt, alas! once renowned for its laws, the commerce of her cities, the grandeur of her buildings, and the fertility of territory, little is left to gratify the laudable curiosity of moderns. Those who have spent much time and labour, in appreciating the worth and merits of the ancients, admit that the earliest nations of the world were fed with the produce of Egyptian soil, and enriched with the wealth and wisdom obtained in that portion of Africa. Upper Egypt furnished the materials of marble and porphyry, with which the most stupendons works of art were reared: and to Hermes Trismegistus, or as he is sometimes called, Thoth, are ascribed among the Egyptians, the inventions of chief use in human life. Their priests maintained, that from the hieroglyphic characters upon the pillars which he erected, and the sacred books, all the philosophy and learning of the world has been derived.

Egypt seems itself to have been indebted for its original population to the northern parts of Arabia and Syria, the Egyptians and Abyssinians having been always wholly distinct from the native nations of Africa. The Copts, or original inhabitants, it has been observed by travellers, have no resemblance whatever to the negro features or form; but a strong likeness may be traced between the make of the visage in the modern Copts, and that presented in the ancient mummies, paintings, and statues. Their complexion, like that of the Arabs, is of a dusky brown. It is represented of the same colour in the paintings which may be seen in the tombs of Thebes. The chief antiquities are the pyramids, and the tombs near Thebes, recently disclosed, with many ruins of temples, and other remains of ancient cities. Dr. White, in the "Egyptiaca," a work which contains much valuable information on the subject, says, the celebrated column ascribed to Pompey, ornamented a space opposite to the temple of Serapis, in which was a great public library. Besides the ancient remains already noticed, we may mention the colossal sphynx, Cleopatra's needle, the marble sarcophagus, reputed to be Alexander's tomb, and the triple inscription from Rosetta, in the hieroglyphic, the vernacular Egyptian, and the Greek characters. The writers on Egyptian antiquities are very numerous. Among the ancients may be noted Herodotus, Pausanias, Strabo, Diodorus Siculus, and Plutarch. Herodotus, Thales, and Pythagoras, were initiated into all the mysteries of the Egyptian priests. The mythology of the country is fully explained in Joblonski's "Pantheon Egyptiacum." On the Egypt of modern times we have the works of Pocock, Niebuhr, Sonnini, and Denon, which may be consulted with advantage. Greaves and Nordon have written on the pyramids, and the mummies are described by the celebrated Kircher.

For the illustration of the antiquities of India, the accessible materials are less numerous. To Sir William Jones we are much indebted for useful and highly valuable information on this subject. Mr. Halhed, in 1776, in the code of Gentoo Laws, gave the first specimen which appeared of the early wisdom of the Indians, and their extensive skill in jurisprudence. In the year 1785, the attention of the world was roused by the publication of the Bhagvat Geeta, edited by Mr. Wilkins, which was said to contain all the grand mysteries of the Hindoo religion, and laid claim to the antiquity of 4000 years. Other works of high reputation have succeeded, among which are the "Indian Antiquities" of the Rev. Mr. Maurice. From Sir William Jones's papers published in the "Asiatic Researches," much solid information on the same subject, may be obtained in a short compass. By that great man, a society was formed for inquiring into the history, antiquities, arts, sciences, and literature of Asia; and having founded the institution, he gave it celebrity by his own admirable discourses, to which our readers are referred for much valuable information on every thing curious relating to India and its inhabitants.

The remains of architecture and sculpture seem to prove an early connexion between India and Africa. Of the ancient arts and manufactures of this widely extended country, little is known, excepting the result of the Indian loom and needle. The Hindoos boasted of three inventions, viz. the method of instruction by "apologues," "the decimal scale," and the famous "game of chess;" and it is thought, that if their numerous works on grammar, rhetoric and music, which are even now extant, could be explained in some language generally known, it would be found that they had still higher pretensions to the praise of a fertile and inventive genius.

Of the antiquities of Greece and Rome, much has been written that merits the attention of the student in literature: these are subjects, in which every well educated youth becomes conversant at an early period. They are taught in all our classical schools, as necessary to the elucidation of those works that are read in the attainment of the ancient languages. Potter on the Greek Antiquities, and Kennet and Adams on those of Rome, are familiar to every ear: in their kind they are truly respectable, though they may be regarded only as elementary treatises, calculated rather to excite a taste for the study, than to satisfy the inquirer in pursuit of knowledge.

The first accounts of Greece, are derived from ages long before the common use of letters in the country, so that it is difficult to distinguish where fable concludes, and real history begins. The antiquities of such a country, which became in after ages so illustrious in the annals of mankind, cannot fail to have excited a considerable degree of interest in every age: they have accordingly been carefully and minutely investigated by writers, celebrated alike for their erudition and industry. Of these we can enumerate but a small portion, in comparison of the many that have treated on the subject. Bishop Potter, to whom we have already referred, Bos, and others, have drawn up systems or abridgments of the whole, or at least of whatever relates to the religion, the gods, the vows, and the temples of Greece: on the public weal and magistracy, Stephanus and Van Dale are well worthy of notice: on the laws and punishments of Greece, we have Meursius and Petit: on military concerns, Arrian and Ælian are well known: on their gymnastic art and exercises, Joubert and Faber may be mentioned: on the theatres and scenic exhibitions, Scaliger and the Abbe Barthelemy have written: besides these, we have many writers on their entertainments, on their marriages, the education of their children, and their funeral ceremonies. The best relics which display the former splendour of the Grecian states, have been preserved by Stuart in his Athens: in the Ionian Antiquities, and in the Voyage Pittoresque de la Greece. The finest specimens of its sculpture in this country, are to be found among the Townley marbles: and of its coinage, in the cabinet of Dr. Hunter.

" Nothing", says Dr. Adams, in the preface to his Roman Antiquities, " has more engaged the attention of literary men, than to trace from ancient monuments the institutions and laws, the religion, the manners and customs of the Romans, under the general name of Roman Antiquities. Scarcely on any subject have more books been written, and many of them by persons of distinguished abilities," We may, as a guide to the student, enumerate the writers from whom Dr. Adams chiefly compiled his own work, as these will be the best authorities for those persons who would enter deeply into the study. To Manutius, Brissonius, and Middleton, he was indebted for his facts relating to the business of the senate: to

Pignorius, on slaves: to Lidonius, and Grucchius, Manutius, Huber, Gravina, Merula, Heineccius, for what relates to the assemblies of the people, the rights of citizens, the laws and judicial proceedings: with respect to the duties and privileges of magistrates, the art of war, the shows of the circus, and the feats of gladiators, he had recourse to Lipsius:—to Sheffer he applied for information on naval affairs and carriages: to Kermannus, on funerals: to Arbuthnot, on coins: to Donatus, on the city: to Turnebus, Salmasius, Grævius, Gronovius, Montfaucon, Gesner, and others, upon different subjects scattered through his work. To these may be added one of the oldest authors on the subject, viz. Dionysius Halicarnassus, who traced the origin of the Romans with great fidelity, back to the remotest ages. His accounts are generally preferred to those of Livy, because they are more ample, and his facts are described with more particulars; and on the ceremonies, worship, sacrifices, manners, customs, discipline, policy, courts, laws, &c. he is perhaps the most authentic writer.

A correct view of the antiquities of Britain, from the earliest period to the end of Henry VIIIth's reign, may perhaps be collected from Dr. Henry's History, and the writers which he refers to, will present the reader with the most authentic sources of inquiry. In connexion with the early history of the Britons, we must not forget the Druids, who have deservedly attracted much curiosity, and whose customs have excited great research, but it would be erroneous to impute to them the whole of our earliest remains. Julius Cæsar took considerable pains to learn every particular relating to the Druids, and he states it as his opinion, that their religion and customs originated in Britain. In justification of this opinion it has been urged, that there is not a single authority for the existence of Druidism any where but in Celtic Gaul, and part of England. In one place, however, the historian and warrior speaks of it as a recent institution, which circumstance has led some authors to suppose it might have come to our ancestors from Phœnicia; but for this there is little foundation. It does not appear that Cæsar was himself a witness to the rites of the Druids in Britain, and Tacitus is the first author who notices them, for the Romans did not meet with any till they had advanced far into Wales.

Of the structures erected by the Britons, Abury and Stonehenge may be deemed the principal. Relics of a smaller kind are continually discovered a few feet beneath the surface of the earth. On these, Stukely and Rowland are the best authorities: the former has written a volume on Abury, a temple of the Druids, in which is a particular account of the first and patriarchal religion, and of the peopling of the British islands: besides his larger work, intitled "Itinerarium Curiosum," being an account of the antiquities, &c. observed in travels through Great Britain, published in 1724. For the history of the Britons under the Roman Government, Horsley's Britannia Romana is a work that may be depended upon. With respect to the antiquities of the Saxons, the illuminated manuscripts are the best records of their manners in the different centuries, and the most interesting information respecting them, has been collected by Turner and Strutt. The best collection of Saxon coins is in the British Museum, and of manuscripts in the same place, and in the Bodleian Library. Mr. King has treated of their military antiquities in his History of Castles; and independently of our works on topography, which are numerous, and many of them of the first respectability, and which throw considerable light on the antiquities of the country, we may refer to the works of Camden, Strutt, and Gough, to which may be added the whole series of the Gentleman's Magazine, and Pinkerton's Geography.

As the antiquities of the United Kingdom are in some respects connected with those of the Danes, and other northern nations, we may suggest to the reader what are the principal remains of those people, as a clue to his future inquiries.

The ancient monuments of Denmark and Norway are chiefly Runic, though it is far from certain at what period the use of Runic characters extended so far north. Circles of upright stones are common in all the Danish dominions, the islands, Norway and Iceland, in which latter country their origin is perfectly ascertained, as some were erected even in recent times of the Icelandic republic, being called domh-ring, or circles of judgment.

Of Sweden the ancient monuments consist chiefly of judicial circles, and other erections of unhewn stone, together with remains inscribed with Runic characters, none of which are imagined to have existed longer than the eleventh century.

In Russia, the ancient monuments are neither numerous, nor afford much variety. There are to be met with the tombs of their pagan ancestors, containing weapons and ornaments. From the writings of Herodotus, we learn that the Scythians regarded the cemeteries of their princes with singular veneration; the Sarmatians or Slavons seem to have imbibed the same ideas. The idols of Pagan Russia, are sometimes found cast in bronze; and Dr. Guthrie has given a good account of the Slavonic mythology, to whose "Dissertations sur les Antiquites de Russie," we refer the reader.

It is not necessary, nor would it accord with our limits, to go farther into this subject, than to add, that Reland has expressly treated on Sacred Antiquities—Fabricius on Hebrew and Ecclesiastical Antiquities—Bingley on Christian Antiquities—Bishop Stillingfleet on the Antiquities of the British Churches—Cave on Apostolic Antiquities—Neineccius on such of the Roman as illustrated the civil law—Mallet on Northern, and Bishop Kennet on Parochial Antiquities.

CHAP. XXVI.

ON THE BRITISH CONSTITUTION.

Civil and political institutions, the growth of time—Rise and progress of the British Constitution—Romans—Picts—Saxons—Danes—Revenues of the King—Parliament—divided into Two Houses.

IN the natural world, it seems to be the general ordinance of Providence, that what is remarkable for solidity and durability, should be slow in growth. While the more succulent plants proceed rapidly to maturity, a long series of years revolves before the oak attains to its appropriate state of perfection. In many instances, the same law appears to be established in the moral world. Civil and political institutions, however skilfully contrived they may seem to be, are seldom the result of a single effort of mind, employed in sketching and completing a pre-conceived plan. These too are generally the growth of time, the products of human skill as exercised at intervals, according to the course of passing circumstances.

This is eminently the case with regard to the British Constitution. "The wisdom of our ancestors," is an expression familiar to our lips; and it is indeed to Britons a subject of legitimate pride, that they are descended from forefathers, who, on various occasions, evinced the utmost sagacity in taking advantage of events for the assertion of their rights, and for the promotion of the general welfare. But we shall form a very erroneous judgment, if we imagine that the glorious fabric of our Constitution was organized centuries ago; or that it was at once erected in all its just proportions. On the contrary, it was raised by almost imperceptible degrees, and happily surviving the period of rudeness and barbarity, it has, from time to time, received those improvements and embellishments, which, in concurrence with the solidity of its foundation, have rendered it the wonder of the civilized portion of the globe.

A brief, but perspicuous review of those circumstances which have given rise to the happy form of government, under which the British Isles have risen to so distinguished an eminence among the nations of the earth, will at once give the clearest view of the principles of our Constitution, and demonstrate the fallacy of those appeals to fanciful standards and maxims in politics, which have tended to mislead the zeal of party, and to bewilder the minds of honest inquirers after correctness of principle.

In tracing the rise and progress of the British Constitution, it is necessary to revert to the time when the Romans withdrew from these islands. By the Lords of the World the aboriginal Britons had been reduced to subjection; but to compensate the loss of independence, they had received from their conquerors the comforts and blessings of civilized life. As, however, the Romans had, during the period of their sovereignty, monopolized all offices civil and military, and had carefully excluded their British subjects from all participation in the management of public affairs: when the exigencies of the empire induced them to abandon this extremity of their dominions, our unwarlike ancestors became the prey of anarchy, and gave themselves up to the most abject despair. Of this their weakness, their turbulent neighbours, the Picts and the Scots, eagerly availed themselves, to spread far and wide the ravages of devastation. It must not, however, be supposed, that these barbarian incursions experienced no opposition. The larger landed proprietors, from time to time summoned their dependants to take the field against the common foe, and this circumstance gave rise to an influential body of aristocracy, from the members of which, upon extraordinary occasions, was chosen a chief, who was vested with that degree of temporary power which the exigency might seem to demand, or which his superior abilities might wrest from the suffrages of his compeers.

One of these chieftains of the name of Vortigern, being hard pressed by the incursions of the Scots and Picts, and listening to the counsels of fear, had recourse to the refuge of weak minds, and adopted the perilous resolution of relying for protection on foreign aid. He accordingly looked for succour to the wilds of Germany; and at his instance, in the year 449, Hengist and Horsa, two Saxon chiefs, came to the assistance of the Britons, at the head of a small band of auxiliary troops. These were soon followed by numerous bodies of their countrymen, who effectually restrained the northern invaders, but soon turned their arms against those whom they had covenanted to protect; and at the end of about one hundred and seventy years, in spite of the obstinate resistance of the Britons, the Saxons made themselves masters of the fairest portion of the Island. Under their domination were established seven independent principalities, known by the general name of the Heptarchy; but by a variety of fortunate contingences, in the year 827, these seven principalities were united under the sway of Egbert, when the kingdom then assumed the appellation of England.

In their native country, the Saxons had been addicted to the pursuits of the pastoral life. For the purpose of affording mutual assistance and protection, they had been accustomed to herd together in rudely fortified villages. The families of which these villages were composed, being incited by a sense of common interest and common danger, appointed a chieftain, whose sole function was to lead them in war. The determination of affairs, interesting to the welfare of the community at large, was left to a general council, composed of the heads of families, who, on important occasions, assembled for the purpose of free debate, and whose decision was final and conclusive.

This circumstance must be noted as of the utmost importance. It had a decisive effect upon the future destinies of our island. For the Saxons brought with them into this country the maxims of civil polity, by which they had been guided in their original establishments. The principles of freedom by which they had been actuated on the shores of the Baltic, they proudly enforced on their own behalf, when they became the masters and possessors of Britain, and these principles, repressed or expanded according to the course of events, have continued to be the animating spirit of our national institutions to the present day.

The grand circumstance which gives a particular character to political institutions is the tenure and the distribution of property. On the arrival of the Saxon chiefs in Britain, they found the inhabitants of the country much more advanced than themselves in the science and practice of agriculture; and enforcing with their swords the right of the strongest, they took possession of cultivated districts, of which they had dispossessed the former proprietors. By degrees they incorporated themselves with the vanquished, and, in consequence of this circumstance, and of the country being over-run by a succession of chieftains, followed by their particular partizans, the captured lands were at first seized in comparatively small portions. Of the estates which were thus acquired, the proprietors held a part in their own hands—other parts they let out to *villeins*—and others they allotted to their relatives and dependents, under the designation of *vassals*, to be held on the tenure of military service. The lands which were possessed by independent proprietors in their own right, were termed *allodial* lands, whilst those which were held by vassals, were distinguished by the epithet of *feudal*; and the possession of lands by these tenures, respectively conferred upon their proprietors the appellation of Greater and Lesser *Thanes*.

In this state of society, the peasantry were for a long period doomed to a condition little short of mitigated slavery. They originally consisted of such persons as had been taken captive during the struggle which took place between the Britons and the Saxons; and though their situation was gradually meliorated, under the appellation of *ceorles*, or *churls*, they were left in a great degree subject to the caprice of their lords.

The measures, adopted by the latter for their mutual defence, gave occasion to a system of internal regulations which continues to modify, at least, the language of the present day. The association of a few allodial proprietors and their dependents for their common security, gave rise to the institution of *Tythings*. The connexion of a number of villages, or towns formed upon the same principle, constituted a *Hundred*; and the association of a reasonable number of Hundreds constituted a *Shire*. Though these associations originated in military views, they were soon rendered subservient to civil purposes, and especially to the administration of justice, and even to the making of legislative provisions; in which processes, each, in the order in which they have been mentioned, was liable, upon appeal, to the control of the other.

But all these subordinate courts were subject to the restraint of a still greater assembly, namely, the Wittenagemot. During the continuance of the Heptarchy, each of the seven kingdoms had its own legislative body, distinguished by that appellation, in which all the allodial proprietors had a right to sit and to deliberate. The powers of the Wittenagemot were ample and extensive. It was authorized to provide for the defence of the country—to superintend the coinage—to act as a high court of judicature to decide upon the quarrels which took place between the great lords—and, in general, to redress grievances, and to correct abuses in the administration of government.

As in the rudest state of society occasions must often arise, when it is expedient to concentrate, as it were, the power of the state, and to delegate to some efficient individual the execution of the general will, this circumstance naturally gives rise to the appointment of a chief magistrate. In the early history of the Anglo-Saxons, this magistrate was entitled *heretoc*, or duke, in place of which appellation, was afterwards assumed that of *king*. This high distinction was originally the meed of valour—a homage paid to power. Its natural tendency was, to increase the possessions of him who was thus elevated, and to extend his influence. The power of the Saxon kings was, however, limited, and yet it was tolerably extensive. In their own domains their authority was absolute. The command of the troops, and the maintenance of the police, gave them extensive sway, and their privilege of summoning the Wittenagemot, and presiding over its deliberations, afforded to prudent and politic sovereigns the means of becoming in a manner the directors of its decisions—in addition to all which, it may be observed, that as their powers were not defined, as occasions arose, they were materially extended.

During the period of which we have been treating, the clergy constituted a kind of separate body in the state, pursuing its peculiar views, and possessing a jurisdiction of its own.

From the time when Egbert became sole monarch of England, A. D. 828, to the Norman Conquest, A. D. 1066, the English were engaged in a course of hostilities with the Danes. Though these hostilities retarded the progress of improvement, and though the country was subdued by Canute the Great, the victor made no alteration in the civil polity of the kingdom. But what was not effected by violence, was brought about by the natural course of events. By a certain, but gradual progress of change, after all England fell under the dominion of one sovereign, the bent of civil polity inclined to the creation of an aristocracy. This was chiefly occasioned by a practice, which now became prevalent, of the smaller allodial lords, for the sake of protection, surrendering their lands to the more powerful ones, and consenting to hold them as their vassals. Hence the greater nobles, surrounded by their retainers and dependants, became so powerful, that they were not unfrequently enabled to brave the authority of the crown itself. One consequence of this accession of influence to the aristocracy was, that the offices of *tythingman, hundreder*, &c. which were formerly elective, became hereditary, and this circumstance accelerated the conversion of allodial into feudal property. The property, however, which had been thus converted, continued to be hereditary under certain stipulations. Another still more important consequence of the changes to which we have been referring, was, that the Wittenagemot, which, on its primitive institution, was numerously attended, became a select body of powerful barons, who, whenever under the influence of the "*esprit de corps*," they made common cause with each other, exercised a degree of authority formidable both to the people and the king.

Among the most valuable of the political institutions of our Anglo-Saxon ancestors, may be mentioned the trial by jury. The precise date of the establishment of this invaluable mode of legal decision is uncertain; but it may be easily conceived, that it would naturally arise from the circumstances of allodial proprietors, who not only felt an interest in the general defence against a common enemy, but also in composing, by their personal interference, those disputes which put to hazard the peace and safety of their several communities.

Such is the outline of the civil polity of our Saxon ancestors. If their institutions are carefully examined, it will be found that they contain excellent principles of government, which were developed and matured in after-times; but we shall be much mistaken if we imagine, that, in reference to the community at large, they were calculated in any peculiar manner to secure the liberty and rights of mankind. According to their provisions, as it has justly been remarked by a celebrated writer,* "the sovereign was, indeed, at no time invested with absolute power. The supreme authority in the state was originally possessed by a numerous body of landed proprietors; but the rest of the community were either slaves, or tenants at the will of their master." It is also a circumstance carefully to be noted, that by the natural tendency to the conversion of allodial into feudal tenures, the numbers of those who took a share in legislation and government, towards the end of the Anglo-Saxon dynasty, were considerably diminished; and several of the great lords acquired a degree of power, the abuse of which rendered them rebels to the king, and oppressors of the people.

One of these, Harold, the son of Earl Godwin, was encouraged by his numerous retainers to lay claim to the throne which was vacated by the death of Edward the Confessor.

Upon the particulars of the contest between this nobleman and his competitor, William, Duke of Normandy, surnamed the Conqueror, it is inconsistent with the object of this essay to dwell. But the political changes which were effected by the accession of the Norman line of kings, claim our especial attention. It has already been remarked, that immediately before this event, the paramount property of the country had fallen into the hands of a few individuals. Of these, many lost their estates in consequence of the forfeitures which were enforced against the friends of Harold, and against the discontented barons, who, from time to time, raised insurrections against the Conqueror. The remainder were so much intimidated by the growing power of the crown, and so much weakened by their internal dissensions, that they deemed it expedient to throw themselves under the king's protection, and to descend from the rank of allodial proprietors to that of vassals. Thus was the feudal system by degrees completed, and "the whole kingdom was united in one extensive barony, of which the king became the superior, and, in some degree, the ultimate proprietor."

* Millar.

As wealth constitutes the sinews of power, it is obvious to remark, that when the sovereign thus became the paramount proprietor of the land of the whole realm, his revenues were considerably increased by the casual emoluments, called *incidents*, which constituted a distinguishing feature of the feudal system. The principal of these incidents are, 1. that of *non-entry*, or the profit obtained by the king on holding estates, during the interval which sometimes occurred between the death of a vassal and the appearance of his heir. 2. That of *wardship*, or the emolument derived from the management of the lands which descended to the heir of a former vassal during the period of his non-age. 3. That of *marriage*, or a pecuniary fee or fine paid by a vassal on his entering into the state of matrimony. 4. That of *aids*, a *benevolence*, or a tax which in certain cases the superior had a right to exact. 5. That of *escheat*, or forfeiture of estates on the failure of heirs, or on the neglect of performing covenants. 6. That of the *fine of alienation* on a premium paid to the lord for the privilege of selling the whole, or any part of a feudal estate. To these was added, in the reign of Henry II. the Incident of *scutage*, or a sum of money paid by the vassal, for relief from the burden of military service.

The influence of the crown being thus extended as it were into all the ramifications of the community, it might have been expected that its influence would at an early period have been matured into the despotism of arbitrary power. Such indeed was the natural tendency of its exercise. But this tendency was checked by the dubious title of some of our monarchs, the consideration of which induced them to court the good will of the people at large, by making concessions in favour of public liberty; and by the feeble character of others, which incapacitated them from resisting even the encroachment of a turbulent aristocracy. In consequence of the remonstrances of the principal nobility, which were not unfrequently backed by the power of the sword, charters were from time to time granted by our kings, which, though they were violated without scruple, by active and ambitious princes, operated upon the whole as a check upon the prerogative. Notwithstanding also these charters provided only for the welfare of the superior ranks of the community, yet as industry increased, and arts and manufactures gradually promoted the accumulation of property in quarters where it had not antecedently been found, there was a gradual increase in the numbers of those who were interested in their provisions.

The most important changes which took place in consequence of the Norman conquest, occurred in the constitution of the great council of the nation. In the reign of William I. the Wittenagemot, which, as has been before observed, consisted of *allodial* proprietors, was, upon the change of tenures from *allodial* to *feudal*, of course abolished, and in its place was instituted the High Court of Parliament. This assembly was composed of the immediate vassals of the crown, that is to say, of the superior clergy, nobility and great landholders. It was convened as the Wittenagemot had been, either at the three great festivals of Christmas, Easter and Whitsuntide, or upon particular emergencies. Though it was generally summoned for some express purpose, and though its deliberations were in a great degree regulated and controled by the royal authority; its influence in public affairs soon became considerable in suggesting improvements in government, and especially in checking the abuses of administration.

The powers of the Parliament were indeed for some time vague and unsettled; and its organization was at first, as might have been expected, extremely imperfect. But in the reign of Edward I. the English government began to be conducted with greater regularity; and our constitution assumed a more definite form, an improvement for which we are indebted to the progress of civilization, and the diffusion of property. It appears by Domesday book, that in the reign of William I. so extensive were the domains which were allotted to the feudal tenants, who held immediately under the crown, that the number of these lordly vassals did not exceed six hundred.

While this was the case, the business of internal regulation could, without much inconvenience, be transacted by them in person. At least, upon important occasions they could be assembled without difficulty, while the more ordinary business was conducted by committees selected from their number, to which may be traced the origin of our superior courts of law. But various circumstances occurred, by the operation of which, the estates of these overgrown landholders were subdivided, and conveyed into the possession of more numerous proprietors. Hence by insensible degrees there arose a class of smaller barons, who, not being able to vie with the wealthier nobles in splendour and authority, regarded attendance in parliament, to which, however, at the king's requisition, they were bound, as an inconvenience and a grievance. Thus circumstanced, they no doubt received as a boon from the crown, permission to absent themselves as a body, and to send a sufficient number of representatives to discharge the duties of parliament on their behalf. As these representatives would be most conveniently nominated by districts, they were naturally referred to the subsisting division of the kingdom into counties, and hence the origin of *Knights of the Shire*, or the representatives of the minor barons and smaller landholders of the realm.

In the mean time, by the progress of civilization, agriculturalists became wealthy; and as they ceased to make for themselves articles of necessity and luxury, artizans and manufacturers were collected in towns and cities, some of which, in consequence of the advantages of their situation on the sea-coast, or on the banks of navigable rivers, became flourishing by means of commerce. As the avarice of power is ever vigilant, these rising communities soon attracted the notice of the executive government, and were summoned to bear the burden of taxation. Hence, with a view of promoting the facility of paying to the sovereign the revenue which he claimed from particular towns, corporations were instituted, which were in a manner responsible to the king for his demands, and were empowered to make the requisite assessments within their respective limits. And when in process of time extraordinary aids were wanted by the crown, these corporate towns or boroughs sent delegates to Parliament, whose principal business was to report the capacity and the views of their constituents, as to the share which they ought equitably to sustain of the public burdens. Such was the origin of that important branch of the English legislature, the *Citizens* and *Burgesses* in Parliament assembled.

At first the Clergy, the Barons, the Knights of the Shire, and the Burgesses, sat and deliberated in one chamber; but as it was soon found, that the nobles who sat in their own right, and claimed a general interest in the ordinance of political regulations, were practically upon a very different footing from those whose department was limited to the offer of pecuniary grants, the deputies for boroughs found it expedient to assemble in a separate chamber, which was early distinguished by the name of the *House of Commons.* For some little time after this the Knights of the Shire continued to sit with the Barons; but soon finding themselves liable to perpetual mortification from a proud aristocracy, who looked upon them as greatly their inferiors, they were led to unite themselves with the Citizens and Burgesses, by whom they were regarded with deferential respect. At the same time an union took place in the upper house, between the nobles and the clergy, who had hitherto voted as distinct and separate orders.

Here then we have a distinct outline of the Constitution of Parliament, as it subsists at this day. And even in many subordinate parts, the resemblance of ancient and modern parliamentary principles is sufficiently striking. At this early period it was the exclusive privilege of the commons to propose taxes, and to impeach the great officers of state who might be guilty of malversation, while it was the exclusive department of the Barons to sit in judgment upon notable state offenders, and in all cases to exercise jurisdiction in the last resort, as a court of appeal. It was also at this time settled, that each house should take cognizance of all questions touching the rights and immunities belonging to their several orders.

The principles upon which the election of representatives of the several boroughs was conducted, varied according to circumstances. In those corporate towns, where opulence was generally diffused, members were returned to parliament by the suffrages of the people at large. In boroughs, in which the bulk of the people were in a poor and servile condition, the right of election was vested in a few individuals.

The knights of the shire, being at first the representatives of the smaller barons, were of course elected by them; but in process of time a most salutary change was effected in the mode of their appointment, by the enfranchisement of the *arriere vassals*, or such landholders as held their estates not immediately from the crown, but from a subject-superior.

As the great barons were the most able, so they were seldom unwilling, to restrain the authority of the sovereign. Hence a jealousy naturally arose between the superior nobles and the king, which, though productive of mischief in its immediate, was useful in its remote effects. For with a view of gaining, as it were, the alliance of a rising power, the princes of the House of Tudor gave franchises to a great number of additional boroughs, which circumstance directly tended to the confirmation and the increase of popular rights. Nor did the people make an ungrateful return for the privileges which were then bestowed upon them. Inspired with a natural dislike of their feudal oppressors, they were ever ready to support the regal dignity. Hence were derived great accessions to the power of the crown, the operation of which was signally manifested in the reign of Henry VII. At this period the families of the nobility were exhausted and reduced by the wars, which had so long been carried on between the houses of York and Lancaster; and as luxury increased in proportion to the increase of trade and commerce, the heads of those families were tempted to supply their wants by the alienation of their estates, the process of which was purposely facilitated by legislative provisions made during the reign. But though the power of the crown increased, as that of the aristocracy declined, it must be remarked, that, as Henry VII. did not exercise his authority in an arbitrary and capricious manner, he never exacted loans from his subjects; and never but twice had recourse to the expedient of benevolences. On all other occasions he regularly imposed taxes by the authority of parliament. Before his time, however, a power had been occasionally exercised by popular monarchs, of dispensing with laws; and the practice of announcing legal regulations by royal proclamations, had been sometimes perverted to the purpose of vesting the legislative authority in the crown alone; but these irregularities were comparatively rare; and when fit opportunities occurred, they were condemned by the declarations of the parliament.

CHAP. XXVII.

BRITISH CONSTITUTION,

Continued.

Changes in the Constitution under Henry VIII.—Elizabeth—James I.—Charles I.—Cromwell—Charles II.—James II.—William and Mary—Present organization of the British Constitution—Regal power.

IN the reign of Henry VIII., the authority of the crown acquired an almost overwhelming influence. On the annulling of the supremacy of the Pope, that monarch was declared head of the English church, and was vested with the extensive power which accrued from the disposal of ecclesiastical benefices; in addition to which, his revenues were for a time materially increased by the produce of the forfeited estates belonging to the monasteries, which his greediness for gain, rather than his religious zeal, prompted him to suppress. It has been remarked, that impetuous as was the temper of Henry, and extravagant as were his claims, he never attempted to raise money upon his subjects without consent of parliament. This remark, however, only points to the fact, that he was not gratuitously tyrannical. In his reign, parliaments were humble and complying. It was only requisite that the king's pleasure should be made known to them, and his wishes were instantly gratified. Nay, to such a condition of degradation was the great council of the nation sunk, at this disgraceful period, that in the thirty-first year of this king's reign, it was enacted, "that the king, with the advice of the council, might issue proclamations, under such penalties as he should think necessary, and that these should be observed, as though they were made by act of parliament." As to the limitation, that "these should not be prejudicial to any person's inheritance, offices, liberties, goods, chattels, or life,"—it was manifestly intended merely as a salvo for the honour of those who passed this infamous statute; and was purposely calculated to be nugatory in point of practical effect.

It was a fortunate circumstance for the inhabitants of these islands, that Henry did not live to consolidate his tyranny, and that the minority of his son, Edward VI., afforded an opportunity of abrogating all proceedings which tended to countenance the late stretches of prerogative. In the reign of Mary, the general attention was occupied by the struggle which took place between the Roman Catholic and the Protestant religion; and she happily did not reign long enough to extirpate either Protestantism or liberty, both of which she regarded with an evil eye.

The glorious reign of Elizabeth was, in the main, conducted upon popular maxims. Relying, indeed, upon her people in the hour of danger, and finding them eager to support her rights, she had full confidence in their duty and loyalty, and never scrupled to refer the general affairs of the kingdom to the consideration of parliament. With the legislative power of that assembly, in the business of taxes, she never interfered. Of her prerogative, however, she was jealous; and confounding the privilege of the sovereign, to refuse his assent to propositions which had been matured by parliamentary discussion, with the right to discuss matters which might be disagreeable to the ruling powers, she occasionally interposed to control the deliberation of both houses, and even went so far as to imprison members, who were pertinacious in agitating questions, the consideration of which she had prohibited. These were, doubtless, unjustifiable stretches of power; and whilst they militated against the rights of the people, evinced the necessity of those rights being more strictly defined than they had hitherto been.

But James I., on whose head were united the crowns of England and of Scotland, seems to have imbibed the highest prerogative notions entertained by the most tyrannical of his predecessors; and to have been insensible of that march of mind which was silently, but decisively preparing the way for resistance to arbitrary power. He did not take into his account the settlement of religion, which left his English subjects more leisure and tranquillity to regulate their civil concerns. He forgot that the very legitimacy of his title to the crown, precluded all fear of that greatest subject of dread to all good citizens, a domestic war. He was not aware that the exercise of theological controversy, had sharpened the acumen of disputants upon politics. He was unconscious of the rapid growth of reason and intellect in his dominions; and if he were apprized that the example of the United Provinces, had diffused throughout his dominions a sense of civil rights, he trusted to his sagacity to find out the means of quelling the rising spirit of freedom among his subjects. Hence his intercourse with parliament was unsatisfactory and unprofitable; and he tried every expedient to conduct the business of the kingdom, independently of the interference of that assembly, which was, on every occasion of its being summoned, found to increase in popularity and power.

Here it may be expedient to observe, that though it had been provided by a statute of Edward III. that a parliament should be holden at least once in the course of every year, this statute had become in a manner obsolete; and for many antecedent reigns, the summoning of the great council of the nation depended on the will of the sovereign.

At his accession to the throne, Charles I. found the revenues of the crown dilapidated, and his finances incumbered with a large debt, which was daily increased by the expenses of the war of the Palatinate. Poverty, however, did not teach him humility. When after a few experiments, he had found parliaments more industrious in stating and enlarging upon the public grievances, than in ministering to his wants, he determined to reign without them. Misled by favourites and flatterers, and drawn into error by dishonest judges, he, on his sole authority, adopted the most arbitrary and the most violent methods of raising money. Soon finding himself involved in the difficulties consequent upon such maxims of government, he was at length reduced to the necessity of applying for aid to that very body, whose scrutiny he had so much reason to dread. In the course of a little time, finding himself stripped, one by one, of his dearest prerogatives, he had recourse to the last appeal of sovereigns. He engaged in a war against his subjects, which ended in his captivity, his trial, and his death. In this dreadful struggle, the Constitution was torn to pieces. The ecclesiastical establishment was superseded—the House of Lords was abolished—all the power of the state was transferred to a Committee, which, branching out into subordinate bodies, diffused throughout the whole kingdom the rancorous activity of democratic sway.

This state of things, however, could not, in its nature, be of long duration. An overstrained democracy always terminates in despotism. In the regular progress of events, the administration of public affairs fell into the hands of a military chief, who ruled the more despotically, because, as his title was new, his powers were undefined. Though it cannot be denied that Cromwell was possessed of many great qualities, neither can it be denied, that his sway was tyrannical. Parliaments he treated with contempt. When they manifested any symptoms of resistance to his will, he dismissed them in part, or in the whole, according to his pleasure.

Such conduct could not fail to diffuse discontent throughout the whole country; and though, after the death of the Protector, his son Richard seized the reins of government, they instantly dropped from his feeble hand. The general voice called for the restoration of Monarchy; and the second Charles returned from his long exile, and was received by his repentant people with the most ardent enthusiasm. On this occasion, as men are ever prone to run into extremes, the spirit of freedom was nearly annihilated; and the public functionaries seemed prepared, in all formality, to vest the crown with arbitrary power. By the interposition of a wise and virtuous few, however, the forms of the Constitution were revived—the hierarchy resumed its dignity—the House of Lords was restored; and the Commons were restricted to their ordinary functions. Thus modified, the Convention which had agreed to the restoration of the monarchy, assumed the name of a Parliament. But, as in the opinion of the court, this parliament stood in need of purification, it had hardly effected the new settlement before it was dissolved; and the House of Commons, on the ensuing election, was replaced by a new one, fully imbued with the obsequious doctrines which constituted the political fashion of the day.

In the reign of Charles I. an act had been passed, which provided, that no longer an interval than three years should take place between one meeting of parliament and another. In the year 1664, this salutary statute was repealed, and the summoning of parliaments was left entirely to the discretion of the king. At this time there was no limit to the duration of the functions of the Lower House. When, therefore, Charles II. had once assembled a body of senators, who seemed to be sufficiently obsequious to his views, he was not in haste to change them, and he allowed his celebrated Long Parliament to sit about eighteen years. In that space of time a great alteration having taken place in the public feeling, and the Commons, influenced by jealousy of the designs of the crown against the protestant religion, manifesting strong symptoms of resistance against the measures of the court, he took a decisive step, and dissolved the parliament in the year 1681. From that period to the time of his death, he governed the kingdom in a great measure according to the dictates of his arbitrary will.

A jealousy, which subsequent events proved to be well founded, of the insidious and despotic views of the Duke of York, the presumptive heir to the throne, had induced the friends of freedom to endeavour, by the Bill of Exclusion, to deprive him of the means of effecting his purpose. Many of the first characters in the kingdom fell victims to the resentment kindled by this abortive attempt in the bosoms of the royal brothers, and for a while they were branded after their death, as factious calumniators. But the conduct of the Duke when he assumed the throne, under the name of James II., fully justified the plans, and vindicated the memories of the martyrs of popular rights. Immediately on his accession he proceeded to levy money, by the authority of a royal proclamation; and though he soon afterwards summoned a parliament, he took care to intimate to the Commons, that if they did not fully enter into his views, he could easily find means of dispensing with their services; to which may be added, that by the exercise of the dispensing power, he attempted to abrogate the fundamental provisions of the constitution. It is a circumstance truly fortunate for these realms, that James II. was in principle not only a despot, but also a bigot. Had he bounded his views to an attack on the civil rights of his subjects, it is a matter of considerable doubt, whether sufficient spirit could have been roused effectually to thwart his designs. But his attachment to the Roman Catholic religion betrayed him into measures which diffused a general alarm. At this crisis the chiefs of the English Church, forgetting their favourite doctrines of passive obedience and non-resistance, plentifully sowed the seeds of discontent; and the leaders of the Whigs applied to the Prince of Orange, whom they invited to repair to this country as the redresser of wrongs, the champion of civil liberty, and the guardian of the Protestant faith.

The pusillanimous James having, on the approach of the

Prince of Orange to London, fled to France, the convention, which on this emergency was summoned to provide for the security of the country, affected to consider this flight as an abdication of the crown. A vacancy of the throne being thus declared, they immediately proceeded to fill it by devolving the succession upon the Prince and Princess of Orange. By this measure they deviated as little from the lineal course of inheritance, as was consistent with the general safety; and gave as little countenance as possible to the principle of elective monarchy. The convention being now converted into a parliament, proceeded under the direction of the most enlightened minds in the kingdom, to ascertain the bounds of the prerogative, and to secure the liberty of the subject, by the justly celebrated "*Bill of Rights.*" In this bill it was expressly declared "that the pretended power of suspending laws, or the execution of laws by regal authority without consent of parliament, is illegal;"—every mode of levying money upon the subject, by mere virtue of the royal prerogative, was pointedly condemned.—It was also laid down as a fundamental principle, "that the freedom of speech, and debates or proceedings in parliament, ought not to be impeached or questioned in any court, or place out of parliament;"—and with a well founded jealousy of military interference in civil affairs, it was declared, "that the raising or keeping a standing army within the kingdom in time of peace, unless it be with consent of parliament, is against law;"—and even in time of war, the maintenance of a military force, was afterwards rendered entirely dependent upon the authority of parliament. These are the principal provisions of the "*Bill of Rights;*" which though it may well be denominated the palladium of British liberties, prescribes no new limitations of the prerogative; but merely asserts those great principles of constitutional law which are to be collected from the practice of the best times.

By one of its clauses a claim is made on behalf of the people of England, to the holding of "frequent parliaments." But this provision not being thought of itself sufficient to guard the interests of the subject, in apprehension of the exercise of undue influence on the part of the crown over the House of Commons, it was enacted in the 6th of William and Mary, that the duration of parliaments should be limited to three years. By the statute 1. Geo. I. St. 2. c. 38.. this term was prolonged to seven.

This brief historical review of the rise, progress and variations of the British Constitution, may with propriety be closed by a still more brief account of its present organization.

Governments which are simple in their forms, are either democratic, aristocratical, or despotic. Each of these systems of political rule has its advantages and its defects. Democracies may be honest in their views, and public-spirited in their resolves; but they are liable to be rash in their decisions, and indecisive in the execution of their measures; to which may be added, that they are liable to all the horrors of factious turbulence. An aristocratical body may be prudent in its deliberations; but it is liable to corruption, whilst the ambitious intrigues of rival chieftains diffuse mutual dissatisfaction, and often give rise to the fury of civil war. And though an arbitrary monarch may be skilful in design, and prompt in action, that thirst for power, which seems to be innate in the human mind, will in all probability incite him to trample upon the dearest interests of his subjects. But the British Constitution, being a mixture of monarchy, aristocracy, and democracy, seems happily calculated to comprehend the good, and to reject the evil, which occur in these simple forms of civil polity. "For," to quote the sentiments of Mr. Justice Blackstone, "as with us the executive power of the laws is lodged in a single person, they have all the advantages of strength and dispatch that are to be found in the most absolute monarchy; and as the legislature of the kingdom is entrusted to three distinct powers, entirely independent of each other; first, the king; secondly, the lords spiritual and temporal, which is an aristocratical assembly of persons selected for their piety, their birth, their wisdom, their valour, or their property; and thirdly, the House of Commons freely chosen by the people, from among themselves, which makes it a kind of democracy; as this aggregate body, actuated by different springs, and attentive to different interests, composes the British Parliament, and has the supreme disposal of every thing, there can no inconvenience be attempted by either of these three branches, but will be withstood by one of the other two; each branch being armed with a negative power sufficient to repel any innovation which it shall think inexpedient or dangerous."

In analysing the component parts of the British Constitution, the regal power claims our first attention.

The crown of the United Kingdoms of Great Britain and Ireland is hereditary in the manner of landed estates, as to the male line. In one material circumstance, however, it differs, from common inheritances, inasmuch as it is not subject to subdivision, but in default of males, it descends entire to the eldest female heir and her issue.

It is nevertheless to be remarked, that though the British crown is generally hereditary, yet, when the welfare of the state requires it, common sense and precedent conspire to prove, that with respect to it, hereditary right may be defeated.

In case of necessity, or of manifest expediency, the lineal heir may be excluded, and the crown may be vested in any one else. And this may be done either by the Lords and Commons alone, as in case of a vacancy of the throne; or by the concurrence of King, Lords, and Commons, in case of the throne being full. Thus, when limitation of the descent became advisable in consequence of the misrule of James II. the two houses of Parliament vested the crown in William III. and Queen Mary; and on failure of issue in the line in which the crown was then limited, the succession was vested by the 12th and 13th of William III. in the heirs of Sophia of Hanover, upon condition that such heirs be protestants of the Church of England, and are married to none but protestants.

The rightful inheritor of the crown of the United Kingdoms, is by the conditions of his inheritance, bound to the discharge of certain duties, as well as vested with certain powers and prerogatives.—And it may be observed in general, that he is solemnly obliged "to govern his people according to law." Nothing is left to his arbitrary will. Nor is this, in the case of British kings, a mere deduction of reason. It is the subject of an express provision of the statute upon which is ultimately founded the right of the present reigning family to the throne of these realms, viz. the 12th and 13th of William III. By this statute it is expressly declared, "that the laws of England are the birthright of the people thereof; and all the kings and queens who shall ascend the throne of this realm, ought to administer the same according to the said laws; and all their officers and ministers ought to serve them respectively according to the same. According to the tenour of this statute, by the oath administered to our sovereigns at their coronation, they solemnly engage to govern according to law; to execute judgment in mercy; and to maintain the established religion, viz. Episcopacy according to the system of the English Church in England; Ireland, and Berwick upon Tweed; and Presbyterianism in Scotland.

To enable the sovereign of these realms to discharge his duties, he is vested by the constitution with ample and extensive privileges. These may be considered as referring to his foreign and to his domestic relations. With regard to the former it may be observed: 1. That as the dignity and power of the state is supposed to center in the king, he is endued with the sole power of sending ambassadors to foreign states, and of receiving within his dominions the ambassadors of foreign potentates. 2. That for the same reason, it is also his prerogative to enter into treaties, and to form alliances with foreign princes and states. 3. That, according to the practice of former times, if any of his subjects were despoiled or aggrieved by strangers, he was empowered to grant them letters of marque and reprisal, which authorized them to redress their private injury. But, in modern days, this private appeal to force is out of use. The wrongs of individuals are made subjects of national resentment, and become a cause of war; the proclaiming, prosecuting, and terminating of which, constitutes the fourth and the most important branch of the royal prerogative, as exercised upon foreign affairs.

In domestic concerns, the regal privileges are so ample, that, did not experience happily prove that they may be checked and counterbalanced, it might, upon an enumeration of them, be supposed that they would soon be heightened into despotism. For, 1. The king has an unquestionable right to put his negative upon all legislative measures proposed by the two other branches of the legislature. 2. As chief of the military power of the kingdom, he appoints all officers of the army and the navy, assigns them their stations in peace and war, and directs all the variety of military movements. He superintends all guards and garrisons, and erects and maintains all forts, fortresses, and places of arms, in these realms and their dependent colonies. 3. He is the fountain of justice, and the general conservator of the peace throughout the kingdom. He has power to erect courts of judicature, and to execute all sentences therein passed, or to suspend, or, with one exception, to remit their execution at his pleasure. The judges of the high courts of judicature are also appointed by him; but with a laudable precaution against a time-serving spirit on the part of those eminent magistrates, it is provided by statute, that they shall not be dismissed at the pleasure of the king, but that they shall retain their places even in the case of a demise of the crown *quamdiu se bene gesserint*. 5. The king is the fountain of honour, office, and privilege. From him are derived all the various degrees of nobility, knighthood, and other titles. He can also erect corporations, and convert aliens into denizens, and "grant place or precedence to any of his subjects, as shall seem good to his royal wisdom." 6. As arbiter of commerce, the king is authorized to institute markets and fairs, and to regulate tolls, weights, and measures, and the public coinage of the realm.

7. And it may be mentioned as the last, though not the least of the sources of royal power, that the king is the head of the English and Irish churches, in which capacity he summons and dissolves all synods and conventions of the clergy; and, in fact, though not in express terms, nominates to all vacant bishoprics, and to various other ecclesiastical offices.

This detail of the main branches of the royal prerogative evinces, that the maxim of the law is not a dead letter, which states, that "in the king is vested the attribute of sovereignty or pre-eminence." As a further support of his dignity and authority, it is a sacred principle of our constitutional law, that "the king can do no wrong." Strange as this principle may appear on its first enunciation, and directly as it may appear to tend to despotism, it is, in point of fact, by its application, one of the main preservatives of public liberty and of general tranquillity. For, whilst it is asserted that "the king can do no wrong," it is provided, that for all his public acts, his ministers and advisers are responsible to the nation at large by the medium of the parliament, and of other legally constituted assemblies. Hence, whilst due respect is paid to the person and the character of the reigning sovereign, the propriety of his measures may be canvassed with strictness, and even with jealousy—and those popular discontents which, in more arbitrary governments, would give rise to all the horrors of a revolution, are generally allayed by the easy and simple process of a change of administration.

The House of Peers is composed of the Lords spiritual, and the Lords temporal. The former consist of two Archbishops, and twenty-four bishops, who are a kind of representatives of the clergy of England and Wales; and of four Bishops, who are taken by rotation, from the eighteen bishops of Ireland. With regard to England, the number of temporal peers is unlimited. At the period of the Union with Ireland, A. D. 1800, it was settled, that from the Irish temporal peers, twenty-eight should be elected by their own body to sit in the Imperial parliament; that they should retain their seats during life; and that each vacancy by death, should be filled by a new election. The Scotch peers are sixteen in number, and are elected by their own body, for one parliament only. The Lords temporal are divided into dukes, marquisses, earls, viscounts, and barons, who hold their respective ranks in the foregoing order, by hereditary descent or by creation. In its aggregate capacity, the House of Peers has a right to a negative upon all legislative proposals. Its members also enjoy the privilege of voting by proxy, and of entering their dissent against the measures adopted by the majority, with the reasons of such dissent, upon the journals of the house. It is the final court of appeal in civil causes; and it constitutes a criminal court for the trial of its own members, and in certain cases for the trial of others who are impeached of high crimes and misdemeanours.

The Commons of the United Kingdoms of Great Britain and Ireland consist, to adopt the language of Blackstone, "of all such men of any property as have not seats in the House of Lords, every one of which has a vote in parliament, either personally, or by his representatives." These representatives, which constitute the House of Commons, or as it is sometimes called, the Lower House of Parliament, are returned by the respective kingdoms in the following proportions:

England	- -	513
Scotland	- -	45
Ireland	- -	100
Total	-	658

The members of the House of Commons are divided into two classes, Knights of the Shire, or representatives of counties; and citizens and burgesses, or representatives of cities and boroughs. The qualification for voting for the former, is the possession of a freehold, of the value of forty shillings per annum, or upwards, situated in the county, for which the elector claims a vote. The right of election in boroughs is very various, depending upon the charters and immemorial usages of each place, or upon solemn decisions made by committees appointed by the House, to decide upon the merits of election petitions. With a view to guard the purity, and to ensure the respectability of this assembly, it is provided by statute, that several descriptions of place-men and pensioners of the crown shall be ineligible to sit in it; and that each knight of the shire, must be seized of a freehold estate in the county which he represents, of the value of £600 per annum; and that every burgess and citizen must possess an annual landed income of £300.

The House of Commons, thus constituted, like the other branches of the legislature, enjoys the privilege of a negative upon all the laws which may be proposed for its consideration. By immemorial custom also, it claims and exercises the right of originating all money bills; that is to say, all bills which levy money upon the subject by way of taxes or assessments. Some fanciful reasons have been assigned for this privilege; but, referring to the history of the Constitution of the Lower House, it should seem, that it originated in the circumstance, that the Commons were first summoned merely for the purpose of informing the king what weight of taxation, their respective constituent bodies would be able to bear. This provision, which was at first in all probability regarded as a great hardship, has by the lapse of time been modified and matured, so as to become the principal safeguard of our liberties, and the main barrier against any inordinate encrease of the power of the crown. Without money the strength of the executive is paralysed; and as all taxation must not only be approved by the Commons, but must originate in their House, while on the one hand the King and the Lords are armed with a negative to defend themselves against any attempt at encroachment on the part of the third estate; so on the other, the Commons can at any time check the measures of ministerial folly, or guilt, by withholding the supplies. At the same time, should it ever happen, that the proceedings of the Commons are manifestly dictated by factious views, which are incompatible with the general interests of the community, the king is invested with a power, not only to negative their proceedings, but to dissolve the parliament; and thus, by submitting their conduct to the revision of their constituents, to appeal against them to the nation at large.

Thus, however complicated the machinery of the British Constitution and Government may appear to be, its operations are regulated by a few grand and simple principles; namely, the sacredness of the king's person, and the responsibility of his ministers—the negative power of each branch of the legislature; and the command exercised by the Commons over the public purse. The forms of parliamentary proceedings provide for the most mature discussion, and the greatest possible freedom of debate; and by those forms, ample opportunity is given to the people at large, and even to individuals, to state to either house, by the means of petitions, their sentiments upon measures which affect, or seem to affect, their immediate and peculiar interests. Notwithstanding then the influence of the crown is occasionally and plainly perceptible in the proceedings of the other branches of the legislature, the constitution has provided a check to that influence by the counterbalance of public opinion. The maxim of the great lord treasurer Burleigh is strictly true, that "England can never be ruined but by a parliament;" but it is equally true, that no parliament will hazard any proceedings ruinous to the liberties, or to the general welfare of the country, while the people at large watch with due vigilance the conduct of their representatives.

CHAP. XXVIII.

MATHEMATICS.

Objects of Mathematics—Use, importance and history of Mathematics. ARITHMETIC; history of—importance of to other branches of science—books of Arithmetic, viz. those by Dilworth—Walkinghame—Vyse—Hutton—Molyneux—Bonnycastle—Joyce—Malcolm and Mair—Arithmetical machines.

THE science of mathematics treats of the ratio* and comparison of quantities, and has been sometimes denominated the science of ratios. The term mathematics is derived from a Greek word signifying discipline, or science, thereby signifying the high idea that we ought to entertain of this branch of human knowledge. The science of mathematics is always accompanied with certainty, an advantage that characterizes accurate knowledge, and the true sciences, with which we must on no account associate conjecture, or even probability.

* Ratio is the relation that two magnitudes of the same kind bear to one another in respect to quantity. Thus the ratio of 2 to 1 is double, of 3 to 1, triple. Ratio has been frequently confounded with proportion, but they are different things, for proportion is the similitude or equality of two ratios. Thus the ratio of 6 to 2 is the same as that of 3 to 1, and the ratio of 15 to 5 is the same as that 3 to 1, and therefore the ratio of 6 to 2 is the same with that of 15 to 5, which constitutes proportion, and it is thus expressed, 6 is to 2 as 15 to 5, or thus 6 : 2 :: 15 : 5. So that ratio exists between two terms, but proportion between two ratios or four terms.

The subjects of which the mathematics treat, are the comparisons of quantities and magnitude, as numbers, velocity, distance, &c. Quantity expressed by numbers is called Arithmetic; but when expressed by letters and signs, it is denominated Algebra.

Geometry considers the relative magnitude and extension of bodies: astronomy, the relative velocities and distances of the planets: mechanics, the relative powers and force of different machines, &c. In all cases there must be some determinate quantity fixed on as a standard measure.

Mathematics are usually divided into the *pure* or *abstract*, and the *compound* or *mixed*. *Pure* mathematics relate to magnitudes generally and abstractedly, and are founded on the elementary ideas of quantity: such is *Arithmetic*, or the art of computation, and such also is *Geometry*, or the science of mensuration and comparison of extensions of every kind. Mixed mathematics consider quantity as subsisting in material substances, as length in a pole or staff, depth in a river, height in a tree, tower, &c. Mixed mathematics are very extensive, and are distinguished by various names, according to the different subjects they consider, and the different views in which they are taken, such as mechanics, hydrostatics, hydraulics, acoustics, optics, navigation, &c.

There is an advantage in *pure* mathematics, which is peculiar to that branch of science: it neither occasions nor admits of contests among wrangling disputants, as happens in other branches of knowledge. For the definitions of the terms are premised, and every person that reads a proposition has the same idea of every part of it. Hence, it is easy to put an end to all mathematical controversies, by shewing, either that the adversary has not kept to his definitions, or has not laid down true premises, or has drawn false conclusions from true principles; and in case some one or other of these can be done, he must acknowledge the truth of what has been proved. In *mixed* mathematics, where we reason mathematically upon physical subjects, our definitions cannot be so strict as in geometry. They are frequently little better than descriptions, which, however, with proper care, will be nearly of the same use as definitions, provided we always mean the same thing by those terms which we have once explained.

Though the application of mathematical sciences is of great importance to the interests of society, yet this is not that which constitutes their peculiar excellency; it is their operation upon the mind, the vigour which they impart to our intellectual faculties, and the discipline which they impose upon our rational powers. The eulogium passed upon this science by the learned Dr. Barrow, may claim the notice of every youth; and those who are capable of appreciating the value of this branch of knowledge, will admit, that he has not gone, in any respect, beyond the truth. "The mathematics," says the doctor, "effectually exercise studious minds, and plainly demonstrate every thing within their reach: they draw certain conclusions, instruct by profitable rules, and unfold pleasant questions. These disciplines inure and corroborate the mind to a constant diligence in study: they wholly deliver us from a credulous simplicity; and most strongly fortify us against the vanity of scepticism: they effectually restrain us from rash presumption, most easily incline us to a due assent, and perfectly subject us to the government of right reason. While the mind is abstracted from and elevated above sensible matter, it distinctly views pure forms, conceives the beauty of ideas, and investigates the harmony of proportions; the manners themselves are sensibly corrected and improved, the affections composed and rectified, the fancy calmed and settled, and the understanding raised and excited to more divine contemplations."

By a certain class of people, mathematical studies are held in contempt; but it may, perhaps, be justly assumed, that those who speak, or even think slightly of them, are the persons who have not patience to investigate the truths which they are capable of unfolding.

A liberal mind excludes, as unworthy of its notice, none of the sciences. They all contribute, by various, and, perhaps, different means to adorn and embellish life, and for this reason, independently of the advantages above enumerated, they ought to be cultivated and improved. "Happy is the mind that is not contracted by the study of philosophy, nor enervated by the charms of the Belles Lettres; that can be strengthened by Locke; instructed by Clarke and Newton; impassioned by Cicero and Demosthenes; and elevated by the powers of Homer and Virgil."

The limits of our work, will not allow us to enter at large into the history of any branch of science; we may, however, briefly notice some facts connected with the early culture of mathematical knowledge. It is generally supposed that the Greeks derived their scientific learning from the Magi of Egypt, long before the time of Thales, who is often styled the father of the Grecian philosophy, only because he is the first of those of whom any decided account has been transmitted to us. This philosopher, according to Herodotus, predicted a total eclipse of the sun, which from subsequent inquiry is ascertained to have happened in the year 610, B. C. At this period, then, astronomy must have made considerable progress in Greece, as the prediction of an eclipse requires much previous knowledge, and a vast number of accurate observations, which could only have been obtained in a long series of years. Pythagoras, who was probably a pupil of Thales, and who flourished about the year 590, B. C., had made considerable improvements in arithmetic, astronomy, and geometry. In arithmetic, he invented the multiplication table, or the Abacus Pythagoricus:—in astronomy, he suggested the idea of the true system, placing the sun in the centre, and making the planets, revolve about that body;—and in geometry, he discovered the forty-seventh proposition of Euclid's first book, well known by the name of the Pythagorean theorem, and which of itself, would have conferred a sort of immortality upon the discoverer. At or about this period, Anaximander flourished, and soon after Anaximenes, Anaxagoras, and others of great note: but passing over these, we come to Plato, who cultivated both geometry and astronomy with great assiduity, nearly four centuries before the birth of Christ. To him, and to his disciple Aristæus, we are indebted for the introduction of the conic sections in geometry. It was almost a century between the time of Plato and Euclid, during which period all the sciences were considerably advanced and extended; and treatises on particular subjects appeared from this time, in which all the propositions then known, were collected and arranged in systematic order, which was the object of Euclid in his celebrated Elements, a work of which we shall shortly have occasion to speak, and which has met with a success vastly superior to that of any other book of science that ever was published. Archimedes, one of the most illustrious geometricians that ever existed, followed soon after the time of Euclid. His genius was as extensive as it was penetrating, and it led him to the contemplation of almost every species of human knowledge, and nearly every branch of mathematical science is indebted to him for most important discoveries. After Archimedes, at the distance of fifty years, Apollonius cultivated the mathematical sciences with the greatest possible success. About this period flourished Eratosthenes, who first attempted to measure the earth; Ctesibius, to whom we are indebted for pumps; and Hero of Alexandria, who invented the clepsydræ, or water-clocks. Hipparchus, the prince and father of astronomy, who flourished about one hundred and forty years, B. C., made the first classification of the stars, ascertained nearly the duration of the year, discovered the eccentricity of the earth's orbit, the precession of the equinoxes, and applied his favourite science to the purposes of geography. Theodosius is the next eminent mathematician; he wrote a work on the sphere, which may be reckoned as the foundation of spherical trigonometry; but after him, we have no account of any great geometrician for nearly three hundred years. Ptolemy began to revive the sciences, about a century and half after the birth of Christ. His principal work was entitled the Almagest, an Arabic word signifying "the Great Collection," because it contained all the ancient observations and theories, which, with the addition of his own researches, may be said to have formed the most complete collection of ancient astronomy that ever appeared. This work, in some measure supplies the place of those that preceded it, and which are now lost to the world; and for the compilation of it, Ptolemy is entitled to the gratitude of all lovers of science. Some years after this period, Diophantus made a new and remarkable step in arithmetic, by the invention of the indeterminate analysis, a species of algebra, which is the first trace we have of this extensive and highly useful branch of science. This work it appears, consisted of thirteen books, only six of which have come down to us: it displays great talents, and has ever been in high esteem among analysts of all succeeding ages; and has accordingly been commented upon and explained by various writers, both ancient and modern—most of the former are lost. Of these, mathematicians have chiefly regretted the commentary of Hypatia, daughter of Theon, who flourished about the four hundred and tenth year of the Christian æra. The talents, virtues, and misfortunes of this illustrious victim of fanaticism, have a claim to the homage of posterity, while the remembrance of the deed,* and the perpetrators of it, will be execrated and abhorred by every friend to science, and admirer of female virtue and talents. About this period we meet with Pappus, who is distinguished for his collections of the various works of his predecessors: these collections contain one of the most valuable monuments of ancient geometry. In them, he has assembled together a number of excellent works, the originals of almost all of which are now lost, and to them he has added several new, curious, and learned propositions of his own.

* Hypatia was murdered in the year 415, under the reign of Theodosius II. by the consent and desire, if not by the direct instigation of Cyril, a Christian bishop. Her cruel and blood-thirsty enemies were not content with her life: they put her to extreme torture, and then treated her dead body with the utmost indignity.

After Pappus, Eutochius flourished about the year 520, who was a great mathematician, and whose commentaries on the works of Archimedes and Apollonius are in high estimation. Other names might be enumerated, had we room to dilate; but we pass on to that period which proved so fatal to the sciences. These had for a long time taken refuge in Alexandria; but, about the middle of the seventh century, a tremendous storm arose, which threatened their total destruction. The successors of Mohammed ravaged an immense extent of the then civilized world. All the cultivators of the arts and sciences, who, from every nation, had assembled in Alexandria, were driven away with ignominy; some fell beneath the swords of the conquerors, others fled into remote countries, to drag out the remainder of their lives in obscurity and distress. The places and instruments which had been so useful in making an immense number of astronomical observations, were involved with the records in one common ruin. The whole of that precious library, which contained the works of so many eminent authors, and was the common depository of every species of human knowledge, was entirely devoted to the flames by the Arabs. From this period, several ages followed of the most wretched ignorance and barbarism, so that it seems wonderful that the sciences ever recovered the deadly blow; but, as has been mentioned, some philosophers of Alexandria escaped the vengeance of their barbarous conquerors, and these of course carried with them a remnant of that general learning for which this school was so justly celebrated. But, destitute of books, of instruments, and almost the means of existence without manual labour, very little farther knowledge could have been accumulated, and still less propagated; so that philosophy and mathematics must have become extinct, had not the Arabians themselves, within less than two centuries from this fatal catastrophe, become the admirers and supporters of those very sciences which they, or, at least, their ancestors, had so nearly annihilated.

Of all the branches of mathematics, astronomy was that

which the Arabs held in the greatest estimation, though they did not wholly neglect the others. Our present system of arithmetic is derived from them, though they were probably not the inventors, but had acquired their knowledge of it from the Indians. It is not in our power to enumerate all the great men among the Arabians that appeared from the period of which we are now speaking, to the beginning of the thirteenth century. Among the Arabian princes, who were also men of science, we may mention Almansor, who flourished about the year 754; Al-Maimon, who reigned from 813 to 833, in whose time, in consequence of the great support and assistance which he afforded the sciences, they made very considerable progress. Alfragan, Thebit, and Albategni, were particularly distinguished about this period. Thebit was a considerable algebraist, geometrician, and astronomer; Alfragan composed elements of the latter branch of science, of which several editions have been published since the invention of printing; and Albategni, in consequence of his numerous and important observations, and very accurate knowledge, was surnamed the Arabian Ptolemy. About the year 1100, Alhazen, a very celebrated Arab, settled in Spain, and composed a treatise on optics; and to him we are indebted for the first theory of refraction and twilight.

Thus have we given a brief sketch of the first rise, the decline, and revival of the mathematical sciences. After this period, they began to be propagated in several European countries, and have continued to be cultivated and improved from that to the present time. The reader is referred to Montucla's History of Mathematics, for a complete account of almost every thing that is valuable and deserving of notice on the subject. Montucla's History was first published in two volumes, 4to. but it was afterwards continued by Lalande, making, in the whole, four volumes.

ARITHMETIC.

Arithmetic, or the art of numbering, is that part of mathematics which considers the powers of numbers, and teaches how to compute or calculate truly, and with ease and expedition. The great leading rules or operations, after we have learnt to name the several figures and combinations of figures, are addition, subtraction, multiplication, and division. Besides these, many other useful rules have been contrived, for the purpose of facilitating and expediting computations, mercantile and astronomical; and which afford the most salutary aid to the philosopher, the man of business, and the political economist.

We know very little respecting the origin and invention of arithmetic; like other branches of knowledge connected with the interests of society, it probably originated in the wants of man, and at first proceeded very slowly toward that point of perfection to which it has long since arrived. History fixes neither the author nor the time when its elementary principles were discovered, or, perhaps, to speak more properly, contrived. Some knowledge of numbers must have existed in the earliest ages of mankind, which was probably suggested to them by their own fingers or toes, by their flocks and herds, and by a variety of objects that surrounded them. Their powers of numeration would, at first, have been very limited, and before the art of writing was invented, it must have depended either on memory, or on such artificial helps as might be most easily obtained.

The introduction of arithmetic as a science, and the improvements it underwent, must, in a great degree, have depended upon the introduction and establishment of commerce; and as that was extended and improved, and other sciences were discovered and cultivated, arithmetic would be improved likewise. Hence it has been inferred, that arithmetic was a Tyrian invention, or, at least, that it was much indebted to the Tyrians or Phœnicians for its progress in the world. Proclus, in his Commentary on the first book of Euclid, says, the Phœnicians, by reason of their great traffic and commerce, were the inventors of arithmetic. This also was the opinion of Strabo. Others, however, have traced the origin of this art to Egypt, and they say that Theut, or Thot, was the inventor of numbers, that from thence the Greeks adopted the idea of ascribing to their Mercury, corresponding to the Egyptian Theut, or Hermes, the superintendence of commerce and arithmetic.

Josephus affirms, that arithmetic passed from Asia into Egypt, where it was cultivated and improved, so much so, that a considerable part of Egyptian philosophy, and theology likewise, seems to have turned altogether upon numbers. Athanasins Kircher shews that the Egyptians explained every thing by numbers. So highly was the art of numbering or arithmetic esteemed by the ancients, that Pythagoras affirmed that the nature of numbers pervades the whole universe, and that the knowledge of numbers is the knowledge of the Deity himself.

From Egypt, arithmetic was transmitted to the Greeks by Pythagoras and his followers, and among them it was the subject of particular attention, as is evident from the writings of Archimedes and other illustrious philosophers; and with the improvements which it derived from them, it passed to the Romans, and from them it came to us.

The ancient arithmetic was very different from that of the moderns, in several respects, and particularly in their method of notation. It has been thought that the Greeks and Romans at first used pebbles in their calculations, and, in proof of this, we find the Greek and Latin words signifying *calculation*, are derived from the words ψηφος and *calculus*, a little stone; and the Greek verb ψηφιζω signifies, among other meanings, to calculate. In confirmation of this theory, it is observed, that the Indians are at this time very expert in computing by means of their fingers, without the use of pen and ink; and that the natives of Peru, by different arrangements of their maize, surpass the European, aided by all his rules, both in accuracy and despatch.

"It is easy to imagine," says the author of the "Origin of

Laws, Arts, and Sciences," p. 218, &c. vol. i. "how, by the help of their fingers and a few little stones, men might perform considerable calculations. If it is demanded how these primitive arithmeticians managed when they were to count a great number of objects, which obliged them several times to recommence the decimal numeration, I answer, that it seems probable they marked tens of units by one symbol, and hundreds by another. Perhaps they expressed tens by white stones, and hundreds by stones of another colour. After this discovery, it would not be difficult to contrive symbols for expressing tens of hundreds, or thousands, &c. &c.

"Perhaps the first arithmeticians might make use of symbols of the same colour to express tens, hundreds, &c. only observing to place them so with regard to one another, as to determine their relative value, as we do with our cyphers, which have different values, according to the rank they hold, and the place they occupy. By such means, mankind might carry the practice of numeration further than their necessities and way of life required. The invention of these methods of numeration would naturally lead men to the knowledge of addition. As soon as they knew how to number with facility a collection of objects, however great, it would require no great effort to number several of these together, that is, to add them. They had nothing to do but to place the symbols of their several numbers under one another, so as to have their units, their tens, and their hundreds, &c. under their eye at once, and then to reduce all these several symbols into one. They would not be long in discovering the art of performing this reduction. They had only to sum up separately first their units, then their tens, and then their hundreds, and to form the symbol of each of these sums as they discovered them; to do that, in a word, by parts, which the weakness of our faculties will not permit us to do at once.

"It was not difficult to proceed from the practice of numeration to addition, it was still more easy to find out the art of multiplying one number by another. There is reason to think, that multiplication was at first performed by means of addition. The steps of the human mind are naturally slow. It requires no little time and labour to pass the medium which divides one part of science from another, however analogons they may seem to be. At first, therefore, it is probable multiplication and addition made but one operation. Had they, for example, to multiply 12 by 4, they formed the symbol of 12 four times, and then reduced these four symbols into one, by the rules just laid down. But this method of multiplication by addition must have been very tedious and perplexing, when either of the numbers was considerable. If they were to multiply 15 by 13, they had to make the symbol of 15 thirteen times, and then to sum up these thirteen symbols. Those who were most practised in calculation, would soon discover that they might abridge this operation, by forming the symbol of 15 three times, and once that of 150, which is the product of 16 by 10; and then sum up these four symbols. Such was probably the first step of the human mind towards multiplication, properly so called, or the art of adding equal numbers with greater facility and expedition. This operation, however, could never be performed with ease, till those who practised calculation had by heart the product of all the numbers under ten."

The Hebrews and Greeks at a very early period, it is well known, had recourse to the letters of their alphabet for the representation of their numbers, and the Romans followed their example. The Greeks, in particular, had two methods; the first resembled that of the Romans, with which we are well acquainted, and is still used in numbering the chapters, and other divisions of books, dates of years, &c. They afterwards had recourse to another method, in which the first nine letters of their alphabet represented the first numbers from 1 to 9, and the next nine letters represented any number of tens, from 1 to 9, that is, 10, 20, &c. to 90. Any number of hundreds they expressed by other letters, in the same, or a similar way, as has been explained above with regard to pebbles, thus approaching to the more perfect decuple or decimal scale of progression used by the Arabians, who, as we have seen, probably received it from the Indians, to whom it was perhaps carried by Pythagoras.

The introduction of the Arabian or Indian notation into Europe, about the tenth century, made a material alteration in the state of arithmetic; and this is thought to have been one of the greatest improvements which this science had received since the first discovery of it. The method of notation was certainly brought from the Arabians into Spain, by the Moors or Saracens in the tenth century. Gerbert, afterwards Pope Silvester II., who died in the year 1003, carried this notation from the Moors of Spain into France, it is believed about the year 960, and it was known in this country early in the eleventh century, or perhaps sooner. As science and literature advanced in Europe the knowledge of numbers was also extended, and the writers in this art were very much multiplied.

The next considerable improvement in this branch of science, after the introduction of the numeral figures of the Arabians, was that of decimal parts, for which we are indebted to Regiomontanus; who, about the year 1464, divided the radius of a circle (see Trigonometry) into 10,000,000, so that if the radius be denoted by 1, the sines, co-sines, &c. will be expressed by so many places of decimal fractions, as there are cyphers following 1. This seems to have been the introduction of decimal parts. The first person who wrote professedly on the subject, and introduced the name "disme" or "decimals" was Simon Sterinus, in a treatise intitled "Disme," subjoined to his arithmetic, published in French, and printed at Leyden in 1585; since which, the method of decimals has been practised by many others, and is now become universal.

Arithmetic, in its present state, is divided into different kinds; our concern with it is only as it relates to *theory* and *practice*. Theoretical or speculative arithmetic is the science of the properties, relations, &c. of numbers, considered abstractedly, with the reasons and demonstrations of the several rules. Euclid, to whom we shall shortly have occasion to refer more particularly, furnishes a theoretical arithmetic, in the seventh, eighth and ninth books of his Elements. The practical part consists in the application of the rules resulting from the theory to the solution of questions or problems, and arithmetic in this respect has been called an art: viz. the art of numbering or computing; that is, from certain numbers given, of finding certain others, whose relation to the former becomes known.

To a person unacquainted with the rules of arithmetic, but who has in his mind an idea of numbers, and at the same time knows how to express those numbers, it may naturally occur to him to ask what is the sum of two or more numbers? hence appears the necessity of the rule *addition*. To obtain the difference of two given numbers, *subtraction* will be required; to find the product of two or more numbers, we want another rule called *multiplication*, and to find how often one number is contained in another, requires *division*. These four rules, viz. addition, subtraction, multiplication, and division, are, in fact, the whole of arithmetic. For every arithmetical operation requires the use of some or all of these. These have been sometimes compared to the simple mechanical powers, which, variously combined, produce engines of different forms and of indefinite force; which, however they may at first strike us with surprise and astonishment, will, upon examination, appear evidently to arise from a proper combination of the simple powers. In the same manner the most complex operations in arithmetic are all effected by the application of the simple rules just described.

Although it may at first appear, that the student, in pursuit of general knowledge, has little to do with arithmetic, excepting, as a branch of science, and that if he understand the theoretical part it will be amply sufficient, experience will teach him a different lesson. To be ready in science, properly so called, he ought to be an expert practical arithmetician, and he cannot lay too broad and solid a foundation in this introductory part of knowledge.

Numerical computations are necessary in almost every step of useful knowledge, though the manner of the operations depends upon the nature of the subject to which they are applied. Arithmetic may, therefore, be regarded as the handmaid to her sister arts and sciences; and, while she is employed in their service, she must be under their direction, be ready at their call, and observe the laws they prescribe. Thus, the calculations of eclipses, the time of the tides, and of the several changes of the moon, are performed by numbers; but the operations must be directed by the precepts of astronomy, which are the results of an extensive knowledge in that branch of science. Reckonings at sea, so useful and necessary to the navigator, are wrought by arithmetic; but the steps of the work are conducted by the rules of navigation. The contents of casks, in the art of guaging, are found by numbers; but the principles of the art depend on plane and solid Geometry. The perpendicular heights of objects are computed by numbers; but trigonometry, which depends on geometry, directs the manner of their application. The Specific Gravities of bodies are obtained by arithmetic; but they could not have been investigated without the aid of hydrostatics. Similar observations would apply to the other branches of science, which shew how important it is, that a person in pursuit of the general principles of knowledge, should be well grounded in arithmetic. It remains now to describe those books from which such knowledge can be readily obtained.

The number of books containing the practice and first principles of arithmetic, is very great; almost any of which, with the assistance of a teacher, will answer the end proposed. We shall mention but few of these, without, however, meaning, by our silence, to depreciate the others.

The principal school-books in Arithmetic, were formerly the "School-master's Assistant," by Dilworth, and the

" Tutor's Assistant," by Walkinghame; these, for many years, kept possession of the majority of schools in this country, and were unquestionably very useful books; and might at that time have been recommended as well to young persons who had no guides, as to tutors, for whose express use the titles seem to denote they were, by the authors, designed. Since which the " Tutor's Guide," by Charles Vyse, became a popular school-book: this is a much more elaborate work than the other two; it includes a number of subjects not necessary as a mere introduction to Arithmetic; such as the mensuration of solids, as well as superfices, the method of obtaining the specific gravities of bodies, the application of the rules of arithmetic to the principles of Chronology, &c. Mr. Vyse published a key to his work, containing solutions of all the questions in the " Guide."

Dr. Hutton's Treatise is used in many schools, to this also there is a key. The same may be said of Keith's, of Goodacre's, Molyneux's, and others. The first part of Molyneux's is excellent, as far as it goes, which embraces the four first rules, Reduction, the Rule of Three, and Practice. We think it not a judicious plan to throw the doctrine and practice of Vulgar Fractions, so far forward as many authors do, because the knowledge of them is required at an early period. The four rules in Vulgar Fractions, are as easily learnt as any other part of arithmetic, when properly taught, and should perhaps be immediately learnt after the same rules in whole numbers.

Mr. Bonnycastle's " Scholar's Guide " is an excellent elementary treatise, in the notes are neat demonstrations of each rule. A few years since the same author published an octavo edition of his work, with various alterations, additions, and improvements; to which he has prefixed a neat historical introduction, and has added a Table of the Squares and Cubes of all the numbers, up to 2000 inclusive, and a table of the square and cube roots of the same numbers. He has likewise given a table of all the prime numbers, from 1 to

100,000, that is, of all those numbers, which cannot be divided into any number of equal integral parts greater than unity; such are the numbers, 3, 5, 7, 13, 17, &c. A much larger table extending to 217,219 is given in Dr. Rees's great work, the New Cyclopedia, under the article PRIME NUMBERS, which, says the author of that article, is double the extent to which they are carried in any other English work, and which it is presumed may be found useful in a great variety of cases connected with arithmetical and numeral problems.

Mr. Bonnycastle's "Scholar's Guide" seems deficient in its examples, which cannot well be too numerous for young beginners: the rules are easily understood, and nothing but considerable practice can give facility in the operations. To obviate this objection, the following work was published, "A System of Practical Arithmetic, applicable to the present state of trade and money-transactions, illustrated with numerous examples under each rule," by the Rev. J. Joyce. A large portion of this work is devoted to examples of all kinds, intended to illustrate the rules, which contain much useful information applicable to the advancing stages of life. The author of this work, after giving reasons for introducing Logarithms, the doctrine of Annuities, Reversions, Leases, &c. into his book, says, "A book of Arithmetic, for schools, should contain every thing necessary to be known, previously to the study of Algebra; and for the sake of those who wish to proceed to that science, it should be introductory to it. This, it is believed, will be found to be one of the characteristics of the work now offered to the public. There are, however, thousands who never trouble themselves to learn beyond the elements of the arithmetic which they acquire at school; who, looking to trade and commerce as the objects of their future lives, seek only for that knowledge which in some way or other is applicable to those objects. These, in almost every rank and situation, have frequent occasion to calculate the interest of money and the discount of bills; and to ascertain the value of annuities on single and joint lives, of survivorships, of leases, of reversionary interests, of funded property, and of freehold estates." To render these subjects familiar to young people was one chief object of the work last mentioned, and it is presumed that it has been attained.

A key to this system of practical arithmetic has been published, into which, unfortunately, several errors crept, owing to the proprietors having employed a person to correct the proofs who was incompetent to the task, instead of consigning the business, as they ought, to the author.

There are besides the introductory books already mentioned, some on a much larger and more expensive scale; among these may be mentioned, one by Malcolm, and another intitled "Arithmetic, Rational, and Practical," by John Mair. We may add, that the most considerable mathematicians have in former times, as well as in modern days, employed their talents in illustrating the rules of arithmetic, and in investigating the properties of numbers.

It may be farther added, that arithmetical operations have been performed by mechanism, and machines of various kinds have been invented to perform the fundamental rules. These, however, can go no farther: in cases where any degree of invention is necessary, the aid of the mind is required. Napier's rods are familiar to every one who has attended to the subject in hand. In the reign of Charles II. Sir Samuel Morland invented two arithmetical machines, of which he published an account under the title "The Description and Use of two Arithmetic Instruments, together with a short treatise, explaining the ordinary operations of arithmetic." This work, which is now very rare, is illustrated with twelve plates, in which the different parts of the machines are exhibited; and from these it should seem that the four fundamental rules in arithmetic are readily worked, and, to use the author's own words, "without charging the memory, disturbing the mind, or exposing the operations to any uncertainty." The present Earl Stanhope about thirty years since invented and caused to be manufactured two machines for the like purposes as those of Mr. Morland. The smallest of these instruments, intended for addition and subtraction, is not much larger than an octavo volume, and by means of dial-plates and indices the operations are performed with undeviating accuracy. The second, and by far the most curious instrument, is about half the size of a common table writing-desk. By this, problems of almost any extent in multiplication and division, are solved without the possibility of a mistake. The multiplier and multiplicand in one instance, and the divisor and dividend in the other, are first properly arranged; then, by turning a winch, the product or quotient is found.

CHAP. XXIX.

MATHEMATICS,

Continued.

Introduction—Algebra defined, and the term explained—History of Algebra—Origin of the Name—of the Science—from whom derived—by whom improved. Modern authors: Ward—Jones—Newton. Algebraical definitions and symbols. Introductory treatises: Fenning—Bonnycastle—Walker—Bridge—Frend—Simpson—Maclaurin—Saunderson—Dodson—Bland—Euler—Hales, &c.

ALTHOUGH a competent knowledge of common arithmetic should be followed by Algebra, yet the student may, and, perhaps, ought to combine, with his analytical studies, a diligent attention to Geometry, of which we shall shortly speak more at large. Algebraical and Geometrical studies should go hand in hand, though for convenience, in this work, we are obliged to speak of them separately; and algebra being but a more general kind of arithmetic, we begin with that.

Algebra is a general method of resolving mathematical problems by means of equations: or it is a method of computation by symbols, which have been invented for expressing the quantities that are the objects of this science, and shewing their mutual relation and dependence. It has been thought that these quantities were, in the infancy of science, denoted by their names at full length, which being found inconvenient, were succeeded by abbreviations, or by their initials. At length certain letters of the alphabet were adopted, as general representations of all quantities; other symbols or signs were introduced to prevent circumlocution, and to facilitate the comparison of various quantities with one another; and in consequence of the use of letters and other general symbols, algebra obtained the name of literal or universal arithmetic.

The origin of the name algebra is not easily ascertained: from its prefix *Al*, it is supposed to be of Arabic original; but its etymology has been variously assigned by different authors. Some have assumed that the word comes from an Arabic term, to *restore*, to which was added another, to *compare*, and hence it was formerly denominated the science of *restitution* and *comparison;* or *resolution* and *equation.* Accordingly, Lucas de Burgo, the first European author on Algebra, calls it the rule of restoration and opposition. Others have derived it from the word Geber, which was either the name of a celebrated mathematician to whom the invention of the science is ascribed; or from the word *Geber*, which forms, with the particle *al*, the term *algebra*, signifying a reduction of broken numbers or fractions into integers. The science has been distinguished by other names besides algebra. Lucas de Burgo calls it *l'arte magiore*, or greater art, in opposition to common arithmetic, which is denominated *l'arte minore*, or the lesser art.

Some writers have defined algebra, as the art of resolving mathematical problems, but this is rather the idea attached to *analysis*, or the analytic art in general, than to algebra, which is only a particular branch of it. Algebra consists of two parts, viz. the method of calculating magnitudes or quantities represented by letters or other characters, and the mode of applying these calculations to the solution of problems. When algebra is applied to the solution of problems, all the quantities that are involved in the problem are expressed by letters; and all the conditions that serve their mutual relation, and by which they are compared with one another, are signified by their appropriate characters, and they are thus thrown into one or more equations, as the case requires: this is called *synthesis*, or composition. When this has been done, the unknown quantity is disengaged, by a variety of analytical operations, from those that are known, and brought to stand alone on one side of the equation, while the known quantities are on the other side; and thus the value of the unknown quantity is investigated and obtained. This process is called *analysis*, or resolution; hence algebra is a species of the analytic art, and is called the modern analysis, in contradistinction to the ancient analysis, which chiefly regarded geometry and its application.

The origin of the science of algebra, like the derivation of the term, is not easily determined. The most ancient treatise, on that part of analytics properly called algebra, now known, is that of Diophantus, a Greek author, who flourished in the fourth century of the Christian æra; and who, it appears, wrote thirteen books "Arithmeticorum," though only six of them are preserved, which were printed together with a single book on multangular numbers, in a Latin translation by Xylander, in 1575, and afterwards in Greek and Latin, with a commentary, in 1621 and 1670, by Gaspar Bachet and M. Fermat. There must, however, have been other works on the subject, though unknown to the moderns, because these do not contain the elements of the science; they are merely collections of difficult questions relating to square and cube numbers, and other curious properties of numbers, with their solutions. To have been able to form these questions, and to have arrived at the solutions, required complete elementary treatises, well known to the author, and something similar, no doubt, to existing elementary books, as will appear from the following considerations.

In his prefatory remarks, addressed to a person by the name of Dionysius, the author recites the names and generations of the powers, as the square, cube, biquadrate, &c. and gives them names according to the sum of the indices of the powers, and he marks those powers with the Greek initials, and the unknown quantity he expressed by the word αριθμος, or *the number*. In treating on the multiplication and division of simple species, he shews what the product and quotient will be, observing that minus, multiplied by minus, produces plus; and that minus into plus, gives minus. Supposing his reader acquainted with the common operations of the first four rules, viz. addition, subtraction, multiplication, and division of compound species, he proceeds to remark on the preparation of the equations that are deduced from the questions, which is now called the reduction of equations, by collecting like quantities, changing the signs of those that are removed from one side of the equation to the other, which operation is termed by the moderns transposition, so as to bring the equation to simple terms. Then depressing it to a lower degree by equal division, when the powers of the unknown quantity are in every term; which reduction of the complex equation being made, the author proceeds no farther, but merely states what the root is, without giving any rules for finding it, or for the resolution of the equations, thus intimating, that rules for this purpose were to be found in some other work or works well known at the time, whether they were the productions of his own or another mind. The great excellence of Diophantus' collection of questions, which seems to be a series of exercises for rules which had been elsewhere given, is the neat mode of notation or substitution, which being once made, the reduction to the final equation is obvious. The work indicates much accurate knowledge of the science of algebra, but as the author reduces all his notations either to simple equations or simple quadratics, it does not appear how far his knowledge extended to the resolution of compound or affected equations.

It has, however, been thought that algebra was not wholly unknown to the ancient mathematicians, long before the age of Diophantus; and there have been those who observed, or who thought they observed, the traces of it in many places, though it seems as if the authors had intentionally concealed it.

Something of this appears in Euclid, or at least in his commentator Theon, who says that Plato had begun to teach it. There are other instances of it in Pappus, and still more in Archimedes and Apollonius, but it must be observed, that the analysis of these authors is rather geometrical than algebraical; and hence Diophantus may be considered as the only author come down to us among the Greeks, who treated professedly of algebra.

Our knowledge of the science of algebra was derived, not from Diophantus, but from the Moors or Arabians, but whether the Greeks or Arabians were the inventors of it, has been a subject of dispute, into which we shall not enter. It is, at any rate probable, that it was much more ancient than Diophantus, because, as we have seen, his treatise refers to, and depends upon works similar and prior to his own existing treatise. But wherever algebra was invented and first cultivated, the science, and also the name of it were transmitted to Europe, and particularly to Spain, by the Arabians or Saracens, about the year 1100, or perhaps somewhat sooner. Italy took the lead in the cultivation of this science after its introduction into Europe, and Lucas de Burgo, to whom we have already referred, a Franciscan friar, was the first author on the subject, who wrote several treatises between the years 1475 and 1510, but his principal work, entitled "Summa Arithmeticæ et Geometriæ," &c., was published at Venice in 1494, and afterwards in 1523. In this work he mentions several writers, and particularly Leonardus Pisanus, placed by Vossius about the year 1400, and said to have been the first of the moderns who wrote of algebra, from whom he derived his knowledge of that science; and from the treatise of Leonardus, not now extant, the contents of that of Lucas were chiefly collected. Leonardus was supposed to have flourished about the end of the fourteenth century, but it is now ascertained from an ancient manuscript, that he lived two hundred years before this, or at the very commencement of the thirteenth century, and of course, that Italy is indebted to him for its first knowledge of algebra. His proper name was Bonacci: he was a merchant, who traded in the sea-ports of Africa and the Levant. Being anxious to obtain an acquaintance with the sciences that were eagerly cultivated among the Arabians, and particularly that of Algebra, he travelled into that country, and it should seem from the authority of the manuscript above referred to, that Leonardus had penetrated deeply into the secrets of the algebraic analysis; that he was particularly acquainted with the analysis of problems similar in kind to those of Diophantus, and that he had made long voyages into Arabia, and other Eastern countries, with the express view of gaining a deeper knowledge of the mathematics.

According to Lucas de Burgo, the knowledge of the Europeans in his time, or about the year 1500, extended no farther than quadratic equations, of which they used only the positive roots;—that they admitted only one unknown quantity;—that they had no marks or signs either for quantities or operations, excepting a few abbreviations of the words or names; and that the art was merely employed in resolving certain numeral problems. If the science had been carried farther in Africa than quadratic equations, which was probably the case, as has been inferred from an Arabic manuscript, said to be on cubic equations, deposited in the library of Leyden, by Warner, the Europeans had, at this period, obtained only an imperfect knowledge of it.

The publication of the works of Lucas de Burgo promoted the study, and extended the knowledge of algebra, so that early in the sixteenth century, or about the year 1505, Scipio Ferreus, professor of mathematics at Bononia, discovered the first rule for resolving one case of a compound cubic equation. Cardanus was the next Italian that distinguished himself, by the cultivation and improvement of algebra: he published nine books of his arithmetical writings, in 1539, at Milan, where he practised physic, and read lectures on the mathematics: six years afterwards he published a tenth book containing the whole doctrine of cubic equations. Cardan denominates algebra, after Lucas de Burgo and others, " Ars magna," or " Regulæ Algebraicæ," and ascribes the invention of it, to Mahomet, the son of Moses, an Arabian. Dr. Hutton, in a curious and very elaborate article, *Algebra*, in his Dictionary, has given a full account of Cardan's treatise, and of the methods which he took to obtain the discovery of solving three cases of cubic equations from Tartalea. To this article we refer our readers, premising, however, that it will not be intelligible to any but those who have made some progress in the science.

Tartalea, or Tartaglia, of Bressia, was, as we have seen, the contemporary of Cardan, and published his book of Algebra, entitled " Quesiti è Invenzioni diverse," in 1546, at Venice, where he resided as public lecturer in mathematics. This work was dedicated to Henry VIII. of England, and consists of nine books, the last of which contains all those questions that relate to arithmetic and algebra. They comprehend exercises of simple and quadratic equations, and evince the great skill of the author in the science of algebra. In 1556, Tartalea published at Venice, a very large work, in folio, on arithmetic, geometry, and algebra, the latter of which was incomplete, going no farther than quadratic equations. Michael Stifelius, and John Scheubelius, were contemporaries of Tartalea and Cardan. The " Arithmetica Integra" of the former, is deemed by Dr. Hutton an excellent treatise on arithmetic and algebra. It was printed at Norimberg, in 1544. Stifelius ascribes the invention of the science to Geber, an Arabian astronomer.

Scheubelius, professor of mathematics at Tubingen, published several treatises on arithmetic and algebra. He is the first modern algebraist who mentions Diophantus, as the person to whom writers ascribe this art. This is recorded in his work, entitled " Algebræ Compendiosa facilisque Descriptio, qua depromuntur magna Arithmetices miracula." Dr. Hutton has analysed the work, and has ascribed to this, and the other authors already mentioned, the chief inventions due to them in perfecting the science, into the minutiæ of which our limits do not permit us to enter. Scheubelius treated of only two orders of equations, viz. the simple and quadratic; but he gives the four fundamental rules in the arithmetic of surds. As he takes no notice of cubic equations, it is probable, that, though they were known in Italy, this author had not heard of them in Germany.

Robert Recorde, in England, published the first part of his arithmetic in 1552, and the second part in 1557, under the title of the "Whetstone of Witte," &c. The algebra of Peletarius was printed in Paris in 1558, with the following title; "Jacobi Peletarii Cenomani, de Occulte Parte Numerorum, quàm Algebram vocant." Peter Ramus published his Arithmetic and Algebra about the year 1560. He expresses the powers by *l*, *q*, c, *b*, being the initials of latus, quadratus, cubus, and biquadratus; nevertheless, he only treats of simple and quadratic equations.

In 1567, Nonius, or, as it is often spelt, Nunez, a Portuguese, published his Algebra in Spanish, though he says it had been written in the Portuguese language thirty years before. Omitting some others, we may observe, that Simon Stevinus, of Bruges, published his Algebra very soon after his Arithmetic, which appeared in 1585, and both were printed in an edition of his works in 1634, with notes and additions by Albert Girard. About the same time with Stevinus, appeared Francis Vieta, who contributed more to the improvement of algebraic equations than any former author. His algebraical works were written about the year 1600; some of them were not published till after his death in 1603. In 1646, all his mathematical works were collected by Francis Schooten. Vieta's improvements comprehend, among others, the following particulars. He introduced the general use of the letters of the alphabet, to denote indefinite given quantities, and he expresses the unknown quantities by the vowels, in capitals, A, E, I, O, U, Y, and the known ones by the consonants, B, C, D, &c. He also invented many terms and forms of expression, which are still in use; as co-efficient, affirmative, and negative, pure and adfected, or affected, and the line, or vinculum, over compound quantities, thus: $\overline{A+B+C}$,

Albert Girard, an ingenious Dutch mathematician, the editor of Stevinus's arithmetic, who died in 1633, deserves notice on account of his work entitled "Invention Nouvelle en l'Algebra, tant pour la Solution des Equations, que pour recoignostre le nombre des Solutions qu'elles reçoivent, avec plusieurs choses qui sont necessaires à la perfection de ceste divine Science." The next person who claims particular notice, is Thomas Harriot, who died at the age of sixty years, in 1621, and whose Algebra was published by Walter Warner, in 1631, under the title of "Artis Analyticæ Praxis, ad Æquationes Algebraicas nova, expedita, et generali methodo, resolvendas," a work which, according to Dr. Hutton, shews, in all its parts, marks of great genius and originality. On the foundation laid by Harriot, says Dr. Wallis, Des Cartes, without naming him, hath built the greatest part, if not the whole, of his algebra or geometry, without which, he adds, "that whole superstructure of Des Cartes had never been." Harriot introduced the uniform use of the small letters, *a*, *b*, c, *d*, &c. expressing the unknown quantities by the vowels, and the known ones by the consonants, joining them together in the form of a word, to represent the product of any number of these literal quantities, thus *a b* c signified that *a*, *b*, and *c*, were multiplied together. Oughtred, contemporary with Harriot, was born in the year 1573, and died in 1660. His "Clavis" was published in 1631; he chiefly follows Vieta, in the notation by capitals. This author, in algebraical multiplication, either joins the letters in the form of a word, or connects them with the sign $\times$, introducing, for the first time, this character of multiplication; thus the three terms $A \times A$, or AA, or Aq, meant the same quantity. He introduced many useful contractions in the multiplication and division of decimals, and he used the following form for the terms of proportion 7 . 9 : : 28 . 36, which is nearly the same as that now in use.

Des Cartes published his Geometry in 1637, which may be considered as an application of algebra to geometry, and not as a separate treatise on either of these sciences. His inventions and discoveries comprehend the application of algebra to the geometry of curve lines, the construction of equations of the higher orders, and a rule for resolving biquadratic equations, by means of a cubic and two quadratics. With a view to the more easy application of equations to the construction of problems, Des Cartes mentions many particulars concerning the nature and reduction of equations, states them in his own language and manner, and frequently accompanied with his own improvements. Here he chiefly followed Cardan, Vieta, and Harriot, and especially the last, explaining some of their rules and discoveries more distinctly, with variations in the notation, in which he puts the first letters of the alphabet, a, b, c, d, &c. for known quantities, and the latter letters, u, x, y, z, for unknown quantities.

Fermat, who published Diophantus' Arithmetic, with valuable notes, was a contemporary of Des Cartes, and a competitor for some of his most valuable discoveries. He had, before the publication of Des Cartes' Geometry, applied algebra to curve lines, and had discovered a method of tangents, and a method of *maximis et minimis*, approaching very nearly to the method of fluxions; to be noticed hereafter. At this period, Algebra had acquired a regular and permanent form, and from this time, the writers on the whole, or detached parts of the science, became so numerous, that it would be impossible in a short article to enumerate all their works; we shall accordingly only mention those that appear the most prominent.

The Geometry of Des Cartes engaged the attention of several mathematicians in Holland, where it was first published, and also in France and England. Francis Schooten, professor at Leyden, was one of the earliest cultivators of the new geometry; and, in 1649, he published a translation of Des Cartes' work into the Latin language. Huygens, illustrious for his many discoveries in mechanics, directed his attention to the algebraic analysis; and, among other works, he published a short piece, entitled "De Ratiociniis in Ludo Alæ," in order to shew the usefulness of algebra. Herigone, in 1634, published at Paris the first course of mathematics, in five volumes, 8vo. containing a treatise on algebra, which, according to Dr. Hutton, bears evident marks of originality and ingenuity. Cavalerius, in the following year, published his "Indivisibles," which introduced a new æra into analytical science, and new modes of computation. In 1655, Dr. Wallis published his "Arithmetica Infinitorum," which was a great improvement on the Indivisibles of Cavalerius, and led the way to infinite series, the binomial theorem, and the method of fluxions.

Mr. Kinckhuysen, in 1661, published a treatise of algebra in the Dutch language, which Sir Isaac Newton, when professor of mathematics at Cambridge, used and improved, and which he designed to republish, with his method of fluxions and infinite series, but was prevented by the accidental burning of some of his papers. In 1665, or 1666, Sir Isaac Newton made several of his most valuable discoveries, though they were not published till a later period; such as the binomial theorem, the method of fluxions and infinite series, the quadrature, rectification, &c. of curves, the investigation of the roots of all sorts of equations, both numeral and literal, in infinite converging series, the reversion of series, &c.

The "Elements of Algebra" were published by John Kersey, in 1675, in two volumes, folio, containing the illustration of the science, and the nature of equations, the explication of Diophantus' problems, and many additions concerning mathematical composition and resolution. This work is thought by Dr. Hutton to be ample and complete. Dr. Wallis's Treatise of Algebra, both historical and practical, time to time, was published in 1685, in folio. In 1687, Dr. Halley communicated in the Philosophical Transactions the construction of cubic and biquadratic equations, by a parabola and circle, with improvements of the methods of Des Cartes, Baker, &c.; and a memoir on the number of the roots of equations, with their limits and signs.

Mr. John Ward published in 1695 "A Compendium of Algebra;" and, in 1706, the first edition of "The Young Mathematician's Guide," which includes Arithmetic, vulgar and decimal; Algebra; the Elements of Geometry; Conic Sections; the Arithmetic of Infinites; and an Appendix of Practical Gauging. This work was, a century ago, extremely popular, and passed through several editions; in the Preface to the fifth edition, in 1722, the author says, that his "book has answered to its title so well, that I believe I may truly say, without vanity, that this treatise hath proved a very helpful guide to nearly five thousand persons, and perhaps most of them such as would never have looked into the Mathematics at all but for it." In describing his plan, Mr. Ward says, "I began with an unit in Arithmetic, and a point in Geometry; and, from these foundations, proceeded gradually on, leading the young learner, step by step, with all the plainness possible."

This book, notwithstanding the high reputation which it had in the beginning of the last century, and to its intrinsic merit we have heard several able mathematicians, now no more, bear most decisive evidence, as having themselves been almost, or perhaps altogether, indebted to it for their delight in science, is now seldom inquired for. It has made way for others, which we shall describe hereafter, and which seem better adapted to the wants of young persons at this period. Perhaps, in nothing, is the present age, including the last thirty years, more distinguished than in the production of elementary works in useful knowledge and real science.

Very similar to Ward's "Young Mathematician's Guide," was Mr. Jones's "Synopsis Palmariorum Matheseos," published in 1706. This compendium contains, though in a shorter compass, the same subjects as those treated of by Mr. Ward, with the addition of the principles of Projection, the elements of Trigonometry, Mechanics, and Optics. The author, who was father to the late illustrious Sir William Jones, said he designed his work for the benefit, and adapted to the capacities of beginners. It appears, however, to have been rather too brief for the purpose intended. Mr. Jones published in 1711 a collection of Sir Isaac Newton's papers, entitled "Analysis per quantitatum series, fluxiones, ac differentias; cum enumeratione linearum tertii ordinis." Sir Isaac Newton's "Arithmetica Universalis, sive de Compositione et Resolutione Arithmetica liber," was published in 1707, since which, it has gone through many editions, and is included in Dr. Horsley's edition of Sir Isaac Newton's works, in five volumes, 4to., the Arithmetica standing first in the collection. This treatise was the text-book of the author at Cambridge, and though not intended for publication, it contains many very considerable improvements in analytics. Commentaries have been published on this work, by S'Gravesande and others. In the year 1769, Dr. Wilder, mathematical professor of Trinity College, Dublin, published a translation of the "Arithmetica Universalis," which had been made by Mr. Ralphson, and corrected by Mr. Cunn. This he illustrated and explained in a series of notes; to the right understanding of which work, thus presented to the public, with an additional treatise upon the measures of ratios, Dr. Wilder says it is only necessary that the student should be well versed in the Elements of Euclid, and be master of common arithmetic, as it is taught in the schools.

Without pretending to enumerate all the introductory works to this science, that have, of late years, been published, we shall point out to our readers a sufficient number to allow them a choice, and mention some of their chief, or distinguishing merits. It is presumed, that the pupil, previously to his entrance upon a course of algebra, is master of the elementary rules of common arithmetic; and if he is conversant with fractions and decimals, he will enter with more advantage upon the study of algebra.

Previously to enumerating particular treatises on Algebra, we may, in few words, explain the nature of the subject generally, and the characters which are used by almost all authors.

Every figure, or common arithmetical character, has a determinate value; thus the figures 5, 7, 9, always represent the same number, viz. the collections of five, seven, and nine units; but algebraical characters must be general, and independent of any particular signification, adapted to the representation of all sorts of quantities, according to the nature of the questions to which they are applied. To answer general purposes, they should be simple, and easy to describe, so as not to be troublesome in operation, nor difficult to remember. These advantages meet in the letters of the alphabet, which are therefore usually adopted to represent magnitudes in algebra; and we have shewn above, in what way, and by whom they were introduced.

In algebraical investigations, some quantities are assumed as known or given, and the value of others is unknown, and to be found out; the former are commonly represented by the leading letters of the alphabet, a; b, c, d, &c.; the latter by the final letters, w, x, y, z. Though it often tends to relieve the memory, if the initial letter of the subject under consideration be made use of, whether that be known or unknown: thus r may denote a radius, b a base, p a perpendicular, s a side, d density, m mass, &c.

The characters used to denote the operations, are principally these:

+ signifies addition, and is named *plus*.

— signifies subtraction, and is named *minus*.

× denotes multiplication, and is named *into*.

÷ denotes division, and is named *by*.

√, the mark of radicality denotes the square root; with a

3 before it, thus $\sqrt[3]{}$, the cube root; with a 4, thus $\sqrt[4]{}$, the fourth, or biquadrate root; thus $\sqrt[n]{}$, the nth root.

Proportion is commonly denoted by a colon between the antecedent and consequent of each ratio, and a double colon between the two ratios: thus, if a be to b as c to d, we state it as follows, $a:b::c:d$.

$=$ is the symbol of equality.

Hence, $a+b$ denotes the sum of the quantities represented by a and b.

$a-b$ denotes their difference when b is the less: $b-a$, their difference when a is the less: $a \backsim b$, the difference when it is not known which is the greater. $a \times b$, or $a.b$, or ab, represents the product of a multiplied into b.

$a \div b$, or $\frac{a}{b}$, shews that the number represented by a is to be divided by that which is represented by b.

$\frac{a}{b}$ is the reciprocal of $\frac{b}{a}$, and $\frac{1}{a}$ the reciprocal of a.

$a:b::c:d$ denotes that a is in the same proportion to b, as c is to d.

$x=a-b+c$ is an equation, shewing that x is equal to the difference of a and b, added to the quantity c.

$\sqrt{a}$, or $a^{\frac{1}{2}}$, is the square root of a; $\sqrt[3]{a}$, or $a^{\frac{1}{3}}$, is the cube root of a; and $\sqrt[m]{a}$, or $a^{\frac{1}{m}}$, is the mth root of a.

a^2 is the square of a; a^3 the cube of a; a^4 the fourth power of a; and a^m the mth power of a.

$\overline{a+b} \times c$, or $(a+b)$ c, is the product of the compound quantity $a+b$ multiplied by the simple quantity c. Using the bar ——, or the parenthesis ( ), as a vinculum, to connect several quantities into one.

$\overline{a+b} \div \overline{a-b}$, or $\frac{a+b}{a-b}$, expressed like a fraction, is the quotient of $a+b$ divided by $a-b$.

$5a$ denotes that the quantity a is to be taken 5 times, and $7.(b+c)$ is 7 times $b+c$. And these numbers, 5 or 7, shewing how often the quantities are to be taken, or multiplied, are called co-efficients.

Like quantities, are those which consist of the same letters, and powers. As a and $3a$; or $2ab$ and $4ab$; or $3a^2bc$ and $-5a^2bc$.

Unlike quantities, are those which consist of different letters, or different powers. As a and b; or $2a$ and a^2; or $3ab^2$ and $3abc$.

Simple quantities, or monomials, are those which consist of one term only. As $3a$, or $5ab$, or $6abc^2$.

Compound quantities, are those which consist of two or more terms. As $a+b$, or $a+2b-3c$.

And when the compound quantity consists of two terms, it is called a binomial; when of three terms, it is a trinomial; when of four terms, a quadrinomial; more than four terms, a multinomial, or polynomial.

Positive or affirmative quantities, are those which are to be added, or have the sign $+$. As a or $+a$, or ab; for when a quantity is found without a sign, it is understood to be positive, or to have the sign $+$ prefixed.

Negative quantities, are those which are to be subtracted, as $-a$, or $-2ab$, or $-3ab^2$.

Like sigus, are either all positive ($+$), or all negative ($-$).

Unlike signs, are when some are positive ($+$), and others negative ($-$).

In every quantity we may consider two things, its value, and its manner of existing with regard to other magnitudes which enter with it into the same calculation. The *value* of a quantity is expressed by the letter or by the character destined to represent the number of its units. But as to the *mode of existence*, with regard to others, some magnitudes may affect the calculation either in the same or in opposite senses; which renders it necessary to distinguish two sorts of quantities, *positive* and *negative*. Thus whether a man have a thousand pounds in property or stock, or be a thousand pounds in debt, may be represented by characters, either arithmetical or algebraical; but since an actual property is directly opposite in its nature to a debt, the two must be marked by different symbols: so that, if property be reckoned a *positive* quantity, and marked +, a debt owed must be estimated as *negative*, and marked −. Again, if, commencing at the same point, motion towards the east be considered as a positive quantity in an investigation, motion towards the west, which is opposite to the former, must enter the same calculation as a negative quantity. If the elevations of the sun above the horizon are considered as positive quantities, the depressions of the sun below the horizon must be treated as negative quantities. It is the same with all quantities, which, when considered together, exist differently with respect to one another.

A residual quantity is a binomial having one of the terms negative. As $a-2b$.

The power of a quantity (a), is its square (a^2), or cube (a^3), or biquadrate (a^4), &c.; called also the 2d power, or 3d power, or 4th power, &c.

The index, or exponent, is the number which denotes the power or root of a quantity. So 2 is the exponent of the square or 2d power a^2; and 3 is the index of the cube or 3d power; and $\frac{1}{2}$ is the index of the square root $a^{\frac{1}{2}}$ or $\sqrt{a}$; and $\frac{1}{3}$ is the index of the cube root $a^{\frac{1}{3}}$ or $\sqrt[3]{a}$.

A rational quantity, is that which has no radical sign ($\sqrt{}$) or index annexed to it. As a, or $3ab$.

An irrational quantity, or surd, is that which has not an exact root, or is expressed by means of the radical sign $\sqrt{}$. As $\sqrt{2}$, or $\sqrt{a}$, or $\sqrt[3]{a^2}$, or $ab^{\frac{1}{2}}$.

One of the easiest and most simple Introductions to this science, is that by Fenning, which, if our recollection serves us, is introduced with an account of fractions by common numbers. It is many years since we have seen this work, and, perhaps, it is not now to be met with but on stalls, or in second-hand catalogues. In lieu of this, we may notice an excellent little treatise by Mr. Bonnycastle, entitled "An Introduction to Algebra, with Notes and Observations for the Use of Schools, &c." This compendium is formed upon the model of larger works, and is intended as an introduction to them. It supposes, however, that the person making use of it, as a first book, on the subject, has the advantage of a living instructor to aid him in difficulties that will inevitably occur to check his progress. To those who have no instructor, we would recommend a work, which, from a slight view of it (for it has but lately come into our hands), appears to obviate all difficulties, by explaining every thing in a full and familiar manner as far as it goes: it is entitled "The Philosophy of Arithmetic, considered as a branch of Mathematical Science, and the Elements of Algebra, &c. by John Walker." This volume is divided into twenty-eight chapters, of which thirteen are devoted to the elucidation of the principles of common arithmetic. Mr. Walker observes, that "the scientific principles of common arithmetic are so coincident with those of algebra, or universal arithmetic, that to persons acquainted with the former, the Elements of the latter offer no serious difficulty. Of the Elements of Algebra, therefore, I have given such a view, as may open that wide field of science to the student, and enable him, at his pleasure, to extend his progress, by the aid of any of the larger works extant on the subject. Having designed this work for the instruction of those who come to it most uninitiated in science, I have aimed at giving a clear and full explanation of the most elementary principles." From the parts that we have examined, it does appear that the author has succeeded in the accomplishment of his object. It must, however, be observed, that Mr. Bonnycastle's "Introduction" includes a number of topics not touched on even by Mr. Walker. Of these, we may mention the Diophantine Problems, and the Summation of Infinite Series, which is a very important part of some of the practical mathematics.

"Lectures on the Elements of Algebra," &c. by the Rev. B. Bridge, A. M. may be safely recommended as a valuable introduction to the science; we admit the truth of the author's assertion, "that the substance of the Lectures is perfectly within the comprehension of students at the age of fifteen or sixteen." In some of these lectures, the learner's ingenuity will, however, be tried; but the subjects are interesting, and worthy the exertion he may be called on to make in the investigation.

In connexion with any of the above-named works, the pupil may read the first part of Maclaurin's Treatise of Algebra, which, though deficient in the number of its examples, is written in a remarkably clear, not to say elegant, style. It proceeds only to Quadratic Equations, and the doctrine of Surds.

"The Principles of Algebra," by William Frend, may be consulted with advantage, but it cannot be recommended, by itself, as an introductory work to the science, because we feel no objection to the usual modes of notation and expression, which Mr. Frend endeavours to exchange for others, as we apprehend, not at all more intelligible. Algebra, like every branch of real science, has, no doubt, its difficulties; and the youth who would make real proficiency in it, either with or without the aid of a tutor, must, in the first instance, be content to advance slowly, feel every step of the ground on which he treads, and fully comprehend every term he may meet with. To such a one, we are sure there can be no real obstacles in the use of the algebraical terms which are found in common books; nor can he be expected to make much progress in the science, who is frightened with the words *plus, minus, sines, co-efficient,* &c. We have, however, said, that the learner may consult the "Principles of Algebra" with advantage; and we regret that the book is become so scarce as rarely to be met with. It was published in two parts. The *first* proceeds to Cardan's rule for the solution of Equations of the third order; the *second* part contains the theory of Equations established on *mathematical demonstration.*

Having gone through the whole, or the introductory parts of either of the foregoing elementary books, the student may take in connexion with his present pursuits, some parts of Mr. Thomas Simpson's Algebra, which treats on topics not to be found in any of the others. Or he may advance to the second part of Maclaurin's Algebra, "On the Genius and Resolution of Equations of all Degrees," &c.

Much curious and valuable mathematical knowledge will be found in Saunderson's "Elements of Algebra," in two volumes, 4to. should they fall in the way of the pupil. Dr. Saunderson, though blind, was one of the ablest mathematicians of the age. He lost his sight when he was only eight years old; yet so great were his talents, and so steady his application to the classics and mathematics, that he could, at an early period of life, take pleasure in hearing the works of Euclid, Archimedes, and Diophantus, read in their original Greek. At the age of twenty-five, he went to Cambridge, and his fame soon filled the University. Newton's Principia, Optics, and Universal Arithmetic, were the foundation of the lectures which he delivered to the students of that seat of learning, and they afforded him a noble field for the display of his genius. Great numbers came, some, no doubt, through motives of curiosity, to hear a blind man give lectures on optics, discourse on the nature of light and colours, explain the theory of vision, the phenomenon of the rainbow, and other objects of sight; but none of his auditors went away disappointed; and he always interested, as well as instructed, those who came for the purpose of gaining knowledge. He succeeded Mr. Whiston in the mathematical professor's chair, and, from this time, in 1711, he gave up his whole time to his pupils, for whose use he had composed something new and important on almost every branch of the mathematics. But he discovered no intention to publish any thing, till, by the persuasion of his friends, he prepared his "Elements of Algebra" for the press.

Dr. Saunderson had a peculiar method of performing arithmetical calculations by an ingenious machine and method, which has been denominated his "Palpable Arithmetic," and which is particularly described in the first volume of the work to which we are now directing the reader's attention. An Abridgment, or Select Parts of Dr. Saunderson's "Elements of Algebra," was published in an octavo volume, in the year 1755, which has passed through several editions, the fourth being printed in 1776. This is a judicious compendium of the larger work, but is not better adapted to learners than Bonnycastle's, Bridge's, or some other introductions to the science, of more modern date. For the sake of beginners, the compiler has prefixed to the Select Parts of Dr. Saunderson's Elements, an Introduction to Vulgar and Decimal Fractions, and a collection of Arithmetical questions, in order that the learner may try his skill in common arithmetic before he enters upon the study of Algebra.

The young algebraist may consult with much advantage some other books not avowedly elementary, but which contain a large number of excellent problems, the solution of which will exercise his ingenuity, and invigorate his powers. Of these, the first is Dodson's Mathematical Repository, three volumes, 12mo. 1748. We refer particularly to the first, and part of the second volumes, the other parts will be noticed hereafter. The early problems of this work are adapted to those who are but just entering on the science; they increase in difficulty as the pupil is supposed to become stronger in the pursuit.

Another excellent work of this kind is entitled "Select Exercises for Young Proficients in Mathematics, &c. by Thomas Simpson, 1752." Of this volume, the first part contains a number of algebraical problems, with their solutions, designed as proper exercises for young beginners, in which the art of managing Equations, and the various methods of substitution, are taught and illustrated.

A much more modern work, but one of considerable utility to the student in Algebra, is the following, "Algebraical Problems, producing Simple and Quadratic equations, with their solutions, designed as an introduction to the higher branches of analytics: by the Rev. M. Bland, A. M. 1812." These problems, of which there are several hundreds, are designed solely to point out the various methods employed by Analysts in the solution of Equations. They are arranged in the usual manner: the *first* part containing simple Equations; the *second*, pure Quadratics, and others, that may be solved without completing the square; and *thirdly*, adfected Quadratics. The author, who has employed much industry and skill in the compilation of the volume, tells his readers that he has consulted many books, and as utility was the sole object which he had in view, he has taken his examples from every source, and has altered them to suit his purpose. At the head of each section he has given the common rules, so that if the reader is acquainted with the practice previously to Equations, Mr. Bland's volume may be considered as a good introduction to the science at that point. Of the Lady's Diary and Leybourn's Mathematical Repository, we shall speak in our next chapter.

Mr. Bonnycastle, in 1813, published a much larger work on this subject, than that which we have already noticed, it is entitled "A Treatise on Algebra in Practice and Theory," in two vols. 8vo. The first volume is devoted chiefly, though in an extended form, to the same subjects as he had already discussed in the smaller work; the second, denominated by the author "the Theoretical part," will afford much exercise to the talents and ingenuity of the student, who has already made considerable progress in the analytic science, and will probably open to him a new field of speculation. To the first volume is prefixed an excellent historical introduction: in the latter part of the second volume is shewn the application of Algebra to Geometry, and the doctrine of curves.

After, or in connexion with, this work of Mr. Bonnycastle, may be taken in hand the second volume of the "Elements of Algebra," by Leonard Euler. This work was published in the German language, in 1770, and has since been translated into the French and English, with notes and additions by the editors. Among the latter there is a very learned and copious tract of the celebrated La Grange, on "continued fractions," and such parts of the indeterminate analysis, as had not been sufficiently treated of by the author; "the whole," says Mr. Bonnycastle, "forming one of the most profound treatises on this branch of the subject that has ever yet appeared."

Before the pupil has arrived at this period of his studies, he will necessarily be acquainted with almost every thing that has been written on the subject, and will of himself know where to look for subjects which may engage his attention. We shall, therefore, only observe, that there is a valuable work in the Latin language, published at Dublin in 1784, entitled "Analysis Æquationum, Auctore Guil. Hales. D. D." The author of which says, that he has endeavoured to follow the tract of Wallis, Maclaurin, Saunderson, De Moirre, Simpson, Clairaut, D'Alembert, Euler, La Grange, Waring, Bertrand, Landen, Hutton, &c. "qui aut scriptis Newtoni illustrandis, aut algebræ limitibus latins proferendis felicissime operam dederunt."

With respect to some of the authors above enumerated, we may observe, in addition to what we have already noticed, that M. Clairaut published his "Elemens d'Algebrè," in 1746, in which he made many improvements with reference to the irreducible case in cubic equations. A fifth edition of this work was published at Paris, with notes and large additions, in 1797. M. Landen published his "Residual Analysis" in 1764, his "Mathematical Lucubrations" in 1765, and his "Mathematical Memoirs" in 1780. The Memoirs of the

Berlin and Petersburgh Academies abound with improvements on series and other branches of analysis by Euler, La Grange, and other illustrious mathematicians. Dr. Waring, late of Cambridge, communicated many valuable papers to the Royal Society, who have caused them to be printed in their Transactions, and many of his improvements are contained in his separate publications, which, it must be acknowledged, are too abstruse for ordinary mathematicians. These are entitled "Meditationes Algebraicæ," "Proprietates Algebraicarum Curvarum," and "Meditationes Analyticæ." Mr. Baron Maseres claims to be mentioned not only as an original writer on the analytical branch of science, but also on account of the labour and expense which he has bestowed on the publication of the "Scriptores Logarithmici," in six large vols. 4to. between the year 1791 and 1807, containing many curious and useful tracts, which are thus preserved from being lost, and many valuable papers of his own on the binomial theorem, series, &c. The Baron's separate publications on Algebra, are, (1). "A Dissertation on the Negative Sign in Algebra." (2). "Principles of the Doctrine of Life Annuities." (3). "Tracts on the Resolution of Affected Algebraic Equations," &c.

CHAP. XXX.

MATHEMATICS,

Continued.

Advantages, History and Province of Geometry—Principles of Geometry. Elementary treatises, Simson's "Elements"—Cunn—Tacquet—De Chales—Whiston—Barrow—Simpson's Bonnycastle's—Payne's and Cowley's Geometry. Matton's—Playfair's—Leslie's—Reynard's; and Keith's. Application of Algebra to Geometry. Simpson—Frend—Bonnycastle—Lady's Diary, and Leybourn's Mathematical Repository.

NEXT to Arithmetic should follow Geometry, in a course of liberal and scientific education. Geometry literally signifies measuring the earth, or parts thereof; and it was probably first invented to enable people to ascertain their own property in land, since which it has been extended and applied to other things and for other purposes, insomuch that geometry, with arithmetic, is now regarded as the foundation of all mathematics.

"Geometry," says an excellent writer, "will enable a person to think justly. Without it there is a certain method wanting which is necessary to rectify our thoughts, to arrange our ideas, and to determine our judgments aright. It is easy to perceive in reading a book, even a moral one, whether the author be a mathematician or not. I am seldom deceived in this observation. The famous French metaphysician would not have composed the *Inquiry after Truth,** nor the famous Leibnitz his *Theodicé*, if they had not been mathematicians. We perceive in their productions that geometrical order which brings their reasonings into small compass, while it gives them energy and method. Order is delightful; there is nothing in nature but what is stamped with it, and without it there could be no harmony. We may likewise say that the mathematics are an universal science, which connects all the rest, and displays them in their happiest relations. The mathematician, at the first look, is sure to analyse and unravel a subject or propositiou with justness; but a man who does not understand this science, sees only in a vague, and almost always in an imperfect manner. Apply yourself then to this great branch of knowledge, so worthy of your curiosity, and so necessary to the uses of life; but not in such a degree as to throw you into absence;—endeavour to be always recollected, whatever are your studies. If I were young, and had leisure, I would acquire a more extensive knowledge of geometry. I have always cherished that science with a particular predilection. My turn of mind made me seek with avidity every thing that was methodical; and I pay but little respect to those works which are only the exercises of imagination. We have three principal sciences, which I compare to the three essential parts of the human composition:—Theology, which, by its spirituality, resembles our soul; the mathematics, which, by their combination and justness, express our reason; and natural philosophy, which, by its mechanical operations, denotes our bodies; and these three sciences (which ought to maintain a perfect harmony) while they keep within their proper sphere, necessarily elevate us towards their Author, the source and fulness of all light. Philosophy without geometry, is like medicine without chemistry. The greater number of modern philosophers reason inconclusively, only because they are unacquainted with geometry. They mistake sophisms

* *Malebranche.*

for truths; and if they lay down just principles, they deduce false conclusions from them."

Herodotus, Diodorus, and Strabo, maintain that the Egyptians were the first inventors of geometry; and that the annual inundations of the Nile were the occasions of it; for that river, bearing away all the bounds and landmarks of men's estates, the people were obliged to distinguish their lands by the consideration of their figure and quantity, and thus formed for themselves a method or art which was the origin of geometry. A farther contemplation of the figures of lands laid down for this purpose, might probably lead them to the discovery of some of the properties of those figures; which speculation continually improving, the art also improved till it laid claim to the rank of a science.

Geometry then, may be considered as the science of extension, or extended things, that is, of lines, superficies and solids. Notwithstanding what has been said above of the Egyptians being the inventors of Geometry, the fact has been disputed, and the honour given, by very respectable authors, to the Hebrews. There is, however, no doubt that the inhabitants of Egypt, in their ancient monarchical state, were acquainted with the elements of geometry, though it does not appear that they had gone deeply into it, since to Pythagoras, who flourished about five hundred and twenty years before the birth of Christ, and who had spent a considerable part of his life in Egypt, was attributed the invention of certain propositions in Euclid, particularly the 47th of the first book, which is called after his name, the "Pythagorean theorem," and for the discovery of which he offered a hecatomb to the gods. Hence it has been inferred, that the great learning of the Egyptians was not geometrical.

From Egypt, geometry, probably in its infant state, passed over into Greece; for Thales, the Milesian, who flourished five hundred and eighty-four years before Christ, was reported to be the first of the Greeks, who, coming into Egypt, transferred Geometry from thence into Greece. He is said to have discovered several of the propositions of the first five books of the Elements which go under the name of Euclid. After Thales, came Pythagoras, already cited, who first of all abstracted geometry from matter, and made many discoveries. Next flourished Anaxagoras, Hippocrates, and many others, till we come to Plato, than whom no one shed a greater lustre on the mathematical sciences; he made many considerable additions to geometry, and upon the entrance to his academy, the inscription "Let no one unacquainted with geometry enter," was written. The fifth book of the Elements is said to have been the production of Eudoxus and to Aristeus, Isidore, and Hypsicles, we are indebted for the books of the solid geometry. After these Euclid came, who collected the inventions and discoveries of others, disposed them into order, in many respects improved them, and left those Elements, by which, in some shape or other, the youth of every succeeding generation, from that time to this, have been instructed in mathematics. Euclid died about two hundred and eighty-four years before the birth of Christ.

The next to Euclid of the ancient writers, whose works are extant, is Apollonius Pergeus, who flourished in the time of Ptolemy Euergetes, about a century later than Euclid. The third ancient Geometer, whose writings remain, is Archimedes of Syracuse, who was celebrated at the same time with Apollonius; to the works of this great man we shall have occasion again to refer. We might mention many other names of great celebrity among the Greeks, which have been immortalized by their skill in ancient Geometry. This people continued their attention to the sciences, properly so called, even after they had been subdued by the Romans. Whereas their conquerors were so little acquainted with this science, even in the most flourishing time of their republic, that they commonly gave the name of mathematicians to those who pursued the chimeras of judicial astrology. Nor were they more disposed to cultivate geometry, it will be readily imagined, during the decline, and after the fall of the Roman empire. The case was different with the Greeks, among whom we find many excellent geometers since the commencement of the Christian era, and even after the translation of the Roman empire. Ptolemy lived under Marcus Aurelius; and we are in possession of the works of Pappus of Alexandria, who flourished in the time of Theodosius; of the Commentary of Eutocius, the Ascalonite, who lived in the middle of the sixth century, on Archimedes' mensuration of a circle; and of a Commentary on Euclid by Proclus, who flourished still later.

The inundation of ignorance and barbarism, to which we have referred in a preceding chapter, was as unfavourable to geometry as to the other sciences; and the few, who even dared to apply themselves to it, were calumniated as magicians. A gleam of light, however, soon appeared, and in those times of European darkness, the Arabians themselves, as we have seen, became distinguished as the guardians and promoters of science; and from the ninth to the fourteenth century, they produced many astronomers, geometers, geographers, &c.; from whom the mathematical sciences were again received into Spain, Italy, and the other parts of Europe, at the close of the fourteenth century. After this period, many editions of Euclid, and many commentaries on his Elements were published.

At the revival of letters, there were few Europeans capable of translating and commenting on the works of the ancient Geometers, and the science of Geometry made little progress till the time of Des Cartes, who published his Geometry in 1637; but from that period to the present, it has abounded with votaries in almost all civilized nations, but in none more than in Great Britain.

The province of Geometry is almost infinite: few of our ideas but may be represented to the imagination by lines, by means of which they become of geometrical consideration: it being geometry alone that makes comparisons, and finds the relations of lines. Astronomy, music, mechanics, optics, and in short all the sciences which consider things susceptible of more or less, may be referred to geometry; for all speculative truths, consisting only in the relations of things, may be referred to lines. Consequences may be drawn from them, and these consequences, again, being rendered sensible by lines, they become permanent objects, which may be constantly exposed to a rigorous attention and examination; and thus we have opportunities both of inquiring into their certainty, and pursuing them farther.

Before we proceed to speak of the elementary treatises on this science, we may observe, that Geometry is founded on certain axioms, or self-evident truths, which none can deny, or fail of understanding, and it is introduced by definitions of the various objects which it contemplates, and the properties of which it investigates and demonstrates; such as points, lines, angles, figures, surfaces and solids. Lines are considered as straight or right, and curved; and in their relation to one another, either as inclined or parallel, or perpendicular to other lines, or to certain given surfaces. Angles are considered either as right, or acute, or obtuse; or external, internal, vertical, &c. Figures are investigated by considering their boundaries, as *triangles,* which in relation to their sides are equilateral, isosceles, and scalene; and in reference to their angles, they are either right-angled, obtuse-angled, and acute angled: as *quadrilaterals,* which comprehend the parallelogram, including the rectangle and square, the rhombus and rhomboid, and the trapesium; as *multilateral,* including all other many-sided figures; as *circles*; and as *solids,* including the prism, parallelepipedon, cube, pyramid, cylinder, cone, sphere, and the frustra of the latter.

In enumerating some of the elementary treatises of Geometry, we shall observe, that to those persons who unite patient attention with a true taste for the ancient method of demonstration, we may, notwithstanding what has been advanced by writers of considerable reputation, recommend as the most useful and valuable work on this subject:

"The Elements of Euclid," viz. the first six books, together with the eleventh and twelfth. The errors of Theon, and others, are corrected, and some of Euclid's demonstrations are restored. Also the book of Euclid's data, in like manner corrected, by Robert Simson, M. D. Emeritus professor of mathematics in the university of Glasgow," 8vo.

The Elements of Euclid, or, as they are frequently termed, "The Elements," are divided into three parts, which respect superficies, numbers, and solids. The first four books treat of planes only; the fifth, of the proportions of magnitudes in general; the sixth, of the proportion of plane figures; the seventh, eighth, and ninth, give us the fundamental properties of numbers; the tenth contains the theory of commensurable and incommensurable lines and spaces; the eleventh, and the following four books, treat of the doctrine of solids. Of these fifteen books, the first six, and the eleventh and twelfth, are not only the most important, but those which are generally considered as the elementary parts of science.

Dr. Simson has added to the eight books of geometry, Euclid's data, which is the first in order of the books that have been written by the ancient geometricians, to facilitate and promote the method of resolution and analysis. Some curious and valuable geometrical notes are subjoined. In the third, and, we believe, all the following editions, is a short but masterly treatise on Trigonometry, entitled "Elements of plane and spherical Trigonometry." The edition from which we write, was printed at Edinburgh, and is uncommonly accurate. There is, besides this, a beautiful edition in quarto, but without the trigonometry, printed by Foulis.

Editions of the same work, by Cunn, Tacquet, Stone, Whiston, and De Chales, have considerable merit. The best edition of De Chales, is that published in 1748, by Mr. Samuel Ashby.

To Cunn's edition is added, a treatise on the construction of logarithms. Andrew Tacquet, a learned Jesuit, has subjoined to his edition, select theorems from the works of the great Archimedes: The editions by De Chales and Whiston are chiefly valuable in having shewn the application of the various theorems in geometry to practical purposes.

Euclid's Elements, the whole fifteen books compendiously demonstrated, with Archimedes' theorems of the sphere and cylinder, investigated by the method of indivisibles. By Isaac Barrow, D. D. To which is annexed, Euclid's data, and a brief treatise of the regular solids. By Thomas Haselden, teacher of the mathematics, 8vo, 1732.

Of this work the learned author shall speak for himself: "My province," says Dr. Barrow, "was not that of writing the Elements of Geometry as I pleased, but of demonstrating, in as few words as possibly I could, the whole works of Euclid. As to the seventh, eighth, ninth, and tenth books, although they do not so nearly appertain to the elements of plain and solid geometry, as the six preceding and two subsequent books, yet none of the more skilful geometricians can be so ignorant as not to know that they are very useful for geometrical matters, not only by reason of the affinity that there is between arithmetic and geometry, but also for the knowledge of both commensurable and incommensurable magnitudes, so exceedingly necessary for the doctrine of plain and solid figures. Besides, I easily persuaded myself, that it would not be unacceptable to any lover of these sciences, to have in his possession the whole Euclidean work."

This, and some of the editions before-mentioned, are only to be purchased from second-hand catalogues; but it frequently happens, that a real treasure may be thus obtained at the expense of half-a-crown, or less.

We shall now direct the attention of the reader to some of the abridgments of "the Elements," of which, indeed, it would be difficult to enumerate the half that have been published from time to time. By many mathematicians, these abridgments, usually known under the title of "Elements of Geometry," are treated with great contempt, as inducing unscientific notions in the learner's mind. By others, however, and those of no mean talents, it is thought high time to discard Euclid's Elements, because they assert that science cannot be exhibited in a more disgusting form than it is in them. They farther contend, that "The Elements" are not, by any means, necessary to lay a good foundation in mathematics, and that few of the eminent mathematicians of Europe have actually been initiated by the study of Euclid. "Non nostrum inter hos tantas componere lites;" but shall proceed to mention some works of considerable and deserved reputation:

"Elements of Geometry, with their application to the mensuration of superficies and solids; to the determination of the maxima and minima of geometrical quantities; and to the construction of a great variety of geometrical problems." By Thomas Simpson, F. R. S. 8vo.

The demonstrations made use of in this work are concise and accurate. The treatise on the maxima and minima consists of nineteen theorems, neatly demonstrated, and well calculated to give the learner a proper taste for this part of science. And the construction of the geometrical problems is an useful application of the elementary books. The edition before me, which I have read more than once, and which is printed with tolerable accuracy, is the third, 1768; but there have been several since that period.

"An Introduction to Geometry: containing the more useful propositions of Euclid, and other authors. Demonstrated in a clear and easy method, for the use of learners." By William Payne.

Of this work, we can also speak with confidence, and will venture to pronounce it a very plain and useful treatise: exceedingly well adapted to the capacity of learners, at a very early age. With this introduction, we know, from repeated experience, that children ten or twelve years old, may, without difficulty, become good geometricians. The first edition was published in small quarto, 1767. The second is in 12mo, and was published in 1768. To this is added a neat introduction to mensuration. The quarto generally sells for about 3*s*. 6*d*. and the other for 2*s*. 6*d*. but it is becoming scarce, and is rising in value.

" Elements of Geometry; containing the principal propositions in the first six, and the eleventh and twelfth books of Euclid; with notes critical and explanatory." By John Bonnycastle, of the Royal Military Academy, Woolwich, 8vo.

The number of propositions in this very excellent work, is about one-fifth less than in Dr. Simson's Elements of Euclid. The enumerations and demonstrations are expressed in a more concise and elegant manner, which, by persons not particularly attached to the ancient mode of geometry, will be thought an advantage to learners—five editions of it have been published.

" Geometry made Easy; or a new and methodical explanation of the Elements of Geometry. Containing a very easy commentary on the first six, and the last five books of Euclid, &c. &c. &c. To which is added, an entire new, curious, and exact method of exhibiting, in miniature, the various kinds of solids, and their sections, by schemes cut out of pasteboards," &c. By John Lodge Cowley. 8vo.

Mr. Cowley makes use of the algebraic mode of reasoning: his propositions are neatly demonstrated, and the method he has introduced of conveying an idea of the nature of the several solids and sections of bodies, by pasteboard, folded up in the forms of those solids, has, by persons of eminence, been thought of considerable use in assisting the ideas of learners. Another edition of this work, with improvements, has been published by Mr. Jones, Holborn.

An Appendix to the last mentioned work, 4to., besides that of facilitating the study of Euclid's Elements, has this advantage, that it is capable of shewing workmen how these solids are to be made; and in what manner they may be divided, for the purpose of making models of them, by lines drawn on paper.

" The Royal road to Geometry; and familiar introduction to the mathematics." By Thomas Malton. 8vo.

This work comprehends every thing that is necessary for the instruction of the learner in the theory and practice of geometry. The first part contains the elements of geometry; the theory of mensuration; and a demonstration of some properties of ellipses. In the second, the author has inserted the problems of Euclid's Elements, with others selected from various writers; and an appendix on the construction of ellipses; proportional scales, and line of chords with problems illustrating their use.

"Elements of Geometry; containing the first six books of Euclid, with two books on the Geometry of Solids. To which are added, Elements of plane and spherical Trigonometry." By John Playfair, F. R. S. Professor of Mathematics in the university of Edinburgh. 8vo.

The four first books and the sixth are, with very few exceptions, the same as in the edition of Euclid, by Dr. Robert Simson before-mentioned. In the fifth the author makes use of an algebraic notation. The seventh book contains solid geometry, but not Euclid's. The rectification and quadrature of the circle are discussed in the eighth book. Mr. Playfair has by this work shewn himself an accurate writer and an excellent reasoner.

"Elements of Geometry, Geometrical Analysis, and Plane Trigonometry," by John Leslie, F. R. S. E. This work, the author informs us, is only part of a plan which he has in contemplation, and which may be comprized in five volumes. Of these, the second is intended to treat of the Geometry of curve lines, the intersection of planes, and the properties of solids, including the doctrine of the sphere, and the calculation of spherical triangles, with the elements of perspective and projection. The third volume will be devoted to Algebra, which is to be preceded by a short tract on the principles of Arithmetic. The fourth and fifth volumes will embrace the differential and integral calculus, with their principal applications.

Mr. Leslie, in speaking of his reasons for introducing to

public notice, a new treatise of Geometry, says, "We should form a wrong estimate, did we consider the Elements of Euclid, with all its merits, a finished production. That admirable work was composed when geometry was making its most rapid advances, and new prospects were opening on every side. No wonder that its structure should appear loose and defective. In adapting it to the actual state of the science, I have, therefore, endeavoured carefully to retain the spirit of the original, but have sought to enlarge the basis, and to dispose the accumulated materials into a regular and compact system. By simplifying the order of arrangement, I presume that I have materially abridged the labour of the student. The numerous additions which are incorporated in the text, so far from retarding, will rather facilitate his progress, by rendering more continuous the chain of demonstration."

Mr. Leslie farther adds, that the view which he has given of the nature of Proportion in the fifth book, will, he expects, contribute to remove the chief difficulties attending that important subject. The sixth book, which exhibits the application of the doctrine of ratios, contains a copious selection of propositions, not only beautiful in themselves, but which pave the way to the higher branches of Geometry, or lead immediately to valuable practical results.

In the part devoted to Geometrical Analysis, the first book consists of a series of the choicest problems, rising above each other in gradual succession. The second and third books are almost wholly occupied with the researches of the ancient Analysis. Of Mr. Leslie's Trigonometry, we shall speak farther on. We have been thus particular in describing the contents of Mr. Leslie's work, but after all, it does not appear so well adapted to beginners as many of the others which have been mentioned before; and should, perhaps, be considered rather as a second, than a first book for those who are studying the science without the aid of an instructor.

One of the latest works of Geometry that have come within our notice, is entitled "Geometria Legitima, or an Elementary system of Theoretical Geometry, adapted for the general use of beginners in the mathematical Sciences," &c. By Francis Reynard.

The author of this work assumes, that the Elements of Euclid is a book not calculated for schools, and particularly unfit to be put into the hands of boys, who might well begin a course of geometry, such as is here presented to them, at the age of twelve. We so far agree with Mr. Reynard, that we would not, in general, put Euclid into the hands of very young persons, yet we must observe, that we have known it taught with success in schools, and we have witnessed lads of twelve or thirteen years of age, who have been instructed in the " Elements" only, able to give a satisfactory account of every step in the demonstrations which they have been called on to perform. This we think it right to state, that unwarrantable prejudices may not be excited against a book that has been in deservedly high reputation so many centuries.

Mr. Reynard, in describing his labours, says, that in order to throw some light on the contents, and to give the student an idea of what he is going to do, and what advantages he will derive, an introduction immediately precedes each book, and by way of exercise, and to try the test of the student's knowledge, after he has read through each book (of which there are eight), there is a suitable collection of questions, which will give the mind ample scope for its exercise, and will afford the best criterion of his industry and attention. Mr. R. states likewise, that he has introduced, in the progress of his work, some new theorems, and that all the theorems through the work are demonstrated by the *direct method,* which he imagines is the safest way of proceeding. If it be the safest method, we cannot help observing, that the reductio ad absurdum very frequently carries with it a conviction equally satisfactory to the mind with the direct method of proof. Our author has added at the end, a selection of miscellaneous questions, chiefly taken from different authors, some of which will demand the ingenuity and knowledge of the skilful geometrician; many are likewise given, with an intention that he may, at the same time, be exercised in solving them analytically. These supplementary questions, and the Questiones Solvendæ at the end of each book, are applicable to almost any other work of Geometry, and may be found useful to those who study this branch of science by means of Simson's, or any other Euclid, or by Simpson's, Bonnycastle's, or the other introductions to Geometry.

"The Elements of Plane Geometry; containing the first six books of Euclid, from the text of Dr. Simson, with notes critical and explanatory; to which are added, book vii. including several important propositions which are not in Euclid; book viii. consisting of Practical Geometry; also book ix. of Planes and their intersections; and book x. of the Geometry of Solids." By Thomas Keith. 1814.

This work, which has not been long before the public, appears to be a very excellent introduction to mathematical knowledge. The notes to the first six books are brief, but much to the purpose, and such as will assist the student in surmounting the little difficulties that may present themselves to him. They are intended to elucidate, improve, or extend the text. The seventh, the author tells us, is an expanded epitome of the theorems in the first six books of Euclid, arranged in the order which the nature of the subject appears to require: it contains some propositions from the tenth, twelfth, and thirteenth books of Euclid, besides a number that are not in his work, some of which are from Pappus, of Alexandria. To these are added, a few propositions relative to the rectification and quadrature of the circle. "Throughout the whole performance," says Mr. Keith, "the utmost care has been taken to render the several subjects accurate, plain, and intelligible to young students. If the author has succeeded in these particulars, his purpose will be answered: and therefore he submits, without apprehension, to scientifical men, the result of his endeavours to elucidate the doctrine and extend the usefulness of Euclid's Elements." We give him full credit for his intentions, and think it will be admitted that he has succeeded.

Thus have we taken a review of a great variety of elementary works on the science of geometry, of which any one will be sufficient as an introduction to that highly important branch of knowledge. As, however, we intend our work for real practical use, we shall offer a few directions respecting the best method of studying geometry. These directions will apply to any of the works which have been mentioned.

In the study of history, and indeed of almost every branch of the belles lettres, the student derives considerable pleasure from the pursuit, even in its first stages. The knowledge of new facts, the contemplation of the diversified customs and manners of different people, or of the same people in the varions stages of civilization, afford at once, amusement combined with instruction.

The case is different in mathematics: many a youth has taken Euclid into his hands, or perhaps some easier treatise on the Elements of Geometry; and has read a book or two, without perceiving even the drift of his author. That such should throw away their books in disgust can be no matter of surprize; though it is probable that with proper directions they might have become good geometricians. To persons of this description, who can derive no benefit from instructors, and who have no scientific friend at hand whom they can consult, our work may stand in the stead of a living monitor.

In the study of geometry, care must first be taken to commit perfectly to memory, the definitions, axioms, and postulates, because to these, reference is perpetually made.

The propositions are to be carefully read and thoroughly understood. The learner must not advance to the second till he is sure that he is master of the first, and so of the rest. After he has thus gone through the first book, it will be an useful and highly advantageous exercise, if he return and commit the enunciation of each proposition to his memory, and then, either having the figure before him, or drawing it out for himself, write out a demonstration in his own words. This he cannot do without being sure that he understands what he is about; and till he can do this, he ought not to leave a single proposition. This method, we will venture to affirm, is, to persons of common capacities, the best and surest to attain a well-grounded knowledge in geometry. It is that mode recommended by the Latins, "Festina lente." Slow at first, but sure. And after the two first books are thus gone through, the remainder will present to the youth great pleasure, and but few difficulties.

The doctrine of ratios in the fifth book, may perhaps retard the learner awhile: it is treated of in Simson's Euclid, in a method less easy than in the several treatises of the Elements of Geometry which we have enumerated, to any one of which the reader of Euclid may be referred for assistance. In the solid geometry, if he would call in the aid of the senses, which is not absolutely necessary, he will do well to have Cowley's figures before him.

The learner will scarcely enter into the spirit of the geometrical notes till he is master of the elements. Euclid's data in the edition of Dr. Simson, Barrow, &c., the maxima and minima, in that of Mr. Thomas Simpson, and the other appendages to the different treatises in this science, will afford the young geometrician much intellectual pleasure, with the expense of little labour, if he has laid a solid foundation in the way recommended.

The pupil having made himself master of the Elementary parts of Algebra and Geometry, will be fully prepared to apply his knowledge in one branch of science to the solution of problems in the other. The application of algebra to geometry is of two kinds: that which regards the plane or common geometry, and that which respects what is usually denominated the higher geometry, or the nature of curve lines. The first of these is concerned in the algebraical solutions of geometrical problems, and in the investigation of theorems in geometrical figures, by means of algebraical investigations or demonstrations. This method of resolving geometrical problems is, in many cases, more direct and easy, than that of geometrical analysis; but of course the solution in this way, depends upon a previous acquaintance with the method of expressing geometrical magnitudes, as well as their mutual positions and relations, by algebraical notation, that is, a line is represented by a single letter, a rectangle by the product of two letters, expressing its sides, a rectangular parallepipedon by the product of three letters; two of which will represent the superficies of the base, and the other its perpendicular altitude: thus, if a and b represent the sides of a rectangle, then $a \times b$ or $a\,b$ will represent the superficies; and if a prison be erected on that superficies, whose altitude is denoted by c, then the solid contents will be expressed by $a \times b \times c$ or $a\,b\,c$. The opposite position of straight lines may be expressed by the signs $+$ and $-$, and segments of lines may be denoted by letters with these signs prefixed, as circumstances require.

In the solution of problems, the following general observations should be attended to. When any geometrical problem is proposed for algebraical resolution, we must in the first place, describe a figure that shall represent the parts or conditions of the problem; then, having considered the nature of the problem, the figure must be prepared for solution, if necessary, by producing and drawing such lines as appear most conducive to that purpose. Then the lines known and unknown are to be represented by proper symbols, and the operation to be proceeded on, by observing the relation which the several parts have to each other. No general rules can be laid down for drawing the lines, and selecting the most proper quantities to substitute for them, so as always to bring out the most simple and direct conclusions. The following general directions, taken chiefly from the Algebra and Select Exercises of Mr. Thomas Simpson, are given and referred to by almost all English writers on this subject.

1. In preparing the figure, by drawing lines, let them be either parallel or perpendicular to other lines in the figure, or

so as to form similar triangles; and if an angle be given, let the perpendicular be opposite to that angle, and fall from the end of the given line, if possible.

2. In selecting proper quantities for substitution, let those be chosen, whether required or not, which lie nearest the known or given parts of the figure, and by means of which the next adjacent parts may be expressed, without the intervention of surds, by addition and subtraction only. Thus, if the problem were to find the perpendicular of a plane triangle, from the three sides given, it will be much better to substitute for one of the segments of the base, than for the perpendicular, though that be the quantity required; because the whole base being given, the other segment will be given, or expressed, by subtraction only, and so the final equation will come out a simple one; from whence the segments being known, the perpendicular is easily found by common arithmetic; whereas, if that perpendicular were first sought, both the segments would be surd quantities, and the final equation a quadratic one.

3. Where, in any problem, there are two lines or quantities alike related to other parts of the figure or problem, the best way is to make use of neither of them, but to substitute for their sum, their rectangle, or the sum of their alternate quotients, or for some line or lines in the figure, to which they both have the same relation.

4. If the area, or the perimeter of a figure, be given, or such parts of it as have but a remote relation to the parts required, it will be sometimes of use to assume another figure similar to the proposed one, of which one side is unity, or some other known quantity, whence the other parts of the figure may be found, and an equation obtained.

The writers on this branch of science are numerous, to several of which we have already referred. In Simpson's Algebra, and the second part of his Select Exercises, there are a good number of Problems. A few pages of Mr. Frend's Algebra are devoted to it, but these are scarcely sufficient to give the pupil an insight into the subject. In the second volume of Mr. Bonnycastle's larger work on Algebra, will be found a variety of problems relating to plane geometry, and also to the doctrine of curves. Almost all the volumes of the "Ladies' Diary," and the "Mathematical Repository," by Mr. Leybourn, will furnish the Mathematical student with abundance of work, from the easiest to the abstrusest problems. The most interesting parts of the "Ladies' Diary," from 1704 to 1773, were selected and published in five volumes, by Dr. Hutton, in 1775. To which the learned editor added a sixth volume, entitled "Miscellanea Mathematica," consisting of a large collection of curious mathematical problems, and their solutions, &c. Mr. Leybourn's Mathematical Repository consists of three volumes, 12mo.

The mathematical student will find an advantage in possessing Hutton's, or Barlow's Dictionary, or Nicholson's "British Encyclopedia;" or, above all, the great national work of the Rev. Dr. Rees, entitled, "The New Cyclopedia," of which nearly sixty parts are before the public.

CHAP. XXXI.

MATHEMATICS,

Continued.

Trigonometry—History of this branch of Science—Ancient writers on Trigonometry: Theodosius—Menelaus—Ptolemy—Purback—Regiomontanus—Copernicus—Maurolicus—Rheticus—Otho—Pitiscus—Clavius,—Ceulen—Napier—Briggs—Gunter—Trigonometry, on what founded—Methods of investigating its principles—Practical rules, Modern authors: Martin—Ashworth—Simson—Simpson—Vince—Leslie—Woodhouse—Bonnycastle—Keith—Kelly; and Walker.

THE art of measuring the sides and angles of a triangle, whether plane or spherical, is called plane or spherical Trigonometry. This is an art of the greatest use in the mathematical sciences, especially in navigation, surveying, levelling, dialing, and geography. By means of trigonometry, we come to know the magnitude of the earth, the moon, the planets, and even the sun: their distances from us, and from one another; their motions and several occultations and eclipses. Hence it is probable, that this art was cultivated from the earliest ages of mathematical knowledge, though no records have been left us, by which we can trace it to a higher age than that of Hipparchus, who flourished about a century and a half before the commencement of the Christian æra; and who is reported by Theon, in his Commentary on Ptolemy's Almagest, to have written a work, in twelve books, on the chords of circular arcs, which was no doubt a treatise on Trigonometry. The earliest existing work on the subject, is the spherics of Theodosius, a native of Tripoli, in Bithynia, who, in the times of Cicero and Pompey, collected the scattered principles of science, which had been discovered by his predecessors, and formed them into a regular treatise, in three books, containing a variety of the most necessary and useful propositions relating to the sphere, arranged and demonstrated with great perspicuity and elegance, after the manner of Euclid's Elements. The first of these books contained twenty-two propositions; the second, twenty-three; and the third, fourteen. They were translated by the Arabians out of the original Greek, into their own language: from which, the work was translated into Latin, and printed at Venice. The Arabic version was found afterwards to be very defective, and a more complete edition was published in Greek and Latin at Paris, in 1558. De Chales printed it in his Cursus Mathematicus. The edition most generally referred to at this time, is that by Dr. Barrow, published in 1675, illustrated and demonstrated in a new and concise method. There is a good Oxford edition, in 8vo, 1709.

The next of the Greek writers, after Theodosius, who has professedly treated on this subject, is Menelaus, an astronomer and mathematician of considerable eminence, who flourished during the first century of the Christian æra. He was author of three books "On Spherics," which have come down to us through the medium of the Arabic language. A Latin version of this work was published at Paris, by Father Mersenne, in 1664, with corrections, restorations, and additional propositions. The Spherics of Menelaus contain besides the first principles of the science, a number of propositions of a more difficult kind. Dr. Halley prepared a new edition of this work, which was published in 8vo, 1758, by Costard, the author of the "History of Astronomy." Menelaus is said to have been the author of another work on the subtenses, or chords, of circular arcs, being, probably, a treatise on the ancient method of constructing trigonometrical tables, which has not come down to the moderns. This loss has been repaired in a good measure by Ptolemy, who, in the first book of his Almagest, published early in the second century after Christ, has given a table of arcs and their chords, to every half degree of the semicircle, in the formation of which he divides the radius and the arc whose chord is equal to radius, each into sixty equal parts; and then estimates all other arcs by sixtieths of that arc, and the chords by sixtieths of that chord, or of the radius. Ptolemy is said to have been the author of the proposition "that the rectangle of the two diagonals of any quadrilateral inscribed in a circle, is equal to the sum of the rectangles of its opposite sides."

After Ptolemy, and his commentator Theon, little more is known on this subject, till about the close of the eighth century after Christ, when the ancient method of computing by the chords was changed for that of sines, which was first introduced into the science by the Arabians, who furnished the several axioms and theorems, which are at present considered as the foundation of trigonometry, as it is now taught. The Arabians, though acquainted with the decimal scale of arithmetic, did not in their trigonometry deviate from the Greeks in the sexagesimal division of the radius, which continued in use till the middle of the fifteenth century, when Purback, a German, constructed a table of sines to a division of the radius, into 600,000 equal parts, and computed them for every ten minutes, in parts of this radius, by decimal notation. The project was carried on by Regiomontanus, his pupil and friend, who computed a table of sines, for every minute of the quadrant to the radius, supposed to be divided into 100,000 parts.

Shortly after this, several other mathematicians contributed to the advancement of this science, among whom was Werner, of Nuremburg, and Copernicus, the illustrious restorer of the true system of the world, who wrote a brief treatise on plane and spherical trigonometry, with a description and construction of the canon of chords, which tract, together with a table of sines, and their differences, for every ten minutes of the quadrant, is inserted in his *Revolutiones orbium cœlestium* published in 1543. Ten years after this, Erasmus Rheinold published his Table of Tangents, and about the same time, Maurolicus published a Table of Secants. The last named author was one of the most considerable mathematicians of his time. He was regarded by his learned contemporaries as a second Archimedes, and was author of many very admirable works.

The most complete work on the subject which had then appeared, was a treatise, in two parts, by Vieta, printed at Paris, in 1579; in the first part of which he has given a table of sines, tangents, and secants, for every minute of the quadrant, to radius of 100,000 with their differences; and towards the end of the quadrant, the tangents and secants are extended to eight or nine places of figures. They are arranged like the present tables. The second part of the volume, contains, besides a regular account of the construction of the tables, a compendious treatise on plane and spherical trigonometry, with their application to a variety of curious subjects in geometry, mensuration, &c., as likewise a number of particulars relating to the quadrature of the circle, the duplication of the cube and such like problems. This work of Vieta is said to be extremely rare. It may be observed, though not strictly connected with trigonometry, that Vieta gave in this work computations of the ratio of the diameter of a circle to the circumference, and of the length of the sine of one minute, to several places of figures, by which he found that the sine of one minute, is somewhere

Between 2908881959
And 2908882056;

and that the diameter of a circle being 1000, &c., the perimeter of the inscribed and circumscribed polygon of 393,216 sides will be as follows: the

Perimeter of the inscribed polygon 31415926535
——————circumscribed—— 31415926537,

and of course that the circumference of the circle lies between those two numbers. See *Mensuration*.

George Joachim Rheticus, a pupil of Copernicus, is the next writer to be noticed on this subject. He formed the design of computing the trigonometrical canon for every ten seconds of the quadrant, to fifteen places of decimals: he was able, however, to accomplish only that part of it relating to the sines and co-sines. The work was finished by Valentine Otho, his disciple, and published under the title of "Opus Palatinum de Triangulis, in 1596." In this work, we have for the first time, an entire table of sines, tangents, and secants, for every ten seconds of the quadrant, to ten places of decimals, with their differences. These tables were afterwards corrected by Bartholomew Pitiscus, and he published his edition under the title of "Thesaurus Mathematicus," in 1613. Previously to this, Philip Lansberg published his "Geometria Triangulorum," in four books, with the usual tables, and Pitiscus had likewise given to the world, in 1599, his own work on Trigonometry, which was reckoned a very complete work, both with respect to the correctness of the tables, and its numerous practical applications.

Christopher Cluvius, in the first volume of his works printed at Mentz, 1612, in five volumes folio, has given an ample treatise on Trigonometry, with tables of sines, tangents, and secants, for every minute of the quadrant, to seven places of decimals.

Ludolph van Ceulen, a Dutch mathematician, published, about the year 1600, his well known treatise "De circulo et adscriptis," &c. in which he treats of the properties of lines drawn in and about a circle, and especially of chords, with the construction of the canon of sines. Francis van Schooten, in 1627, published at Amsterdam, a table of sines, tangents, and secants, for every minute of the quadrant to seven places, which has been esteemed a very accurate work.

These are the principal writers on Trigonometry, and the tables of sines, tangents, and secants, before the change that was made in the subject by the introduction of the logarithmic calculus, which was first employed in this science about the commencement of the seventeenth century, by the inventor, the celebrated Baron Napier, of Merchiston, in Scotland, who, in 1614, published his work entitled "Mirifici Logarithmorum Canonis Descriptio," which contains the logarithms of numbers, and the logarithmic sines, tangents, and secants, for every minute of the quadrant, together with the description and use of the tables. But the person to whom we are chiefly indebted, for the new and more advantageous form which the mode of computation has since assumed, is Mr. Henry Briggs, at that time professor of geometry in Gresham college, who has the merit of having first proposed, both to the public in his lectures, and to the illustrious inventor of the doctrine himself, the improvement in the system of these numbers, which consists in making the radix of the system 10, instead of 2.71828, &c. as was done by Napier; or which is the same thing, by changing them from the hyperbolic to the present common, or tabular logarithms. In 1624, Mr. Briggs published his "Arithmetica Logarithmica," which contains the logarithms of all the numbers from 1 to 20,000 and from 90,000 to 100,000 to fifteen places of figures. This table was completed by Adrian Valcq, of Gouda, in Holland, who calculated the seventy intermediate chiliads, and republished the "Arithmetica Logarithmetica," at that place, with these additional numbers, in which state it contained the logarithms of all numbers from 1 to 100,000 to ten places of decimals, together with a table of logarithmic sines, tangents and secants, to the same extent, for every minute of the quadrant.

Mr. Briggs completed a table of logarithmic sines and tangents for the hundredth part of every degree, to fourteen places of decimals, together with a table of natural sines for the same parts to fifteen places, and the tangents and secants of the same to ten places, with an account of the construction of the whole; which work was likewise printed at Gouda by Valcq, in 1633, and upon his death a preface to it was supplied by Mr. Henry Gellibrand, who added to it the application of logarithms to plane and spherical trigonometry, which he published in the same year under the title of "Trigonometry Britannica." Valcq at the same time published his own great work, entitled "Trigonometria Artificialis," which contains the logarithmic sines and tangents of every ten seconds of the quadrant, to ten places of figures, besides the index, and the logarithms of the first twenty thousand numbers, to the same number of places, with the differences of each; the whole being preceded by a full description of the tables, and the application of them to some of the principal problems in plane and spherical Trigonometry. Several smaller tables of these logarithms were also published about this time by Gunter, Wingate, and others. Gunter, it should be noticed, first applied the logarithms of numbers, together with those of the sines and tangents, to a ruler, in the form of a two foot scale, which is still known by his name; by which proportions in trigonometry, navigation, and other subjects, may be performed, to a degree of accuracy sufficient for many practical purposes, by the mere application of a pair of compasses.

The common logarithmic canon was first reduced to its most convenient form by Mr. John Newton, in his "Trigonometria Britannica," printed in 1658, which contains the logarithms of the first 100,000 numbers to 8 places of decimals, arranged in the same manner as they are in our tables at present, as also the logarithmic sines and tangents to the same extent. The greater part of these tables are superseded by those of a later date, some of which we shall have occasion to notice in the sequel.

Trigonometry, or the resolution of triangles, is founded

upon the mutual proportions which subsist between the sides and angles of triangles, which proportions are known by finding the relations between the radius of a circle, and certain other lines drawn in and about the circle, denominated chords, sines, tangents, secants, &c. We have seen that the ancients performed their trigonometry by means of chords, which have been long since abandoned for the use of sines, tangents, and secants.

The proportion of the sines, tangents, &c to their radius, is sometimes expressed in common or natural numbers, which constitute what are called the tables of natural sines, tangents and secants. Sometimes it is expressed in logarithms, being the logarithms of the natural sines, tangents, &c. These last constitute the table of artificial sines, tangents, secants, &c.: and sometimes the proportion is not expressed in numbers; but the several sines, tangents, &c. are actually laid down upon certain scales. In trigonometry, as the angles are measured by arcs of a circle described about the angular point, so the whole circumference of the circle is supposed to be divided into 360 parts, called degrees, and each degree is divide dinto 60 parts, called minutes, and each minute, into 60 seconds; sometimes by a similar division, the seconds are divided into *thirds*, and so on. An angle therefore is said to consist of so many degrees, minutes and seconds, as are contained in the arc that measures the angle, or that is intercepted between the sides or legs of the angle.

The sines, tangents, secants, co-sines, &c. of every degree, minute, second, &c. of a quadrant, are calculated to the radius of 1, and ranged in tables for use, as also the logarithms of the same; forming the triangular canon.

There are two methods used in investigating the principles of trigonometry: viz. by geometry and algebra. By the former, the various relations of the sines, co-sines, tangents of arcs or angles, and those of the sides and angles of triangles, are deduced immediately from the figures to which the several inquiries are referred, each particular case requiring its own method, and resting on evidence peculiar to itself. By the algebraical method, the nature and properties of the linear-angular quantities being first defined, some general relation of these quantities, or of them in connexion with a triangle, is expressed by one or more equations, and then other theorems of use in this branch of science, are developed by the simple reduction of the first equation. Thus it is observed, "the rules for the three fundamental cases in plane trigonometry, which may be deduced by three independent geometrical investigations, are obtained algebraically, by forming between the three data, and the three unknown quantities, three equations, and obtaining, in expressions of known terms, the value of each of the unknown quantities, the others being exterminated by the usual processes. Each of these methods has its peculiar advantages. The geometrical method, in this, as in all other cases, carries conviction at every step; and, by keeping the objects of inquiry constantly before the eye, serves to guard against the admission of error. The algebraical method, on the contrary, requiring little aid from first principles, excepting at the commencement of the process, is rather mechanical than mental, and requires frequent checks to prevent any deviation from the truth. The geometrical method is direct and rapid, in producing the conclusions at the outset of trigonometrical science; but slow and circuitous in arriving at those results which the modern state of science requires: while the algebraical method, though sometimes circuitous in the developement of the mere elementary theorems, is very rapid and fertile in producing those curious and interesting formulæ, which are wanted in the higher branches of pure analysis, in mixed mathematics, and more particularly in physical astronomy."

In practice, three things, in every plane triangle, must be given to find the rest: and of these three, one, at least, must be a side. There are three cases which include all the varieties that can happen: (1) When two of the three given things are a side, and its opposite angle. (2) When two sides and their included angle are given. (3) When the three sides are given. Each of these cases may be resolved in three different ways, viz. by geometrical construction—by arithmetical computation—or instrumentally. In resorting to the first of these methods, the student will find himself well prepared for the pursuit, if he has before attended to the Geometrical construction of Problems, of which there are many excellent examples in the latter part of Mr. Thomas Simpson's Geometry. In this method, the triangle is constructed by laying down the sides from a scale of equal parts, and the angles from a scale of chords, or a protractor, and then measuring the unknown parts by the same scale or instrument from which the others were taken.

In the mode by arithmetical computation; having stated the proportion according to the proper rule, multiply the second and third terms together, and divide the product by the first, and the quotient will be the fourth term required; that is, when the natural numbers are used. In working by logarithms, the logarithms of the second and third terms are to be *added* together, and from the sum, the logarithm of the first term is to be *taken*, and the number answering to the remainder, will be the fourth term sought.

In the third method, or instrumentally, as by logarithmic lines, on one side of a common two-foot scale, the legs of the compasses are to be extended from the first term to the second or third, as they may happen to be of the same kind, and that extent will reach from the other term to the required fourth term, taking both extents towards the same end of the scale.

Among the many works on trigonometry that may be recommended to the student's attention, the following require to be noticed.

"The Trigonometer's Guide, by Benjamin Martin," in two volumes, 8vo. In the course of this work, the examples are very numerous, and applied to the various departments in natural philosophy. They are worked according to the three methods mentioned above.

On nearly the same plan, but on a much more contracted scale, is a small work, entitled "An Easy Introduction to Plane Trigonometry: the application of it to the measuring Heights and Distances; to the several branches of Natural Philosophy, Land Surveying, &c. by C. Ashworth, D. D." This treatise is practical, and, like the last, adapted for persons who have not gone deeply into mathematical studies. It contains a great number of examples, and, being of a small price, may be used in connexion with those which are more theoretical, and some of which are very scanty in their exemplifications.

"The Elements of Plane and Spherical Trigonometry," by Dr. Robert Simson, consist of only about forty pages, and are attached to his Elements of Euclid. This treatise contains the elementary part, and is, says the author, "much the same as the common treatises, excepting that the demonstrations of several of the propositions are changed into others that were thought better."

"Trigonometry, Plane and Spherical, with the construction and application of Logarithms." By Thomas Simpson, F. R S. This, like the last, is brief, but, for the most part, clear and perspicuous. The section on the nature and construction of logarithms, with their application to the doctrine of triangles, is short, but satisfactory. The author having exhibited the manner of resolving all the common cases of plane and spherical triangles, he subjoins a few propositions for the solution of the more difficult cases which sometimes occur.

A larger and somewhat plainer disquisition on the nature and use of logarithms stands as an introduction to "A Treatise on Plane and Spherical Trigonometry," by the Rev. S. Vince, now Doctor Vince. This is intended as part of a mathematical course, recommended to the students at Cambridge, and is therefore adapted particularly to the views of the professors of that learned University; it may, however, answer all the purposes of other persons who are in pursuit of trigonometrical knowledge.

The "Elements of Plane Trigonometry" are neatly and clearly stated by Mr. Leslie in his work on Geometry, of which we have before spoken; and to which we mean to make ourselves indebted for certain illustrations on several of the branches of science flowing from the principles of trigonometry. As an introduction to this little piece, the learned professor observes, the sides of a triangle are measured, by referring them to some definite portion of linear extent, which is fixed by convention. The mensuration of the angles is effected by means of that universal standard derived from the partition of a circuit. Since angles are proportional to the intercepted arcs of a circle described from their vertex, the subdivision of the circumference, therefore, determines their magnitude. A quadrant, as it corresponds to a right angle, hence forms the basis of angular measures; but these measures depending on the relation of certain orders of lines connected with the circle, he sets out with previously investigating these; and, in order the more clearly to discern the connexion of the lines derived from the circle, Mr. Leslie traces their successive values, while the corresponding arc is supposed to increase. Having thus taken his preliminary steps, his whole tract is comprised in a few theorems and problems, which will not present any serious obstacles to the young mathematician, if he be well grounded in the principles of geometry. This, in mathematics, is, what Demosthenes said, pronunciation was to oratory, the first, the second, and, in short, every thing.

"Elements of Trigonometry, plane and spherical, applied to the most useful problems in heights, distances, Astronomy and Navigation," By William Payne, author of Elements of Geometry, already referred to, is a very easy and useful treatise adapted to the use of learners.

Mr. Woodhouse's Treatise on Plane and Spherical Trigonometry, may be recommended; but it is less easy than most of those already noticed.

There are, no doubt, other tracts of the smaller kind, of real value on trigonometry, of which our own knowledge does not allow us to speak; and such, we are persuaded, is that by Mr. Bridge. We shall close our account by mentioning two, which are carried to a much greater extent than any of those of which we have already spoken.

"A Treatise on Plane and Spherical Trigonometry, with their most considerable applications." By John Bonnycastle.

"An Introduction to the Theory and Practice of Plane and Spherical Trigonometry, and the Stereographic Projection of the Sphere, including the Theory of Navigation," &c. By Thomas Keith.

To Mr. Bonnycastle's introduction, the historical part of this chapter in our work is much indebted, he having more neatly and concisely stated the rise and origin of the trigonometrical and logarithmic calculus than any other author in our recollection. The author, as will be seen in the foregoing pages, has attributed to the respective authors the honour due to them on account of their several discoveries. The work itself is furnished with a great variety of rules and examples; and, in the second edition, which is much enlarged, nearly all the practical questions that had been before given, and many of which, he says, had passed in the same state from one work to another for more than a century; he has re-proposed, with new data, "and in every case," the author adds, "where it was judged necessary, both the examples, and the rules upon which they depend, have been carefully attended to, and reduced to their most commodious and approved forms."

"The Introduction," by Mr. Keith, though not larger in the number of its pages, by its mode of printing, contains a deal more matter, perhaps double the quantity. The author means it for a complete treatise in itself; and, in answer to those who may suppose it too much extended for an introductory treatise, he says, "the student is here supplied with three distinct treatises, which are all essential towards his future progress in the science: 1st. A Treatise on Logarithms, and the necessary Tables; 2d. A Treatise on Practical Trigonometry; and 3d. A Theoretical Treatise on the Subject." In the part of the volume which comprehends Spherical Trigonometry, the Stereographic Projection of the Sphere is given; and among many other things, two chapters, that will be found very useful to those who are desirous of studying practical Astronomy. The fourth book includes a brief treatise on the theory and practice of Navigation, which, as we observed in the beginning of this chapter, is one of the branches of practical science that depends almost wholly on trigonometry. The volume concludes with a number of extremely useful tables, among which are a table of logarithms from 1 to 10,000 to five places of decimals; a table of natural sines to every degree and minute of the quadrant; and a table of logarithmical sines and tangents also to every degree and minute of the quadrant.

Besides the works avowedly on Trigonometry, we have an excellent work entitled "A Practical Introduction to Spherics and Nautical Astronomy, being an attempt to simplify those useful sciences." By P. Kelly, LL.D: and another "On the Doctrine of the Sphere," in six books, by the Rev. George Walker, F.R.S., containing Preliminary properties of the cone—the general doctrine of the Sphere—and spheric triangles—Projection, orthographic and stereographic, and a treatise on Spheric Trigonometry. This work is, we believe, very scarce, and has at no time been appreciated according to its merit.

It is usual to have tables of Logarithms in a separate volume; of these there are many entitled to commendation; and, in speaking of them, we cannot follow a more respectable authority than that of Mr. Bonnycastle, who, in his trigonometry, says, "among the most accurate and convenient of which, for common use, may be reckoned the edition of Vlacq's small volume of tables, printed at Lyons in 1670 and another work of this kind, printed at the same place, in 1760; but more particularly the edition of Sherwin's Mathematical Tables, in 8vo. 1742, as revised by Gardiner; also Hutton's Mathematical Tables, in 8vo. first printed in 1785; the Tables of Vega, 2 vols. 8vo. printed at Leipzig, in 1797; and the first edition of the Tables Portatives de Logarithms of Callet, in small 8vo. printed at Paris, 1783;* all of which are adapted to the sexagesimal division of the circle, used by Valcq and most of the later compilers.

" Besides these, several other tables, of a different kind, have been lately published by the French; in which the quadrant is divided, according to their new system of measures, into 100 degrees, the degree into 100 minutes, and the minute into 100 seconds; the principal of which are the second edition of the Tables Portatives of Callet, beautifully printed in stereotype, at Paris, by Didot, 8vo. 1795, with great additions and improvements; the Trigonometrical Tables of Borda, in 4to. an. ix, revised and enriched with various new precepts and formulæ by Delambre; and the tables lately published at Berlin, by Hobert and Ideler, which are also adapted to the decimal division of the circle, and are highly praised for their accuracy by the French computers.

" Among the various tables, however, of the sexagenary kind, none have been more esteemed for their usefulness and accuracy than those of Gardiner, printed in 4to. at London, in 1742; which contain the logarithms of all numbers from 1 to 102100, and the logarithmic sines and tangents for every ten seconds of the quadrant, to 7 places of decimals, with several other necessary tables; a new edition of which work was also printed at Avignon, in France, in 1770, under the care of Pezenas, who added to it the sines and tangents of

* This neat portable work, which is now become extremely scarce, contains all the tables in Gardiner's 4to. volume, hereafter mentioned, with several additions and improvements; and is, by far, the most useful and convenient performance of the kind that has yet been offered to the public.

every single second, for the first 4 degrees, and a small table of hyperbolic logarithms, taken from Simpson's Fluxions.

" But of all the trigonometrical tables hitherto published, the most extensive and best adapted for obtaining accurate results, in many delicate astronomical and geodetical observations, are those of Taylor, printed in large 4to. at London, 1792; which contain the logarithms of the first common numbers from 1 to 1260, to eight places of decimals; the logarithms of all numbers from 1 to 101000, to 7 places; and the logarithmic sines and tangents of every second in the quadrant, to 7 places; as also a preface, and various precepts for the explanation and use of the tables, which, from the author's dying before the last sheet of his work was printed off, were supplied by Dr. Maskelyne, the late astronomer royal.

" It may here likewise be observed, that besides the common tables hitherto mentioned, which contain the logarithms of numbers in their usual order, others, of a different kind, have been constructed, for the more readily finding the number corresponding to any given logarithm; of which the principal one, of any considerable extent, is the Antilogarithmic Canon of Dodson, published at London, in 1742; which contains the numbers corresponding to every logarithm, from 1 to 100000, to eleven places of figures, with their differences and proportional parts; and, though little used at present, is a performance of great labour and merit."*

With respect to the new division of the circle, by the French, referred to in the preceding page, and the advantages of which have been so highly applauded by many authors, we may observe, that, though it would unquestionably facilitate calculation, yet it would render useless all existing trigonometrical and astronomical works, as well as the most valuable mathematical instruments, which have been constructed and divided by

* Dr. Wallis informs us, in the 2d vol. of his mathematical works, that an antilogarithmic canon was began by Harriot, the algebraist (who died in 1621), and finished by Warner, the editor of his works, about the year 1640; but which was lost for want of encouragement to print it.

the most eminent artists. The best instruments in all the observatories of Europe, have been made by British artists, as Ramsden, Troughton, &c., and they are all graduated according to the sexagesimal division of the circle, therefore, supposing the change to take place, recommended by the French, it is manifest that all observations, made with these instruments, must be reduced to the centesimal division of the circle, before they can be used in calculation. All the latitudes and longitudes of places on the globe must likewise be changed, which change would render the different works on Geography, in a great measure, useless; or otherwise, those in the habit of making trigonometrical calculations, must be perpetually turning the old divisions of the circle into the new, or the new into the old. The same may be said of all the logarithmical tables of sines, tangents, &c., so that the change from the sexagesimal division to the centesimal is a matter of doubtful advantage, when balanced with the difficulties that must necessarily attend it.

CHAP. XXXII.

MATHEMATICS,

Continued.

Conic Sections—Method of obtaining the several sections—History of the Science. Writers upon it—Apollonius—Pappus—Wallis—Hamilton—Robertson—De la Hire—Simson—Boscovich—Newton—Vince—Jack Trevigar—Steel, &c.—Fluxions—rules for finding the fluxions of quantities—application of fluxions—writers on fluxions—Newton—Rowe—Vince—Simpson—Maclaurin. Doctrine of Chances—Annuities, Insurance, &c.

CONIC Sections are such curve lines as are produced by the mutual intersection of a plane, and the surface of a solid cone. The nature and properties of these figures were the subject of an extensive branch of the ancient geometry, and formed a speculation well adapted to the genius of the Greeks. In modern times the conic geometry is intimately connected with every part of the higher mathematics and natural philosophy. A knowledge of the great discoveries of the last century, cannot be attained without a familiar acquaintance with the figures and properties of the conic sections. These sections are derived from the different ways in which the solid cone is cut, by a plane passing through it;

and they are, a *triangle*, a *circle*, an *ellipse*, a *parabola*, and an *hyperbola*. The last three of these, are peculiarly called *Conic Sections*, and the investigation of their nature and properties, is generally denoted by the term " Conics." The mode of obtaining these sections is as follows:

(1.) If the cutting plane pass through the vertex of the cone, and any part of the base, the section will be a triangle.

(2.) If the plane cut the cone parallel to the circular base, the section will be a circle, provided the cone be a right one.

(3.) The section is a parabola when the cone is cut by a plane parallel to the side; or, when the cutting plane and the side of the cone make equal angles with the base.

(4.) The section is an ellipse, when the cone is cut obliquely through both sides, or when the plane is inclined to the base in a less angle than the side of the cone is.

(5.) The section is an hyperbola, when the cutting plane makes a greater angle with the base than the side of the cone makes, and if the plane be continued to cut the opposite cone, this latter section is called the opposite hyperbola to the former.

(6.) The vertices of any section are the points where the cutting plane meets the opposite sides of the cone. Hence, the ellipse and the opposite hyperbolas have each two vertices, but the parabola only one.

There is no work of antiquity which professedly treats of the history of conic sections, that has reached our time, and there is little to satisfy curiosity in this inquiry, excepting some incidental notices collected from different authors. The discovery of the curves, denominated the conic sections, is attributed to the philosophers of the school of Plato, or even to Plato himself. The theory of these curves probably grew up gradually from small beginnings, increasing in magnitude and importance, by the successive improvements of many geometricians. The history of the mathematics mentions two problems, famous in ancient times, and both of them so difficult as to surpass the limits of plane geometry. These problems were the duplication of the cube, and the trisection of an angle; and there is no doubt, but that the theory of the conic sections received great additions, and was enriched with many new properties, by the researches that were undertaken for resolving these problems. Two solutions of the former problem, derived from the conic sections, are preserved by Eutochius, in his commentary on the works of Archimedes, which are attributed to Menechmus. Some solutions of the latter problem, by means of the conic sections, are likewise extant in ancient authors, for which, science is thought to be indebted to the ingenuity of the followers of Plato. Hence it has been inferred, that great progress must have been made in investigating the properties of the conic sections before the time of Archimedes. This conclusion is confirmed by the writings of that celebrated mathematician, the best and most splendid edition of whose works was printed at the Oxford press, in 1792. In these works many principal propositions are there expressly said to have been demonstrated by preceding writers, and are spoken of as truths commonly known to mathematicians. Archimedes himself, perhaps the greatest genius of antiquity, and deserving to be ranked with Galileo and Newton, enriched the theory of the conic sections, with many noble discoveries. After a lapse of two thousand years, the quadrature of the parabola is even yet the most remarkable instance in the science of geometry, of the exact equality of a curvilinear to a rectilineal space. To this discovery must be added, the determining of the proportions of the elliptic spaces to one another, and to the circle; and likewise the mensuration of the solids generated by the revolution of the conic sections about their axes.

We are principally indebted to the preservation of the writings of Apollonius, for a more perfect knowledge of the theories of the ancient geometricians, on conic sections. He was instructed in geometry in the school of Alexandria; and under the successors of Euclid, he there acquired that superior skill in the science which distinguishes his writings. Besides his great work on conic sections, he published many smaller treatises, relating chiefly to geometrical analysis, which have all perished, and are known to us only by the account given of them in the seventh book of the collections of Pappus.

The treatise of Apollonius on the conic sections, is written in eight books, and it was a work in such high estimation among his contemporaries, that it obtained for him the title of "The great mathematician."

The four first books of the conics of Apollonius, is the only part of that work that has come down to us in the original Greek. But in the year 1658, Borelli, passing through Florence, found an Arabic manuscript in the library of the Medici family, which he judged to be a translation of all the eight books of the Conics of Apollonius. Transported with joy, he had interest enough to prevail on the Duke of Tuscany to entrust him with the manuscript, which he carried to Rome, where he published a translation of it in 1661. The manuscript found by Borelli, was entitled "Apollonii Pergæi Libri Octo," and was at first supposed to be a complete translation of the work of the ancient geometrician; but on examination, it was found to contain the first seven books only. Two other Arabic translations of the conics of Apollouins, have since that period been discovered, but both these have the same defect as that found at Florence. Hence it is imagined, that since all the three manuscripts agree in wanting the eighth book, that it was not in existence when the Arabic translations were made. It cannot be ascertained when the original of Apollonius's work disappeared, but it is certain that it was extant in the time of Pappus of Alexandria, as in his "Collectiones Mathematicæ," is given an account of the contents of the eight books, and he has even added the lemmas required for the demonstrations of the propositions which they contain: and this circumstance enabled Dr. Halley to annex to his edition of the conics of Apollonius, published in 1710, a restoration of the eighth book, executed with so much talent as to leave little room to regret the want of the original.

The mathematicians who followed Apollonius, seem to have been content with the humble task of illustrating his treatise. We shall not attempt to enumerate all the commentators who, at different times, have written on his work, and have endeavoured to render the important truths contained in it, of more easy access to the general class of mathematicians. Among the number, however, was the learned and accomplished Hypatia, whose praises we have already recorded; and we are still in possession of the lemmas of Pappus, and of the commentary of Eutochius on the four first books. Since the revival of learning, the theory of Conic Sections has been much cultivated, and is the subject of a great variety of works.

There is, says a writer on this subject, a relation subsisting between all parts of human knowledge, which frequently connects speculations the most abstracted, and seemingly the most barren, with inquiries that are highly interesting to us, and most fertile in its consequences. In studying the properties of the Conic Sections, the followers of Plato sought merely to gratify a contemplative mind, without the most distant regard to practical utility; but, among the moderns, they have been employed to explain many of the most remarkable phenomena of the material world. The doctrine of the Conic Sections has been found of utility in the science of optics, as well as in determining the path of a projectile body. This branch of mathematics, however, derives its chief importance from the application that is made of it in modern astronomy.

There are different modes of treating this branch of science; before Dr. Wallis, all writers on Conic Sections followed the ancient geometricians in making the solid cone the common origin and foundation of their theories. But that great mathematician, in a work entitled "De Sectionibus Conicis," published at Oxford in 1655, deduced all the properties of the curves from a description of them on a plane; since which, authors have been divided as to the best way of defining the curves, and demonstrating their elementary properties. Many, in imitation of the ancient geometricians, make the cone the foundation of their theories; while others, equally respectable for talents and learning, have followed the example of Dr. Wallis.

The latest and most approved writers, who have deduced the properties of the Conic Sections from the cone itself, are Dr. Hugh Hamilton, whose work, originally published in the Latin language in 1758, was translated in 1773, under the title of "A Geometrical Treatise of the Conic Sections, in which the properties of the sections are derived from the nature of the cone, in an easy manner, and by a new method;" and Dr. Abraham Robertson, professor of Oxford, whose work was published in the Latin language in 1792. Dr. Hamilton, in treating on this subject, explains the nature of the conic surface in such a manner, that, as soon as the several curves are defined by the intersection of a plane with this surface, it appears what their principal properties are. "Accordingly," he says, "before the sections are defined, certain properties of the Conic Sections are demonstrated, which contain in them most of the fundamental properties of the Sections. Then, since it appears from their definitions, that these sections are curves, all the points of which are placed on a conic surface, it is manifest that every right line which any way meets these sections, must, in the same manner, and in the same points, meet the conic surface; and, therefore, all the properties which are proved to agree with right lines meeting the conic surface, are immediately transferred to those which meet the Conic Sections. Thus the principal and most general properties of the sections being laid down in the beginning, he expects that their particular properties will be more easily deduced.

Besides these, we have, as has been already observed, many treatises on the Conic Sections, in which the cone is entirely laid aside, and the curves are given and defined from descriptions *in plano*. M. De la Hire, in his treatise entitled "Nouveaux Elémens des Sections Coniques," published in Paris in 1679, is the first author who successfully treated on Conic Sections in this new view of the subject. "He derives his description of the parabola from the equality that subsists between two lines meeting in any point of the curve, one of which is drawn to the focus, and the other is perpendicular to the directrix; and he describes the ellipse and hyperbola from the analogous properties, that in the former, the sum of two lines drawn from any point in the curve to the two foci, and, in the latter, the difference of two such lines, are equal to their transverse axis." In these fundamental properties, De la Hire is followed by most of the later writers, who have treated of the Conic Sections independently of the cone; and in particular by Dr. Robert Simson, of Glasgow, who published in 1735, an extensive treatise on this subject, entitled "Sectionum Conicarum," lib. v. a work which is entitled to high commendation, on account of its elegance and geometrical accuracy. An English translation of the first three books of this work, in 8vo. was published in London in 1775, and again in Glasgow in 1804, entitled "Elements of the Conic Sections."

Besides the method of De la Hire, another way of defining curves *in plano* has been proposed, founded on a general property of the directrix, first discovered, or at least given, by Pappus, viz. the ratio that subsists between the distances of every point in the curve from the focus and the directrix. The Abbé Boscovich has drawn his definitions of the curves from this fundamental property, in his treatise entitled "Elementa Matheseos Universæ;" and we have a work in our own language, which is founded on the same primary definitions, viz. "A short treatise on the Conic Sections, in which the three curves are derived from a general description on a plane, and the most useful properties of each deduced from a common principle," by the Rev. T. Newton. This is an admirable little performance, and may be recommended to those students who wish to get a sufficient insight into the subject without much expense of money or time. The demonstrations are neat, and frequently elegant. The author has compressed into about a hundred pages all those propositions with which every one ought to be acquainted, previously to his entering on the Principia of Newton, and the other branches of natural philosophy; and he has taken care that the demonstrations should be strictly geometrical, and such as the young student will find no difficulty in understanding, provided he be well acquainted with the Elements of Euclid, and plane trigonometry. It should be observed also, that Dr. Hamilton intended the work, described above, as an Introduction to the Newtonian philosophy; and he gives frequent references to certain propositions in the *Principia*. With a similar view, the following work, still more concise than that of Mr. Newton, was published, of which the first edition was entitled "The Elements of the Conic Sections, as preparatory to the reading of Sir Isaac Newton's Principia," by the Rev. S. Vince. In the subsequent editions, Dr. Vince has dropped the latter part of the title, and, in its stead, has inserted "Adapted to the Students in Philosophy." It will be found an useful treatise, as introductory to larger works.

"Elements of Conic Sections, in three books," &c. by Richard Jack, we remember to have read many years ago with satisfaction.

The propositions of Trévigar's work on this subject in Latin, and those in Steel's, in English, are demonstrated algebraically. Besides the above works, there are many others, viz. one by Milne, in Latin, others by Muller and Emerson, and one of the latest by Dr. Hutton, adapted chiefly to the students at Woolwich. By some moderns likewise, the subject has been treated of in a very elaborate manner, as by Euler, Prony, and Lacroix, who have inferred the chief properties of the Conic Sections from the different modifications of the general algebraic equations of lines of the second order, and the established analogies between the properties of equations, and those of curves.

FLUXIONS.

To form a proper idea of the nature of fluxions, all kinds of magnitudes are to be considered as generated by the continual motion of some of their bounds or extremes, as a line by the motion of a point, a surface by the motion of a line, and a solid by the motion of a surface. Every quantity so generated is called a *variable,* or flowing quantity; and a fluxion may be defined as the magnitude by which any flowing quantity would be uniformly increased in a given portion of time, with the generating celerity at any particular instant, supposing it from thence to continue invariable, which is thus explained by Mr. Thomas Simpson, in his work entitled "The Doctrine and Application of Fluxions:" Thus, let the point *m,* plate 1, fig. 1, be conceived to move from A, and generate the variable right line A*m,* by a motion any how regulated; and let the celerity thereof, when it arrives at any proposed position R, be such *as would,* was it to continue uniform from that point, be sufficient to describe the distance, or line R*r,* in the given time allotted for the fluxion; then will R*r* be the fluxion of the variable line A*m,* in that positiou.

The fluxion of a plane surface is conceived in like manner, by supposing a given right line *mn,* fig. 2, to move parallel to itself, in the plane of the parallel, and immovable lines AF and BG; for if Rr be taken to express the fluxion of the line A*m,* and the rectangle RrsS be completed, then that rectangle, being the space which *would be* uniformly described by the generating line *mn,* in the time that A*m would be* uniformly increased by *m*r, is therefore the fluxion of the generated rectangle B*m,* in that position, according to the true meaning of the definition.

If the length of the generating line *mn,* fig. 3, continually varies, the fluxion of the area will *still* be expounded by a rectangle under that line, and the fluxion of the abscissa, or base: for let the curvilineal space *Amn* be generated by the continual and parallel motion of the (now) variable line *mn*, and let Rr be the fluxion of the base, or abscissa, *Am* (as before); then the rectangle RrsS will, here also, be the fluxion of the generated space *Amn;* because, if the length and velocity of the generating line *mn* were to continue invariable from the position RS, the rectangle R*rs*S would then be uniformly generated, with the very celerity wherewith it begins to be generated, or with which the space *Amn* is increased in that position.

From what has been hitherto said, it will appear, that *the fluxions of quantities are always in proportion to the celerities by which the quantities themselves increase in magnitude;* whence it will not be difficult to form a notion of the fluxions of quantities otherwise generated, as well such as arise from the revolution of right lines and planes, as those by parallel motions.

In the application of algebra to the theory of curve lines, we find that some of the quantities which are the subject of consideration, may be conceived as having always the same magnitude as the diameter of a circle; the parameter of a parabola; and the axis of an ellipse, or hyperbola; while others are indefinite in respect of magnitude, and may have any number of particular values; such are the ordinates, &c. of a curve line. This difference in the nature of the quantities which are compared together, takes place in other theories, and on other subjects, in pure and mixed mathematics, which suggests the division of all quantities whatever, into those that are *constant,* and those that are *variable.*

A *constant* quantity is that which retains always the same magnitude, although other quantifies with which it is connected, may be supposed to change; and a *variable* quantity is that which is indefinite in respect to magnitude, according to its position. Thus the radius of a circle is a constant quantity, while the siue, co-sine, tangent, secant, &c. of an arc, are variable quantities, depending upon the magnitude of the arc for their relative value. In Conic Sections likewise, the axes, and the parameters of the axes, are constant quantities, and the abscissas and ordinates are variable quantities. To determine the values of these variable quantities, the doctrine of fluxions, invented by the illustrious Newton, when he was only twenty-three years of age, is perfectly adapted; and, by this doctrine, as it has been explained and illustrated by various authors, many difficulties, insurmountable by any other known method, are solved with expedition, ease, and elegance. We shall just give our reader an insight into the science, by shewing, in a few of the simplest cases, which the young algebraist will readily understand, how fluxions are adapted for determining the maxima and minima of bodies—for drawing tangents to curves, &c. by which he will readily understand in what way the science may be made to extend to the investigation of the most abstruse and difficult problems in the various branches of mathematics and natural philosophy.

Constant quantities are usually denoted by the early letters of the alphabet, as a, b, c, &c. and those that are *variable*, by the latter letters, as u, w, x, y, and z. The diameter of a given circle may be represented by a, and the sine, tangent, &c. of an arc or angle of it, by x.

The fluxion of a quantity represented by a single letter, is usually expressed by the same letter with a dot over it; thus the fluxion of x is represented by $\dot{x}$, of y by $\dot{y}$, of z by $\dot{z}$, and so on.

The rules for finding the fluxions of any flowing quantities are as follow, $\dot{x}$ being the fluxion of x.

1. To find the fluxion of a given fluent, in which there is but one variable quantity. Rule.—Mark the letter that represents the variable quantity with a dot over it, and you have the fluxion required. Thus the fluxion of ax is $a\dot{x}$. For, if we suppose the variable rectangle AS, fig. 2, to be generated by the given line RS, setting out from the situation

AB, and moving along with a parallel motion between the parallel and indefinite lines BG and AF, it is evident that the velocity with which the rectangle flows, is equal to the generating line RS multiplied into velocity with which the point R moves along the line AF; that is, the fluxion of the rectangle AS is equal to the invariable line RS, multiplied into the fluxion of the variable quantity AR. Therefore, if AB, or its equal RS, be denoted by a, and AR, or BS$=x$, then the fluxion of the rectangle $a\,x$, will be equal $a\times\dot{x}=a\,\dot{x}$.

2. To find the fluxion of the product of two or more flowing quantities multiplied into each other. Rule.—Multiply the fluxion of each quantity separately, by the other, or the product of the rest of the quantities; and the sum of these products will be the fluxion required. Thus the fluxion of $x\,y=\dot{x}\,y+x\,\dot{y}$; of $x\,y\,z=\dot{x}\,y\,z+x\,\dot{y}\,z+x\,y\,\dot{z}$, &c. The reason of this and the following rules, is given in all the introductory books to the science, to several of which we shall presently direct the attention of the reader.

3. To find the fluxion of a fraction. Rule.—Multiply the denominator into the fluxion of the numerator; from the product of which, subtract the numerator multiplied into the fluxion of the denominator; then divide the remainder by the square of the denominator, and the result is the fluxion of the fraction required. Thus the fluxion of $\frac{x}{y}=\frac{\dot{x}\,y-x\,\dot{y}}{y^2}$; and the fluxion of $\frac{x^2}{y^3}=\frac{2\,x\,\dot{x}\,y^3-3\,x^2\,y^2\,\dot{y}}{y^6}=\frac{2\,x\,\dot{x}\,y-3\,x^2\,\dot{y}}{y^4}$.

The following examples will shew the application of fluxions to the solution of problems de maximis et minimis, and to the drawing tangents to curves.

Ex. 1. To divide a given right line A B in two such parts, A C and B C, that the rectangle of their parts may be the greatest possible.

Suppose the whole line A B $=a$
———- the variable part equal x
then the other part will be $a-x$

of course the rectangle required will be $\overline{a-x}\times x = ax - x^2$, of which the fluxion is $a\dot{x} - 2x\dot{x}$ which being put equal to o; we have $a\dot{x} = 2x\dot{x}$ or $a = 2x$ and $x = \frac{a}{2}$. Therefore the rectangle will be the greatest possible, when the line is equally divided.

2. To determine the greatest rectangle that can be inscribed in a given triangle. See fig. 4.

Put the Base AC of the given Triangle $= b$, and its Altitude BD $= a$; and let the Altitude (BS) of the inscribed Rectangle *mc* (considered as variable) be denoted by x: Then, because of the parallel Lines AC, and *ac*, it will be as BD (a): AC (b):: DS $(a-x)$: $\frac{ba-bx}{a} = ac$: Whence the Area of the Rectangle, or $ac \times$ BS will be $= \frac{bax-bx^2}{a}$: Whose Fluxion $\frac{ba\dot{x}-2bx\dot{x}}{a}$ being put $=$ o, we shall get $x = \frac{1}{2}a$. Whence the greatest inscribed Rectangle is that whose Altitude is just half the Altitude of the Triangle.

A tangent is a right line which coincides with a curve in a point, and there shews its direction, that is, the inclination which it bears to the axis, or the angle it makes with the ordinate. Now, in general, what is requisite in order to draw a tangent to any point, is to find the right line, called the sub-tangent, or the distance of the point from the ordinate through which the tangent must pass.

Ex. I. To draw a Tangent to a Circle. See fig. 5.

Put the radius EA or ED $= a$, absciss AC $= x$, and ordinate CB $= y$; then, CD $= 2a - x$. Now, by 35 E. 3. $AC \times CD = CB^2$, that is, $2ax - x^2 = y^2$; and this equation put into Fluxions is $2a\dot{x} - 2x\dot{x} = 2y\dot{y}$; which, divided by $2a - 2x$, makes $\dot{x} = \frac{y\dot{y}}{a-x}$; which substituted for $\dot{x}$ in the general expression found by other means, for the Subtangent, *viz.* $\frac{x\dot{y}}{\dot{y}}$, makes the Subtangent $CT = \frac{y^2}{a-x}$ (which, by writing $2ax - x^2$ for its above value, *viz.* y^2, is) $= \frac{2ax - x^2}{a-x} = \frac{CB^2}{EC}$. Wherefore, if the distance signified by this expression be set off from the point C, in the diameter D A produced, we shall have the point T through which the Tangent to the point B must pass.

Construction. Through the point B describe the semicircle E B T: then will T be the point from which the Tangent to the point B is to be drawn. For, by 31 E. 3. the angle E B T will be right; and therefore, by 8 E. 6. the triangles E C B and B C T will be similar, and by 4 E. 6. $EC : CB :: BC : CT$; $\therefore CT = \frac{CB^2}{EC}$.

Ex. II. To draw a Tangent to a Parabola. See Fig. 6.

Suppose F to be the focus; and P R the parameter, which put $= a$; also, put the absciss $AC = x$, and ordinate $CB = y$. Now, by a well known property of the curve, $PR \times AC = CB^2$, that is, $ax = y^2$; the Fluxion of which equation is $a\dot{x} = 2y\dot{y}$; therefore, $\dot{x} = \frac{2y\dot{y}}{a}$; which substituted for $\dot{x}$, makes the general expression for the Subtangent $CT = \frac{2y^2}{a} =$ (by substituting ax for y^2 its value,) $\frac{2ax}{a} = 2x$. So that, the Subtangent CT is double the absciss A C; and consequently, A T is = A C.

Of the several works written on this subject, the following seem to require particular notice.

"The method of Fluxions and infinite Series, with its application to the Geometry of curve lines, by the inventor, Sir Isaac Newton, to which is subjoined, a perpetual Comment upon the whole work," &c. by John Colson. This will always be regarded as a standard work, but it is not exactly suited to young persons entering upon the subject.

Mr. John Rowe's "Introduction to the Doctrine of Fluxions," is divided into two parts, the first treats of the direct method of fluxions, and the second of the inverse method. This latter, which is unquestionably the most difficult part of the fluxionary calculus, viz. that of finding the fluent from the fluxion being given, is introduced with the doctrine of infinite series. The whole is written in so plain and perspicuous a manner, that the learner, who is previously well acquainted with the arithmetic of surds, need not be deterred from entering upon the study of Mr. Rowe's treatise. Of this the third edition was printed in 1767.

The same may be said of "The Principles of Fluxions," by the Rev. S. Vince, D. D. F. R. S., which is a neat introduction to this branch of science. The third edition of which was published in 1805.

A more elaborate and more difficult piece is entitled "The Doctrine and Application of Fluxions, &c., in two parts, by Thomas Simpson, F. R. S." But the principal work is Mr. Maclaurin's "Treatise of Fluxions," in two volumes, 4to. In this the subject is handled agreeably to the method of reasoning used by the ancient mathematicians, without having recourse to algebraic solutions. To his demonstrations of this doctrine he has added many valuable improvements of it, and has applied it to so many curious and useful inquiries, that the work has been denominated a store-house of mathematical learning, rather than a treatise on one branch of it. Throughout the whole there appears a masterly genius and uncommon address. The biographer of Mr. Maclaurin, speaking of him in connexion with his Treatise on Fluxions, says, "he had a quick, comprehensive view, taking in, at once, all the means of investigation, he could select the fittest for his purpose, and apply them with exquisite art and method. This is a faculty not to be acquired by exercise only; we ought rather to call it a species of that taste, the gift of nature, which in mathematics, as in other things, distinguishes excellence from mediocrity."

DOCTRINE OF CHANCES.

The doctrine of Chances being of great importance, when applied to the solution of questions in life-annuities, insurance, reversions, &c. it is necessary briefly to point out those works in which its principles are laid down and investigated.

This subject, no less useful than interesting and curious, does not appear to have engaged the attention of mathematicians in former times, so much as its importance may seem to have required. The writers upon it, in our own language, are comparatively few. To M. Huygens we are indebted for the first regular tract on this subject, which was in the Latin language, and entitled "De Ratiociniis in Ludo Aleæ;" this work, however, from the comparatively few problems which it contains, and the want of demonstration to some of them, cannot be regarded as an elementary treatise. To this succeeded a small anonymous tract entitled, "on the Laws of Chance," published in London in 1692, and a French publication entitled "L'Analyse des Jeux de Hazard," written by M. Monmort, and published in 1708. This author, following the mode of M. Huygens in the solution of his problems, M. de Moivre, who objected to it, published his work "On the Doctrine of Chances," which was first published in 1717, but which has been twice or thrice reprinted since. The edition of 1756, is, it is believed, the best. M. De Moivre proceeds from the most simple to the most complicated cases; so that, by the variety of his problems, as well as by the improvements and additions which he made in two subsequent editions, he has rendered his work the best and most copious that has ever been written on the subject. In the year 1740, Mr. Thomas Simpson published a very thin and small quarto, on "The Nature and Laws of Chance, illustrated with a great variety of Examples," which, like his other publications, is not only clear and concise, but contains some problems, the solutions of which had never before been communicated to the public. Mr. Dodson, in the year 1753, rendered the subject still more accessible to persons not far advanced in analytical studies, by publishing in the second volume of his "Mathematical Repository," a number of questions with their solutions, but chiefly with the view of applying them to the doctrine of annuities and survivorships. In addition to these, may be mentioned a small tract, "De Mensura Sortis," given by M. De Moivre, in his "Miscellanea Analytica," and some papers published at different times in the Transactions of the Learned Societies on the Continent, and those of the Royal Society of London. "Among which," says Mr. Morgan, in the article *Chances*, in the New Cyclopedia, "may be particularly mentioned an "Essay on the Method of calculating the exact probability of all conclusions founded on Induction," and a "Supplement" to that Essay; the one preserved from the papers of the late Rev. Mr. Bayes, and communicated with an appendix, by Dr. Price, to the Royal Society in the year 1762, and the other chiefly written by Dr. Price, and communicated in the following year. "These tracts contain the investigation of a problem, the converse of which had formerly exercised the ingenuity of M. Bernoulli, De Moivre, and Simpson. Indeed both the problem, and its converse, may be considered not only as the most difficult, but as the most important that can be proposed on the subject, having no less an object in view, than to shew what reason we have for believing that there are in the constitution of things, fixed laws, according to which events happen; and that therefore, the frame of the world must be the effect of the wisdom and power of an intelligent cause, and thus to confirm the argument, taken from final causes, for the existence of Deity."

Besides the above-named works on the Doctrine of Chances, which is of very great consequence in this country, where the valuation of an immense property, and the future provision of many thousands, entirely depend on the right knowledge of it, we may mention a treatise just published, entitled "The

Doctrine of Chances, or the Theory of Gaming made easy to every Person acquainted with common Arithmetic, so as to enable them to calculate the probabilities of events, in Lotteries, Cards, Horse Racing, Dice, &c. with tables on Chance never before published, by Wm. Rouse." The principles of the Doctrine of Chances cannot be altered—they are invariable; but Mr. Rouse may have made them more intelligible to the unlearned, among whom we presume gamblers are usually to be reckoned, who require a strong stimulus to engage their attention, but who have not sufficient energy to make study either the business or amusement of life. The tables, mentioned in the title, are intended to shew, at one view, the Chances for and against winning any assigned number of Games, at any kind of play, out of a given number, &c. How far this volume has a claim to the character of accuracy we know not, it being too recent a publication to admit of its having been read.

If the doctrine of Chances could be applied only to the principles of Gaming, it would be of comparative little value; but as upon that doctrine depends every thing relating to Annuities, to Survivorships, and to Reversions, we shall endeavour, in a few words, to state the connexion of these several subjects.

Chance is particularly used for the probability of an event, and is greater or less, according to the number of chances there are by which it may happen, compared with the number by which it may either happen or fail. Thus, if an event has three chances to happen, and two to fail, the probability of its happening may be estimated at $\frac{3}{5}$ths, and of its failing, $\frac{2}{5}$ths. Hence it appears, that if the probability of its happening and failing be added together, the sum is equal to unity. The expectation of obtaining any thing is estimated by the value of that thing, multiplied by the probability of obtaining it. The risk of losing any thing is estimated by the value of the thing multiplied by the probability of losing it. Applying this to *gaming*, we say, if from the expectations which the gamesters have upon the whole sum deposited, the particular sums they deposit, that is, their own stakes, be subtracted, there will remain the gain, if the difference is positive; or the loss, if the difference be negative. Again, if from the respective expectations which either gamester has upon the sum deposited by his adversary, the risk of losing what he himself deposits be subtracted, there will likewise remain his gain or loss.

ANNUITIES, INSURANCE, &c.

In the application of the subject to insurance and life-annuities, we say, if there is a certain number of chances by which the possession of a sum can be secured, and also a certain number of chances by which it may be lost, that sum may be insured for that part of it, which shall be to the whole, as the number of chances there is to lose it, is to the number of all the chances.

From the bills of mortality in different places, tables have been constructed, which shew how many persons, upon an average, out of a certain number born, are lost, or have died at the end of each year, to the extremity of life: from such tables the *probability* of the continuance of a life of any proposed age is known. Hence we have tables calculated, shewing the *Expectation* of human life at every age, according to the probabilities of life at every age; and from these tables, founded upon the doctrine of chances, the value of Annuities, and of the insurance of single and joint lives, &c. is ascertained.

The present value of a life-annuity is the sum that would be sufficient, allowing for the chances of life failing, to pay the annuity without loss: of course, if money bore no interest, the value of an annuity would be equal to the sum, to be yearly paid, multiplied by the number of years, equal to the expectation of life. But since money is capable of being improved at interest, the sum just mentioned, would be more than sufficient to pay the annuity; and it will be as much more than sufficient, according as the interest is greater. Thus it is found, that the expectation of a life of twenty, is equal to thirty three years and a half, therefore to purchase an annuity of £1 per annum, for such a life, a person must pay, if there were no interest on money, the sum of £33. 10s. but money improved at 5 per cent. interest, doubles itself in about fourteen years; and from this, and other circumstances which we cannot here enter into, the sum to be paid, will not be more than about £14. From the principles now described, methods are obtained for calculating the value of an annuity for a person of any given age—for the longest of two or more lives, &c. Or the value of a given sum payable at the decease of a person, whenever that shall happen, that is, the value of an assurance of any given sum on the whole duration of life, which is the principal object of several most respectable insurance offices in London. On the same principles as those already described, the value of reversions is found, and the sum necessary to be paid to insure property from the risk of fire, and loss by sea, &c. This may at first sight appear very strange, and on that account we shall transcribe the following paragraphs from an admirable critique, in the Edinburgh Review, on a work entitled "Essai Philosophique sur les Probabilites. Par. M. Le Compte Laplace." "The way in which probability is affected by the indefinite multiplication of events, is a remarkable part of this theory. If out of a system of events governed by chance (or by no perceivable law) you take a small number, you will find great irregularity, and nothing that looks like order, or obedience to a general rule. Increase the number of events, or take in a larger extent of the domain over which you suppose chance to preside, you will find the irregularities bear a much less proportion to the whole; they will in a certain degree compensate for one another; and something like order and regularity will begin to emerge. In proportion as the events are farther multiplied, this convergency will become more apparent; and in summing up the total amount, the events will appear adjusted to one another, by rules, from which hardly any deviation can be perceived.

"Thus, in considering the subject of life and death; if we

take a small extent of country, or a few people, a single parish for instance, nothing like a general rule will be discovered. The proportion of the deaths to the numbers alive, or to the numbers born; of those living at any age to those above or below that age,—all this will appear the most different in one year, compared with the next; or in one district compared with another. But subject to your examination the parish registers of a great country, or a populous city, and the facts will appear quite different. You will find the proportion of those that die annually out of a given number of inhabitants, fixed with great precision, as well as of those that are born, and that have reached to the different periods of life. In the first case, the irregularities bear a great proportion to the whole; in the second, they compensate for one another; and a rule emerges, from which the deviations on opposite sides appear almost equal.

"This is true not only of natural events, but of those that arise from the institutions of society, and the transactions of men with one another—Hence insurance against fire, and the dangers of the sea. Nothing is less subject to calculation, than the fate of a particular ship, or a particular house, though under given circumstances. But let a vast number of ships, in these circumstances, or of houses be included, and the chance of their perishing, to that of their being preserved, is matter of calculation founded on experience, and reduced to such certainty, that men daily stake their fortunes on the accuracy of the results.

"This is true, even where chance might be supposed to predominate the most; and where the causes that produce particular effects, are the most independent of one another.

"LAPLACE observes, that at Paris, in ordinary times, the number of letters returned to the Post Office, the persons to whom they were directed not being found, was nearly the same from one year to another. We have heard the same remark stated of the Dead Letter Office, as it is called in London.

" Such is the consequence of the multiplication of the events least under the controul of fixt causes: And the instances just given, are sufficient to illustrate the truth of the general proposition; which LAPLACE has thus stated.—

" The recurrences of events that depend on chance, approach to fixt ratios as the events become more numerous, in such a manner, that the probability of the mean results not differing from those ratios by any given quantity, may come nearer to certainty than the smallest limit that can be assigned."

One of the first treatises on the subject of interest and annuities, that requires to be mentioned, is Ward's " Clavis Usuræ," published in 1709, and which, on account of its scarcity, is published as the last tract in the fifth volume of the " Scriptores Logarithmici" of Mr. Baron Maseres, with an appendix by the Baron himself, who considers Ward's tract as the most complete treatise that has ever been published on the subject. We may farther observe, that in this fifth volume of the Scriptores Logarithmici, there are several other pieces on the same subject, by De Moivre, Robertson, Dr. Halley, and others.

Mr. Smart, in 1727, published some very valuable tables on interest and annuities, which have been in use from that time to the present, and which Mr. Francis Baily has inserted in a work of his, shortly to be noticed. The late learned and very excellent Dr. Price, besides some papers in the Transactions of the Royal Society, published two volumes, though at different times, entitled " Observations on Reversionary Payments—on schemes for providing annuities for widows, and for persons in old age—on the method of calculating the values of assurances on lives, with Essays on different subjects, on the Doctrine of Life Annuities, and Political Arithmetic, Tables," &c. &c. Although this cannot be deemed an elementary work, yet it contains a vast fund of valuable matter, connected with all those subjects which have their foundation on the Doctrine of Chances and Annuities. The tables are numerous, and methods of forming are clearly given.

"The doctrine of Annuities and Assurances on Lives and survivorships," was explained by Mr. William Morgan, in a 8vo volume, published in 1779. Besides these, Mr. Dodson, in his Mathematical Repository, Mr. Thomas Simpson, M. De Moivre, and Baron Maseres, have all treated on the subject; and it must be observed, that those who would enter deeply into it, should be well acquainted with algebra and fluxions.

Mr. Francis Baily, in 1809, published, as an introductory book, "The Doctrine of Interest and Annuities analytically explained," &c. The reasons which Mr. Baily assigns for the publication of his work, which is a good and useful performance, may be applied generally as a recommendation of the science itself to the attention of the mathematical student: "At this time," he says, "a more than ordinary degree of attention has been given to it, arising from the great variety and extent of property, which is affected by circumstances, involving the consideration of this subject. For, when we consider the numerous cases of daily occurrence, in which the question of interest is unavoidably concerned, both simple and compound; when we consider the great and extensive business which is constantly transacting, in the purchase and sale of annuities of various kinds, immediate and reversionary, temporary and perpetual, increased no doubt by the numerous offices which have sprung up within these few years, for that very purpose;—when we consider also the immense quantity of lands which are held on leases, for different terms of years, and which leases are continually required to be exchanged, sold, or renewed;—but above all, when we consider its application in regard to our finances, and the state of the National Debt, with the help it affords us in pointing out the easiest and most effectual method of alleviating our present incumbrances—the subject assuredly acquires a degree of importance which it never before aspired to."

Mr. Baily's work treats of the doctrine of Interest, Annuities, Reversions, and the Renewal of Leases, and of various subjects of Finance.

Mr. Baily, in the year 1810, published a much larger and more comprehensive work on this subject, to which, in 1813, he added an appendix, making together two volumes, 8vo. It is entitled "The doctrine of Life Annuities and Assurances, analytically investigated and practically explained," &c. Of this treatise, he says, it must be considered as a continuation of the other work, and will, he believes, contain all that is useful or interesting on the science, and he adds, that he has taken care to comprehend in it "such additional information as a more improved analysis, and more recent discoveries in the science have been able to afford." It contains the elementary principles of the Laws of Chance, with remarks on the probabilities of life—Methods for determining the value of annuities on single or joint lives; and on the longest of any number of lives—problems for the solution of cases of absolute and contingent Reversionary annuities—cases of annuities depending on survivorships, between two and three lives—a full explanation of the doctrine of Assurances, and other interesting matter.

We have, by the same author, a smaller work, entitled "Tables for the purchasing and renewing of leases, with rules for determining the value of the reversion of estates," &c. &c.

MATHEMATICS,

Continued.

Navigation—What the art comprises—History of—Ancient writers on, viz. Medina—Cortes—Frizius—Nunez—Coignet—Norman—Mercator—Wright—Napier—Norwood—Bond. Modern writers recommended—Mackay—Mendoza—Robertson; and Maskelyne. Mensuration—History and Practice of—Writers on—Hawney—Robertson—Hutton; and Bonnycastle. Surveying—writers—Leslie—Hutton—Crocker—Davis and others. Marine *Surveying*. Levelling, practice of. Dialling, practice of, and writers on.

THE word *Navigation* is derived from two Latin words, viz. *navis*, a *ship*, and *ago*, to manage, and the great end of the art of Navigation, is to instruct the mariner how to conduct a ship through the wide and pathless ocean, to any given country, by the safest and shortest way. This art comprises the method of giving to the vessel the desired direction, by means of the sails and a rudder, which has been denominated seamanship, as well as the mode of ascertaining the relative situation of the ship at any assigned time, and its future course. For the performance of this, much previous instruction is necessary; such, for instance, as will give a perfect knowledge of the figure of the earth, with the various real or imaginary lines upon it, so as to be able to ascertain the distance and situation of places, with respect to one another. The mariner must also know the use of the several instruments employed in measuring the ship's way, as the log and half-minute glass; also of the quadrant, to take the altitude of the sun and stars, the compass to represent the sensible horizon, and the azimuth compass, to take the azimuth or amplitude of the sun, in order to ascertain the variation of the needle. He must be conversant with maps and sea-charts, and should know the depths of water in particular places, the times of the ebbing and flowing of tides upon the coasts that he may have occasion to approach. These and other things will, perhaps, be best learnt by practice, but an able sailor should be well grounded in the elementary principles of mathematics, which will teach him the reason and foundation of his whole art.

The antiquity and general utility of the art of Navigation will not be disputed: its very early history it is impossible to ascertain, but it is known that the Phœnicians were skilful navigators, at a period when other nations had scarcely ventured from the shore. From Phœnicia it may be traced to Egypt and Greece, but the Carthaginians soon eclipsed the inhabitants of those countries in nautical knowledge and experience, and by this means acquired those vast resources that enabled them so long to withstand the Roman power. It was during the struggle between Carthage and Rome, that the first traces of the art may be discovered in Italy. The subsequent destruction of Carthage consigned navigation, and with it commerce, to the Romans: the latter was left to the exertions of the conquered provinces, and the former was chiefly cultivated to aid their favourite views of universal dominion, and upon the ruin of that empire, navigation shared the fate of literature and the other arts. When Attila destroyed Mantua, Verona, and other adjacent cities, such of the inhabitants as escaped the bloody slaughter, fled to the islands off their coast, where they took up their residence, and in process of time they founded Venice. Here navigation and commerce revived, and from hence they passed successively to Genoa, the Hans Towns, Portugal, Spain, England, and Holland.

Navigation was very imperfect till after the discovery of the mariner's compass, which was known about the close of the thirteenth century, after this the navigator launched boldly into the ocean, having a guide to direct his operations, and the means of returning to the place from which he set sail. At this time, however, the kindred sciences, geometry, trigonometry, and astronomy, which now constitute the groundwork of navigation, were not sufficiently cultivated to afford the assistance, which they have since been found calculated to impart. The impulse being given, the human genius soon saw in what way the mathematical sciences might be applied to the art of navigation, this, with the invention of suitable instruments, enabled the navigator to proceed, not only to the most remote places on the globe, but at length to circumnavigate the earth.

There are various methods of sailing described in books, of which the most ancient is denominated *plane* sailing: this is defined to be the art of navigating a ship upon principles deduced from the supposition that the earth is an extended plane, and is, in fact, no more than the application of Plane Trigonometry to the solution of the several variations, or cases, in which the hypothenuse is always the rhomb line, that the ship sails upon. This method was soon found to be inaccurate.

The mariner's compass was not applied to the art of navigation till about the year 1420, and fifty years afterwards tables of the sun's declination were calculated for the use of sailors, and the astrolabe was then used for taking observations at sea. After this the use of the cross-staff was introduced among sailors, for observing the distance between the moon and any given star, in order thence to determine the longitude. At this time navigation was very imperfect, on account of the inaccuracies of the plane chart, which must have greatly misled the mariner, especially in voyages far distant from the equator. About the year 1545 two Spanish treatises were published on the subject, one by Pedro de Medina, the other by Martin Cortes, the latter contained a complete system of the art as far as it was then known. About the same time proposals were made for finding the longitude by observations of the moon. Previously to this, in 1530, Gemma Frisins advised the keeping of time, by means of small clocks or watches, then, as he says, newly invented. This author contrived a new sort of cross-staff, and an instrument called the nautical quadrant.

In 1537, Pedro Nunez, or Nonius, published a book in the Portuguese language, in which he exposes the errors of the plane chart, and gives the solution of many curious astronomical problems; among which is that for determining the latitude from two observations of the sun's altitude, an intermediate azimuth being given. In 1577, Mr. William Bourne published a treatise, in which he advises, in sailing towards the high latitudes, to keep the reckoning by the globe, as in those cases the plane chart is most erroneous: he also advises to keep an account of the observations, as useful for finding the place of a ship, which advice was prosecuted at large, by Simon Stevinus, in a treatise, published at Leyden in 1599, the substance of which was printed in the same year at London, in English, by Mr. Edward Wright, entitled "The Haven-fiuding Art." In this tract is described likewise the way by which our sailors estimate the rate of a ship in her course, by an instrument called the *log*, so named from the piece of wood or log that floats in the water, while the time is reckoned, during which the line that is fastened to it is running out. The author of this contrivance is not known, nor was it noticed till 1607, in an East-Indian voyage, published by Purchas, and from this time it became famous, and has been noticed by almost all succeeding writers in navigation.

In 1581, Michael Coignet, a native of Antwerp, published a treatise, in which he shewed, that as the rhombs are spirals, making endless revolutions about the poles, numerous errors must arise from their being represented by straight lines on sea-charts. Among other things he described the cross-staff, with three transverse pieces, as it is at present made, which was then in common use on ship-board. He likewise gave an account of some instruments of his own invention, among which was the nocturnal.

About this period Mr. Robert Norman discovered the dipping needle, and he made considerable improvements in the construction of compasses themselves. To this work of Norman's is always prefixed a discourse on the variation of the magnetic needle, by Mr. William Borrough, in which he shews how to determine the variation in many different ways.

Globes of an improved kind, of a much larger size than those formerly used, were constructed, and many improvements were made in other instruments, still the plane chart was continued to be followed, though its errors were frequently complained of. The methods of removing these was pointed out by Gerard Mercator, who proposed to represent the parallels of latitude and longitude by parallel straight lines, but gradually to augment the number of the former as they approached the pole. Thus the rhombs, which otherwise ought to have been curves, were now extended into straight lines, and accordingly a straight line drawn between any two places marked upon the chart, would make an angle with the meridians, expressing the rhomb leading from one to the other. In 1569, Mercator published an universal map, constructed in this manner, but it does not appear that he was acquainted with the principles on which it was founded, and it seems generally agreed, that the true principles, on which the construction of what is still denominated Mercator's chart depends, were first discovered by our countryman, Mr. Edward Wright,* who published, about the year 1600, his famous treatise, entitled "The Correction of certain Errors in Navigation," &c. in which he explained very fully the reason of extending the length of the parallels of latitude, and the uses of the chart thus improved, to the purposes of navigation. In this second edition, printed in 1610, he proposed a method for determining the magnitude of the earth, and suggested the idea of making our measures depend upon the length of a degree on the earth's surface, and not upon the uncertain length of three barley-corns. He also gave a table of latitudes for dividing the meridian into minutes, having, before this time, been divided into every tenth minute only. Among many other improvements, he contrived an amendment in the tables of the declination and places of the sun and stars, from his own observations, made with a six-feet instrument in the years 1594, 5, 6, and 7. The improvements of Mr. Wright soon became known abroad, and a treatise, entitled "Hypomnemata Mathematica," was published by Simon Stevinus, for the use of Prince Maurice. In that part relating to navigation, the author having treated of sailing on a great circle, and shewn how to draw the rhombs on a globe, mechanically, inserts Mr. Wright's tables of latitudes and rhombs, in order to describe these lines with more accuracy, pretending even to have discovered an error in Mr. Wright's table, which, however, the author shewed arose from the slovenly manner of Stevinus's mode of calculation.

About this period, Lord Napier published an account of his logarithms, from which Mr. Edmund Gunter constructed a table of logarithmic sines and tangents to every minute of the quadrant, which he published in 1620. In this work, he applied to the art of navigation, and other branches of mathematies, his ruler, known by the name of Gunter's scale. He

* See Robertson's Elements of Navigation.

improved the sector for the same purposes, and shewed how to take a back observation by the cross-staff; he described likewise another instrument of his own invention, called the cross-bow, for taking the altitudes of the sun and stars. Gunter's rule was projected into a circular arch by Mr. Oughtred, in 1633, who explained its uses in a tract, entitled "The Circles of Proportion." It has simee been made in the form of a sliding ruler.

Napier's tables were first applied to the different cases of sailing, by Mr. Thomas Addison, in a work entitled "Arithmetical Navigation," printed in 1625. Mr. Henry Gellibrand published, in 1635, his treatise, entitled "A Discourse mathematical, on the variation of the Magnetical Needle," in which he pointed out his own discovery of the changes of the variation.

In the year 1635, Mr. Richard Norwood put into execution the method recommended by Wright, for measuring the dimensions of the earth, and found a degree on the great circle of the earth to contain 367,196 English feet, an account of which he published in his treatise, entitled "The Seaman's Practice," published in 1637; in this tract, he points out the uses to be made of the fact, in correcting the errors committed in the division of the log-line; describes his own method of setting down, and perfecting a sea-reckoning, by using a traverse table; and how to rectify the course, by considering the variation of the compass; and how to discover currents, and to make a proper allowance on their account.

About the year 1645, Mr. Bond published, in Norwood's Epitome, an improvement on Wright's method, by a property in his Meridian line, by which its divisions were more scientifically assigned than by the author himself, which he afterwards fully explained in the third edition of Gunter's works, printed in 1653.

After the true principles of the art had been settled by the foregoing writers, the authors on navigation became so numerous, that it would not at all agree with the limits of our work, to attempt an enumeration of them. Navigation has, however, been much indebted to Dr. Halley, who perfected Wright's chart; to Mr. Henry Briggs, who improved the logarithms invented by Napier; to Mr. Hadley, for the invention of the quadrant that bears his name; and to the late Dr. Maskelyne, who was more than forty years Astronomer Royal, for devising and establishing, under the Commissioners of Longitude, the Nautical Almanac. Among the later discoveries in this branch of practical science, that of finding the longitude by lunar observations, and by time-keepers, is the chief. Dr. Maskelyne put the first in practice, and the time-keepers constructed by Mr. Harrison, were found to answer so well, that he obtained the parliamentary reward.

Among the modern authors on navigation, we must mention Dr. Andrew Mackay's "Theory and Practice of finding the Longitude at Sea and Land," in two volumes; this, with his other works, particularly his "Complete Navigator," and "Collection of Mathematical Tables," form, it is said, the most correct and practical system of navigation and nautical science hitherto published in this country. These, then, with the "Tables for Navigation and Nautical Astronomy," by Jos. de Mendoza; Mr. John Robertson's "Elements of Navigation," in two vols. 8vo; the "Nautical Almanac," and the Tables requisite to be used with it, and the "British Mariner's Guide," may be considered as a complete library for a young navigator. Among practical men, Hamilton Moore's "New Practical Navigator," has long been very popular, and is still much used. The sixteenth edition was published in 1804.

MENSURATION.

Mensuration is the art of finding the dimensions and contents of bodies, by means of others of the same kind; thus the length of bodies, or distances, is found by lines, as yards, feet, inches, &c.; surfaces by squares, as square inches, feet, or yards; solids by cubes, as cubic inches, cubic feet,

&c. The invention of this art cannot be traced to any particular person; it has usually been given to the Egyptians, by whom it was probably invented for the purpose of ascertaining the magnitude and relative situation of their lands, after the waters of the Nile had subsided. Euclid's Elements, it has been thought, were originally directed to this object; and many of the beautiful and elegant geometrical propositions in that work, it is almost certain, arose out of the simple investigations directed solely to the theory and practical application of mensuration.

Notwithstanding the perfection to which Euclid attained in Geometry, the theory of Mensuration was not, in his time, advanced beyond what related to right-lined figures, which might be reduced to that of measuring a triangle; for since all right-lined figures may be divided into a number of triangles, it was necessary only to know how to measure these, in order to find the surface of any other figure whatever, which was bounded by right lines. After Euclid, Archimedes took up the theory of mensuration, and carried it to a great extent. He first found the method of ascertaining the area of a curvilinear space, unless the *Lunules* of Hippocrates are excepted, which, however, required no other aid than that contained in the Elements of Euclid. Archimedes found that the area of a parabola was two-thirds of its circumscribing rectangle. He also determined the ratio of spheres, spheroids, &c. to their circumscribing cylinders, and left behind him an attempt at the quadrature of the circle. He investigated, and determined to a considerable degree of accuracy, the approximate ratio between the circumference and diameter of a circle. He moreover determined the relation between the circle and ellipse, as well as that of their similar parts, besides which, he left a treatise on the Spiral.

Little more of importance was done to advance the science of mensuration, till the time of Cavelleri, an Italian mathematician, who flourished in the seventeenth century. Before his time, the regular figures circumscribed about the circle, as well as those inscribed in it, were always considered as being limited, both as to the number of sides, and the length of each. He was the person that introduced the idea of a circle being a polygon of an infinite number of sides, each of which was, of course, indefinitely small; he also considered solids as made up of an infinite number of sections indefinitely thin. This was the foundation of the doctrine of *indivisibles*, which was very general in its application to a variety of difficult problems, and which was embraced by many eminent mathematicians, such as Huygens, Wallis, and James Gregory. It was, however, disapproved by other men, celebrated also for great talents and deep geometrical learning, and particularly by Sir Isaac Newton, who, among his numerous and brilliant discoveries, produced his method of fluxions, the excellency and generality of which, almost instantly superseded that of indivisibles. Hopes were now revived of squaring the circle, and the quadrature was attempted with great eagerness; but, after many ineffectual efforts, it was abandoned; and mathematicians began to content themselves with finding, by means of fluxions, the most convenient series for approximating towards the true length of this and other curves, and the theory of mensuration began to make a rapid progress towards perfection. Many of the rules were published in the Trausaetions of Learned Societies, or in separate and detached works, till, at length, Dr. Hutton formed them into a complete work, entitled "A Treatise on Mensuration, in which the several rules are all demonstrated." Before this time, Hawney's "Complete Measurer," and a treatise on the subject by Mr. Robertson, were the only works that could be referred to, either by the artizan or mathematician. Since Dr. Hutton's publication, which was first given to the world in 4to, and has since been printed in 8vo, Mr. Bonnycastle has published an excellent little work on this subject, entitled "An Introduction to Mensuration and Practical Geometry, with Notes, containing the reason of every rule concisely and clearly demonstrated." The author has very judiciously given in the text the rules in words at length, with examples to exercise them; the remarks and demonstrations are confined to the notes, and may be consulted or not, as shall be thought necessary; but, to those who would wish to be acquainted with the grounds and rationale of the operations which they perform, the demonstrations will be found extremely useful; and Mr. Bonnycastle has done all in his power to make them easy. He has, he says, through the whole, "endeavoured to consult the wants of the learner, more than those of the man of science," and hence his work may be strongly recommended to those who would study the subject from the beginning.

SURVEYING.

THE art of surveying consists in determining the boundaries of an extended surface. When applied to the measuring of land, it comprises the three following parts, viz. taking the dimensions of the given tract of land; the delineating or laying down the same in a map or draught; and finding the superficial content or area of the same. The first of these is what is properly called surveying; the second is called plotting or protracting, or mapping; and the third, casting up or computing the contents.

Surveying, when performed in the completest manner, says Mr. Professor Leslie, "ascertains the positions of all the prominent objects within the scope of observation, measures their mutual distances and relative heights, and consequently defines the various contours which mark the surface. But the land-surveyor seldom aims at such minute and scrupulous accuracy; his main object is, to trace expeditiously the chief boundaries, and to compute the superficial contents of each field. In hilly grounds, however, it is not the absolute surface that is measured, but the diminished quantity that would result, had the whole been reduced to a horizontal plane. This distinction is founded on the obvious principle, that, since plants shoot up vertically, the vegetable produce of a swelling eminence, can never exceed what would have grown from its levelled base. All the sloping distances, therefore, are reduced invariably to their horizontal lengths, before the calculation is begun."

The instruments usually employed in surveying, are the chain, the plain-table, the cross, and the theodolite. The English chain is twenty-two yards in length, that is, the tenth part of a furlong, or the eightieth part of a mile. The chain is divided into a hundred links, each 7.92 inches in length. An acre contains ten square chains, or 100,000 links.

When land is surveyed by means of the chain simply, the several fields are divided into large triangles, of which the sides are measured by the chain; and if the exterior boundary happens to be irregular, the perpendicular distance or offset is taken at each bending. The surface of all the triangles is then computed by the elements of plane geometry, and the exterior border of the polygon is considered as a collection of trapezoids, which are measured by multiplying the mean of each pair of offsets or perpendiculars, into their base or intermediate distance. In this method, the triangles should be chosen as nearly equilateral as possible; for, if they are very oblique, small errors in the lengths of their sides will occasion very large ones in the estimate of the surface.

The usual mode of surveying a large estate is, to measure round it with the chain, and observe the angles at each turn by means of the theodolite; but the observations must be taken with great care. If the boundaries of the estate be tolerably regular, it may be considered as a polygon, of which the angles, being necessarily very oblique, are apt, unless much attention be exercised, to affect the accuracy of the results. The best method of surveying is, undoubtedly, to cover the ground with a series of connected triangles, planting the theodolite at each angular point, and computing from some base of considerable extent, which has been selected and measured with as much precision as the nature of the case will admit; for angles can be measured more accurately than lines; and hence it has been recommended, that surveyors should generally employ theodolites of a good construction, and trust as little as possible to the aid of the chain.

In surveying, for sale or other purposes, large tracts of land in rude and uncultivated countries, the contents are usually estimated by the square mile, which includes six hundred and forty acres: thus in the back settlements of North America, the lands are divided and allotted merely by running lines north and south, and intersecting them by perpendiculars at each interval of a mile.

We may farther observe, that where any degree of nicety is required, as is the case in surveying estates of value, the operator will have frequent occasion for calculation, and therefore it is necessary that he should be familiar with the four first rules of arithmetic, and the rule of proportion, as well in fractions and decimals as in whole numbers; he should be conversant with the nature and practice of logarithms; and if he is acquainted with the elementary parts of algebra, he will find the advantage of it. As he will have to investigate and measure lines and angles, and to describe them on paper, he should well understand and be quick in the application of the principles of geometry and plane trigonometry.

Dr. Hutton's mensuration will be found to contain an outline of the theory and practice of the art of Surveying. There are several other very respectable treatises on the subject, by Leadbeater, Wilson, and Stephenson: but the two works with which we are best acquainted, is one by Mr. Abraham Crocker, in which will be found several improvements in the art; and "A Complete Treatise on Land-Surveying by the Chain, Cross, and Offset-staffs only. By William Davis." This treatise is divided into three parts: (1.) It gives an outline of Practical Geometry, at least such parts of it as are requisite for Surveying; and Plane Trigonometry, with its application to measuring heights and distances. (2.) It goes through the whole practice of Surveying by the different methods; and (3.) it points out the practical method of obtaining the contents of Hay-ricks, Pits, Timber, and all kinds of Artificers' works: likewise the method of levelling, conveying water from one place to another, and of draining and flooding land.

Another, but very different branch of this art is denominated *Maritime Surveying*, which determines the positions of the remarkable headlands, and other conspicuous objects that present themselves along the coast, or its immediate neighbourhood. It likewise ascertains the situations of the various inlets, rocks, shallows, and soundings, which occur in approaching the shore. The method of performing this, given by Mr. Professor Leslie, is as follows: "To survey a new or inaccessible coast, two boats are moored at a proper interval, which is carefully measured on the surface of the water; and from each boat the bearings of all the prominent points of land are taken by means of an azimuth compass; or the angles subtended by these points and the other boat, are measured by a Hadley's sextant. Having now on paper drawn the base to any scale, straight lines radiating from each end at the observed angles, will, by their intersections, give the positions of the several points from which the coast may be sketched.—But a chart is more accurately constructed, by combining a survey made on land, with observations taken on the water. A smooth level piece of ground is chosen, on which a base of considerable length is measured out, and station staves * are fixed at its extremities. If no such place can be found, the mutual distance and position of two points conveniently situate for planting the staves, though divided by a broken surface, are determined from one or more triangles, which connect with a shorter and temporary base assumed near the beach. A boat then explores the offing; and at every rock, shallow, or remarkable sounding, the bearings of the station staves are noticed. These observations furnish so many triangles, from

* These staves will be described in the next article, *levelling*.

which the situation of the several points are easily ascertained. —When a correct map of the coast can be procured, the labour of executing a maritime survey is materially shortened. From each notable point of the surface of the water, the bearings of two known objects on the land are taken, or the intermediate angles subtended by three such objects are observed. To facilitate the last construction, an instrument called the *Station-Pointer* has been invented, consisting of three brass rulers, which open and may be set at the given angles."

LEVELLING.

LEVELLING is the art of finding a line parallel to the horizon at one or more stations, to determine the height or depth of one place with respect to another, for the purposes of laying out grounds, draining morasses, conducting water, &c. Two or more places are on a true level when they are equally distant from the centre of the earth. Of course one place is higher than another, or out of the level with it, when it is farther from the centre of the earth; and a line equally distant from that centre, in all its points, is called the true level. Hence, since the earth is spherical, that line must be a curve, and make a part of the earth's circumference, or at least one that is parallel, or concentrical to it.

The practice of levelling therefore consists: 1. In finding and marking two or more points that shall be in the circumference of a circle, whose centre, and that of the earth, shall coincide; and 2. In comparing the points thus found with other points, to ascertain the difference in their distances from the earth's centre.

With respect to the theory of levelling, the following observations may be set down: A plumb line, hanging freely in the air, points directly towards the centre of the earth; and a line drawn at right lines, crossing the direction of the plumb-line, and touching the earth's surface, is a true level only in that particular spot; but if this line, which crosses the plumb, be continued for any considerable distance, it will rise above the earth's surface; and the apparent level will be above the true one, because the earth is spherical, and this rising will be as the square of the distance to which the said right line is produced, that is, as much as it is raised above the earth's surface at one mile's distance, it will rise four times as much at the distance of two miles, nine times at the distance of three miles, and so on. This circumstance is, as we have already observed, owing to the globular figure of the earth, and the rise is the difference between the true and apparent levels, the real curve of the earth being the true level, and the tangent to it, the apparent level. It appears that the less distance we take between any two stations, the truer will be the operations in levelling; and as soon as the difference between the true and apparent levels becomes perceptible, it is necessary to make an allowance for it, even if the distance between two stations does not exceed a few chains in length.

Levelling may be performed very expeditiously by the assistance of a large theodolite, capable of measuring with precision the vertical angle subtended by a remote object; the distance being known or calculated, and allowance made for the effect of the earth's convexity, and the influence of refraction. But the better method is to employ a *spirit-level*, accompanied by a pair of square staves, each of which is composed of two parts that slide out into a rod of ten feet in length, every foot being divided centesimally. A vane slides up and down upon each set of these staves, which, by brass springs, will stand at any given height. These vanes are about ten inches long, and four broad: the breadth is first divided into three equal parts, the two extremes painted white, the middle space divided again into three equal parts, which are less; the middle one of them is also painted white, and the two other parts black; and thus they are suited to all common distances. These vanes have each a brass wire across a small square hole in the centre, which serves to point out the height correctly, by coinciding with the horizontal wire of the telescope of the level.

Levelling is distinguished into two kinds, the simple and the compound; the former, which rarely admits of application, assigns the difference of altitude by a single observation; but the latter discovers it by means of a series of observations carried along an irregular surface, the aggregate of the several descents being deducted from that of the ascents. The staves are therefore placed successively along the line of survey, at proper intervals, according to the nature of the ground, and not exceeding three or four hundred yards, the levelling instrument being always planted nearly in the middle between them, and directed backwards to the first staff, and then forwards to the second. The difference between the heights intercepted by the back and the fore observation, must evidently give at each station the quantity of ascent or descent; and the error occasioned by the curvature of the globe may, in very short distances be overlooked, as it will not amount at each station to the hundredth part of a foot. The final result of a series of operations, or the differences of altitude between the extreme stations, is discovered by taking the measures of the back and fore observations collectively, and the excess of the latter above the former, indicates the entire quantity of descent.

The following observations will render the whole subject easy and clear to any comprehension.

To find the distance between the apparent and true level at the distance of a mile.—In the right-angled triangle A B C, fig. 7, the side A C, the semi-diameter of the earth, is given, suppose 3,982 miles, and the side A B = 1 mile; to find the hypothenuse C B.

$$CA^2 = 15856324$$

$$AB^2 = \qquad\qquad 1$$

$$CA^2 + AB^2 = 15856325 = CB^2$$

$$\text{And } \sqrt{15856325} = 3982.0001255 = CB.$$

Consequently the apparent level at the distance of one mile from the observer's station is higher than the true level by $EB = CB - CE = .000125$ of a mile $=8$ inches nearly.

The same thing may be done another way. By Eucl. III. 36. $\overline{2\,EC + EB} \times EB = AB^2$; consequently, $2\,EC + EB : AB :: AB :: EB$. But EB in the first term is so small in comparison of EC, that it may be neglected, therefore it will be $2\,EC : AB :: AB : EB$, and $EB = \frac{AB^2}{2EC} = \frac{AE^2}{2EC}$ nearly; that is, the difference between the true and apparent level is equal to the square of the distance between the places, divided by the diameter of the earth; and since the diameter of the earth is a given quantity, it is always proportional to the square of the distance.

The diameter of the earth $=7964$ miles, if AE be equal 1 mile as before, then the difference of levels will be $\frac{AE^2}{2EE}$ $= \frac{1^2}{7964} = 8$ inches nearly. If $AE = 2$ miles, then the difference of levels will be $\frac{2^2}{7964} = \frac{4}{7964} = 32$ inches, &c.

Hence, proportioning the excesses in altitude according to the squares of the distances, the following Table is obtained, shewing the height of the apparent, above the true level, for every 100 yards of distance on the one side, and for each mile on the other.

TABLE I.

Dist. or A E.	Diff. of Level, or E B.	Dist. or A E.	Diff. of Level, or E B.		Dist. or A E.	Diff. of Level, or E B.		Dist. or A E.	Diff. of Level, or E B.	
Yards.	Inches.	Miles.	Feet.	In.	Miles.	Feet.	In.	Miles.	Feet.	In.
100	0.026	½	0	2	4	10	7	10	66	4
200	0.103	1	0	8	6	23	11	12	97	7
1000	2.571	2	2	8	8	42	6	14	130	1

As, however, levelling is usually performed by measures consisting of *chains* instead of yards, the following Table is calculated, shewing the difference of a true and apparent level, in distances of from 5 to 100 chains.

TABLE II.

Dist. in chains.	Diff. lev. sub. in.	Dist. in chains.	Diff. lev. sub. in.	Dist. in chains.	Diff. lev. sub. in.	Dist. in chains.	Diff. lev. sub. in.
5	0.03	30	1.12	55	3.78	80	8.00
10	0.12	35	1.53	60	4.50	85	9.03
15	0.28	40	2.00	65	5.31	90	10.12
20	0.50	45	2.53	70	6.12	95	11.28
25	0.78	50	3.12	75	7.03	100	12.50

Example. It is required to find if water can be brought from a spring on the side of a hill at R, fig. 8, to the house S, by means of pipes laid under ground.

Fix the theodolite *x* at any convenient distance from the spring, suppose five chains, then enter on a paper, the difference between the true and apparent level from the table No. II, 0.03 inches: let an assistant place a staff at *a*, the spring, and another assistant, a staff at *b* towards S: the spirit level is to be directed to *a*, and the assistant there is to place the vane so as, when the staff is held perpendicularly, the hair in the telescope may cut the middle of the vane, suppose at 6.5 inches, which is to be entered in the paper, under the back-sights: let the other assistant now take the fore-sight at the staff *b*, which suppose to be 3 feet, 6.4 inches, which is to be entered under the fore-sights: then take the measure of the distance of the instrument to the staff *b*, suppose 15 chains, which enter in column *Dist.* and in the next column against it, is the difference between the true and apparent level taken from the table, or 0.28 inches. Measure next to the second station suppose 10 chains, which enter, and against it write the difference between the true and apparent level 0.12; take the back-sight to the staff *b*, viz. 1 foot, 2.7 inches, which is to be entered as before, then take the fore-sight to the staff c, and so on, whatever be the number of stations. When the observation is carried to S, and the level finished, the columns in the paper, or field-book, are to be added up; and from the sum of the heights, under the back-sights, take the sum of the differences of the level under the same, the remainder will be the correct sum of the heights of the vane: the same is to be done under the fore-sights, and the difference of these corrected heights gives the difference of the true level; and the sum of the distances under both distances will be the whole distance from R to S, thus:

The first Assistant's Notes, or Back-Sights.					The second Assistant's Notes, or Fore-Sights.				
Station.	Height V. Feet.	In.	Dist. in chains.	Diff. lev. inches.	Station.	Height V. Feet.	In.	Dist. in chains.	Diff. lev. inches.
1	0	6.5	5	0.03	1	3	6.4	15	0.28
2	1	2.7	10	0.12	2	2	6.9	10	0.12
3	2	0.8	15	0.28	3	4	6.5	13	0.12
	3	10.00	30	0.43		10	7.8	38	0.52
	0	0.43				3	9.57	30	
	3	9.57				6	8.23	68	

Here it is evident, that the sum of the heights of the vanes in the fore-sights exceeds those of the back-sights, by rather more than 6 feet 8 inches, and so much is S below the true level of R, and the whole distance from R to S being 68 chains, water may be readily brought from the spring on the hill, to the house in the valley.

The table, No. I, will answer several useful purposes, as follow,

1. To find the height of the apparent level above the true, at any distance. If the given distance be contained in the table, the correction of level is found on the same line with it: thus at the distance of 1000 yards, the correction is 2.57, or somewhat more than 2½ inches; but at the distance of 10 miles, it is 66 feet 4 inches. If the exact distance be not found in the table, multiply the square of the distance in yards by 2.57, and divide by $\overline{1000}|^2$, or cut off six places on the right hand for decimals: the rest are inches; or multiply the square of the distance in miles by 66.4, and divide by $10^2=100$.

2. To find the extent of the visible horizon, or how far can be seen from any given height on a horizontal plane at sea, as on the frozen ocean. Suppose the eye of an observer be at the height of 6 feet above the surface of the earth, he will see 3 miles every way. Hence it is plain, that a man thus situated, will be able to see another person of the same height at the distance of 6 miles. If the eye be situated on a ship's mast 130 feet high, it will see an extent of 14 miles every way. If a light house be 130 feet above the level of the sea, it will be visible to an eye on the surface at the distance of 14 miles; but if the observer mount the mast 97 feet, then the distance is increased 12 miles, consequently the light-house will be visible at 26 miles distant.

3. Suppose a spring be on one side of a hill, and a house on an opposite hill, with a valley between them: and that the spring seen from the house appears by a levelling instrument to be on a level with the foundation of the house, which is at a mile distance from it: then is the spring 8 inches above the true level of the house; and this difference would be barely sufficient for the water to be brought in pipes from the

spring to the house, the pipes being laid all the way in the ground.

4. If the height or distance exceed the limits of the table: then if the *distance* be given, divide it by some aliquot part till the quotient come within the distances in the table, and take out the height answering to the quotient, and multiply it by the square of the divisor for the height required. So if the top of a hill be seen at 40 miles distance, then $\frac{40}{4} = 10$, to which $66\frac{1}{3}$ answers in the table: now $66\frac{1}{3} \times 4^2$, or $66\frac{1}{3} \times 16$, gives $1061\frac{1}{3}$ feet for the height of the hill.

When the *height* is given, divide it by one of these square numbers, 4, 9, 16, 25, 36, &c. till the quotient come within the limits of the table, and multiply the quotient by the square root of the divisor, that is, by 2, 3, 4, 5, 6, &c. for the distance sought. Thus when the top of Teneriffe, said to be 15840 feet high, just comes into view at sea, divide 15840 by 225, or the square of 15, and the quotient is about 70 feet, to which $10\frac{2}{7}$ miles will answer: and $10\frac{2}{7} \times 15 = 154\frac{2}{7}$ miles for the distance of the mountain from the place of observation.

DIALLING.

DIALLING is the art of drawing dials on the surface of any given body, whether plane or curved: it is founded on the apparent motions of the heavenly bodies, or rather on the real diurnal motion of the earth.

A dial is a plane, upon which lines are described in such a manner, that the shadow of a wire, or of the upper edge of a plate, called a *stile*, or *gnomon*, erected perpendicularly on the plane of the dial, may shew the time of the day.

The universal principle on which dialling depends, is this: if the whole earth *a P c p*, fig. 9, were transparent and hollow, like a sphere of glass, and had its equator divided in twenty-four parts by so many meridian semicircles, *a, b, c, d,* &c.; one of which is the geographical meridian of any given place, as London, which may be supposed to be at the point *a;* and if the hours of XII. were marked at the equator, both upon that meridian and the opposite one, and all the rest of the hours in order on the other meridians, those meridians would be hour-circles answering to the latitude of London: then if this glass sphere had an opaque axis P E *p* terminating in the poles P and *p*, the shadow of the axis would fall upon every particular meridian and hour, when the sun came to the plane of the opposite meridian; and would consequently shew the time at London, and at all other places on the meridian of London.

If this sphere were cut through the middle by the plane ABCD, in the rational horizon of London, one half of the axis EP would be above the plane, and the other half below it; and if straight lines were drawn from the centre of the plane, to those points where the circumference is cut by the hour circles of the sphere, those lines would be hour lines of a *horizontal* dial for London; for the shadow of the axis would fall upon each particular hour-line of the dial, when it fell upon the like hour circle of the sphere.

If the plane, which cuts the sphere, be upright at AFGG, fig. 10, touching the given place at F, and directly facing the meridian of London, it will become the plane of an erect south dial; and if right lines be drawn from its centre E, to those points of its circumference where the hour-circles of the sphere cut it, these will be the hour-lines of a vertical or direct south dial for London, to which the hours are to be set, as in the figure; and the lower half E*p* of the axis will cast a shadow on the hour of the day in this dial, at the same time that it would fall upon the like hour-circle of the sphere, if the dial plane were not in the way.

Without entering into the minutiæ of inclining and reclining dials, &c., we may observe generally, that the plane of every dial represents the plane of some great circle upon the earth, and the gnomon the earth's axis, whether it be a small wire, as in the figure just referred to, or the edge of a thin plate, as in common horizontal dials.

Dialling may be performed by a common globe, which is to be elevated to the latitude of the given place, and turned about until any one of the twenty-four meridians cuts the horizon in the north point, where the hour of XII is supposed to be marked, the rest of the meridians will cut the horizon at the respective distances of all the other hours from XII. Then if these points of distance be marked on the horizon, and the globe be taken out of the horizon, and a flat surface be put into its place, even with the surface of the horizon, and if straight lines be drawn from the centre of the board to those points of distance on the horizon which were cut by the twenty-four meridian semicircles, these lines will be the hour-lines of a horizontal dial for that particular latitude, the edge of whose gnomon must be in the very same situation that the axis of the globe was, before it was taken out of the horizon: that is, the gnomon must make an angle with the plane of the dial, equal to the latitude of the place for which the dial is made.

For the practice of dialling either with the globe, or by the principles of spherics, we must refer the reader to the works now to be mentioned. Of these, for persons not conversant in mathematics, the second volume of Brewster's edition of Ferguson's Lectures will be reckoned quite sufficient. Leybourn's Dialling—Bion in his Use of Mathematical Instruments—the works of Leadbeater and Emerson may be consulted with advantage. Mr. W. Jones has a work on Instrumental Dialling, and Dr. Horsley has treated on the subject in his mathematical tracts. Several ingenious constructions of dials are to be found in Montucla's Recreations, as well as in Ferguson's Lectures.

END OF VOL. I.

J. M'Creery, Printer,
Black-Horse-Court, Fleet-Street, London.

Lightning Source UK Ltd.
Milton Keynes UK
UKHW011329221118
332792UK00010B/799/P

9 781333 759742